the cinema of SALLY POTTER

DIRECTORS' CUTS

the cinema of
SALLY POTTER

a politics of love

sophie mayer

WALLFLOWER PRESS LONDON & NEW YORK

First published in Great Britain
in 2009 by

Wallflower Press
6 Market Place, London W1W 8AF
www.wallflowerpress.co.uk

A catalogue record for this book is available from the British Library

ISBN 978-1-905674-67-1 (paperback)
        978-1-905674-68-8 (hardback)

Series design by Rob Bowden Design

All production images reproduced by permission © Adventure Pictures

Printed and bound in India by Imprint Digital

CONTENTS

ACKNOWLEDGEMENTS

This book is deeply concerned with the significance of collaboration, and it is just as deeply a product of collaboration with Sally Potter, who not only gave me many hours of interviews and conversations, but also access to (and context for) her private, working archives. While closely attentive to the book's progress, she was extraordinarily, generously and completely open to my questions and interpretations. The book could not have existed without her willing and inspiring collaboration, but all errors – whether factual or interpretive – remain mine.

That collaboration would not have been possible without the staff and associates of Sally Potter's production company, Adventure Pictures. Production team members Jimmy Barnett, Mike Manzi, Steve Masters and Amos Field Reid, Sally's assistants (chronologically) Alex Johnson, Elias Millward, Rachael Castell and Sarah Fox, interns Maya Puig and Thom Coates Welsh, and especially Christopher Sheppard, Potter's long-term producer, have been this book's most invaluable resources and cheerleaders. I am also very grateful for the opportunity to speak to two of Potter's collaborator-performers, Leda Papaconstantinou and Julie Christie, who very graciously shared her thoughts in the wonderful foreword for this volume.

Based on my access to the archives, I advised Adventure Pictures on the development of SP-ARK, the Sally Potter Online Archive, which engendered valuable discussions with the staff and students of the Screen Studies department at Goldsmith's – especially Julian Henriques and Jacqueline Haigh – and the Film Studies department at Queen Mary's, especially Charles Drazin, Annette Kuhn and Lucy Bolton. These conversations continued those about feminist authorship begun with my PhD supervisory committee at the University of Toronto – Linda Hutcheon, Elizabeth Harvey and Barbara Havercroft – all of whom commented on and supported this book's process, as did my external examiners, Corinn Columpar and Emma Wilson.

Corinn Columpar has also been my co-editor on the anthology *There She Goes: Feminist Filmmaking and Beyond*, wherein I was able to test my thoughts on Potter and the archive, beginning with a panel at the Society for Cinema and Media Studies (SCMS) Conference 2007. I am also grateful for the opportunities to present work on Potter offered by the organisers of *Screen* 2007 and 2008, by Lee Wilson and Mary Jacobus at CRASSH (University of Cambridge), by Sarah Barrow at Anglia Ruskin University, and by Sanja Bahun and Marina Warner at the University of Essex. Previous attempts and versions have also appeared in *Literature/Film Quarterly*, *Little*

White Lies, Plan B, roundtable review, Screen, Shebytches, Trans/forming Feminisms and *Vertigo*. Gareth Evans at *Vertigo* earns a particular vote of thanks for his insights into and enthusiasm for Potter's oeuvre, and for the opportunity to receive and transmit John Berger's insights into *Carmen*.

I wrote most of this book as an independent scholar, and thanks are due to the Andrew W. Mellon Foundation for a year-long postdoctoral fellowship at the University of Cambridge, and to my postdoctoral supervisors Emma Wilson and David Trotter, who enabled me to complete my research and to refresh it by teaching Potter's films. I undertook my initial research at the University of Toronto, with the support of a Metcalf Research Fellowship from Victoria College (enabling me to work with their library's Virginia Woolf collection) and a School of Graduate Studies Postdoctoral Teaching Fellowship, which gave me the opportunity to discuss the relationship between tango, crying and red with the students of 'Short Talks: Reading Anne Carson'. My determination to write about Potter began in teaching *Orlando* to the students of 'Introduction to Film Studies' (2002–03, 2003–04) at Innis College in the University of Toronto, under the mentorship of Charlie Keil.

Wallflower Press have guided the book on its journey from teaching notes on *Orlando* to *The Cinema of Sally Potter*. Their support for cinema and cinephilia is unfailing, and I am honoured to be part of their respected list. Thanks in particular to Yoram Allon and Tom Cabot for their support and attention to detail. Jacqueline Downs has been a truly collaborative editor, and this book owes much to the generous gift of her attention at a time of mourning. The editing process was infused with thoughts of her mother, and I hope the book can stand in some small way in memory of Eileen Downs.

The staff of the British Library (and the Newspaper Reading Room), Haringey Libraries, Innis College Library, the Toronto Film Reference Library and especially the British Film Institute Library, as well as the staff of the Toronto Women's Bookstore and Prospero's Books, all contributed their assistance and expertise, as did a number of friends and colleagues who generously read material and discussed ideas, including: Michele Byers, Ted Chamberlin, Jasmine Chan, Kieron Corless, Ben Crowe, Michelle Girouard, Natalie Harrower, Daniel Heath Justice, Claire Laville, Michelle Neilson, Julian Patrick, Katy Price, Shelagh Rowan-Legg, Davina Silver, Sophie Thomas and Emily Thornton.

I count myself lucky to have such intelligent and engaged friends, and particularly lucky in Preti Taneja, who not only offered her editorial incisiveness (and steely support) at a crucial juncture, but also her brilliant theological and affective insights which I have adopted as my own. My mother, Victoria Ainley, raised me to look closely, love wisely and ask questions, and she brought all these skills to our conversations about Potter's work. SF Said read the book with the careful eye of a fellow writer and cinephile, and debated its themes with the loving engagement of a comrade.

This book is for SF, who said 'yes'.

London, 2009

FOREWORD

Julie Christie

I first heard about Sally Potter through a friend who was involved, along with Sally, in a group that did performance art. It all seemed terribly alternative to me, although they probably didn't think so. My friend told me that Sally would like to meet me, and I thought, 'Oh dear, I'm going to meet one of these clever people and I won't know what she's talking about.' The day came and I didn't know what to do as, to my horror, *three* clever women walked in. By clever, I mean utterly original. The three were Rose English, the comedienne and performer, Lindsay Cooper, a wonderful musician and composer, and Sally. There were these three original minds sitting on my sofa, asking if I would be in their film. They then sent me a script, which I didn't understand, and I wasn't sure whether I could work in their performance art style, but I thought 'I'd better do it – I might become a clever woman, too!'

One of the things that most impressed me about Sally was her disinclination to take things at face value, her practice of digging under the surface, as indeed she was doing in *The Gold Diggers*. At that time, people were not familiar with the darker side of corporatism; so when I went into Sally's bathroom and saw her Tom's of Maine toothpaste, I thought, 'Here's a woman who understands!' Sally was also ahead of her time shooting *The Gold Diggers* in Iceland. I've subsequently shot two other films there, and seen how it has become the hippest place on earth.

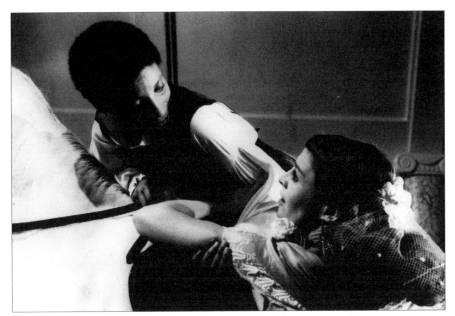

Ruby (Julie Christie) follows Celeste (Colette Laffont) into Sally Potter's experiments with cinema

What I remember most about *The Gold Diggers* is working with an all-woman crew. Sally had perceived the absence of women in film other than as performers. It was very marked at that time: film was, as it always had been, a male arena. I had become used to this, and to the division that comes about when you talk mainly to people who are outside your own experience, so you divide yourself and don't talk about your life and opinions while working. Suddenly, on *The Gold Diggers'* set, everyone there knew what it was like not to be part of a powerful majority; most had had to struggle to do their work. In my case, it made for an unself-conscious and relaxed experience, as well as an educative one, and I was very happy on the film.

We were paid equally, the way things should be in an ideal world. Sally was trying to make real her commitment to equality in a world – filmmaking – where equality was a low priority. I loved her for pursuing these difficult routes, and for even conceiving of them. I don't know if anybody else could have brought it about. Sally made it happen through her unwavering determination that it was *going* to happen. Her tenaciousness is breathtaking. She sets herself an impossible task and, through sheer resolve, will see it brought to fulfilment.

I didn't wholly understand *The Gold Diggers* at the time, but I loved it for its visuals and complex ideas, two areas in which Sally excels. I loved the way she uses pantomime and performance in it. It's the most complicated film she's made. *Orlando* shares with it the elements of fun, display and a great aesthetic. That, however, comes from an already-conceived edifice, a novel by a great writer. *The Gold Diggers*, however, is more like gold dust in the wind, motes that settle but don't form a cohesive whole.

That doesn't bother me, I don't need that from a film. It's visually so beautiful. Little shots stay in my mind: Colette on her white horse in the ballroom; Hilary in her long skirt moving across the ice.

I also remember the scenes we shot in a former hospital, the old Royal Free in London, in these great, big, spacious rooms with *huge* windows. The relative spacing and size of the panes was very beautiful and Sally brought all that out, its austerity particularly. Great, undervalued quality – austerity. It's going to become a positive, rather than negative, description again, in the face of current global economic collapse. It's happening already: Sally has been shooting some of her new film as if on a camera-phone. Very little money has been spent on it.

An austere eye can produce the most beautiful images of all. Sally's films are, at times, heartrendingly austere, which leads you into a comparison with Bresson or Herzog. On the other hand, they have the scope of Bertolucci or Visconti – their lushness and fullness, an overflowingness. The combination marks her aesthetic out as very particular. You see it in the objects she chooses to surround herself with, which are few. I've learned and watched as she practised it, and been astounded because, like all great gifts, it's not common. She's born with it: it came from her family, in her genes, this extraordinary aesthetic practice.

But anyone who's spent time with Sally knows that she is basically someone who is reaching for the humour in life. She laughs all the time. She takes serious things and looks at them from a wry point of view. She's great fun to be with. She has a lightness about everything, including her interest in shoes and clothes (she has enormous style). She's curious about them, as she is about everything else. Nothing exists by itself; everything is made by someone, and the more you enquire, the more you know about the world. She loves to learn by encountering the new. She's never passive – whatever someone is talking about, from tennis to science, Sally wants to know more. She asks very focused questions. When she's gathered all the information, she comes out with her own opinion of what people have been discussing, very well-digested and very *layered*, and all in a short space of time.

As with Godard, she uses entirely divergent forms for her films, according to their content. You never know what brave new structure you are going to encounter. In *Yes*, for instance, the issues were those familiar ones of race and imperialism. Framing them in a classical structure made the experience of the ideas totally original, so that the film was like a piece of music, rather than a dialogue. It's really tough for a filmmaker like Sally to survive in the film world, especially as it gets more commercial and unsurprising. Films that are more oblique and ambiguous, daring to question received information, to be truly modern, such films are extremely hard to finance, and I admire Sally for continuing to make them and delighting her audiences with the thrill of the truly original.

Most of us want a lot of things and we live in the muddle of the pursuit. Sally always knows what she's doing; what she wants to do she realises fully. Almost invariably, however long it takes and however secret the pursuit, she gets there. She takes a definite, unrelenting route. It comes from her *clarity*: if only we could all see our goals as clearly as she can. It makes things difficult for her, because she can't veer off the path and take a rest. Each attempt is very tough because she doesn't compromise. Of course, she *does* compromise, because one can't make a film without doing so; what I mean is that she's a perfectionist.

She works other people as hard as she works herself. Yet – and I really envy this – she has the ability to give people their own space. Whoever she works with, not only actors, but people in much less exalted jobs who are responsible for the mechanics of a whole unit or office functioning, she is always asking them questions. Having learned about their abilities through this two-way communication, she is very specific about what she asks them to do. It's a non-authoritarian, non-hierarchical way of being. The manner in which she solicits what she wants is extremely sweet and sunny, which is a wonderful ability in someone who knows so clearly what she wants. She has an understanding of human psychology, so she sees and comprehends how people react immediately. She responds very tenderly, never judging, as is the case with many great directors. She becomes the person whom everyone turns to – not because of her authority, which she does carry well, but because she listens.

Julie Christie
London, 2009

Becoming (Part I)

Transformation is a key word in my films. There's an invitation to ask the questions: 'What do you see in other people, do you really see in them what they are? Who are you, what are you really?' You're not a fixed given. Take up the pen and write your own life or self-description: abandon it or explode it. You can change. That leads to the broader political principle: whole societies can change. It's an anti-despair way of thinking. Nothing's fixed, everything's impermanent, everything's in flux. We can influence events. Choice is involved – perhaps not complete choice – but we can be part of the transformation, at least.

– Sally Potter, interview with author, September 2006

Sally Potter's film *Orlando* (1993) was the first arthouse film that I saw at the cinema. I left the cinema transformed – so changed that I cannot now imagine what prompted my 15-year-old self to pick it out of the listings on a sunny Sunday in the Easter holidays. Maybe it was that Billy Zane, who played Orlando's lover Shelmerdine, had been throbbing teenage hearts as the daredevil pilot Jack in the final episodes of *Twin Peaks*, my then-favourite TV show. David Lynch's venture into serial television, which screened in the UK from October 1990 to spring 1992, was as close as my friends and I got to alternative culture beyond the grunge bands we discovered, like

Twin Peaks, through American magazines. As the lights went down on my first visit to an arthouse cinema (London's Screen on the Hill), I had no idea what to expect. I did not know *Orlando* had wowed audiences at Venice and Toronto in autumn 1992. I did not know that Tilda Swinton, who played Orlando, was Derek Jarman's muse and the face that launched British alternative cinema, nor that Quentin Crisp, who played Queen Elizabeth I, was one of 'the stately homos of England', as he expressed it. Jimmy Somerville was a familiar voice and face from his appearances with hi-NRG dance group Bronski Beat on *Top of the Pops* but unrecognisable in doublet and hose as the Queen's Herald.

Their presences layered the film with jokes about gender and sexuality that were largely obscure to me. Yet the film filled me with joy. As a nascent feminist and poet, I was thrilled by a fellow-feeling with the eternally young Orlando as s/he journeyed through history from his first appearance as a male Tudor courtier and hopeless Metaphysical poet to a society lady being taunted by writers Addison and Pope, finally becoming a motor-biking contemporary writer and single mother. The fiercely policed boundaries of gender, art and desire were suddenly thrown open: no mean feat under the Iron Lady. As British prime minister from 1979 to 1990, Margaret Thatcher earned her nickname through her vitiation (continued under John Major's government until 1997) of all aspects of care, emotion, expression and affect that form society's connective tissue, not least through the notorious Section 28. An infamous article of the Local Government Act 1988, Section 28 forbade the promotion of homosexuality by local authorities (including schools and public programming). This largely limited the 'corrupting' effects of the gay British arts explosion of the early 1980s to *Top of the Pops*. Fourteen years of Conservative economic policies had also obscured and vitiated the politically and culturally alternative scenes out of which directors like Potter and Jarman emerged. As the tail-end of Generation X, my friends and I had swallowed Thatcherite policy: we were resolutely opposed to 'culture' and had little sense of history. To us, the 1970s had been about the orange velour and Farrah Fawcett hair we saw in our parents' photo albums, not liberation movements.

Researching this book, I discovered what we had been 'protected' from. It was an incredible opportunity to understand how and why Potter was celebrating and continuing these movements, not least through her polymorphously perverse casting choices in *Orlando*. Making Somerville the Herald to Crisp's Virgin Queen was a bold statement that queer alternatives were right there in British history, and had always been part of British culture as a fierce and exciting undercurrent of difference *within* the mainstream. In the same year that *Orlando* opened at Venice, Jarman, who had adapted *The Tempest* for film in 1979, painted an imagined letter from a queer 14-year-old to William Shakespeare that read, 'I'm queer like you ... I want to be a queer artist like Leonardo or Michelangelo' (1996: 126), inscribed into bright yellow paint over layers of tabloid homophobia. *Orlando* makes a subtler argument for a redefinition of Britishness as queer, feminine, Eurocentric, downwardly mobile and experimental. It does so through its carnival of art forms, high and low, from Tudor painting through chamber opera to ice dance. By opening my eyes to the idea that all art forms could change the individual and society, *Orlando* became part of a cavalcade of popular culture that altered my relationship with power and hierarchy in all its forms: not only gender and sexuality, but also nation, class and ethnicity.

In Potter's work cinema is celebrated as an artform capable of making change because it incorporates all the arts without losing its specificity. This multi-art cinema is both a representation of and a metaphor for her astonishingly diverse career. When *Orlando* was the surprise hit of the Venice Film Festival in 1992, mainstream entertainment publications fell over themselves to profile its hip young director. As canny *Film Quarterly* interviewer David Ehrenstein notes, many found themselves engaged in the irony of 'declaring a writer/director with a 25-year-long career a "debutante"' (1993: 2) because of the ten-year gap between *Orlando* and her first feature film *The Gold Diggers* (1983). Ehrenstein's hindsight dates Potter's career back beyond its 'established' starting point of *Thriller* in 1979, her first narrative film and the first to receive extensive if informal distribution in the UK and US. He takes account of her portfolio of short films, beginning with *Daily* in 1968, many of which were created as part of live dance or Expanded Cinema events organised by the London Filmmakers' Co-op (LFMC).

Founded in 1966, the LFMC provided a space for experimental, hands-on filmmaking inspired by the 1950s and 1960s American avant-garde. Potter joined in 1969, where she was one of the few women filmmakers, as well as one of the only filmmakers to emerge from the LFMC into feature exhibition with *Thriller*. She made three multiscreen installations – *Jerk* (1969), *Play* (1970) and *Black and White* (1970) – that were stringently focused on form, with mathematical editing; all three were clearly influenced by the dominant structuralist ideals of the LFMC. She toured with them around the UK and to galleries in the Netherlands as part of a programme with LFMC filmmaker Mike Dunford, in whose 1979 short film *Weeds* she would later appear. By 1969, the LFMC had incorporated a second influential centre, the Arts Laboratory, where Potter had attended many screenings in her late teens. It had been an events space at 182 Drury Lane, London, described by its founder Jim Haynes as 'an experiment with such intangibles as people, ideas, feelings and communications' (1969). ArtsLab introduced a generation of filmmakers and viewers to avant-garde film from contemporary North American practitioners like Stan Brakhage, Andy Warhol, Michael Snow and Joyce Wieland, and 1930s radicals such as Sergei Eisenstein and Dziga Vertov, as well as hosting performances by companies like Human People.

In the same way that ArtsLab had been a cinema, theatre, gallery and live space, Potter bridged many of the experimental art scenes that bloomed in London during the 1960s. Born in 1949, Potter began making 'visual poems' as an adolescent, with a camera loaned by her uncle, whose 'then companion, Sandy Daley ... later made *Robert* [Mapplethorpe] *Having His Nipple Pierced* ... They were independent-film aficionados, and they gave [her] as a young teenager, a 14-year-old, the status of an artist doing her work, which was the most incredible gift!' (Potter in MacDonald 1998: 401). She dropped out of secondary school at 15-years-old to study art. After taking classes at Camden Art Centre, she entered a pre-diploma foundation course in draughtsmanship at Central St Martins in 1967, switching to Jim Haynes' class at Chelsea School of Art in 1968. In 1967, she had become involved with Group Events, a situationist theatre company founded by Thom Osborn. With them, she performed at art schools and in urban spaces as part of the political and cultural uprising that took place in London in 1968. The influence of their site-specific, physical, comedic and political acts can be seen in Potter's subsequent training as a dancer and performance artist.

While the worlds of experimental dance and avant-garde film were distinct, Potter had briefly bridged them by making three short films for projection with performance; in 1968 *Daily* and *The Building* were both performed at the ArtsLab, and two years later *Hors D'Oeuvres* appeared at The Place. Expanded Cinema, a movement associated with the LFMC, provided a home for just such experiments in combining cinema and live performance, and both *Daily* and *The Building* screened as part of Expanded Cinema programmes at the National Film Theatre. In 1971, Potter took a one-year course in choreography and dance at the London School of Contemporary Dance, based at the Place Theatre, where the British New Dance was being conceived. She studied and worked alongside Richard Alston and Siobhan Davies, whose eponymous companies remain influential forces in British contemporary dance. Once Potter undertook serious dance training, she made films only for projection with dance performances. Dance historian Stephanie Jordan comments that *Combines* (1972), a triple-screen projection for Richard Alston's Strider company, 'was the most radical of [Alston's] pieces, and extraordinary in the context of the LCDT repertoire' (1992: 106). From 1971, Potter focused on choreography, creating several increasingly large-scale pieces for Strider and other Place-based artists, and in 1974 she won a scholarship from The Place. She used it to form her own performance company with regular collaborator Jacky Lansley, who would later choreograph the eloquent ice dance in which Orlando spurns his appropriate but horse-faced fiancée Euphrosyne for the beautiful Russian Sasha.

Limited Dance Company (LDC), so called because their work contained limited amounts of dance, produced dozens of works over the following three years which spoofed high art such as Verdi's opera *Aïda*. Many of the pieces also contained references to film. *Why Film?* (1974) literally turned structuralist cinema into pure performance: the piece was lit by film projectors, and all the performed tableaux occurred in the rectangles of light they cast. The performance was in two halves, black-and-white and colour, with an interval when ice-cream boxes containing optical devices were handed out. The first section used black-and-white costumes and props and was about film processes; the second section used Technicolor costumes and props, and was about audience experience (a curious parallel with Potter's use of black-and-white and colour film in her later career, as chapter 6 explores). One performer built a huge 'camera' structure from junk found locally, and the piece moved from a visually 'pure' statement to a 'vulgar' and chaotic one, mixing structuralist analysis (LDC often performed as lecturers) with vaudevillian play.

LDC's final performance *Mounting* (1977) was performed to disrupt a Frank Stella exhibition at the Museum of Modern Art in Oxford. Among other satirical gestures, it sent up the artist by shouting his surname in imitation of Marlon Brando in *A Streetcar Named Desire* (1951). LDC's performances were reviewed in small dance magazines and, according to Lansley, gathered 'a larger and more sophisticated audience [than their earlier choreographic work with London Contemporary Dance Theatre] ... among visual artists' (in Mackrell 1992: 23). *Berlin* (1976), Potter's final live performance show, was a serial performed over four nights in four different locations, including a squatted house, a swimming pool and an ice rink, on which Potter stood naked apart from a tutu skirt made of leaves, and delivered a monologue on gender politics. *Berlin* attracted audiences including influential critics and practitioners such as Laura Mulvey and Simon Field, who would go on to become supportive viewers of *Thriller* (Potter, interview with author, September 2006).

Between 1977 and 1978, when a first cut of *Thriller* was shown at the National Film Theatre, Potter moved artform again, to improvisatory music performance and avant-jazz. She had worked on dance pieces in 1972 with the Portsmouth Sinfonia, a ramshackle artists' orchestra, and with pianist and composer Michael Finnissy, whose 60th birthday was marked in 2006 by a Finnissy Weekend broadcast on Radio 3. For the August 1975 Serpentine Gallery Festival of Performance Art, LDC created a weekend-long performance piece called *Park Cafeteria*, for which Potter formed an orchestra of female artists and musicians to improvise in Hyde Park. One of these was Lindsay Cooper, with whom Potter would tour in several improvised music groups, and who composed the score for *The Gold Diggers*. In the early 1980s Potter also toured as a singer with musicians including Fred Frith, who would go on to co-compose pieces for *Orlando*, *The Tango Lesson* (1996), *The Man Who Cried* (2000) and *Yes* (2004).

Moving across forms, Potter continues to draw diverse collaborators distinguished in their own fields, who bring their artistic and political energy to her work. As well as Frith, she worked with leading contemporary composer Osvaldo Golijov, tenor Salvatore Licitra, contemporary musicians the Kronos Quartet and Roma orkestar Taraf de Haïdouks on the soundtrack to *The Man Who Cried*. Pankaj Mishra, author of *An End to Suffering: The Buddha in the World* (2004), wrote an introduction to the *Yes* screenplay that reads the film through his work on spirituality, politics and changing culture in modern India (see 2005: xv–xx). The screenplay also includes a letter from influential writer and activist John Berger, who had contacted Potter after seeing *The Tango Lesson* (2005: xi–xiii). She had long been a fan of his politically-incisive novels and art criticism, and asked if he would read a draft version of *Yes*. He did, and – as chapter 11 will explore – his comments shaped the film's developing narrative. Collaboration is at the heart of Potter's work – not only with those involved in the films' production, but with the viewer.

The films resonate with a question that Berger asked in 1960: 'Why should an artist's way of looking at the world have any meaning for us? Why does it give us pleasure? Because, I believe, it increases our awareness of our own potentiality' (1960: 16). The question proposes a kind of pleasure distinct from the easy satisfactions of eye-candy and happy endings. It is a radically utopian idea, still vivid more than forty years after the artistic uprisings of 1968. Rather than espousing militant revolution, it returns to the original sense of revolution: the constant wheel of change. As a Marxist (a descriptor he stands by proudly in *Hold Everything Dear* (see 2007: 113)), Berger locates pleasure in art's ability to stimulate consciousness of individual and social transformations. Both communism and feminism produced more or less didactic forms aimed at dictating change, but Berger's questions suggest something more subtle, that the viewer can be awakened to the potential for change within themselves by the pleasure of understanding an artist's investigations. Pleasure comes from working in concert with the artist, and from being worked on by the art object that represents how the artist has been worked on by the world.

That which is transformational in Potter's films draws on what she learned from live performance and improvisation to invite the viewer into just such a collaboration where both film and viewer can realise their 'own potentiality'. Berger's term 'potentiality' neatly entwines political change and its roots in the spirit or private self. In the 1960s Berger struggled to see film as an artform capable of creating such change, because in its dominant form it is an industrial product that depends on corporate circuits of global (or nationalist) finance. Film, like many other activities, is increasingly mediated by technology and big business. Experimental work that deliberately takes place on the margins of dominant funding, production and distribution models can be like 'slow food', an experience that can offer us a moment alone in the dark to reconnect. In her 'untold history of people power' *Hope in the Dark*, Rebecca Solnit asks, 'What is the purpose of resisting corporate globalisation if not to protect the obscure, the ineffable, the unmarketable, the unmanageable, the local, the poetic and the eccentric? So they need to be practiced, celebrated and studied too, right now' (2005: 96).

It is these 'unmarketable … unmanageable … local … poetic' films that Vivian Sobchack (1992) and Laura U. Marks (2000; 2002) have used to develop different versions of film phenomenology, which claims that film takes place in the world, not just in the cinema, and affects us as real experience can. They call this affect 'haptic', alluding to film's ability to touch us somehow, although it has no tactile dimension. For Sobchack, this occurs through the way in which feminist films, in particular, rethink ways of seeing that link the viewer into the body of the protagonist. Marks is drawn to experimental films that privilege visual and aural textures, which encourage the viewer to patch narrative gaps by sensing and feeling. In both cases, they describe a meshing of the physical body and what Potter identifies as 'the subtle body', the body composed by our minds and memories. There's a suggestion that these 'local … poetic' films attract audiences who are open to being touched, but are regarded as 'unmarketable … unmanageable' because they infringe on a society that, in general, does not want to be touched.

Potter's films develop ways of touching the viewer as a repudiation to the argument that film, because it is technologically and commercially produced, always disembodies us. There are two contrasting strategies that 'touch' us haptically: firstly, her performers use their bodies in ways that carry over from her live work; and secondly, her use of film forms such as the close-up and rhythmic editing shows us those bodies in motion. Through the intersection of performance and cinematic techniques, the films reach out and affect our bodies. Avant-garde film historian

Rachel O. Moore argues that 'the paucity of bodily felt and contingent experience [in the modern world] accounts for why films "touch". If this is so, it is also the reason why cinema needs to touch those parts of us that are most in danger of atrophy' (2000: 159). 'Movies ... like other aspects of our lives, [can be] "events that have happened to us, experiences that are inalienably ours", ones that we revisit in our memory and make up who we are' (Elsaesser in Keathley 2006: 21). It is through their association with live performance – its gestures, its immediacy, its work with the audience – that Potter's films become 'events that have happened to us'. More than that, like the 'happenings' of 1970s performance art, they are events in which we have participated. They do not just happen to us: by experiencing, we co-author them, inviting them to alter our perception of ourselves.

With Orlando's first gaze to camera – an outrageous gesture coming from live performance that breaks every rule of conventional film – I was electrified and altered. My perception of what film could do was changed. And not only film, but my 'potentiality', my sense of what I could possibly do through art and politics. Something in the film had summoned me and compelled me, as Queen Elizabeth magically compels Orlando to immortal youth by telling him: 'Do not fade. Do not wither. Do not grow old.' How did the film reach out through the screen and affect me so profoundly that I think back on it as a moment of personal and political epiphany? The notion that film affects us deeply is shadowed by negative ideas about film as a kind of mesmerism, either cheap entertainment that distracts us or propaganda that browbeats us. Ideas such as disavowal, voyeurism and masochism are the inheritance of psychoanalytic film theory, while Marxism added distraction and interpellation. All of them suggest that there is – or should be – something displeasurable in film viewing which is covered up by bright lights and spectacle that suck us in and bamboozle us like hucksters at a fairground.

'That is, I': Orlando (Tilda Swinton) welcomes the viewer

In Orlando's gaze to camera, Potter finds a different answer for what might draw us in with our permission, rather than against our will: *apostrophe*. Found in lyric poetry, apostrophe is a device in which the poem addresses 'a thing, a place, an abstract quality, an idea, a dead or absent person ... as if present and capable of understanding' (Cuddon 1997: 55). Often introduced by an 'O', apostrophe was used widely by Romantic poets such as Percy Bysshe Shelley, whose work is quoted twice in *Orlando*. The second quotation comprises the first lines of the poem 'An Indian Girl's Song': 'I arise from dreams of thee / In the first sleep of night.' At the end of the poem's second stanza, the speaker cries that she must die on her lover's heart: 'O beloved as thou art! / O lift me from the grass!' (1977: 369–70). Overcome by emotion, she first apostrophises her sleeping lover. The apostrophe then becomes an urgent call for the lover to wake from his absentness and rescue her. Orlando's glance to camera uses humour to mitigate the insistence of apostrophe's urgent demand that we be present.

According to Jonathan Culler, apostrophe is neglected in contemporary poetry because it exemplifies 'all that is most radical, embarrassing, pretentious, and mystificatory' (1981: 137). Apostrophe foregrounds an embarrassing fact about art, one that is doubly true of cinema: it is made to address an audience that is absent, so at root it shares a mood or attitude with prayer. Through finding an apostrophic language for film that addresses rather than seduces, distracts or instructs, Potter's work deliberately and specifically trespasses into this radically embarrassing area. Like the Indian girl's apostrophe, cinema walks the fine line between an emotional, abstract call to the 'beloved' audience and an urgent summoning to be involved.

Oh Moscow, the celebrated song cycle that Potter wrote with Cooper, apostrophises the Russian city in its title. Its lyrics point to, and reverse, apostrophe's impossible summoning: 'Oh Moscow, I forgot / You were there, I was not.' Rather than the singer being present, she is '[in]capable of understanding' because she was absent. *Oh Moscow* inverts apostrophe by acknowledging the liveness of the apostrophised 'thing ... place' or person. Potter's films do the same. Orlando's gaze to camera breaks the 'fourth wall' convention of the cinema screen in which actors must never acknowledge the presence of the camera. By letting us *know* that we are watching a film, it also invites us to do so by recognising our presence. Apostrophe 'wills that ... particular objects function as subjects', encouraging viewers to be active subjects in the world beyond the screen (Culler 1981: 140). Orlando's gaze is startling because it asks us to be present in our bodies in the moment of watching the films in a way that is similar to meditation.

As Potter expresses it:

In the act of surrender to it, what the film experience can offer is the possibility of saying 'There you are! This is your life: your life is this and more. This is a journey inside your brain, or your experience, or your relationship with people, things, places, spaces.' It's not just through identification or projection onto characters, it's the totality of experience itself being thrown back at you. With the best [films], you come out with the feeling that you took a walk through your own brain and remembered that you were alive in the big, spacious universe that you're occupying. (Interview with author, September 2006)

For me, that apostrophic call to move through the film and into the world worked dramatically. Several hours after seeing *Orlando*, I told an armed security guard at Heathrow airport to 'Bend my gender'. It seemed like an appropriately inappropriate response to his sexist banter, which ranged from my physical attributes to my mental incapability. Rather than reacting with silent frustration or ineffectual rage, I tried Potter's strategy of cool, witty provocation. To my dismay and delight, it turned out that bending gender upset those with power more than I could have guessed. I narrowly escaped being arrested – only because the guard found it difficult to explain what had flustered him. My parents let me know I was in big trouble, but I was triumphant. The film's mischievous politics and verbal wit had enlarged my grasp on the universe. It inspired the first of many acts of insurrection around issues of gender and power.

While this book cannot be as pithy as that cheeky imperative, it derives from the same impulse to challenge received notions in a spirit of play. Film theory is not as heavily policed as airports, so I hope that the unusual frame of reference through which I explore how the films' apostrophe actually reaches out to the viewer will be seen as arresting rather than an arrestable offence. I trace what I learnt about the performance and politics that shaped Potter's early work through to her most recent film, *Rage* (2009). That arc is informed by two opportunities, sparkling with the aura of the live event, to see the films bracketing Potter's career: an archival screening of her early shorts and the premiere of *Rage* (2009). On a magical afternoon in July 2008, as I was polishing the manuscript, Potter's short films were unreeled from their cans, some for the first time in three decades, at a screening organised by Maggi Hurt and Will Fowler at BFI Southbank as research for a planned retrospective.

Both the book, and the retrospective, were delayed by an announcement a few weeks later: that *Rage* (2009) was complete, and would be screening in competition at the 2009 Berlin International Film Festival, which offered the exhilarating, if unnerving, challenge of weaving the film into what I had thought was a finished manuscript. My rejigged deadline gave me barely a month after *Rage's* (2009) premiere in the enormous Filmpalast, on a brilliantly cold Berlin evening, to unpick and rebraid both film and book. I had some inklings about the film, whose development kept pace with this book, through interviews that Potter generously gave me in between writing, shooting and editing, and through conversations with the team at Adventure Pictures, Potter's production company: Christopher Sheppard, Mike Manzi, Jimmy Barnett and Sarah Fox. It was an incredible opportunity to observe, from a distance, the auteur-as-collaborator and art as process. Both the premiere and the sense of process strengthened my argument that Potter invests film with the liveness of performance, not only in its presentation but onscreen. This was further corroborated by Catherine Fowler's brand-new study, *Sally Potter*, which arrived on my desk shortly before I went to Berlin. Drawing on Fowler's acute knowledge of 1970s avant-garde and feminist film, the book offers an extended reading of the liveliness of Potter's Expanded Cinema as a framework for her feature work and is a complement to this book in its focus on the milieu and genesis of the early shorts.

Although my focus is on the features, like Fowler I offer a chronological reading of Potter's films, interwoven with thematic chapters that take up the challenge highlighted by *Rage* (2009): the way in which the films rework each other across time. There are actually three *Rages* to be accounted for: the first (chronologically) being the final programme in the television documentary series *Tears, Laughter, Fears, and Rage*, broadcast in 1987, the second being the unmade film-within-a-film in *The Tango Lesson*, and the third being the new feature. In order to talk about all three, often in relation to one another, I refer to them by date, to indicate their historical context and their place in Potter's oeuvre: *Rage* (1987) is the documentary segment; *Rage* (1996) is the film within *The Tango Lesson*; while *Rage* (2009) is the feature film. There are threads that bind all three together, and also connect across the films from *Thriller* to *Yes*, showing Potter's development as a filmmaker even as they indicate preoccupations and image clusters that appear throughout her work.

Rage (2009), a film about fashion, is equally and perhaps more significantly about refashioning film. It looks, and feels, like no other film I have seen. Its visual, narrative and ethical boldness can be read as the complex simplicity of a formal reponse to an interconnected world, which Potter has been reaching towards throughout her work. Combining the look of documentary, the immediacy of live performance and the heightened verbal and visual languages of Potter's features, it is told through a series of monologues (and equally telling silences) delivered in front of a greenscreen and addressed to the cellphone camera of the invisible, inaudible schoolboy protagonist Michelangelo, taking Potter's exploration and inversion of cinema further than any previous film. Like *Yes*, it is insistently political within a dramatic framework complemented by seductively beautiful visuals and poetic language. Spoken in monologues, it is suggestive of the arias heard in *The Man Who Cried*, and, like that film, it is deeply concerned with the ethical and narrative relationship between parent and child. It takes place in New York, whose fashion history can be traced back to the sweatshop where the protagonist of *The Man Who Cried* finds the clue that leads her to her father. New York, layered with history as if with clothing, is like *Rage* (2009) itself, a project that Potter has been dressing and undressing since *The Tango Lesson*. New York is also like Orlando's oak tree, wrapped about with contradictory and intertwining histories, and *Rage* (2009) reprises both Orlando's love of costume and her gaze to camera. Through that gaze and the bodies it challenges us to think about, *Rage* (2009) goes right back to *Thriller*'s concern with the connection between femicide, fashion and self-fashioning, and *The Gold Diggers*' witty, impassioned, prescient tirade against the bankers and strip-miners.

The fashion industry is, on the surface, an easy target, but it is just the cover for an all-out attack on patriarchal capitalism in its strip-mining of everything from language to human lives. With her sharp ear for everyday speech, Potter has fun exposing how fashion's deformation of labouring (as well as modelling) bodies is paralleled and furthered by the pompous and meaningless deformation of language in the hands of the marketing men. Besuited Bradley (Bob Balaban) is an updated version of the comic financial Expert in *The Gold Diggers*, speaking in circular inanities about the new brand of perfume being launched at (and overshadowing) the fashion show that is the dramatic engine of *Rage* (2009). As if signalling the inflated importance of marketing itself, the scent is called *M*, at once an empty signifier (and signifier of marketing's emptiness) and a rich, poetic mine. It could stand for Merlin (Simon Abkarian), the fashion house's controversial designer, and for all that his name implies about the contradictory nature of the creative artist: he is magical, masterful, mercurial, mystificatory, and (like Arthur's Merlin, the spinner of nationalist myths) morally ambiguous.

M is, of course, also for marketing itself, the promotion of the brand above the product described by Naomi Klein in *No Logo* (2000). True to form, Bradley suggests that it evokes 'mystery', while tyro intern Dwight (Patrick J. Adams) posits 'muthafucka … for the African-American market'. Film fans will guess that *M* is for murder, recalling Fritz Lang's *M* (1931) and Alfred Hitchcock's *Dial M for Murder* (1954). The branding of ethnicity and the (dis)pleasures of the classical thriller are both there in *M*'s mix. Unseen, *M* evokes the golden arches of one of the most famous American brands, and the transformation of visual and verbal language into meaningless logos and marketing-speak. The only brand mentioned in the film is Starbucks, whose marketing director Scott Bedbury remarked in 1996 that the coffee chain wants to '"align [itself] with one of the greatest movements towards finding a connection with your soul"' (in Klein 2001: 138). Yet Bradley, for all his platitudes, is not the villain, but a henchman for the genial, yet tentacular, mogul Tiny Diamonds (Eddie Izzard) who owns the fashion house and various media outlets, among other unspecified businesses. The film subtly reveals that he controls – and may eventually own – Michelangelo's documentary. That this apparently undercover investigation of labour abuses at the company is part of Diamonds' plan becomes clear when Tiny states that he never imagined *M* could be associated with murder and adds, with a confidential wink more threatening than any Bond villain's grimace, 'You got that? Good.' To Tiny, the young protestors enraged by Michelangelo's film into activism against the company are nothing more than a potential market, primed by their media saturation.

Rage (2009) exists in the same media landscape that it excoriates, where the value of labour and art is erased by the almost-impossible situation in which every aspect of film, from the manufacture of cameras to distribution (even online), has converged in the subtle hands of global conglomerates. As Klein argues, these companies (like Starbucks) speak of 'community' and 'empowerment', to be achieved through consuming, rather than working or thinking, together. *Rage* (2009) explores the possibility of a communitarian audience connected by more than buying in to the same brand. That audience is the complement to, and reflection of, Potter's continuing redefinition of herself as an artist maintaining a critical distance from the market. Alive to a situation in which a cappuccino brewed from plantation-labour beans sells itself as a connection with your soul, *Rage* (2009) rages at the narrowing zone in which independent art – art that is not focused on chasing the market – can operate.

Refashioning film (back) into an artisanal industry, *Rage* (2009) had the smallest budget, in real terms, of any of Potter's full-length features. The on-set crew consisted of Jean-Paul Mugel, recording and mixing the live sound. Director of Photography Stephen Fierberg was on hand to adjust the lighting; producer Christopher Sheppard acted as first assistant director and clapper loader; and Jimmy Barnett attended to the downloading of rushes and other digital technology. Potter shot the film, as well as writing and directing, returning to the place behind the camera from which she started in making her shorts and *Thriller*. As an independent writer/director (who has also edited, choreographed, composed, sung for and performed in various of her films), Potter is regarded as an auteur. Scott MacDonald (1998) included her in his series of interviews with internationally-regarded independent auteurs, published as the *Critical Cinema* series. Auteurist magazine *Cineaste* likewise included her in an interview collection (see Dowell 2002). She is listed in Yvonne Tasker's *Fifty British Filmmakers* (see Ciecko 2002), as well as the international dictionary of *Women Filmmakers and their Films* (Glaessner 1998), *The Cinema of Britain and Ireland* (Lucas 2005) and *Fifty Key British Films* (McNeill 2008). *The Cinema of Sally Potter* is, as its title suggests, obviously in the auteurist tradition, searching for the threads that run through Potter's work from her earliest films to projects in the making. Archival material and long quotations from interviews season the chapters, neither in order to mandate a biographical reading, nor to cede to Potter control over the meanings of her films. Instead, they present an investigation of what it means to be identified as an auteur by the system, but to be committed to collaboration and conversation.

While Potter's films have been used to establish her as an auteur who exemplifies (or bucks) trends in British, independent and feminist filmmaking, there are few critical accounts that have approached her oeuvre as a whole, rather than focusing on single films. Scant consideration has been given to the way in which the films work with each other, or with her non-feature work in performance, short film, documentary and music. Yet there are potent connections on a large scale in narrative patterns and world view that are visible in the repetition and reshaping of small details such as gestures, colours and framings. As her cinematic style develops, it does not move away from experiment, but integrates it into narrative filmmaking in order to bring her political concerns to larger audiences. Through the emphasis that her films place on aspects of cinema that are often neglected by mainstream film theory, Potter also draws attention to communities and issues that are considered marginal by dominant culture. These cinematic repetitions make visible the interrelated themes that are taken up in a series of chapters that range across Potter's oeuvre while paying attention to aesthetic and historical shifts.

The first thematic chapter, 'Working', considers how Potter brings artisanal (hand-made) filmmaking practices into feature film, and reflects the labour of filmmaking by showing workers on film. Representations of work in each of the opening scenes of each film argue that the filmmaker is a worker engaged, and inviting the viewer to participate, in a joint endeavour. 'Moving' looks more specifically at the work of the artiste, or the live performer using her body to connect with an audience. It asks why performance is such a neglected aspect of film, and observes that far from being pure spectacle, song and dance signal that Potter's characters are sharing their interiority with us *through* the body. Performance's riposte to realism is underlined by Potter's stylised and spectacular use of colour. 'Colouring' explores the films' connections to art history through their symbolic colour palettes. Potter's films have frequently been called 'postmodern' for their abundance of literary and cinematic as well as artistic intertexts. In *The Poetics of Postmodernism*, Linda Hutcheon amply discusses the relationship between referential texts and their readers who may or may not get every reference (2004: 141–57). At fifteen, I don't think I consciously 'got' *Orlando*'s intertexts, apart from the parodic charm of Toby Stephens delivering Othello's final lines in a Shakespeare on Ice show. Colour, which is layered with cultural meanings, italicises moments of intertextuality in the films by thickening them, allowing audiences to *feel* the significance of the moment whether they know the reference or not.

Like work and performance, the particular use of colour operates as a signature across the films. 'Listening' looks at the idea of the auteur's 'signature' literally, by considering the films' use of verbal language in writing, dialogue and song. Potter's deft and passionate attention to language makes her films particular, as they work through the difficulties of communication in relation to the writer/director's practice. Rather than speaking from a confessional 'I', Potter's films reinvent the auteur as a listener. They do this by modelling audience, as each film includes multiple scenes in which one character listens to another as a witness. The films' protagonists all learn to listen, not only to communicate with the Other, but in order to understand their individual and cultural memories. To foreground this process, Potter uses many different genres of music to tell her stories. Music is a particular trigger to the embodied, emotive memory that is the subject of 'Feeling'. Rather than the performer's body, this chapter focuses on the viewer's, looking specifically at how sound can break the fourth wall and 'touch' what we have forgotten or repressed. The films listen to and record forgotten histories, awakening memories of that which has been excluded from dominant culture or the official archives because it is marginalised or considered ephemeral.

Forgotten histories are also sounded out in 'Loving', which considers the place of place in Potter's films, looking in particular at the way that the temporary, marginal places in which her characters find themselves shape their intimate relationships. When Orlando falls asleep in England for seven days, he wakes embittered by his break-up with Sasha; when he falls asleep in Uzbekistan for seven days, he wakes up as a woman. Place matters, especially in relation to ideas of home and exile that shape both individuals and their romantic relationships. Certain spaces that are displaced by being the same everywhere, like hotel rooms and theatres, become the setting for moments of transformation. Cinema, too, becomes one of these spaces, in which the audience is offered the opportunity to be transformed.

In the conclusion, I return to and reimagine the introduction's theme of 'becoming', drawing together the threads relating to transformation that run through the book. Rather than a biographical or film-historical trajectory, it imagines an ongoing change spiralling out through Potter's work, traced through her use of elemental imagery. I situate cinema in the world through Potter's use of deep symbolic structures shaped by hidden histories and philosophies. From anarcho-syndicalism to alchemy, these have been suppressed by dominant culture because they hold out the promise of transformation at every level, from the individual's body to systemic power. Each of her central characters starts out complicit with and oppressed by dominant culture's use of gender, class, race and sexuality to divide and conquer. Orlando is perhaps the most extreme of these, as he is trapped by being on the 'right' side of the divide at the start of the film: as an upper-class, wealthy, handsome white male he appears to want for nothing. Encountering a series of lovers and artists, he discovers that he is lonely and that the loneliness of the poet isolated by his class and wealth does not make for very interesting art. Through the encounters, he changes – most obviously by becoming female after refusing to kill in battle. The characters come to see that by changing within intimate relationships, they begin to change the world. The films end with that beginning, a gesture outwards that asks the audience to carry on the change.

A brief history of Potter's films will demonstrate how they contain and encourage this change as they emerge from conscious and conscientious engagement with the historical circumstance of their making based in the filmmaker's active commitment to social transformation. *Thriller* was shot on a small Arts Council grant while Potter and her *Berlin* collaborator Rose English moved from squat to squat in 1978, as she had throughout the 1970s (see Rich 1993). She had been a team leader and spokesperson in the infamous squat behind Heal's department store on Tottenham Court Road, London, which was infiltrated by police informants. Potter was instrumental in getting the case against the squatters thrown out of court when she was able to identify the informant (interview with author, September 2006). As part of LDC, Potter had participated in a 'happening' to protest against the 1973 coup in Chile as well as a growing number of feminist performances, conferences and actions. *Thriller* came out of a euphoric and effusive moment in which feminism, film and theory connected to alter the landscape of cinema radically (see Potter 1981).

When *Thriller* screened at the Edinburgh Film Festival in 1979, it was part of a moment of historical significance: the second Women and Film week, following the 1975 conference that launched Laura Mulvey's influential article on gender and spectatorship, 'Narrative Pleasure and Visual Cinema' (see MacKintosh & Merck 1979). In *Thriller*'s retelling of *La Bohème* from the point of view of its female working-class tragic heroine, Mimi, many viewers saw an exemplary working-out of the ideas for a feminist counter-cinema put forward by Mulvey. While the film's investigation of labour politics and the hidden histories of women's lives shared a political will with the feminist direct cinema documentaries of the mid-1970s, *Thriller* had a distinctive wit, verve and range derived from Potter's knowledge of both dance and the works of Russian anarchist Peter Kropotkin. It had, in many senses, *form*: Potter's background in music and performance allowed her to use the structure of the opera to make her points, framed by specifically cinematic traits inherited from the LFMC like looped footage, repeated images, close-ups and a voice-over, all of which pointed to what was missing from the opera.

The film's voice-over narration quoted influential ideas from Michel Foucault and Karl Marx, but it also gave voice to grassroots feminist rage at the invisibility of poor, working-class, ageing women, and particularly women of colour, symbolised by Potter's re-conception of Mimi. Potter split the role between black performer Colette Laffont and white performance artist Rose English. With Laffont delivering the voice-over that spans the film, *Thriller* was the first British film with a black female protagonist. This was one of the reasons that *Thriller* generated enough excitement to play at the Ritzy in (predominantly black) Brixton and to tour the US. While little has been written about its anarchic anti-racist and anti-capitalist politics, early articles about *Thriller* capture the excitement that the film caused in the feminist community. In 1980, feminist filmmaker Jane Weinstock wrote the first academic article on *Thriller* for an early issue of feminist film journal *Camera Obscura*, reading it through the groundswell of French theory that was reshaping the study of the humanities in the US. B. Ruby Rich, meanwhile, reviewed it in the weekly *Chicago Reader* specifically as a reworking of the kind of gendered film conventions that Mulvey had so brilliantly identified (1998: 227–32). Both of them argue that the film's heady brew of feminist anger, humour, love and courage is transformative, as it imagines Mimi reaching out in friendship and desire to Musetta, the opera's 'bad girl'.

Such a friendship is at the heart of Potter's next film, *The Gold Diggers*, which arrived at a different kind of euphoric moment. It was being shot in London and Iceland, with £250,000 of British Film Institute funding, as the Academy Awards resounded to the cries of 'the British are coming!' after the success of *Chariots of Fire* (1981). Thatcherite politics – nationalism as well as capitalism – subsequently took the opportunity to bring film into 'the religion of the market' (Quart 2006: 15), shaping British film policy towards competing for the mainstream with Hollywood. *The Gold Diggers* was a late flourish of what Rich called, in 1983, 'The Very Model of a Modern Minor Industry' of independent British cinema, based in 'the emergence of a post-Godardian political modernism at the BFI [production board]' in the late 1970s under Peter Sainsbury (Wollen 2006: 41). *The Gold Diggers* was modernist in its focus on formal strategies, while its politics were, like Jean-Luc Godard's, directly and didactically critical of 'the religion of the market'. It emerged stridently from the politics and practices of the performance scene: written collaboratively by Potter, English and Cooper, it was the first film to be shot with an all-female crew, all – including star performer Julie Christie and renowned cinematographer Babette Mangolte – working for equal, and minimum, wage.

Nothing could have been more different from *Chariots of Fire*'s heroic story of male friendship and sporting achievement than *The Gold Diggers*' black-and-white fairy tale of two girls lost in late capitalism. Celeste (Laffont) is a bank employee by day and an investigator by night. Her investigations into the circulation of money lead her to discover a ritual in which the beautiful Ruby (Christie) is paraded through the streets along with gold bars, and then taken to a ball. Celeste rescues Ruby from the ball – and challenges her to rescue herself from the trap of money and femininity by recovering memories of her mother. Ruby takes up the challenge, only to find herself locked tighter in the interlocking meanings of gold and women. Celeste rescues her again and they ride off into the night.

Vaudeville, dance and madcap chases make the film Potter's closest homage to her beloved Marx Brothers. She had been touring with a music improv group of that name in between *Thriller* and *The Gold Diggers*, and the film has a wonderful score by fellow Brother Cooper, which she subsequently played in concert to sold-out houses (see Merck 1984: 51). The film packed in audiences at film festivals – including the feminist film festivals then in their heyday, such as Cinémama in Québec – but its critical take on capitalism, heterosexuality and a mainstream film industry which promoted both unthinkingly left it out in the cold. The girls found each other, but their unusual romance lost many members of the film's audience – or rather, lost a vocal section of (predominantly male) critics, who railed against the film so harshly that Potter withdrew it from circulation. Even the most disdainful reviewers noted a glowing performance by Christie in the role of a screen icon who challenges her own objectification. Influential alternative and feminist critics such as Pam Cook (1984b) hailed it as a breakthrough for counter-cinema, taking pleasure in the freshness of its two central narratives: a sweetly-suggested lesbian romance between Celeste and Ruby, and Ruby's imagined reconciliation with the mother who had abandoned her as a child.

The icy wastes in which Ruby and her mother lived were shot in Iceland with characteristic style and vigour by Mangolte, Chantal Akerman's regular cinema-tographer. That unforgiving landscape could be seen symbolically as Potter's home for the following ten years, as she pitched projects to Channel Four and the Arts Council to little avail. Channel Four did commission two documentaries in the late 1980s: *Tears, Laughter, Fears, and Rage* was a four-part series broadcast in a primetime slot on Saturday evenings in September and October 1987, opposite ratings-winner *Blind Date*. Through a combination of film clips from British and international cinema, and talking heads interviews with a weird and wonderful range of people (from the Chief Rabbi of Britain to *Carry On* films actor Barbara Windsor), *Tears, Laughter, Fears, and Rage* examined the kind of emotions that were generated by its rival on ITV. Interviews with psychoanalytic theorist Juliet Mitchell and Irish trade union organiser Inez McCormack had a feminist focus, and the series also began Potter's investigation of masculinity, asking the director of *Peeping Tom* (1960), Michael Powell, and politician Paul Boateng, among others, about whether and why boys cry.

As it screened, Potter was gathering footage for another documentary that would not screen until 1990. Taking advantage of *glasnost*, she travelled to the Soviet Union, which she had visited several times previously and to which she felt a strong artistic and political connection, to explore the state film archives. *I am an Ox, I am a Horse, I am a Man, I am a Woman: Women in Russian Cinema* (1990) introduced

British television viewers to some of the masterpieces of Soviet cinema that had been trapped behind the Iron Curtain. It looked at the mythic figure of Mother Russia as well as at the lived realities of making art under communism, emphatically fore-grounding the equal role of women as directors, writers and performers. The trips to Russia were preparation for more than the documentary, however, as Potter initially planned to shoot *Orlando* at Mosfilm in Moscow, where Eisenstein had made many of his films. The winds of political fortune that buffet Orlando from England to Khiva and back again also affected the film; as between 1988 when Potter began drafting and 1991 when she began shooting, the status quo throughout Eastern Europe changed utterly.

As Potter's plans altered, so too did the political mood of the screenplay. Early drafts of *Orlando*, among other differences, are much more explicitly and polemi-cally concerned with property and class. The finished film has the liberatory light-ness of post-1989 politics in its theme of freedom (although it cannot and does not resist a welcome dig at the shiny new corporate London being constructed in Dock-lands). Many reviewers and theorists were newly excited by Potter's work, generating a massive amount of writing on *Orlando*, much of which focuses on its adaptation of Virginia Woolf's novel. Woolf's status as a feminist icon, the novel's play with gender and costume, and Potter's previous expressions of feminist politics created an engaging combination that saw theorists Patricia Mellencamp and Maggie Humm embrace the film to the extent of using stills on the covers of their books, *A Fine Romance* (1995) and *Feminism and Film* (1997).

The focus on adaptation and costume positioned the film in a discussion about genre and gender, specifically the changing face of costume drama and its relation to literature (see Garrett 1995; Pidduck 1997; Ciecko 1998; Ouditt 1999; Vincendeau 2001a). Some Woolf scholars, such as Leslie Hankins (1995), professed themselves disappointed by the film's alterations and challenges to the novel, and saw the film's playful tone and 'visual pleasure' as a betrayal of their previous support for what they saw as Potter's anti-pleasure experiments. Others, like Stella Bruzzi (1997), celebrated its playful, sensuous embrace of a new, expansive feminist erotics. As I have discussed elsewhere, more recent readings go beyond costume drama to wonder whether Orlando, time-travelling and gender-blending, might have been shaped by the idea of the cyborg put forward in 'The Cyborg Manifesto' by Donna Haraway in 1985 and republished in 1991, as Potter was shooting the film (see Mayer 2008). For Haraway, the wired woman – like Orlando – is a new figure of pleasure who defines her own embodiment, at once historically aware and fully in the present, connected to a global network of labourers, and always on the move.

Starting in the late 1990s, *Thriller* and *The Gold Diggers* have been re-evaluated for the pleasures that they offer, and Potter's political self-definition has also shifted with the times. The meaning of 'feminist' altered as the economic and cultural struc-tures that had supported *Thriller* and *The Gold Diggers*, as well as organisations such as women's filmmaking co-operative Circles, shifted or disintegrated under the pres-sure of Reaganomics and 'family values'. The backlash had begun. Talking to Potter in 1993, David Ehrenstein concludes his *Film Quarterly* interview with three key questions about feminism and the politics of filmmaking whose answers are worth quoting at length for their coherence and honesty:

DE: Do you think that *Orlando* speaks to issues related to today's gay and lesbian politics?

SP: I'm so wary of making any sort of generalisation because of what happened to the feminist movement. 'Feminist' has become a sort of trigger word that closes down thinking rather than opening it up. I was very interested to see a recent issue of *New York* magazine with k. d. lang on the cover and the headline 'Lesbian Chic' – as if it were all just fashion. Still, these public moments of shifts in acceptability have significance. Perhaps it's a result of the long, slow burn of activism, and the courage of a great number of people, and of course AIDS … I think that [there] are really significant gains, and gay and lesbian cinema can be seen in relation to them. As for *Orlando* and where it fits in, I really think that the film's contribution to that area is not so much about gaining identity as it is blurring identity. It's about the claiming of an essential self, not just in sexual terms. It's about the immortal soul.

DE: You were speaking of feminism as a 'trigger word'…

SP: Feminism is a really difficult thing to talk about. I've been asked so many times by the, let's say, populist sort of journalists: 'Are you a feminist?' It's like laying the gauntlet down. If I say yes … it would slot in with their definition, which was a cliché of a protesting radical – everything they fear. But I've learned that to win, you've got to have cover. You've got to be clever. You've got to speak freshly with nice juicy words that intoxicate, not trigger jargon words that turn people off. If I talk about treating women with respect and dignity, not as second-class citizens, able to make a contribution with freedom and without limitation – it gets the point across. The other thing that I think is problematic about the word 'feminist' at this point – at least in England, I imagine it's different in the US – is that it doesn't necessarily imply linking up with other liberation struggles … it leads to a cheap, commercialised view of liberation.

DE: It seems that now you're in a situation that's the opposite of where you were after *The Gold Diggers*.

SP: It's a lot nicer to be wanted than not wanted! I think I'm just about old enough to remain fairly centred and unseduceable by certain things … Orson Welles said filmmakers have to be like cotton pickers – go where the harvest is. It comes down to the project and the terms, and the only terms I know how to produce are the ones where I'm in complete control. (1993: 6–7)

Filmmaking could no longer operate 'in sexual terms', as audiences and debates changed. Moreover, Potter redefines feminist as intersecting with other battles for equality, and with larger questions of the 'immortal soul' rather than glass ceilings. Orlando does not end the film with the fame, respect and fortune that Woolf's protagonist accrues. Instead of fighting her way into the boardroom, she bikes out of the rat race, refusing the strictures of capitalist society altogether. Her choice is based in her recognition that her 'essential self' is not singular, but plural, and therefore not able to be described or contained by the shorthand of an -ism, even as Potter and her work remain committed to the struggle for equality and justice.

The relationship between this precise redefinition of political art and the politics of making art shaped Potter's subsequent film. *The Tango Lesson* tells the story of a filmmaker called Sally (played by Potter) who is in demand in Hollywood because of the success of her previous film. Struggling to write her new film, *Rage* (1996), she decides to take tango lessons with Pablo (Pablo Veron), a well-known young Argentinean dancer living in Paris. Her film and the relationship proceed apace, as Pablo happily imagines his new career as a screen star and Sally takes delight in both dance and dancer, until a disastrous poolside meeting with producers in Hollywood. Sally suddenly finds that being wanted can be more of a bind than not being wanted and she abandons her film to throw herself headlong into a tango exhibition performance with an increasingly volatile Pablo. Like the meeting, the performance is not the crowning success that a conventional film narrative would demand, and Sally has to start again. She aligns her liberation struggle as a white woman from the developed world with Pablo's as an exile from the Global South. Through this reconciliation, she starts again, planning a new film that becomes the film we are watching.

When Sally truly commits to the new film, she does so through a dance that lifts *The Tango Lesson* into the musical's 'feeling of freedom, in which people can fly through space' (Potter, interview with author, January 2007). After spending an exhausting day looking for locations for her tango film, Sally, Pablo and their two male friends slump, disconsolate, outside a locked room. Sally tells Pablo to set up a tap rhythm and teach it to the other men. After a while, he breaks out into a pirouetting solo, leaping through the closed doors into an immense, empty warehouse. First the male dancers, then Sally, join him, and they link arms in a unique dance figure, a *pas de quatre*. This wreathing, spiralling group soars the length of the warehouse in a long take, while the camera responds, like a dance partner, to the complex interweavings, progressions and regressions, circlings and leaps of the four dancers as they invent a four-person tango. The soundtrack to their dance is Astor Piazzolla's 'Libertango', and the freedom with which Potter and her dancers explore and expand the conventions of both tango and cinema is spectacular. As a plea for life, liberty and happiness through respect for the other, the film moved audiences worldwide, playing at dozens of film festivals and garnering awards, including a nomination for a BAFTA. *The Tango Lesson* won Best Film at Mar del Plata in Argentina in 1997, which marked the second year of the revival of Latin America's largest film festival, after it was closed for political reasons from 1971 to 1995. The film's themes of openness and collaboration, as well as its documentation of the struggle to make meaningful art, must have seemed pointed and poignant in post-*junta* Argentina recovering from dictatorship, censorship and economic disarray.

The Tango Lesson uncovers the potentially dictatorial nature of 'complete control'. On the one hand, Sally is a successful filmmaker and Pablo a brilliant dancer; on the other, neither is good at opening up to the other within their artforms. While they can have deep philosophical conversations, they have to learn to transfer that energy of vulnerability to collaborative creation. By daring to fail with each other, a new kind of virtuosity is found, in which the determination that lies behind the desire for complete control is balanced by a self-confidence that enables the artist to realise that to write her own life is a collaborative process. Yet the film was also charged with the kind of narcissism it critiques, because Potter herself – a middle-aged non-professional actor – dared to play Sally in a narrative that seemed autobiographical. Sally is and is not, of course, also Sally Potter who *did* write and shoot the scenes from *Rage* (1996). The joke fell flat with many male reviewers who conversely celebrated Woody Allen playing (with) himself in *Deconstructing Harry*, released the same year (see Columpar 2003: 108). As Corinn Columpar writes: 'if Harry were to meet Sally, it would be on a textual terrain reserved for male subjectivity' (2003: 109). Like Meg Ryan's Sally in the famous orgasm scene in Rob Reiner's film, Potter and her eponymous character lay claim to a bodily autonomy and pleasure that confused male reviewers who 'conflate[d] female autonomy and authorship with narcissism' (ibid.).

Columpar instead interprets the 'dancing body' as a route to an understanding of self through its negotiations with the other. Theorist and *tanguero* Erin Manning puts forward tango as a 'politics of touch' because it 'calls out to the night-world to re-orchestrate its systems of governance and exchange through bodies that exist not, first and foremost, for the outside world, but for the inner exchange between two silent partners, moving quietly, eyes half closed, towards dawn' (2007: 2). So *The Tango Lesson* ends, with its characters and the film itself transformed through the 'inner exchange' of tango's improvisation and collaboration. Concerned with 'the immortal soul', *The Tango Lesson* moves exactly in the embarrassing and mystificatory territory of apostrophe. Film theorist Sylvia Harvey suggests that 'one of the challenges of current secular criticism is to reconstruct or re-invent a sense of the sacred and the immortal, and perhaps to find other words than these to refer to the constant presence of the extraordinary within the ordinary' (1996: 233). Potter's films are looking exactly for forms, words or images 'to re-invent a sense of the sacred and the immortal'. Her films resonate with the historical and ongoing presence of the Abrahamic faiths in many aspects of daily life in the West, from the way we think about cleanness and dirt to specific stories and images, such as the angel.

Sally talks to Pablo about God, saying that she does not 'believe our lives are already written … Therefore, I suppose I'm an atheist. But…'. The film's exploration of the immortal soul hinges on and works through that 'But…'. Sally and Pablo's journey towards each other will take them to two monuments of Western religion: Saint Sulpice in Paris and one of Buenos Aires' fifty synagogues. Rather than God and religion providing a home or way of locating oneself, in Potter's films they are way-stations on a journey. Saint Sulpice, where Sally goes to look at Delacroix's famous painting *Jacob Wrestling the Angel*, is a Parisian tourist destination, while the synagogue – where Sally's and Pablo's eyes finally meet as equals – is one of those displaced spaces in which the films and their characters find themselves, mirroring

Pablo's double displacement as a Jewish Argentinian in Europe, and as a European Jew in Argentina.

The film tangos with the question of Jewish identity and the idea of diaspora as a location from which to speak and listen. It takes up Jewish philosopher Martin Buber's 1958 mystical text *I and Thou* to suggest that tango's 'inner exchange' can be 'about the immortal soul'. In Potter's words, '*I and Thou* is like a key that unlocks a lot of the dance, the story, the metaphysics that lie behind the whole idea, and that's, in a way, part of the key to the door' (in Vollmer 2006: 214). It is part of the key to understanding how the films engage their viewers in a conversation. Buber argues that there is no way to say 'I' as we are always speaking in relation to an object and a listener. On an everyday basis we say 'I-It', making our relation unequal with the object of our speech, whether they are human, animal or mineral. In speaking of and to the divine, we have to say '*I-Thou*', to speak with the Other as an equal participant.

Buber deeply influenced psychotherapist Carl Rogers in his conception of patient-centred practice, and can be seen as part of a similar, secular but spiritual viewer-centred practice in Potter's work. The films' respectful regard offers audiences who are willing to follow it a cinematic language that takes the place of ingrained and exclusory religious ways of approaching the world. In a significant sense, film's abilities to render things visible and to change points of view makes saying '*I-Thou*' possible. As Potter puts it, 'seeing, therefore, becomes a kind of worship in the sense of really recognising, acknowledging what's there, or trying to see beyond the three dimensions into some other dimension. By seeing, absorbing and interpreting what's there we create or recreate the world anew; it is born through our eyes' (in Vollmer 2006: 217).

Potter's characters are intensely watchful. Sally, the film director who tells Pablo that she loves him 'with my eyes' is the model for all the searching female protagonists who use their eyes to discover themselves and their worlds. More than that, Potter's characters boldly and levelly engage each other's gaze and the audience's. Feminist philosopher Donna Haraway draws a distinction between the destructive penetrative 'gaze' theorised by psychoanalytic feminists in the 1970s, and regard, which she relates to the Latin *re-spicere*, to look again, the origin of the English word *respect*. She comments that writing was her 'effort to gain the father's regard – not the father's gaze, but that regard of holding in mutual esteem, that richochet specularity of *re-spicere*, of respect, the holding and mutual regard that is the exact opposite of that which critical theory has learned to theorise best … *Respicere, respectus*, to take heed, to take care, to have care for' (Haraway 2006; author's transcription). Potter's films work to respect, 'to take heed, to take care, to have care for' their viewers.

Many scenes in *The Man Who Cried* proceed entirely through a conversation of eyes shown in close-up. With no more than searching glances, to-camera gazes and averted eyes an operatic drama is played out. This watchfulness occurs in the context of Paris, 1940, just before the Nazi invasion and occupation. Betrayal and danger are everywhere for the film's protagonist, Suzie (Christina Ricci), a Jewish refugee from Russia via Depression-era London. Like Pablo, she is a figure for diasporic Jewishness in the twentieth century. She has left behind the shtetl where she grew up with the Yiddish name Fegele. As she escapes a pogrom, Fegele (Claudia Lander-Duke) takes a ship, thinking that she is following her father to America, only to dock in England. Renamed Susan for her black eyes by a customs official and immersed in a new language, Suzie uses her singing voice to get a job in a cabaret in Paris where she saves money to get to America. The anti-semitism that she fled as a child catches up with her, first through Dante (John Turturro), a talented Italian tenor whose voice has given him a sense of superiority, and then through the invasion. After she is betrayed to Dante by her friend and flatmate Lola (Cate Blanchett), Suzie's only ally is Cesar (Johnny Depp), a Roma horse wrangler who works for the opera company where all four perform. Cesar and Suzie are about as shy as each other and it is their passionate exchange of glances that draws the viewer into the film.

What sets *The Man Who Cried* apart from the melodramas to which it is a love letter is its insistence that love can unify across all barriers. Where Sally and Pablo worked towards an equality, Suzie and Cesar are united by their position on the margins of the opera company and by their sense of displacement. Lola befriends Suzie because she has a spare bed in her apartment and pursues Dante because he is wealthy and successful, but Suzie is attracted to Cesar because he is excluded by being Roma from Lola's marketplace thinking. Their relationship is not motivated by pity or by kooky oddball attraction, but by a fierce pride in being outsiders. With very few lines, they have the kind of 'inner exchange' that Manning sees in tango.

It is this exchange that Potter identifies as the most desirable and powerful form of spectatorship when she talks about the often emotional reactions of audiences at festival screenings:

> People's tears and fears, I welcome them, I'm unafraid, and I know how important that can be. I've been on the other end of it, where I've been deeply and profoundly affected by somebody's work, and wanted to have that little moment of exchange. In those rare moments where it's happened, it's been *so* significant. I met [influential British filmmakers] Michael Powell and Emeric Pressburger for maybe thirty seconds after a performance – I think it sustained me for about three years, and continues to. It's a symbolic exchange, it's more than itself. (Interview with author, September 2006)

Potter's films recognise and work outwards from the power of that 'little moment of exchange'. Not every viewer can meet or speak to the director, even with the new media technology allowing the development of interactive websites for *Yes* and for the filmmaker. Instead, the films offer symbolic versions of such an exchange.

The word 'exchange' has become tied up with ideas of market value and use value, with the kind of Exchange where gold is stored, as seen in *The Gold Diggers*, or the kind that Lola makes when she gives Dante her body for his money. In his classic study *The Gift*, Lewis Hyde suggests another meaning that links moments of intimate exchange back to the idea of the gift by looking at potlatch customs where giving causes giving. He argues that 'when you give a gift there is momentum, and the weight shifts from body to body' (1983: 9). This is exactly the exchange seen in Potter's films: between characters, and between the film and the viewer. Potter's idea of a moment of exchange is one where the feelings and thoughts inspired by a film lead to a connection, which leads not to a closed circuit between viewer and film or fan and director, but to the viewer being 'sustained' by the exchange into making their own mark on the world. For Hyde, the gift is always on the move – it is perhaps better to call it 'giving', like the back-and-forth of tango (1983: 4).

In a similar way, perhaps Potter's films could be called 'viewings' or 'happenings', not only because of their fascination with human movement but because of their unique time signatures. Ursula K. Le Guin writes that narratives structured by dance will be told through 'steps, gestures, continuity, harmony, the spiral' (2001: 484). *Thriller* and *The Gold Diggers*, each of which repeats its central narrative three times, are most obviously spirals. *Orlando* begins and ends in the same setting, with the closing scene an inversion of the opening scene. *The Tango Lesson* spirals in on its own making as Sally moves from writing *Rage* (1996) to shooting *The Tango Lesson*. While *The Man Who Cried* appears to be linear, it is a spiral inwards and back outwards from Suzie's near-death experience. *The Man Who Cried* appears to be Suzie's memories as she struggles against death.

Stephanie Jordan attributes the subversion of linear narrative in which the past keeps happening again until it comes right, to Potter's citation of 'the influence of Gertrude Stein, borrowing her use of repetition to suspend time into a continuous present, to isolate the moment being observed' (1992: 106). There is a pun implicit in the double meaning of 'present': the films' sense of 'now' is part of their gift. Jay Griffiths describes the gift of the moment that Potter's films offer when she writes of 'a wild idea of time that demands a sense of being right at the edge of the moment, just at the point where the moment meets the eternal … In this momentous now is the freedom of uncountable choices: spontaneity, caprice and the absolute freedom of wild time' (2007: 298). The spiral makes time wild by bringing past events into the present, not through clearly-defined flashbacks, but by allowing memories and dreams to leak into the apparently 'linear' narratives.

As Potter said in an interview about *Orlando* with her story editor Walter Donohue, she 'found that you can be much bolder than [she] ever thought in the way you jump, cinematically, from one period to another' (in Donohue 1993: 12). Rather than tying themselves to the tight temporal structure of classical Hollywood cinema, where tension is racked up by deadlines, train times and ticking clocks, Potter's films use cinematic form to loosen time towards 'the point where the moment meets the eternal'. Time, in film, is made linear by image and sound editing: there are few match-cuts in Potter's films; we rarely follow a character walking from one space directly into another. Similarly, voice-over and music often have an unstable source, or none at all. Only small, bodily clues initially tell the viewer that the voice-over on *Thriller*'s soundtrack is being delivered by Laffont. Both voice and music can move from being diegetic – spoken or heard by the characters in the frame – to non-diegetic, heard only by the viewer, or they can be somewhere in between, heard internally only by one character. Sound often moves between the three when it bridges one scene into another, which gives a sense of wild time's '"simultaneity", the sensation that others are doing at the same time things that are meaningfully related to your own experience' (Boyarin 1994: 17).

More than any other Potter film, *Yes* uses formal play to create a sense of the 'absolute freedom of wild time' as its simultaneity between two lovers makes possible the moment of exchange. Yet, more than any other, it is urgently embedded in the moment of its making. Potter began writing the story of love between a white American woman and an Arab man, both displaced in contemporary London, on 12 September 2001. It is the only one of her films to make such explicit reference to contemporary events, although unlike many films concerned with 9/11, it has no direct reference to or re-imagining of particular terrorist attacks or illegal wars. While it speaks insistently of and from its present moment, it suspends direct references in order to put political and cultural relations between the Arab and Euro-Western worlds into a wider historical perspective. Through its use of gardens, numbers and music, the film refers to Sufi poetry, which is at once about erotic and spiritual love. Sufism emerged in the Golden Ages of Islam in Spain and Baghdad when European Crusaders were the *jihadis*. Historical time and individual time meet in the story of two people, called He and She. We watch their relationship progress through scenes that have only the most tenuous markers of conventional narrative time. This is the time of love, in which days and hours are marked by being in the presence of the beloved. It is also, the film suggests, cinematic time, as film – like love – makes each moment we spend with it more intense.

Yes notifies us of its intensity from its first few lines which, like all the lines in the film, are in iambic pentameter, the rhythm of Shakespeare's plays and sonnets, which some argue is the deep rhythm of English itself. Made up of five feet with two beats each, iambic pentameter is a regular metre that suggests the origins of lyric poetry in song and dance. It connects language back to the body. Like Potter's spiralling, searching films, lyric poetry feels deeply, bodily familiar (its beats are like a heartbeat) but its formal pressure on language can make things wonderfully unfamiliar. 'Language, [Elaine Scarry] argues, is what makes us subjects; it allows us to take a distance from our bodies. A lover's promise is to take the beloved to that point where he or she has no distance from the body – and then to let the beloved come back, into possession of language and personhood' (Marks 2002: xvi). Associated with love poetry in particular, lyric works like love, that *I-Thou* connection, to show us things anew.

Deeply concerned with the erosion of both visual and verbal language, *Rage* (2009) extends *Yes*'s lyric evocation of *I-Thou* in the specific setting of the fashion industry. The film simultaneously seeks to subvert, and invert, the industry's emphatic narcissism and the diminution of charged words such as fashion, material, fabric, thread. Investigating and invested in the metaphors of clothing, knotting, knitting, stitching, seaming that we use to describe the process of making both life and story, *Rage* (2009) recognises art's location in material history. It takes place in *Yes*'s post-9/11 world whose connectedness and violence ask us to recognise that, as Judith Butler says, 'we're undone by each other … and if we're not, we're missing something' (2004: 23). Thus,

Rage (2009) essays an undoing: unseaming the cinematic suture that makes us passive viewers, unpicking the stitches that hold patchwork lives together, unbraiding the tangled threads of global finance that keep us poor and powerless. Frayed and afraid, the characters – given the gift of Michelangelo's rapt attention – begin to remake themselves: Bradley, fired from his marketing job, dreams of taking up dancing to the delicate sound of a quotation from the soundtrack to *The Tango Lesson*. In these exchanges, where the filmmaker is figured as a listener, *Rage* (2009) gives cinema back to itself and time back to its audience.

When I began to look anew at my memories of seeing *Orlando*, I remembered a final, telling detail. I would not have been confronting that security guard if we had not shown up a day late for the flight. The film may well have been gone by the time we returned, or my attention might not have been caught without that gift of a day with nothing to do. I may have become someone completely different. The gift of the moment, like the lover's promise and the inner exchange, are all ways of thinking about what happens when I watch Sally Potter's films. What they have in common is their openness and generosity – without which this book would not exist. While I was working on a PhD thesis chapter on *Orlando*, *Plan B* magazine offered me the opportunity to interview Potter before the release of *Yes* in the UK in July 2005 (see Mayer 2005). That hour-long interview sustained me through the final months of my graduate work, and became the seed of this book. It was a generous allocation of time to a neophyte reporter and, more generous still, Adventure Pictures sourced some high-quality stills from *Orlando* for my thesis and sent them on to me with an additional surprise gift, a VHS copy of *The Gold Diggers*, the only film of Potter's that I had not seen. As I saw threads of continuity and change between the 'lost' film and those that had been more successful, it prompted me to wonder why there was no single study that drew out these themes across the body of her work.

Published as *Rage* (2009) becomes the sixth feature film in Potter's forty-year career as a filmmaker, *The Cinema of Sally Potter* is about an 'inner exchange' between one viewer and the films. Many current theorists, from conservative Bazinian Christian Keathley to psychoanalytic feminist Kaja Silverman, have attested to the loss of what Silverman calls 'the cure by love' in film studies and in film itself. Ever-narrower spaces exist for alternatives to commercial cinemas, which are full of sentimentalised conventions in the guise of romantic love. At the same time, love has resurfaced as a concept in philosophy and political theory for thinking beyond the stalemate of identity politics. Michael Hardt, co-author of a new post-colonial politics of change in *Empire* (2000) and *Multitude* (2004), says boldly that:

> One has to expand the concept of love beyond the limits of the couple, even the psychoanalytic limits of coupling. One good model is through Christian and Judaic traditions, where love means, in a way, a constitution of the community. Premodern notions of love have this political character. As it has gained in sentimentality, love has lost its political efficacy ... It seems to me a summation of various things that interest me to think of politics as a project of love. (In Smith & Minardi 2004)

Potter's films have the radical potential to restore to love its political efficacy. Loving with her eyes, she tells stories about how community comes together through the exchange of looks, time and gifts. The exchange between two selves is not a closed circuit but a spiral that keeps opening outwards to the world. This book is constructed as such an exchange, in which the thematic chapters explore the spiralling relations between films, encouraging the reader to think backwards and forwards to make their own connections. Part of the motivation for this book was to continue to circulate the films' gift, what Sylvia Harvey calls 'the constant presence of the extraordinary within the ordinary'. My project is to say *I-Thou* with the films, in tune with their own politics of love.

CHAPTER ONE

Thriller

There's so many ways of thinking how a piece of art works on the subtle body of the viewer. If workers at the end of a hard day's revolution can sit down and sing a song together that makes them feel better, they'll get up the next day re-energised and revitalised to get on with the revolution. An anthem like the *Marseillaise* can unite people together around an idea and energise collectively. A song can also bring out the deep emotions of an individual, and that can provide the ground from which to take action. A Billie Holiday song is more than a victim's cry. It's a recognition that only by acknowledging, playing out and mourning the reality can you move on and look at it in another way. A blues song about the end of a relationship is a very gentle way of looking at death, at the loss of all things. That's why you weep. It's not just about being jilted by a lover, it's about being alive and dying.

— Sally Potter, interview with author, September 2006

Thriller is about nothing if not the life-and-death realities of the politics of love. It takes up – and takes issue with – one of the classics of nineteenth-century Romanticism, Giacomo Puccini's 1896 opera *La Bohème*. In adapting Henri Murger's *La vie de Bohème* stories for the operatic stage, Puccini shaped a narrative that would dictate all subsequent imaginings of artists and lovers. His theme is the impossible co-existence of love and art: Rodolfo, an artist sharing a garret with three other young Bohemians, falls in love with his downstairs neighbour Mimi, a poor seamstress dying of consumption. Poverty complicates their relationship and Mimi leaves Rodolfo, only returning to die by his side. She is carried up to the artists' garret by Musetta, a showgirl and the former lover of Marcello, another of the artists. After Mimi dies in his arms, Rodolfo sings Mimi's name in a magnificent closing statement of mourning. Music, love, poverty, creativity and loss are bound up in Puccini's powerful vision of life on the margins. If the story sounds familiar, it is because it has proved resonant for many late twentieth-century artists looking to describe the ongoing struggle between poverty and love, between art and money, and between men and women. Most recently Baz Luhrmann retold *La Bohème* in his spectacular film *Moulin Rouge!* (2001), in which the music is updated to saccharine pop songs but Satine (Luhrmann's version of Mimi) still dies.

Mimi's endlessly repeating death-by-love is the narrative puzzle that *Thriller* sets out to solve. Its thirty-minute retelling of the opera is narrated in voice-over by Mimi (Colette Laffont) who investigates her own death. She tells the story three times: firstly, as if writing programme notes for a performance (illustrated by stills from productions of the opera); secondly, beginning to break down and re-imagine various narrative incidents through performance art-like tableaux (what if Mimi had been the hero? what if she had studied critical theory?); and lastly, by recovering the real historical figure behind Mimi, the working poor woman who has no real place in the opera. Mimi realises (as she turns the story this way and that) that it was the collusion of male power and money – patriarchal capitalism, or sexism and classism – what done her in, not least by coming between her and Musetta, setting them up as opposites and competitors. At the end of the film, Mimi wonders what would have happened if the two women had become friends.

Thriller's Musetta was played by Rose English, Potter's collaborator on a number of Limited Dance Company pieces and a distinguished performance artist in her own right. Their brief, radical reworking of *La Bohème* was shot and edited in a London squat in a building that had formerly been a sweatshop for female garment workers, and that was close to the squat where they were then living (see Mellencamp 1995: 157). Traces of both its production circumstances and its attitude can be found in Jonathan Larson's *Rent*, a surprise Broadway hit musical that adapts *La Bohème* to tell stories of the artists, strippers and squatters of Avenue A in New York. Larson, who auditioned the original cast in the unheated loft where he lived, based his adaptation (which premiered off-Broadway in 1993) on aspects of his own experience, but the musical's book stays fairly close to the opera, while updating it to reflect late 1980s New York in the grip of AIDS and gentrification. Perhaps in a reflection of *Thriller*, Musetta has become Maureen, a polyamorous, bisexual performance artist. Whereas Puccini's Musetta sings a waltz (boldly referenced in both the music and book of *Rent*), Maureen offers a (pastiche of feminist) performance that is intended to satirise the wealthy landlords who want to kick the artists out of their lofts. It is hard not to see a nod to *Thriller*'s energy and wit in Larson's cross-dressing Angel, feminist performance art, and a Mimi who survives.

Most pointedly, Musetta's ex-lover Marcello is no longer an artist, but an experimental filmmaker called Mark, whose attempt to document a year in the lives of his friends gives the musical its shape. Mark has become the choral character, the narrative point-of-view, a radical change from the opera's focus on the lovers. In his opening song, he sings: 'from here on in, I shoot without a script / See if anything comes of it, instead of my old shit'. It is a neat description of the prevailing countercultural energies at the time of *Thriller*'s making. Throughout the decade of punk, Potter and LDC created dance performance 'without a script', using the energy of improvisation and juxtaposition to parody the 'old shit' of a European high culture that seemed like it was about to split under the pressure of re-invention. Organisations like Rock against Racism and the feminist collective Spare Rib were tearing up the old rulebook that Mimi reads and laughs at in *Thriller*. In *Jubilee* (1977), Derek Jarman ripped up the screen by casting punks like Adam Ant and Toyah Willcox in a time-travel narrative in which Queen Elizabeth I meets Anarchy in the UK. Jon Savage titled his seminal history of British punk rock *England's Dreaming*, arguing that punk was an alarm clock. 'Dramatising catatonia, the Punks showed up the rest of the public: they were not narcotised by England's dreaming, and they flaunted the fact' (1991: 274). Mimi, too, dramatises the dangers of unconsciousness when she awakes at the start of the film from Puccini's dream of the tubercular heroine and her supposedly beautiful, inspiring death.

La Bohème is punk at heart, with its story of making art out of chaos in the face of a cold world. But the question remains as to why Potter decided to rework a narrative that was part of the 'old shit' by virtue of being an opera as well as its Romantic belief in love (to say nothing of its gender and class politics). In fact, punk's DIY mentality specifically drew on the cut-up practice of William Burroughs to rip up the 'old shit' and paste – or rather safety-pin – it into new configurations. The shock value of the Sex Pistols' infamous first single for A&M, 'God Save the Queen' (1977), derived from its juxtaposition of something culturally impeccable and the utter fury and disdain to which the band subject it. *Thriller*, while less violent, offers a politically critical cut-up of *La Bohème* that was shot with DIY energy and resources. Unlike the punks, however, Potter is not a nihilist: within her source material she finds another story – a woman's self-realisation through friendship – that offers a new politics of love, rather than snarling hate.

In doing so, she was in tune with a burgeoning feminist and postmodern practice that understood stories as being at the root of culture, and retelling stories as the root of change. *Thriller* was shown at the Edinburgh Film Festival in 1979, the same year as Angela Carter published *The Bloody Chamber*, her era-defining collection of wickedly feminist and sexy short stories that delved into traditional fairy tales and brought out both their historical contexts and their uncanny violence and desire. *Thriller*'s Musetta, whom the film describes as 'the bad girl, the one who didn't die', combines punk's performance energy and Carter's fascination with women who use their wits to survive. Carter's approach echoed Kate Bush, who became the first female solo artist to top the charts in the UK with a self-penned song, which spent four weeks at number one in 1978. 'Wuthering Heights' packs the love story from Emily Brontë's sprawling novel into a few dramatic verses. Bush sings as the story's female romantic heroine Cathy, sounding out her wild desire for Heathcliff. Like Mimi, Cathy addresses us from 'the other side', after her death, and yet the song is ecstatic, almost orgasmic in its swooping vocal lines.

It is a stretch to call Bush's song, with its almost classical orchestral backing, punk, but its strangeness owes something to the rip in the mainstream made by the Sex Pistols and others. Likewise, *Thriller* combines punk's attitude with searing strings rather than anarchic, delirious noise. Puccini is the main source, although his opera is cut up musically as well as narratively. Potter told *Undercut* magazine that she had 'a fairly contradictory attitude to the opera, because the debunking aspect is about the more overt levels of romanticism that I think are primarily destructive … However, there's an aspect about death and loss and love which doesn't transcend those but is not entirely collapsible into them. When I was working with the music, and had heard it ten million times, I suddenly found myself crying during the death scene' (in Swanson & Moy-Thomas 2003: 197).

The death scene is where the film begins, with Rodolfo's aching cry, 'Mimi, Mimi' over a black screen. In *Opera, or the Undoing of Women*, Catherine Clément writes of Rodolfo's final music that it 'is a last spiral, all wrapped back on itself; already the notes are unable to climb to the top of the scale, already the voice is singing a single infinite repetition' (1989: 87). Rodolfo's voice moves – or 'thrills' – the audience because of this 'single infinite repetition' at the edge of the performer's range. It is also thrilling because it reaches back across the opera to echo Rodolfo's first duet with Mimi in Act I. In the opera, Mimi's death (and Rodolfo's inspired composition) are present, fated from the very first moment they sing together. Potter untwists the seductive spiral and turns it the other way: starting the film with its final notes *cues* Mimi to investigate its meaning, and so to save herself.

Mimi's musical investigations are even more essential in uncovering the intent of the second source of music that Potter entwines into Puccini's spirals: Bernard Herrmann's shrieking string theme from the shower scene in *Psycho* (1960). The Puccini/*Psycho* mash-up suggests that the opera is as much of a femicidal thriller as the film, allowing Mimi – and Potter's film – to take on and investigate both. Potter chose her source texts and named her film *Thriller* because 'women's death as a cultural obsession is … not something that's going to go away … Current campaigns, like "Reclaim the Night" are organising against this fear … In all those fear/exploitation films we get the superior knowledge of the attacker, even if we are supposed to be identifying vicariously with the terror of the heroine. In *Thriller* Mimi is looking at it from the other side' (in Swanson & Moy-Thomas 2003: 196). Potter's comment connects cultural forms that legitimise violence against women to actual violence and women's mobilisation against it. Feminist filmmaker Yvonne Rainer recalls that feminist film theory was inspired by and incited real-world activism, describing Laura Mulvey's 'Visual Pleasure and Narrative Cinema' (1975) as 'a *cri de coeur* [against sexual violence] that was echoed in protests on both sides of the Atlantic' (2006: 168). Mulvey argued that films like

Hitchcock's demanded women's punishment through objectification, constriction or death in order to create narratives satisfying to male viewers, and that cultural texts reinforced social gender hierarchies.

Mulvey's article ended by calling for a feminist counter-cinema that would revolutionise not only content but film form. It was not enough to tell women's stories; like punk, feminist cinema had to rip up the old stories and tell them differently. Mulvey pointed to the techniques of the transatlantic avant-garde (which included the work of Potter and other LFMC alumni) as a potential source of disruption and reconstruction. The techniques, she advocated, could enable both filmmaker and viewer to stand back from the overwhelming emotions associated with classical film (or opera), in order to analyse them and untangle their association with what Potter called 'overt levels of romanticisation'. Filmmakers like Rainer and Mulvey herself engaged in exploring the feminist, psychoanalytic and Marxist film theories of the time through formal practices, which included non-linear narrative and a refusal of the kinds of framing and lighting associated with the 'visual pleasure' used to contain women in Hollywood cinema.

Rainer speaks of the 'electrifying fervour' of films that believed they could change the world, which they did in no small measure (2006: 169). *Thriller*'s charge is perhaps harder to register today in a political and cultural climate that appears to have altered significantly. But appearances are deceptive: in July 2008, the UK's equality chief told 'overwhelmingly white' broadcasters that they must 'diversify or die' (Gibson 2008). *Thriller* remains one of the few British films to have had a black female lead; not only that, but as Mimi, Colette Laffont gets to play one of the great Romantic heroines *and* to survive her fate. The feminist counter-cinema that responded to Mulvey with alacrity and invention has often been called 'theory film' for its commitment to analysis. Yet as Potter argues, analysis and investigation lie at the heart of the thriller's narrative pleasures: 'there's another layer in the suspense genre which is … about literally suspense and about mystery and … the real thrills of thinking, of getting it sussed … Suddenly you get a clue and the mystery unfolds: why you are the way you are and other people are the way they are and how things are held together' (in Swanson & Moy-Thomas 2003: 196).

Rereading the film in 2004, Elena del Rio listens carefully to the heartbeat and cough on the soundtrack that bring us into the narrator's consciousness. *Thriller*'s use of sound takes away the emphasis on '*visual* pleasure' that Mulvey critiqued, embedding the viewer in her body where the film's sounds – musical and corporeal – reverberate. It is Potter's response to 1970s feminist film theory's turn away from the physical to the psychoanalytic, as borne out in early articles on the film by Joan Copjec (1980) and E. Ann Kaplan (1981). Their readings celebrated the film and formed an important basis for the development of a feminist aesthetic in cinema. In order to do so, however, they identified *Thriller* as something Other, and – in Copjec's reading – as largely a theoretical tract in itself. Potter argued that 'theoretical work which describes … how women are outside culture … can lead to a very pessimistic place where all you can do is define your absence in psychoanalytic terms and redefine your "lack"' (in Agostinis 1981: 7). In place of psychoanalysis's argument for women's bodily 'lack', Potter places a profusion of the kind of sounds that Julia Kristeva identifies with the maternal and bodily. *Thriller* uses the acoustic, as well as visible, body to bring the opera's historical and political absences to the fore.

As well as feminism's commitment to social change, Potter was influenced by other movements and moments in which radical experiments in film form connected to revolution. Discussing 'what was thrilling about the Russian formalists', Potter commented that 'they weren't just formalists. They were trying to, in parallel, reinvent the language of how you see and think about the world through their medium, and in its own right. That was a Utopian moment when there was a sense of freedom of the intellect, not a whiff of anti-intellectualism in it, thrills and spills of big ideas' (interview with author, September 2006). Part of the thrill is the way in which *Thriller*, like the Russian Formalists, relates its big ideas to and through lived experience. Rather than a textbook, *Thriller* offers the cinematic equivalent of the Soviet theatre train: a carnival of dance and music with political intent.

Lucy Moy-Thomas asked Potter whether 'opera limited the number of people who would want to make up [the film's] audience' (Swanson & Moy-Thomas 2003: 194). Potter was still 'grappl[ing] with [her] own ambivalence about taking on an art form so steeped in tradition, so strangely lumbering and usually so expensive, and – above all – performed for so few' when she came to direct *Carmen* for the English National Opera in 2007 (Potter 2007). Her irreverent suggestion to the ENO of an opera she would love to stage – the Marx Brothers' *A Night at the Opera* (1935) – explains something of opera's comedic and political value in *Thriller*. She describes the classic comedy as 'an opera, played out by anarchists, danced and sung with love and irreverence, teasing out the big themes, freed from the constraints of crawling realism by its music, its big numbers and its jokes' (ibid.). The film had been an inspiration for LDC performances that also brought opera into unusual performance situations and down to earth. In *Aïda* (1974), Potter and Jacky Lansley sang a duet from the Verdi opera, while a nude woman sitting on a plinth quietly read Karl Marx's *Das Kapital*; in *Death and the Maiden* (1974), Potter played a silent film heroine about to be shot. *Death and the Maiden* riffed on Schubert's music and the tropes of *film noir* in a way that prefigures *Thriller*'s mash-up of opera and thriller.

Like Mimi, *Thriller* aims to take up something perceived as dead (whether opera or theory, depending on the audience member) and make it alive. It also reanimated the *noir* genre, which had been repopularised by films like *Klute* (1971). Whereas *Klute* takes up the old story of deadbeat detectives and dead (or deadly) dames, made more violent and explicit for a 1970s audience, *Thriller* uses the genre to undo itself: the dead dame becomes the detective and befriends the brassy Musetta. Mimi's case files include the genre of *noir* itself, figured in the use of high-contrast black-and-white cinematography and in Herrmann's psychotic strings. The first time they are heard, they play over a shot of a closed door, followed by a shot of the same door cracked open. The strings appear to have their classic warning function. The viewer knows that Mimi is dead, and that she is investigating her murder: the music suggests that the perpetrator is about to appear.

But the case is not closed. The shots of the door repeat several times through the film, which is built out of such repetitions; each time, they have a slightly different meaning. In the first instance, the door shot suggests an opening within Mimi, as she begins her investigation. The voice-over narrator identifies herself with Mimi, whom we have seen dead on the attic floor, and states that she will investigate her death. She then tells the opera's story straight over a series of production stills intercut with still images of the four performers engaged in tableaux suggestive of moments in the opera. The tableaux grow more frequent and parodic in the second narration, which is the main investigation and questioning of the romanticised narrative. The film is largely composed of stills that were subsequently filmed in long takes with slow fades between them. This gives the viewer a sense that particular characters belong in particular spaces, according with the structure of classical cinema, in which – for example – women belong in the home, and men in the outside world. As the film works through its three retellings of the opera's narrative, however, the characters move in and out of each other's spaces, blurring the lines.

The third retelling refocuses on the attic as lived, rather than performance, space, in order to situate Mimi historically as a garment worker growing older in poverty. It considers her alternate fates had she survived the end of the opera's narrative, naming a catalogue of women who are absent from opera: older women, mothers, poor women and women of colour (such as Laffont herself). It makes the viewer aware that the film has rectified this: throughout the film, only Laffont has been shown in close-up, often in dramatically-lit, tightly-framed and canted shots that show her contemplating her reflection. The deep blacks of her skin and almost abstract sheen of white light on the top side of her face are utterly different from the Vaselined, angelic Hollywood close-up of the female star. Other characters usually appear in the middle distance, with frontally-positioned and level shots dominating. This theatrical framing draws particular attention to the lines like those of the door, which create frames within the frame.

The door is a liminal space that appears to divide inside and out, so, like the window in *Rear Window* (1954) it threatens the gendered division of spaces and their stability. Both thrillers and horror films, following in the tradition of Bluebeard's Castle, contain an inordinate number of close-ups of mysteriously locked doors, doors creaking open or door handles moving. Potter plays with the manipulative thrills attendant on the door as she repeats the shots, but it quickly becomes evident that the person entering is not the murderer but (possibly) another victim, a woman in a ballet skirt who performs an arabesque while the woman who we had seen dead on the floor at the start of the film sits in a chair and contemplates her reflection in the mirror.

Laffont is framed by or in the mirror in approximately half the shots. Mirrors are another generic thriller space, used for trick shots in which something or someone unexpected appears behind the shoulder of the person looking at themselves. This happens only once in *Thriller*, shortly after English comes through the door for the first time: she is reflected, ghost-like, behind Laffont's shoulder. The mirror and the door, both frames within the frame, express the potential for a women's counter-

Mimi (Colette Laffont) and Musetta (Rose English) were framed

cinema as a risky space where the gaze that appears threatening can be redefined as liberatory and connective. From these boundary places women can think their way into owning the larger space of the narrative and the attic.

The attic becomes a character in itself. Bare of everything but the mirror and a chair, the attic is mainly presented from a medium-long frontal shot, as if the camera were the proscenium arch of a stage. In the opera, the artists' garret is the set for Acts I and IV; in the film, it becomes the place where the opera repeats until it falls apart. To emphasise this, shots of the film's bare attic are contrasted with a number of production stills from the Royal Opera House's archive. The stills show detailed, perspectival sets and hundreds of historically-appropriate props and costumes that define the characters as Bohemian artists. *Thriller* ironises this set (over)dressing, arguing that the verisimilitude of traditional opera stagings is bourgeois and materialist, underlining the artists' own adherence to the conventions of bourgeois society even as they claim to resist it.

These stills are juxtaposed with another set, images of women garment workers taken from the National Museum of Labour History. These unstaged photographs show Mimi's historical referents: seamstresses working in shabby rooms. As for the artists, those rooms are zones of both work and daily life. In one, a seamstress is surrounded by her children. Whereas Potter can list production details and performers for the opera in the film's closing credits, the women garment workers are nameless, dateless. 'The eternal woman bec[omes] historical women' (Mellencamp 1995: 158). Mimi gives the invisible historical women her name, and they give a body and history back to Puccini's Mimi, whose visibility hid the real lives from which her character was drawn. Their real lives are hauntingly suggested as cuts from the labour museum's images to the film's bare garret connect the space to its lived history: sweatshop workers (like Mimi) laboured where the film's performers strike their poses.

Laffont asks of the male artists, 'Do they really suffer to create in the way I must suffer to produce?' The attic becomes a space that is used to reflect on that question. Mimi makes flowers to decorate wealthy women's clothes with accessories that refer to the association of women with both nature and ornamentation. Flowers, suggestively, are never placed in the vase that is one of only two props in the film. The first time we see the Artist (the two male characters in *Thriller* are simply called The Artists, played by Tony Gacon and Vincent Meehan), he comes into the empty attic and places an empty vase on the mantelpiece. The vase is an overdetermined curvilinear symbol for the female form, and for femininity *as* form waiting to be filled with matter by the male, whether in terms of reproduction or artmaking. That is Mimi's role in the opera, the Muse who gives form to Rodolfo's music.

Potter argued that the film called attention to the 'disguising of class relations, in that [Mimi] is working class and her labour is never represented, while the artists and the nature of their work is romanticised' (in Swanson & Moy-Thomas 2003: 197). It does this in two ways: by making Mimi's work, and the asymmetries of power that mark her life as a working-class woman, visible; and by deromanticising the male artists. In an article written the year after *Thriller*, during a series of tours to feminist conferences and classes in the US, Potter argues that 'in the nineteenth century, during the consolidation of class difference to serve the new industrial capitalism, the word artist became distinct both from artisan (craftworker) and artiste (performer) … artiste usually implied entertainer; for women this usually meant a connection with prostitution, for the display of the female body in performance was considered a form of sale' (1980: n. p.).

Thriller shows Potter working out her place in this triangle as she moved from live performance into feature filmmaking. In a sense, she inhabits or is divided between three roles from the opera simultaneously: Rodolfo, the artist/filmmaker; Musetta, the dancing girl/performance artist; and Mimi, the working poor seamstress/squatter. *Thriller* suggests a potential collaboration between the (middle-class male) artist, the (prostituted female) artiste and the (working-class) artisan – if the artist can remove the artiste from the pedestal on which he places her and stop looking down on the artisan. Film needs to incorporate an idea of itself as both performance and labour in order to begin again telling the stories missing from opera. Between the silk flowers that Mimi suffers to produce and the empty vase (perhaps an allusion to Keats' meditation on a Grecian urn), Potter reimagines a counter-cinema that is neither the dragging labour that kills Mimi, nor the Bohemian aestheticism indulged by Rodolfo.

Thus the attic is altered from a site for the privileged male artist to Mimi's (intellectual and physical) workspace and a rehearsal room. At one point, the Artists strike a ballet pose in tutus while Laffont, in combat trousers, catches one of them in a ballet lift. Predominantly, it is where a female performer practises an arabesque. With this gesture, English is at once Musetta, the showgirl, and the Romantic, balletic heroine Mimi. Unlike Laffont, the investigator, who mainly sits in her chair or lies on the floor, English moves and is moved from space to space. She performs the arabesque in two distinct settings: in the corner of the room, where she is supported, then contorted and carried out, by the Artists, and in the doorframe. It becomes clear that the arabesque in the corner, which is interrupted by the Artists who separate the two women, is a rehearsal for the final, unsupported arabesque in the doorframe which will bring the two women together. The curves of her body soften the frame, as English turns her Mimi/Musetta as an artiste breaking out of domestic and performance space by reclaiming the pleasures of her body.

In the final arabesque, her leg points out of the doorframe towards the camera in a visual echo of the first mention of Musetta in the film. It comes over a shot from a stage production in which the singer playing Musetta is finishing her waltz and showing her cold, 'tiny foot', as described in the libretto (see Clément 1989: 86). It is intended to invoke Musetta's tenderness and vulnerability, as well as her feminine wiles as she shows off her body to charm her lover(s) into buying her shoes. In the film, the female body's thrilling role as a consumer object and fetish is under investigation. As it cuts between English's foot, and that of the Royal Opera House performer, the film asks what the difference between the two performances might be. Elena del Rio sees the doubled foot as Potter signalling her background as a dancer and her pleasure in the expressive female body (2004: 12). Musetta's 'shoeless foot', Clément claims, 'is also [Puccini's] opera [with its] … whiff of operetta' (1989: 86). So the foot's coquettishness *and* its demonstration of labour associate it with operetta, purview of the working-class audience and the low-brow artiste, whose performing female body puts the *show* in shows. Puccini's Musetta uses her foot to gain material possessions and affection from men; through its depiction of rehearsal, the film positions the foot as a sign of labour, and the female performer's body as a labouring one.

Incorporating dance into film shows the body working hard; by association, and through scenes such as the inverse-gendered ballet lift, gender is shown to be bodily labour rather than biological essential. *Thriller* suggests that film (and performance) can open up a thrilling new *vie de Bohème* in which – as in *Rent* – gender, sex and sexuality can be productively explored and confused, leading to the creation of new forms of art. The body marks where Puccini's themes of love, death and art remain entwined in *Thriller*, but is also the site where the film summons up some of the 'thousand different stories' imagined by viewers and apparently excluded from *La Bohème* (Potter in Swanson & Moy-Thomas 2003: 197). Rather than inventing an ending, Potter works, like Angela Carter retelling fairy tales, to 'extract the latent content from the traditional stories' (Carter in Haffenden 1985: 80) and locate a possibility implicit within the opera. That possibility is signalled in the opera by the women's bodies: when Musetta carries the dying Mimi to Rodolfo's garret, she sells her earrings to buy medicine and, in a reverse of her earlier request for shoes to warm her 'tiny foot', gives Mimi a muff to warm her hands. *Thriller* takes that moment of connection between Mimi and Musetta as the key to unlocking Mimi's death. The female characters not only connect, but refuse to stay in their allocated roles (as good girl/bad girl). Laffont's voice-over switches pronouns between I, You and She to refer to Mimi and Musetta, sometimes addressed to herself and sometimes to English.

When Laffont describes her own actions in a dissociated second person as English, playing Mimi, tries to connect with her, the fracturing effect of sex, class and race as they come between the women, and even confuse their self-images, is most marked. In one of the few sequences of moving images in the film, as Laffont reads from a book (the only prop other than the vase), English places her hand on Laffont's shoulder but Laffont ignores her. In the subsequent still image, English is being carried out of the attic in arabesque. After commenting that 'you were immersed in the text', describing herself in the second person, Laffont switches to speaking in the first person, the transition marked by the use of a frequently repeated extreme close-up in which she leans her head against the mirror. Rather than being singular and isolated (like the typical post-Enlightenment self), Laffont's 'I' is plural: it refers to the character who had been reading, to her reflected self in the mirror, and to English who was carried past the mirror. The 'I' unites the victim and the investigator, and the two in the character of Mimi.

'I was,' says Laffont, pricking up the ears of feminist theorists, 'searching for a theory that would explain my life.' Laffont's textual investigations of herself, however, should have given theorists pause. Immediately after Laffont announces her search for a theory, the moving-image sequence picks up where it left off. English, her hand on Laffont's shoulder, turns away as she is rejected for the text. At the back of the room she performs an arabesque, leaning against the wall, in rhythm to Laffont's reading in French, in a rare instance of external diegetic sound rather than voice-over. Laffont reads from Tel Quel's 1968 collective manifesto, *Theorie d'Ensemble*. Although the theory was formed in the crucible of the 1968 uprising in France, and contained contributions by politically-engaged critics such as Julia Kristeva and Phillipe Sollers, Laffont's focus on finding the reasons for Mimi's death in the outdated theoretical text stops her from saving English. Despite espousing collective action, *Theorie d'Ensemble* prevents Mimi and Musetta from coming together or performing as an ensemble.

The Artists enter, and carry English out as Laffont reads about 'surrealisme, formalisme', closing the door very carefully behind them to indicate that this is a deliberate, planned action. The door is firmly closed for the first time since the early, thrilling sequence of stills in which it appeared to open to the rhythm of Herrmann's strings. The possibilities for connection appear to be cut off. But it is not the end. When she finishes her reading, Laffont claps the book shut and laughs warmly and lengthily, rocking backwards and forwards in the chair, engaging the audience through frequent looks directly to camera. The laugh has several resonances: it replays Musetta's infuriating laugh from Act III of *La Bohème* in which the showgirl's coarse laughter offstage interrupts Rodolfo and Mimi's romantic duet onstage; it is the murderous, insane laughter of the 'madwoman in the attic', the quintessential figure of nineteenth-century literature identified by Sandra Gilbert and Susan Gubar in their influential book published under that title in 1979; and, as Gilbert and Gubar suggest, it is the madwoman's protest at the double bind that traps women, what Hélène Cixous called the laugh of the Medusa as she confronts her own reflection and does not turn to stone. Laughing as she slams the book shut, Laffont refuses the 'retreat to burgeois [sic] aesthetic criteria, to formalism, which ignores the way pleasure works for a wider audience' (Potter in Agostinis 1981: 7). The eruption of the laugh signals the film's commitment to 'the way pleasure works for a wider audience' at the same time as it replaces classical narrative conventions with the intellectual and sensory thrill of following Laffont in working out a complex series of meanings from clues that cannot be found in books.

After Laffont's laugh, there is a cut to black. Laffont's rejection of theory seems to have completed the investigation, as English's carrying-out, signalled by many visual hints of similar shots scattered throughout the film, appears to be the climax. There is a beat, and then the voice-over cautions or invites the audience: 'No, wait! The clue!' It will be found specifically in that which Laffont ignored: Mimi's hand on her shoulder. 'Suddenly', continues Laffont over a close-up on a seamstress's hands, 'I understand.' The close-up shows, in detail, a fragment of one of the labour archive images seen earlier in the film. A cascade of similar images follows as Laffont realises how and why the opera ended as it did: 'If they had let me live, I would have become an old woman. And an old seamstress would not be the proper subject for a love story.' So the love story itself needs to change, and with it the narratives and ideas of art with which it has been bound up in the West. In the final moving-image sequence of the film, English's exit is reversed as she enters through the door in arabesque, and the women embrace. In place of the violence of the thriller, and of punk's vicious, vital attack on a calcified culture, comes another kind of wake-up call: a gentle touch, further evidence of the centrality of the body.

All three of the possible roles that the film offers the filmmaker are embodied, and related to touch's new politics of love: while the artisan manifests in close-ups of women's hands, and the artiste in shots of women's feet, the artist is in the shadow. In the final still image following the embrace, Laffont's shadow, which had previously fallen to the left of her, now falls directly onto her, suggesting a reunion of the dead and living Mimis, of the investigator and the shadow-self. Subtle play with the direction of the performers' shadows within still images repeated with a difference offers a series of clues to the developing narrative. Shadows point to the thriller's origins in *film noir*, whose B-movie production mode often dictated minimal lighting, cheap film stock and night-for-night shooting that created its stark, high-contrast look. *Noir*'s motif of crime and punishment is evoked in a moving-image sequence that recurs periodically through *Thriller*. The camera bears down interrogatively on one or other of the performers seated in the chair in which Laffont reads her theories, and the camera operator's shadow falls onscreen over the performer. Potter, operating the camera, makes her mark as a hands-on filmmaker by breaking one of the basic rules of filmmaking, crossing the divide between behind and in front of the camera.

The first time it happens, the Artist is sitting in the chair, and the shadow falls on him and blots him out as Laffont, on the voice-over, says the word 'hero'. The shadow *knows*, in the old radio catchphrase. It is the trace of the thinking, analytic, witty artist behind the camera who is framing this story as *her* take. In a figure that will repeat in different forms throughout Potter's work, the artist (behind the camera) cannot remain in her pure, isolated position, but reveals herself as artisan (operating the machinery of cinema) and artiste (a performing body caught onscreen). The shadow enmeshes the three positions, which had become alienated from one another, in the obliquely-reflected body of the female filmmaker. Inscribed directly into the text, the shadow makes it impossible to erase the filmmaker from the product of her labour, as so many female artists and artisans have been erased. It also 'reclaim[s] the night' as Bush's 'Wuthering Heights' does, singing out in the shadow-space of desire and intellect where women are not supposed to operate. 'We get so used to making little strategies and diversions to make sure we don't go too close to the shadows … that kind of fear … is undoubtedly one of the ways in which women are kept in line' (Potter in Swanson & Moy-Thomas 2003: 196).

Thriller crosses that line in the body of the artisan. Just as Mimi moves from a dead body to a live one through her many forms of reflection, the film exchanges the artistic work of deconstruction for the artisanal work of reconstruction (see Rich 1998: 228–9). Investigations into shadow, space, sound, laughter, hands and feet recover the vibrant Mimi who was always hidden in Puccini's opera. Each of those traits derives from Potter's artisanal approach to filmmaking: shooting in a squat with one light and limited film, working with friends and collaborators, reusing existing images and music. *Thriller* is engaged in the bodily labour of making film, like Potter's dance film *Hors D'Oeuvres*, for which three minutes of 8mm footage of three dancers each performing a single domestic movement was projected onto a ground glass screen and refilmed on 16mm (see Glaessner 1972: 46). *Thriller* expresses affinity with its home-working seamstress Mimi. Her voice-over stitches together the film as the story of her work is told through still shots filmed into sequence on Potter's kitchen table. Ending with an embrace, *Thriller*'s love of labour highlights its labour of love.

CHAPTER TWO

Working

How people situate themselves in relation to work in a story is always terribly telling. Are they about effort or the cult of cool? I've always enjoyed effort: working up a sweat, or trying and failing, or working late into the night. And I'm always moved by watching other people work – somebody digging in the road, or a cleaner in an airport. If I'm passing and I see somebody working, I stop and I watch. After a while, the person looks round, worried, but if you give them an appreciative look, or say thank you ... Suddenly the invisible become visible, and something happens.

– Sally Potter, interview with author, September 2006

Potter's films begin with work. Labour and effort act as an introduction to both films and characters, placing work at the heart of identity and spectatorship. Labouring bodies define the scale of opening scenes, replacing grandiose establishing shots. The scenes align us with their protagonists' subjectivity through techniques such as to-camera address, extreme close-ups, bodily sounds and questioning, unstable voice-overs. These unconventional openings act as traces of the performer's labour. They create what Laura Marks calls 'haptic images [which] do not invite identification with a figure so much as they encourage a bodily relationship between the viewer and the image' (2002: 3). Highlighting physical work, the films' opening scenes also acknowledge cinema's effort to reach out and touch us, using labour to create a 'bodily relationship' that connects the viewer, through memories of effort and its gestures, to the character. These gestures are often related to, or mimic, making art; for example, a dancer rehearsing reminds the viewer that the film's performers rehearse, while a scene showing sous-chefs chopping vegetables echoes the film editor's cuts. In relating haptically to the characters' (and performers') hard work, we also feel (with) the film.

In an ethics derived from Marxism, Potter casts a cinematic eye over work; by making it visible – and often beautiful – she also makes it valuable. In the gestures of cleaners and dancers, chefs and writers, she discovers both the beauty of work, in and of itself, and an analogy for the work of making the self. Foregrounding this self-fashioning, her films stop to watch workers and to thank them. Sometimes this is literal, as in *The Tango Lesson*, when Sally, returning to her Buenos Aires hotel at dawn after a night's dancing, stops to say 'Buenas días' to an elderly male cleaner as she enters her room to work through a pile of faxes from her new film's American producers. The camera hangs back in reception, watching Sally walk down the hall, which is radiant with the effort of the cleaner. This pooled light is a happenstance moment of grace as beautiful as any of the film's tango scenes. Created by the labour of the cleaner as an onscreen metaphor for the labour of the production designer, lighting designer, cameraman, actor and director, it draws attention to the work of filmmaking, reminding the viewer that Potter began as – and remains – an artisanal filmmaker.

Artisanal filmmaking is 'the most direct relationship an artist can have to this highly technological medium. This individual mode of production not only emerged from economic necessity but, by the 1960s, was also articulated as a political and aesthetic stance intended as an implicit critique of the industrial modes of film production' (Skoller 2005: xxiii). The American filmmakers whose work Potter encountered through ArtsLab would have recognised this as a description of their work. Their 'implicit critique' of the mainstream, along with economic developments like the growth of the multiplex, meant that few artisanal filmmakers would extend their practice to commercial cinema. Beginning with *Thriller*, however, Potter balanced the desire to reach a wide audience with the aesthetic and political rigours of artisanal filmmaking. None of her subsequent films were cut on a kitchen table, but she has retained a high degree of creative control as a writer/director who also composes and sound mixes. Deferring her pay cheque and shooting with a small crew, Potter brings the spirit of artisanal filmmaking into the big leagues (see Potter 2009b). She works with a close team of regular collaborators, including producer Christopher Sheppard and designer Carlos Conti, and with relatively small budgets. *Thriller* cost about £4,000 in 1978 while *Yes*, in 2004, was made for £1 million: a massive increase in real terms, but not a change of scale.

Economic constraints themselves inspire Potter's aesthetic, which in turn reveals the origin of its grace in labour. By aligning art-makers with workers, her films recast creative effort as artisanal and labouring, and at the same time envision manual and menial labour as containing, when recognised, the possibility of grace. The films explicitly do not romanticise labour or poverty: from *Thriller* onwards, Potter's films recognise that artisanal effort is largely unrewarded because it is denigrated and feminised in capitalist societies. Across eras and identities, her films ask what it means to work, and they suggest that 'worker' is an identity that can bring people together. Potter's father, Norman Potter, was an anarchist and celebrated designer who worked to return design from its commercial and industrial applications to its artisanal roots. *Thriller* similarly draws a strong connection between a capitalist form of high commerce – fashion – and the invisible artisanal labour behind it in Mimi's flower-making. Potter returns to this tension in its current, urgent form of globalised sweatshop labour in *Rage* (2009), as protestors shouting 'Justice for Workers!' converge on a catwalk show.

In *Live Working or Die Fighting*, Paul Mason concurs with the need to historicise labour struggles in the era of globalisation by telling the story of the earlier *Internationale* of working class uprisings, beginning with the Peterloo Massacre of 1819. Mason's second key revolt is that of the silk weavers of Lyon in the early 1830s, which ended royalist authority in France. As an epigraph to the Lyon chapter, he quotes a contemporary witness, John Bowring, who comments that he was 'exceedingly surprised at finding among the weavers ... an attention devoted to everything which was in any way connected with beauty' (in Mason 2007: 25). It is this surprise at the connection between the artisan and aesthetics that Potter both exploits and explodes. Work's grace in her films is a revolutionary gesture, reconnecting 'work' and 'art'. The terms have been estranged from each other through the cult of the Romantic genius producing in a fit of inspiration, which drives the commercial art market, but also through commercial cinema's determination to obscure human and mechanical labour in favour of 'the cult of cool'.

In his famous 1936 essay 'The Work of Art in the Age of Mechanical Reproduction', Walter Benjamin draws a distinction between the politicisation of aesthetics, which he saw and praised in the work of Bertolt Brecht, and the aestheticisation of politics, in which work is erased by the celebration of gleaming machines, and which he prophesies as 'the logical result of fascism' (1992a: 234). Benjamin's vision of fascist art is that of the grand gesture: the mass movement of peoples and technology conceived on an epic scale. He argues that it is 'attributable to the discrepancy between the tremendous means of production and their inadequate utilisation in the process of production – in other words, to unemployment' (1992a: 235). His arguments have been applied both to the cinema of Nazi Germany and to the spectacles of Hollywood: both make labour invisible in an attempt to glorify a dangerous 'cult of cool'. Through this cult, the performer is alienated from his labour. Benjamin writes that:

> While facing the camera [the actor] knows that ultimately he will face the public, the consumers who constitute the market. This market, where he offers not only his labour but also his whole self, his heart and soul, is beyond his reach. During the shooting he has as little contact with it as any article made in a factory ... The film responds to the shrivelling of the aura with an artificial build-up of the ... cult of the movie star, fostered by the money of the film industry. (1992a: 224)

The actor's image has become separated from him, a commodity whose value does not accrue to his labour. Like a factory worker, he works repetitiously, in response to mechanical promptings.

On *Rage* (2009), a film about alienated labour, Potter found an elegant solution that 'takes away the alienation' (interview with author, December 2008). The reformulation of actors as workers engaged equally in making began in the process of refining the script through workshops. Potter said that as she had 'got to know Simon Abkarian while making *Yes*, [she] was able to ask him to come and test the idea a couple of times. Because of his background in theatre, he knows how you develop something in the privacy of a workshop, the freedom it affords you' (ibid.). The success of these collaborative workshops led her to understand fully the impact of having a single character onscreen at any one time. This visual solution also allowed the filmmaker to work with one actor at a time, acting as the receptive and responsive audience for their live performance as they play through their scenes in chronological order. Potter argues that it 'probably takes filmmaking closer to the feeling of theatre, the sense of a family come together for a period of time' (ibid.). Each actor worked alone with Potter for two days, receiving Equity (or Screen Actors Guild) minimum wages – in several cases, the actors supplied their own costumes and did their own make-up. While these practices are common for first-time indie filmmakers, they represent a striking riposte to commercial cinema from an experienced director working with prestige actors such as Dame Judi Dench, Jude Law, Steve Buscemi and Dianne Wiest.

The magic cast by the star, argues Benjamin, is 'the phoney spell of a commodity', used to draw consumers to a film (1992: 224). It is a spell that Potter's films resist. They cut against Benjamin's concept of the actor (and filmmaker) as alienated labourers, restoring them to artisanal status. While many films show their protagonists at work, few take it as a theme or framework, so Potter's choice is deliberate and stands out. 'It's always hard to put work on screen', she says. 'It always ends up being sustainable only for very short periods, unless the characters are working whilst doing something else' (interview with author, September 2006). The 'something else' that contains and enlivens scenes of work is not only to be found in the framing, sound and dialogue or narrative that give them form and meaning, but in work's ability to create connection between the characters, and between them and the audience. These pleasures show labour itself as something in which labourers find grace: both beauty and thanks. The delight with which work is shown at each film's beginning makes grace a gift, an invitation to visual pleasure, that supplants the economic value of labour. Perhaps Benjamin might have found in Sally's thanks to the cleaner a model for cinematic spectatorship that politicises aesthetics.

Not only is aesthetic pleasure produced through thoughtful representations of labour, but it is the reward for the viewer's willingness to work. It is no secret that Potter's films invite the audience to work with her: *Thriller* and *The Gold Diggers*, informed by a Marxist feminist moment that wanted viewers to work for their pleasures, offer non-linear narratives with non-psychologically realist protagonists. For too long, however, the idea of labouring as a viewer has been associated with a deliberate withholding of pleasure by the filmmaker, or an experience of displeasure by the viewer. Potter's films demonstrate that aesthetic pleasure, like Lyon silk or a spark-lingly clean floor, is the product, and trace, of effort: the mark of human care and labour. This invites the viewer's attention and suggestively asks the audience to put themselves within reach of the onscreen performer.

It is easiest to accept this reading as it refers to *Thriller*, but it applies powerfully to the opening of *Orlando*, which announces the way that the film has been worked out of Virginia Woolf's source text. Work is the difference. At the beginning of the novel, two pages are devoted to Orlando play-fighting against a Moor's head swinging from the rafters of the Great House's attic (see Woolf 2000: 11). At the beginning of the film, however, Orlando is striding back and forth under a tree, muttering to himself. At first, this seems like the self-indulgent behaviour of a wealthy nobleman, but a few scenes later it becomes clear that Orlando was in fact working for a living: rehearsing a poetry performance whose outcome will decide whether his family retains the right to their house and lands.

His dangerously unflattering choice of lines from Sir Philip Sidney inappropri-ately characterise the ageing Queen Elizabeth I as a once-'virgin rose' now fading. Orlando's failure to perform appropriately paradoxically secures his success with the haughty Queen. 'Trying and failing' positions each of Potter's protagonists as workers. Her films do not simply record and celebrate failure in the manner of 1990s slacker comedies such as *Clerks* (1994), in which pleasure derives from inventive resistance to alienated labour. Orlando works, rather, to reinvent labour and his relation with its products. His first line to camera – 'That is, I' – encapsulates the labour he will undertake: to be able to say 'I' coherently *and* to say it as *I-Thou*. By opening with work, the films thank the viewer for theirs. Their grace is related at root to gratitude, the attitude of welcome that the films extend to and through work.

I: Solo Performance

Thriller ends with an act of artisanal gratitude, inscribed on the film in the form of handwritten end credits. Potter gives her performers, sources and friends a hand-clapped round of applause in writing out their names. These scripted titles appear from behind still photographs from the Royal Opera House and National Museum of Labour History, bringing both high art and history out of the dusty archive, and into the liveness of handwriting. Film hovers and crosses the boundary between the liveness of performance and the recorded documentation of the archive, a productive tension explored further in chapter 10. That boundary crossing is a signature whose hybrid nature can be seen in the way that the opening scene of each film works as an invita-tion. The viewer is positioned between the future audience of cinema and the present audience of live spectacle with its possibility of interaction. Opening scenes often offer a portrait of the protagonist as working artist, whether a writer like Orlando or Sally, or the Cleaner in *Yes*. They are shown working alone, but with an audience in mind.

Potter specifically shows art-making as *work* in her films, particularly figuring the dancer's body as a labouring one. Dance is not the ahistorical perfection of ballet or the mass production chorus line of Busby Berkeley films, but an individual's work on herself, through the repetitive, difficult process of rehearsal and failure required to produce creative expression. It is through the focus on this embodied labour that Potter stitches the audience into the film, by showing work as a structuring element of the narrative. The term 'stitches' consciously invokes Jean-Louis Baudry's 1970 theory of 'suture', the combination of exhibition circumstances and cinematic verisimilitude that absorbs the audience into the film. Baudry links our absorption to an identification with the male protagonist whose point-of-view shots dominate classical cinema, placing the audience member in 'his' position through shot/reverse-shot. Potter, in making her first film about a female garment worker, refuses to 'stitch' us conventionally. She does not give a single shot from her protagonist's point of view, nor employ reaction shots or glance-object cuts. These traditional forms of editing form the basis of suture, which Baudry and followers such as Christian Metz argue is an unconscious process that audiences cannot resist or escape. Instead, Potter makes suture visible as invisible women's work. Potter's investigation moves away from the literalness of Annabel Nicolson's Expanded Cinema piece *Reel Time* (1973), in which Nicolson ran a piece of film through a sewing machine and then through a projector. Instead, Potter formulates a solely cinematic language that seeks to invite an active, rather than entrap a passive, viewer.

Thriller makes its invitation by reworking a well-known artwork that had been widely adapted from short fiction to theatre to opera, and into the first of many films in 1926, starring Lillian Gish as Mimi. Potter explicitly confronts the work of art as it has been laboured over, altered and renewed by multiple authors. The photographs of stagings of the opera also situate the film's audience in a continuum of audiences who have experienced *La Bohème*. The viewer is invited to be one of many, even as the film pares down *La Bohème* to stage it inside Mimi's head. Potter likewise elects to join a union or commune of fellow workers, rather than lay claim to solo auteur status and, in doing so, stands alongside Mimi the garment worker, rather than Rodolfo, the heroic artist. Her choice highlights the fact that Puccini's opera is already a reworking filled with nostalgia for a different set of working relations.

Between the first appearance of the *La vie de Bohème* stories, in Henri Murger's magazine articles in the early 1800s, incorporated into a book in 1849, and Puccini's opera in 1896, a series of profound changes had occurred among the community of workers in Paris, most significantly the Paris Commune of 1871. Mason traces its grassroots mobilisation to the garment workers' strike in Lyons (see 2007: 52–78). Workers – and particularly women – rather than bourgeois, Bohemian Proudhonists (the 1860s equivalent of 'champagne socialists') played a significant part in the Commune's formation. Montmartre was transformed from the setting for Murger's stories of Bohemia to a radical communist separatist state for a few months, because it was the base of many of the working-class activists that joined the commune. One such activist, Louise Michel, was a radical teacher who organised her district and fought hand-to-hand. Michel was executed in the last days of the Commune, but in 1946, after the liberation, a Paris Métro station was named after her in recognition of her courageous example to the Resistance. Puccini's *fin-de-siècle* opera glosses over the potential Mimis of 1867–71, harkening back nostalgically to the 1800s Mimi who

Forbidden Reflections: Mimi (Colette Laffont) works it out

knew her place. By contrast, Potter's Mimi stands alongside Michel on the brink of revolution, united with the images of garment workers from the labour archives.

In *Thriller*, Mimi investigates her life, which is at once a life of the hands and of the mind. The mirror which dominates the film's imagery acts as a hyphen between body and mind, through the dual physical and metaphysical meanings of reflection. When the film's title is spelled out in jagged letters at the bottom of the screen, Laffont faces the camera with her hand over her mouth. The same image, facing forward, is impossibly repeated again and again in the mirror behind her. Echoing René Magritte's painting 'La Reproduction Interdite', the shot could be titled 'Forbidden Reflection' as it changes the terms from Magritte's male figure – who cannot reproduce – to Potter's female figure, who conversely cannot reflect *because* she is supposedly all body and no mind (see Sobchack 1992: 282–3). Laffont adopts the classic pose of the thriller's female protagonist as she is confronted (with her bodily vulnerability) by the killer. The image's endless and impossible re-reflection draws attention to cinema's constant reproduction of the rules forbidding women from reflecting, and thus working, on themselves.

Potter also uses the mirror to invert Benjamin's suggestion that it symbolises the actor's alienation from his labour. 'The feeling of strangeness that overcomes the actor before the camera, as Pirandello describes it, is basically the same kind as the estrangement felt before one's own image in the mirror. But now the reflected image has become separable, transportable' (Benjamin 1992a: 224). By returning repeatedly to these moments of reflection, Laffont reclaims her image as *not* separable or transportable. The undoing of the mirror moment is suggested by the presence of another element in the title frame: a shadow on the wall beside Laffont, one that is separate from her and distorted. Like the reverse mirroring, this announces the film's play with the image through error, because later sequences will reveal it to be the shadow of the camera operator, Potter. This apparent mistake marks the filmmaker as the performer's shadow (rather than vice-versa). Laffont uncovers her mouth to speak for the filmmaker, and for cinema.

What is surprising about the title shot is not so much that it is Laffont's face reflected rather than the back of her head, but that given the angle of the mirror and the trick shot, the viewer expects to see *herself* reflected. The title shot suggests another way for the viewer to inflect the film, as Mimi's (not quite) shadow, paralleled with the filmmaker. Film is marked symbolically as a solo performance in which the protagonist, through her investigation in collaboration with the filmmaker, can come to speak for all the Mimis silenced behind her in the mirror, and before her in the audience. That this will be the film's work is corroborated by the shot following the title screen. Wearing the black dress that had been seen on Mimi's dead body, Laffont leans her head on the mirror. The blackness of her dress blends in to the blackness of the mirror, isolating her face as a heartbeat sounds on the score. The viewer is privileged to enter into this woman's reflections, her intimate negotiation with her own image as she investigates her own death. Yet the use of the mirror also doubles the 'I' engaged in solo performance: an extreme close-up of the mirror shot shows two eyes looking into each other, punning visually on Laffont's two I's (Mimi and Musetta), the real body and the reflection.

Both viewer and filmmaker are multiple subjects who speak in concert, but always as more than one. Another Mimi is carried by two men. The transportable, separable body has returned. It will be the work of the film to bring the two Mimis together before the other Mimi is carried out of the door for good. The very first image of the film parallels the mirror with the open door beside it. As the film progresses, the open door will become the site of potential connection between Laffont and English. Mimi moves away from the mirror towards affinity and alliance with Musetta who comes through the open door. The film simultaneously suggests its openness and its need for an active viewer. 'Do *you* remember being in the room?' asks Laffont, casting the audience as Mimi and making them witnesses to her investigation.

You: The You the Singer Sings To

When Mimi leans against the mirror, her eye is reflected back in an almost cubist shot as she tries to define herself as an 'I' who contains multitudes. The pun on the I/eye undoes the supposed effect of suture, which links the viewer into the perspective of the protagonist. Instead the film looks back at the viewer, and causes the viewer to look critically at cinema. More like songs, Potter's films invite their viewer by saying 'you'. Most pop songs specify one particular listener, the 'you' who is the romantic Other in the song's narrative, but the non-specificity of the pronoun allows it to refer to the listener as well.

'Seeing Red', the song Potter herself sings over the opening images of *The Gold Diggers*, apostrophises no less an Other than cinema itself, as a microcosm of society. 'Please please give me back my pleasure' asks the chorus, while the verses describe the relentlessly misogynist narratives that the singer encounters when trying to relax at the cinema or with a book. The song infers that films and novels marketed as mindless entertainment are actually hard and unpleasant work for anyone with the least political sensibility. Pleasure might then consist in a film that presents itself as hard work through which it respects and refreshes the viewer's intellect by challenging the status quo. Certainly, the elliptical story told by the stunning images that play under the song suggests that *The Gold Diggers* is just such an answer to the singer's quandary. The opening scene works like music videos, which became regular practice after the success of Queen's 'Bohemian Rhapsody' (1975), made for about the same amount of money as *Thriller*. As in a music video, the images sometimes match the lyrics of 'Seeing Red' and sometimes counterpoint them. Our intimations of the film's work rise in the play between the two.

Like many pop songs, 'Seeing Red' is sung from the singer's 'I'. The singer, however, sings of 'my feet' and 'my pleasure', but elides the 'I' that should appear before each verb. 'Went to the pictures' is a colloquial first line, but its missing subject pronoun points to one of the film's key themes: female viewers struggle to say 'I' because they do not see themselves reflected onscreen as agents. The film's protagonist, Ruby, has to find a form that will allow her to become a coherent, active self. At first, she has no 'I', no sense of herself because she thinks she has no memories. When the opening shots are repeated from Ruby's point of view, it becomes clear that they are fragments of her memories. Yet at the start, they are 'owned' by the singer, and the song suggests that they are memories of films she has seen. This begins the process by which Ruby and cinema are identified with one another. The viewer first sees Ruby's memories in this 'pure' form while Ruby must work to recall them at all. Ruby and the viewer share the work of putting the memory shards together into a narrative. The labour of art and the labour of memory are intertwined.

The film states this by opening with a daring reference to the paradigmatic film about the labour of memory, art and self: *Citizen Kane* (1941). In an early shot, a dark object pokes out of the snow by some wooden rails. The object forms a graphic match with a broken-down wall or fence in the previous shot, which is itself an echo of the mountains in the opening panorama. The dark object, hauntingly reminiscent of Charles Foster Kane's Rosebud, which provides the key to his life, will be revealed later as child Ruby's toy wooden horse. It marks the scale of the film as human craft and play rather than landscape, and its appearance cues the song. The next shot shows a straight path trodden into the snow and heading to the horizon. A woman in a dark coat (Hilary Westlake) enters the frame from lower screen right and walks towards and along the path, as the song's first line is heard. The figure in black walks in rhythm to the song along a strip of white ground like a representation of cinema itself.

This ravishingly simple shot continues until the song begins to tell the story of the film that the singer saw, which is revealed as the core narrative of *The Gold Diggers* itself. The shot of a woman walking cuts to a shot of a pair of masculine boots dusted in snow entering through a wooden door. The shot inverts the balance of black and white, with the boots, door and floor interrupted only by the smatterings of snow. 'Then / A man with a gun / Walked through the door', as the singer sings. In her review of *Thriller*, B. Ruby Rich contrasted the film to the kind of thriller Raymond Chandler famously described: 'When in doubt, have a man come through the door with a gun in his hand' (in Rich 1998: 230). Instead of a gun, the man is shown to be holding the gold nuggets that act destructively to separate mother and daughter. We have entered into Ruby's childhood memories. When the singer announces that she 'couldn't take it any more', the film cuts to an over-exposed shot of wintry land and sky with the path proceeding to the horizon, followed by a shot of the dark-haired woman cradling a blonde-haired girl, whom the film will establish to be Ruby's younger self.

Seeing Ruby for the first time raises questions about whose point of view we have been in and are in now. Point-of-view ambiguity is intensified by the voice-over that follows the song, in which an unidentified voice (which can later be identified as Ruby's) poses a riddle that asks what we see when we watch a film and how we see it:

> I am born [or borne] in a beam of light.
> I move continuously yet I am still.
> I am larger than life, yet do not breathe.
> Only in the darkness am I visible.

After this initial description, the riddle reverses to involve the viewer in the game as an active investigator, like the pronoun switches in Laffont's voice-over in *Thriller*:

> You can see me but never touch me.
> I can speak to you but never hear you.
> You can know me intimately, and I know you not at all.
> We are strangers and yet you take me inside of you.
> What am I?

The answer at first seems to be cinema, and also the cinematic heroine who will be embodied by Ruby.

Ruby recites her riddle over a shot of mountain snowfields cutting each other with darkly delineated diagonals. The shot is in contrast to the stark simplicity of the straight white path down which the dark-haired woman strode towards the horizon. Here, too, there are people walking: a line of tiny black figures proceeding along a left-right diagonal that bisects the right-left diagonals of the dark paths between the snowfields. As the film proceeds, we will learn that these figures are gold miners, including Ruby's father, going to pan a stream high in the icy mountains. They are searchers, like the singer looking for her pleasure. Their labour is the vehicle for the film's metaphor of searching, embodied in the riddle of an I and a You with, as Celeste says, 'ninety minutes to find each other', searching through the screen.

He/She: Difference

The gendered division of labour in *The Gold Diggers* (men dig, women are gold) is rethought in *Orlando*, in which gender itself is the protagonist's hard work. Potter wrote and shot a sequence of black-and-white scenes, discarded in the edit, which would have rolled backwards through Orlando's life as she went into labour in the penultimate section of the film. Each one reverses the outcome of key scenes – Orlando gets married, he fights in the Khan's war – each pointing out how Woolf and Potter have written their way out of gender expectations. The last one described Orlando's mother giving birth to Orlando as a girl; the black-and-white scene would have cross-faded into a colour scene of Orlando herself giving birth to her daughter. In its dizzying reflection on how being female from birth would have changed Orlando's destiny, the spiral of possibilities that could not possibly exist with one another shows up the impossibility of gender difference. In labour herself, Orlando revisits the labour of living gender differently. As an aristocratic member of the leisure classes, Orlando seeks work that is appropriate to his station and gender, whether as patron, ambassador, wife or writer. The film argues that it is through this search for labour that he becomes herself, offering more than a postmodern confection of gender as play. Gender is *labour*, graceful and received with gratitude.

That labour is most evident onscreen in the hard work around donning and bearing costumes that signify both gender and class. Whether male or female, as an aristocrat Orlando is dependent on servants to dress him/her, providing this intimate service of constructing his/her outward appearance as well as running the Great House with which he/she is identified. That this dependence is part of Orlando's attempt and failure to become a coherent self is evident from the film's post-credit sequence. Orlando has fallen asleep under the oak tree where he was supposed to be working. When he awakens and runs across the fields, the scene cuts to show the Queen's barges arriving, with the Herald singing from the prow. Orlando's flight is set into the context of his failure to do his share of work, as sailors pole the barges while, on the banks, servants of the Great House run out with torches. Orlando bobs and weaves through these workers in his family's employ, running against the tide, to be dressed by further servants. The sumptuous ceremony and banquet are shown to be the product of labour that most costume dramas either take care to disguise or stage as a kind of set dressing that ornaments the protagonists (see Pidduck 2004: 121–2). Orlando works to divest him/herself of the property and class values that entail this servitude, whereas the novel has a comedic chorus in the form of the housekeeper and butler. Angela Carter uses these figures as chorus and comic foils in her operatic adaptation (sadly never produced), *Orlando: or, the Enigma of the Sexes*. While Potter uses the Cleaner to expatiate upon the lives of her protagonists in *Yes*, in *Orlando* the speaking roles for servants are largely excised to focus on Orlando as a labourer. Orlando embodies a class spectrum, as well as a gender spectrum, coded through his/her relationship to work. He/she works because of this multitude of identities, and his/her work is to bring them into unity.

This is what Orlando is meditating towards under the oak tree at the start of the film. A cut in from long shot to close-up adds to the sense of Orlando as a multiple yet unitary collection of selves. There are two gazes occurring in the opening of *Orlando*: the first is the camera's, which is unattributed despite the swaying shot being quite ostentatious; the second is Orlando's. When Orlando looks to camera and suddenly speaks, we realise that it is his voice we have been hearing describing himself in the third person on the voice-over. At the same time, we sense that he is controlling the camera's gaze, which, throughout the film, falls on Orlando, or something that s/he sees. The camera's gaze is partial: it mainly takes in what Orlando sees or does, and – Orlando being Orlando – it often does so quizzically. There is a witty tension between the image of Swinton as Orlando reclining beneath the tree in doublet and hose and the voice-over's assertion that 'there can be no doubt about his sex'. Of course there can be, produced rather than prevented by the voice-over's subsequent sly disavowal: 'despite the feminine appearance that all young men of the time aspire to'. Double-edged, this comment brings with it a spiralling set of doubts about what exactly sex might mean in different eras and how we perceive it, warning us to be on our guard.

The black-and-white scenes of undoing were not necessary because it is Orlando's gaze to camera that invites the audience, at key moments, to imagine his/her fate differently. His first line to camera 'that is, I', unites the first-person pronoun with a third-person singular verb form, an intriguing metaphor for the gaze to camera. It echoes Arthur Rimbaud's famous statement, 'Je est un autre' (my self is other), to imply Orlando's unsettling multiplicity of identities – he, she and s/he. Its productive indeterminacy is immediately highlighted by the first music in the film: the Herald singing Edward Thomas's poem 'Eliza'. Heard as Orlando awakens, it is unclear whether the music is in his head, in the air or simply on the soundtrack. The camera's close identification with Orlando suggests the first, and it is only when the film cuts to show the Herald on the prow on the Queen's barge that its source is established.

When the Herald appears again at the end of the film, Orlando is seated once more beneath the oak tree to which her identity is so tied in Woolf's novel. Orlando has become a woman, and the Herald has become an angel (*angelos* is the ancient Greek for herald). His appearance to Orlando, recently a single mother, is a reverse Annunciation, and a reverse *enunciation*, full of mixed-up pronouns. Like Laffont's voice-over in *Thriller*, the Angel's closing song has a changeable relationship to identity that suggests, perhaps, that the Angel and Orlando are one. At the start, the song speaks from I to You, summoning a 'moment of unity' from which it hymns a first-person plural that cancels out He/She politics:

Neither a woman nor a man –
We are joined, we are one
With a human face.

Orlando is the focus of the frame at this moment, and the song slides into being an internal meditation.

This is intensified by Swinton's 15-second, unbroken look to camera, compelling the viewer to hold her gaze to the point of tears. Unblinking is a trace of the performer's bodily work, a reminder of the film's dedication to merging labour and aesthetics. Here, we are reminded, are bodies working (at gender) for our pleasure, and taking pleasure in their work, not least in the Angel's powerful falsetto voice. When zhe sings of being between genders, hir identity becomes plural (*zhe* and *hir* are currently used as pronouns by many people who identify as intersex). Or perhaps zhe assumes the singular royal 'we', returning to Quentin Crisp's 'Queen' Elizabeth, whose queer male body bears the narrative freight from the film's opening, suggesting that the film will be 'coming across the [he/she] divide to you' to gather the (un-)suspecting viewer into its 'we'.

We: Travelling Companions

Orlando's opening voice-over monologue asserts that 'it wasn't privilege he sought, but company'. Throughout the film, Orlando has travelled to make connections, only to see them fall away. The concluding scene suggests that s/he has found company by accepting his/her plural identity, one that is not only gendered but contains historical multitudes. This imaginative plurality (is the Angel one of Orlando's imaginings?) is picked up by the opening of Potter's next film, *The Tango Lesson*. It may seem odd to describe a scene, and indeed a film, that appears on the surface to be about the solitude of writing, under the heading 'We'. The film invites such a perverse reading by opening with a stark, almost blank close-up on an arm sweeping clean a round table, which cuts to an aerial shot confirming that this is a woman, cleaning. A solitary labourer cleans the slate for the credits to appear. It seems like the witty introduction of a minor character preparing the scene for the main actors, visually imitating the Rank gong-striker. Viewers recognising the performer as Potter may think the scene is a pun on the director's work, preparing the scene for the actors. When the brief credits end, Potter re-enters as the protagonist Sally. There is paper on the table, and a pencil. Sally sits, squares the paper and places her hands on either side of it. The score starts up with similar sighing voices to those on the *Orlando* soundtrack. Cut in to an extreme close-up of a pencil lead snapping as it meets paper.

That amplified crack signals to us that we are not only in the presence, but in the consciousness of this character. The extreme close-up is her point of view focused in on the page where she is about to write. The sharp sound ricochets in her ears in the silent studio. As in the openings of *Thriller*, *The Gold Diggers* and *Orlando*, it appears that we have tripped into the intimate mind-space of a solitary protagonist, a writer who cleans (or a cleaner who writes). Indeed, Potter worked as a cleaner in the late 1960s and early 1970s to support her creative work (interview with author, September 2006). The artist's solitude is emphasised, for those familiar with Potter's work, by the bare study with its wooden floorboards and angular shadows, shot in black-and-white, that evokes the attic room of *Thriller*. Nothing could be more auteurial: the filmmaker alone, her genius signalled by the minimalist set of her first film and the score of a previous successful film. There is a shocking intimacy to watching the act of writing begin; as Potter told Kristy Widdicombe, the studio in the opening scene 'was actually a set of this room [Potter's own studio, where she writes] built by Carlos Conti in a studio in Buenos Aires' (2003).

After the pencil lead snaps, there is a brief flash, even more intimate, of what the writer is imagining. In full, blazing colour, we see a beautiful woman in a long red *haute couture* gown with a long red train, fleeing screen left to right against a verdant background. There is no context for the image, as there is none for the scene of the writer writing: there are no names, no locations, no story. This, the film suggests, is the pure moment of creation. The pencil writes – and the high voices sing – the word *rage*. As Sally continues to write on, and discard, pieces of paper, there are cuts to further colour scenes from the projected film, but there are also cuts to further credits, white type on black, for *The Tango Lesson*. A long interpolated *Rage* (1996) scene shows the red-dressed woman, now partnered with women in blue and yellow dresses, being arranged for a photo shoot on a flight of stone steps. A photographer and a director or designer are in attendance, along with several minders, wittily paralleling the crediting of the cinematographer, editor and art director. Along with the intercut credits, this scene gives the lie to the myth of the auteur: a film cannot be made by one person, any more than a fashion shoot can be staged solo. The model who appeared alone at first has brought with her an entire context and crew. When the film cuts back to the black-and-white of Sally's studio, there has still been no dialogue, no sense of a narrative. Yet the intertwining of writing and imagining has the viewer hooked into a labour of decipherment and discovery that parallels the writer/director's. The paired scenes underscore the effort behind making artistic products and aesthetic images, as is fashionable and conventional, appear effortless.

The room is now, in a sense, filled with two sets of people who mirror each other: the characters of *Rage* (1996), and the cast and crew listed in the credits of *The Tango Lesson*, two communities developing side-by-side. A third community is suggested by the pencil's audibility: not only the imagined figures and the real crew that make Potter a plural 'we' engaged in creating the film, but also the viewers for whom the sound of the pencil is created. In the first scene of the film proper, the viewer will share another auditory experience with Sally, watching a tango performance by Pablo. Sound makes the viewer party to the experience: the scene opens with a shot tracking Sally as she walks along a busy road in Paris, and an orchestral tango is faintly audible as she passes a revolving door. Cued by the music, there is a cut to medium close-up; the music becomes louder, bringing us closely into Sally's attention as she pauses to listen. She passes through the gilt doors and there is a cut to show her entering a packed auditorium. Sally becomes a member of the onscreen audience's 'we' by following the music, as if following the interest of the offscreen audience.

This responsive listening characterises Potter's work, and it provides a clue to the first-person plural enunciated by *The Tango Lesson* from its very first moments. Over the production credits of the film, an instrumental tango plays. At first, this suggests little other than that the film will be about tango. At the end, when the underlying theme that it takes two (or more) to tango becomes clear, the tune acquires words written by Potter, and sung by Sally to Pablo:

You are me
And I am you
One is one
And one are two.

This is similar to the conjoining ecstasy of the Angel's song, to Ruby's riddle and to Laffont's shifting speech. Distinctions are blurred, resulting not in homogeneity but in plurality.

The song answers an earlier exchange with Pablo, in which Sally says she loves him 'with [her] work', and he responds petulantly, 'Work. Only work?' There is nothing 'only' about her work: it is always plural, making one into two, I into we. Tango historian Marta Savigliano writes that this is the work of the tango itself:

> Tango expresses, performs, and produces Otherness erotically through exoticism, and in doing so, it plays seductively into the game of identification – an attempt at 'selving' by creating anti-selves ... but it actually takes three to tango ... [the two dancers] and a gaze to watch these occurrences ... expectant, engaged in that particular detachment that creators have towards the objects of their imagination. (1996: 213)

The viewer is a necessary working element of the 'we', crucial to Potter's 'attempt at "selving" by creating anti-selves'. It is music, and the act of listening, that brings the viewer/listener across the 'particular detachment' exhibited by the opening of the film, with its dialogue-free aerial shots of a woman working, alone.

You, plural: Open Your Ears

Listening carefully is as much work as performing. While *The Tango Lesson* suggests this in several of its lessons, *The Man Who Cried* makes it very clear. Diverse characters, from different backgrounds, speaking different languages, populate the film and make connections despite the poisonous atmosphere of Europe in the 1930s. They find each other by listening. *The Man Who Cried*, like *Orlando* and *The Tango Lesson*, ends with a character singing a song, in this case the protagonist Fegele/Suzie. Unlike the other songs, this one does not hymn the profusion of pronouns and confusion of identities, although like the others it celebrates the end of the character's search for self. It is a melody heard many times in the film, but its lyrics do not reach 'across the divide' to us – or only to an 'us' constituted by the language of the song: Yiddish speakers, suggesting a culturally plural audience for the film. A lullaby written by Potter and translated into Yiddish by Barry Davis, 'Close Your Eyes' is faithful to the second person of its title. Its aim is not to constitute a 'we' sharing an identity, but to welcome a 'you, plural' of allies including those prepared to listen without, or before, full understanding. Sung as a lullaby to Fegele by her father, its gentling effect is recalled when the adult Fegele – now called Suzie – unites her plural self before her father in their mutual language. This kind of listening is an active commitment to an identity shared across barriers of language and memory.

Listening's hard work could shape a 'collective politics ... which places a particular emphasis on the "painstaking labour" of working for each other and speaking to (not for) others in order to find out what ... we might yet have in common' (Ahmed 2000: 180). As Elaine Aston and Geraldine Harris comment about this 'painstaking labour', 'encounters in this process must be premised on a recognition of the *absence* of knowledge … allowing for both surprise and conflict' (2006: 12–13; emphasis in original). Each of Potter's films begins in this absence of knowledge, not only for the audience, but for the protagonist who is searching for a self that will be constituted in community. This search for commonality through 'speaking to (not for) others' who are the audience is the work that threads through Potter's films from the openness of their opening moments. The audience, in turn, are not allowed to rest easy as complacent voyeurs of a performance of Otherness. Mimi's heartbeat, Orlando's gaze and Sally's writing draw us in by moving us from the third-person audience of cinema to the collectively-constituted second-person audience of live performance. As the liveness of the bodies is expressed through the close-ups and sound mixing of cinema, we are also a unique hybrid: a first/third-person audience *within* the protagonist's body and mind.

The first sound heard in *The Man Who Cried* suggests that its music is all in Suzie's head. The film opens with a rushing noise over a black screen, which is revealed to be rolling water that reflects and bears flames. A dark-haired girl's head moves up and down at the water line, the camera dipping under as she does, suggesting that the rushing sound is in her ears. There is a series of shots moving from medium long to close-up, coming into proximity with the girl (Christina Ricci), who is clearly nearing death. An indrawn breath is audible on the soundtrack, and then orchestral music begins, acting as a sound bridge to the credits, over which a man's voice begins to sing in Yiddish. Slow and operatic, the song continues through the credit sequence, in which white on black credit intertitles are interspersed with slow motion, sepia shots of a bearded man singing to an audience. The movement of his mouth and the joyousness of the scene suggest that he is singing a different song or at a different tempo. He is accompanied by a band and the shots alternate between the singer and the partygoers who listen to him. Most of the audience of women in headscarves are laughing or clapping and dancing. There is one still face, a young girl, sitting and listening raptly behind the dancers. The singer reaches towards the audience and in the next shot the girl smiles at his recognition of her. In the final shot, the man is singing passionately, or laughing, or crying, embodying the title of the film.

This is the most immediate opening of any of Potter's films, although it echoes the way that *The Gold Diggers* opens with Ruby's memories of her mother. We are watching the memories of a young woman fighting for her life. Their particularity and their foreignness reminds the viewer of her difference from the unnamed drowning girl, whose dark hair connects her to the young girl watching the singer. Suzie's fate, to be at once agent and audience, is foreshadowed by this opening. At the start of the film, she is a passive 'you' listening to her father, who is the active protagonist leaving for America; later, she is the silent, watchful foil to the bright, brittle showgirl Lola who speaks half a dozen languages. Suzie's silence keeps the audience at a distance, as does the film's repeated use of unsubtitled Yiddish and Roma. It reminds the viewer of the way in which plural communities are constituted through listening. We have to work through being prepared, initially, not to understand.

A fragmentary, haunting image or tune is the guiding principle for the viewer as it is for the protagonist of each of Potter's films. In the film's first post-credit scene,

Fegele (the young Suzie) runs off into the silver-grey pine forest where she is playing with her father, and sees a gypsy caravan passing through the next break of trees. Distant music is heard. Later encounters with a gypsy caravan in England and a stand of Christmas trees in Paris point back to the pine forest, providing Suzie with a key towards uncovering the mystery of her identity. Both fragmentary sense-memories enable her to build affinity by using her half-understood childhood memories to protect herself from various bullies large and small. The audience is encouraged to do the same, allying ourselves with the film rather than standing against it: a reminder that 'you, plural' stands between 'us' and 'them'.

They: There Is No They

The Man Who Cried is concerned, from its opening, with what it means to fail to hear. Suzie's silence in the vast wartime ocean implies that her death is imminent, but she is saved throughout the film by her ability to listen and to overhear. Those who refuse to listen are those who consider Jews and Roma to be 'them', excluded from a community designated by a dominant language and culture. The film makes use of popular knowledge about the Nazi genocide to fill in the background to its more complex story of betrayals and alliances across faiths and nationalities. It does not, however, claim that the politics of 'us' and 'them' is all in the past. Potter's subsequent film, *Yes*, reflects on and responds to resurgent racism and religious hatred post-9/11 by including everyone and everything in its sights. Its supple, flowing verse lines draw equally on Shakespeare and The Streets to broaden the definition of English. Although iambic pentameter is the metre of high art, the film says from the beginning that nothing and no one is too small to be noticed. If we are prepared to give the world this effortful quality of attention, the result will be not only in aesthetic pleasure, but community. It draws on the politics of the labour union movement: there is no 'they'. No one is excluded from a caring look that the film contrasts with the dispassionate gaze of the surveillance camera.

The film begins with a monologue by the Cleaner (Shirley Henderson), reflecting on what she knows about the lives of her employers, known as She (Joan Allen) and Anthony (Sam Neill). The first word of the film is 'They'. Pankaj Mishra, in his introduction to the screenplay, suggests that the film is about discovering the humanity of 'the usually obscure figure of the house-cleaner' (2005b: xix). The Cleaner, however, is a fully realised character from the first moment: her investigation, and our curiosity, is focused on discovering the humanity of 'They', which is initially obscured by their 'cool' bourgeois typicality. They live in an all-white house with minimal personal detail. It is the Cleaner's revelation of the secret details of their lives through her work, which makes them more than façades. Art's work of balancing the mass of humanity against the stories of individuals is made visible in the first shots of the film: 'microscopic images of the smallest visible particles of matter danc[ing] and float[ing] across the screen', which become lines of static, then cells, then 'tiny grains of dust – drifting and sparkling in a beam of sunlight' (Potter 2005b: 1). These are the same grains of dust that dance in the light that falls on Orlando at the moment of her sex change.

The character who appears beneath them, like Orlando, is one who commands our attention with a direct gaze to camera.

Orlando's pithy one-liners have been replaced with the Cleaner's run-on lines and internal rhymes. Unlike Orlando who resists visibility, the Cleaner wants to be visible. She wants her work to be recognised, and she makes visible that which those who refuse to see her also refuse to see. She is, moreover, a philosopher of the visual field (or film theorist), arguing that there is no space in which there is nothing to see. What can be seen is us:

> …Those of us who clean
> As a profession know the deeper source
> Of dirt is always there. You can't get rid
> Of it. You cannot hide or put a lid
> On it, as long as human life is there.
> It's us. The skin we shed, and then the hair.

The film returns repeatedly to the Cleaner to listen to her metaphysics of the dirt that makes us visible. Her work remains unrecognised by her employers, as does the work of the other cleaners and waiters shown in the film. Anthony, the husband, 'flings [his used condoms] / Into the toilet and thinks [she] won't see', debasing her. Fishing them out and holding them up to the camera, she celebrates her investigative skills, aligning herself with Potter's other investigatory protagonists, Mimi, Celeste, Ruby and Sally. Restoring work to visibility, she also points to the failure of the dirt and mess associated with labour to disappear.

All of Potter's films include and even celebrate the mess of failure, from Mimi's death and failure to bond with Musetta, through failed performances by Ruby and the Dancer in *The Gold Diggers*, the failure of *Rage* (1996) from the moment that Sally's pencil lead breaks, to the repeated failure of disappearance in *Yes*. Towards the end of the film, both She and her Lebanese lover He (Simon Abkarian) disappear from their lives in London, returning to the roots they had tried to erase. In Belfast, She is driven past the haunting Shanklin Road 'peace wall' that has failed to disappear from the landscape and marks the failure of the political process to erase barriers to peace. In Beirut, He stands in a square of collapsed buildings, marked with constellations of bullet marks, marking the potential erasure of lives, as well as suggesting the designation of 'failed state'. At the mid-point of the film, She and He had compared experiences of sectarian violence while He cooked for her – a mark of failure, as He had been a doctor in Lebanon and now works as a chef in London. His memory, in particular, speaks of failed labour: his failure to uphold the Hippocratic oath in the face of gunmen arguing about who should be saved. This 'us' and 'them' sectarian mindset causes the failure of He's medical expertise, and of his belief in his country. Returning to Beirut, he picks up a scalpel in his friend's surgery, as if remembering how he 'cut the flesh to save the life', leaving traces of his labour in the bodies of his patients. Read in this way, the crumbling buildings and barriers are scars: traces of the determination to rebuild, repair, continue, to unthink 'they' by insisting on visibility. His fingers on the scalpel recall the haptic sensibility of the film editor. The doctor/chef is a worker whose efforts not only make beauty, but recognise that beauty is a political strategy to 'save the life'. It is this sensibility that invites the viewer into Potter's films as the 'invisible becomes visible'.

Ubuntu: Theorie d'Ensemble

Beauty is omnipresent in *Rage* (2009): beautiful faces, beautiful costumes, beautiful colours, as one would expect from a film set in the fashion industry. Such a peacock display, sparkling with witty banter, initially presents a striking contrast to the metaphysics of *Yes*. Yet *Rage* (2009) is as serious of purpose, as committed to a thoughtful, vivid investigation of (in)visibility. Through reappropriating beauty from its dulled, vapid commodification in the 'beauty industry', it redefines it as the product (and reward) of labour. Each of the ensemble characters speaks as part of a choral symphony about work, and each speaks as protagonist when describing their own labour. Vijay (Riz Ahmed) identifies himself as delivering pizzas; he speaks with as much precision and passion of his bike as a tool that enables his work as designer Merlin speaks of his models and fabrics.

Despite the stringent similarity of monologues presented in single takes divided by straight cuts, spoken against a greenscreen background in medium close-up framing, the voices – speaking into Michelangelo's silence – do not meld into one, authoritative stream. *Rage* (2009) speaks (of its characters' history and labours) in a dozen accents that invite us variously. The protagonist is invisible; there is no single figure among the 14 visible characters who dominates to the extent of securing our point of view, so there are as many points of entry and identification as there are enunciation. Most likely, the viewer will shift in their response and alignment to the characters as the cleverly-paced writing offers revelations – not of facts pertaining to the thriller story, but to the real mystery of memory and identity.

In this ensemble of ever-changing voices, *Rage* (2009) unlaces the strict hierarchy of the business that it documents, removing the labourers from subjection to their overseers into a community made equal by access to expression. Potter describes the form as 'about giving equal weight to the unsung as to the famous, as an antidote to hierarchy based on celebrity power or wealth. Within any industry or sector there is an interdependence that is not reflected in how we perceive the value of different work; the ensemble is a reflection of the mosaic nature of the structure in which these individuals find themselves' (interview with author, December 2008). This inclusive speech suggests the Bantu maxim of *ubuntu*, brought into EuroWestern awareness by Archbishop Desmond Tutu who advocated it as an ethical path to dialogue in post-apartheid South Africa. Tutu's widely-quoted definition from *No Future Without Forgiveness* holds that ubuntu means that '"a person is a person through other people ... I am human because I belong". I participate, I share. A person with ubuntu is open and available to others' (2000: 35).

Ubuntu not only suggests a narrative form that depends on listening respectfully to all the voices, but one in which the imagined future audience has a voice in the narrative as well. As the characters speak from their identities as workers, they extend the same identity to Michelangelo – as filmmaker – and to the viewers engaged in working out the film's mystery, building the story that occurs in offscreen space from the dialogue and soundscape. Philosopher Mogobe B. Ramose links ubuntu to the production of harmony in music and argues that 'passive spectatorship on hearing the music of be-ing is understandable only as a necessary posture for the [post-Enlightenment] fragmentation of being' (2003: 235). Ubuntu includes the spectator in its harmony, a powerful metaphor for the way in which *Rage*'s (2009) unique enunciation – with the characters and the audience separated by a present-yet-invisible filmmaker who has become the screen – creates the sense of an invitation into the frame. Ramose underlines the fact that ubuntu is not just a community composed of the visible, living people we are accustomed to think of as the human community, but also the unseen dead and yet-to-be-born. This 'ontology of invisible beings is thus the basis of ubuntu metaphysics' (2003: 236). It offers a way to think about how Potter reinterprets her inclusive, interactive live performance work before palpable spectators in order to extend that community to the imagined audience who hover over the film as 'invisible beings' – and for whom the filmmaker and actors as labourers are rendered invisible by the beautiful fabric of the film that they create.

As the Cleaner says, describing herself and/as a filmmaker: 'invisible, we work our magic'. She speaks for all labourers: for the performer, for the filmmaker and for the audience who watch, and for the difference that Potter's films make. Most films summon an audience that is, in the Cleaner's words, 'Indivisible / One from the other; we're a mass, no soul.' Restoring the soul to the labourers whose work opens her films, Potter renders both the labourer(s) behind the camera and the audience before the screen more than a mass 'they'. She asks them to grace her films with their effort by recognising what John Bowring saw among the Lyon silk makers: 'an attention devoted to everything which was in any way connected with beauty'.

CHAPTER THREE

The Gold Diggers

DEar SalLY POtter
hear is the script for your new flim
once upon a time there were two grills
they were searching for the golden fleas
[camera pans over fleas]
their search took them all over the wirled
[humming] and to some other planets as well [cut to m.s. of planets]
just as they were about to discover a cosmic conspiracy [gnashing]
against the working class [l.s. of working class]
they bit each other very hard [c.u. teeth]
and it was all over [fade to black]
from a frend

— Anon., *The Gold Diggers* draft, undated

Two 'grills' searching for the golden 'fleas' discover a cosmic conspiracy against the working class: *The Gold Diggers* mixes mon(k)ey business and serious pleasure to show how beauty works and work can be beauty. It is a fantastic film – at least, that is how I encountered it even before I saw it. I read and was tantalised by ecstatic descriptions calling it the future of film in three important books that set out alternate histories of women's cinema: Kaja Silverman's *The Acoustic Mirror* (1988), Patricia Mellencamp's *A Fine Romance* (1995) and B. Ruby Rich's *Chick Flicks* (1998). Yet tantalise was all these detailed accounts could do: Potter withdrew the film from circulation in 1993, fearing conflict with the release of *Orlando*, so I only had the fantasias on a theme composed lovingly by Silverman, Mellencamp and Rich, with support from David Ehrenstein's slice of avant-garde film history in *Film: The Front Line/1984* (see 1984: 119–27) and Jonathan Rosenbaum's early and invigorated review for *Camera Obscura* (1984). Rosenbaum continues to place *The Gold Diggers* on his top one hundred list, calling *Yes* 'the best film Sally Potter's made since *The Gold Diggers*' when selecting it for his 2005 top ten for the *Chicago Reader*. Mellencamp ends her account by wondering 'what feminist film theory would be like in the 1990s [when she was writing the book] if, *in 1983*, we had taken this film as our model' (1995: 164; emphasis in original). For Ehrenstein, *The Gold Diggers* is cinema's fantasia, 'what characters in other films do while they are asleep … where they go when they leave the shot … [into] an unchartered [sic] region of desire – of pleasure – musing over what possible direction [film] might take' (1984: 127). Even now, the film inspires the thought that another world is possible: in a recent *Sight and Sound* article, Rich suggests that 'with [experimental silent filmmaker] Guy Maddin at the height of his fame, it's tempting to imagine a different fate for such a daring experiment' (2007: 23). *The Gold Diggers* did not only critique the old rules for women in cinema but used film history to discover and shape new ones. Shot in black-and-white, it features an investigation, chase sequences, shadowy urban landscapes and a *femme fatale* who, having learned from Musetta, does not die.

How and why did a film that was heralded for its fantastic visions of a different kind of cinema and a different world disappear? Rich's brief note for *Sight and Sound*'s review of 75 lost classics points the finger at 'anti-BFI forces opposed to subsidies [for the arts] and anti-feminist and homophobic forces in general' (ibid.). As her review suggests, these are also the economic and social forces that the film's protagonists fight against. Had the film been shot with a small budget raised on a grant from the Arts Council, as *Thriller* was, and had it been released two years earlier, its battle against capital may have been more widely cheered. Larger events had conspired to give voice and confidence to the forces Rich identifies. When the film was conceived in 1981, the Reagan/Thatcher era was just beginning and the BFI Production Board offered evidence that the political aspirations of the 1960s and 1970s were still alive and hopeful. *The Gold Diggers* now seems prescient in implying that the excesses of late capitalism could not endure and showing that international trade was rooted in systemic violence against the land and its inhabitants.

Its critical prescience was its undoing. 1983 was a bad time to be critical of capitalism and of nationalism, especially in a film funded with UK government money. The film's concern with gold mining and/as colonialism could be seen as an oblique reference to what the British claimed was the first offensive act of the Falklands War, in which Argentinian scrap metal merchants raised their national flag on South Georgia. The Falklands War gave rise to a new conservatism in the UK, both social and economic. Jingoistic tabloid newspaper headlines harked back to the Britain of World War Two and created a wave of popularity that returned Thatcher's government to power in 1983 when the film was released. *The Gold Diggers*, as Rich says, 'became a convenient proxy' for a newly conservative culture looking to divest itself of reminders of the wild 1970s, as the government was looking to sell itself and its (family and market-friendly) films to the newly conservative US. Through its investigations into gold, the film protests against the endless circulation of meaningless numbers that maintain national economies and the status quo.

The research into gold by the protagonist Celeste is based on interviews with economists, bankers, jewellers and financiers undertaken by Potter and her collaborators on the film, Rose English and Lindsay Cooper, as well as being informed by Potter's reading of Marxist and anarchist thinkers (interview with author, September 2006). In an interview with Pam Cook, Potter quoted Michel Foucault on 'the metaphysics of money', saying that the film went beyond Marxist analysis to understand what Foucault called the 'equivocal glitter' of gold (in Cook 1984a: 14–15). Not only does the film critique capitalism, but it returns gold's lure to the realm of fantasy. At the heart of the film is a story of gold mining that has the look and feel of the California Gold Rush, the hidden narrative behind Hollywood's location and success. Capitalism and the emergence of commercial cinema are connected in these scenes, and are linked to colonialism, environmental destruction and the marriage market that renders women, like films, objects for sale.

All that glistens come together in the film's other protagonist, Ruby. Embodied by Julie Christie, the character plays on the idea of the star whose presence in a film means big box office because of her classical beauty. Ruby is part of a chain of associations: whiteness, beauty, desire, wealth, gold, the cinematic icon, cinema as industry, the big-budget Hollywood musical, costume, all adding up to the oppression of women. Christie embodies both meanings of the artiste: perceived as the woman for sale, she is the escape artist(e) who refuses to play dumb. She remains an outspoken feminist and conscientious objector to the Hollywood game whom Rich calls the 'film star as outstanding human being' (see 1998: 326–36). As the most iconic star of her era, she was the gold standard against which other actresses were measured. By putting her on a pedestal, the media and industry tried to reduce her to the pretty face on a billboard that she played in *Darling* (1965). Her leftist politics, which were seen as a threat to films' reception and takings, were silenced by turning her from a human being into a promissory note with an exchange value. 'The star phenomenon is an actual form of investment and in real financial terms is a kind of circulation of the face' (Potter in Cook 1984a: 15). The cinema's fascination with the female star is revealed as its obsession with money.

Ruby is instrumental in discovering how she is being used and removing herself from circulation, a narrative twist that delighted many viewers. As Rich points out, that twist was, however, 'reviled for taking Christie away from the boys who reviewed it' (2007: 23). The ideal woman – white, beautiful, dolled-up and pliant – is shown to be no more than a fantasy construction of the capitalist patriarchy which controlled not only the film's production and distribution, but its reception. Potter was not naïve enough to imagine the film meeting a rapturous reception from mainstream critics. It uses a theatrical performance to symbolise the mainstream world of feature films, in which male critics determine reception. Ruby performs the role of the wide-eyed innocent beloved of D. W. Griffith in a stage play. In the grand auditorium, a row of men in identical suits harrumph and cross their legs in unison. They become a chorus line whose disapproval is stereotypical, unthinking, repeated and collectively conceived, in a prescient mirroring of the film's reception.

On the other side of town another kind of performance takes place in a bar. On the dance floor, women in white shirts and braces dance in pairs to the rhythms set up by the bartender as she drums on the wall. The dancers are Potter's contemporaries and collaborators from the London Contemporary Dance Theatre, Siobhan Davies and Maedée Duprès, while the drumming bartender is celebrated percussionist Marilyn Mazur, who played with Potter in a number of improv groups. This performance takes place in Celeste's dream of her love for Ruby, which is allegorised by this all-female space reminiscent of the performance world from which Potter emerged into filmmaking. Although it is an intimate dream, it is also a manifesto for a new, democratic and inviting space in which performance could take place away from the harrumphs. This is a performance in which anyone could participate, but it also showcases the performers' virtuosities. The dancers use a combination of everyday movements and female-female lifts, the bartender drums with whatever she can lay her hands on. In contrast to Ruby's performance, these women dance together spontaneously in a social space. There is a stage in the bar, but they are dancing amidst the tables and chairs.

This shared and joyous dance makes Ruby's stage debut shortly after seem all the more painful. She is dressed up like a child and forced into a mime with no preparation. Instead, she has to rely on the stagehand (George Yiasoumi) in the wings, whose gestures she copies. Missing cues that she does not know are there, her delayed and exaggerated actions cause the all-male audience to laugh and boo. She even performs a sad version of a happy dance, her lugubrious skip prompting more laughter. As the booing rises in volume, Ruby stands stock-still on the forestage. Lindsay Cooper's bassoon score swells in to drown out the audience's comment on Ruby's performance. Ruby, emboldened by the companionship of this collaborator (it is unclear whether she can hear the music or not), laughs in the audience's faces. Like the rest of her performance, the laugh is silent, exaggerated, dramatic. The film cuts between her laughter and the heckling audience three times, emphasising her bold response to their uncomprehending criticism of her failure to live up to the character into whose too-small outfit they have forced her.

It is also the film's response to the political infrastructure in which it was made and to its future critics. Perhaps this determination to laugh in the face of power was what upset those critics more than anything that the film says explicitly. While other radical feminist films of that period, such as Marleen Gorris's *De Stilte Ronde Christine M.* (*A Question of Silence*, 1982) and Lizzie Borden's *Born in Flames* (1983), advocated the violent overthrow of the powers that be, *The Gold Diggers* finds humour a more potent weapon. 'The level on which these things are dealt with in the film is on the level of … a cinematic pun, which means deep play with the language of film' (Potter in Cook 1984a: 15). Like its jokey early sketch (quoted as epigraph to this chapter), the film staged intentional puns whose deliberate outrageousness sends up the conventions of cinema. Critics unwilling to credit Potter with the depth of knowledge that clearly sustains her play read the puns as errors deriving from a basic lack of film grammar.

Yet Potter provided evidence of the depth and breadth of her cinematic knowledge, and a primer for *The Gold Diggers*' dizzying catalogue of references, when she was asked to programme a season at the National Film Theatre to mark the film's release. It ran to 23 separate programmes, including D. W. Griffith's *Way Down East* (1920) and Charlie Chaplin's *The Gold Rush* (1925), both of which inform *The Gold Diggers*' homage to silent cinema. Julie Christie in an austere winter landscape featured in *Doctor Zhivago* (1965). *Darling* also screened, as part of a series of investigations of the female icon and the possibility of friendship between women, across different genres and eras, including *Queen Christina* (1933), *The Lady Vanishes* (1938), *Madame de…* (1953), *Lola Montès* (1955), *Une femme est une femme* (1961), *Persona* (1966) and *Julia* (1977).

The film's avant-garde intentions were highlighted by the inclusion of a short by Joyce Wieland, as well as *La Souriante Madame Beudet* (*Smiling Madame Beudet*, 1923) and *Alexandr Nevskiy* (1938). Postwar experimental masterpieces *Rekopis znaleziony w Saragossie* (*Saragossa Manuscript*, 1965) and *Die Macht der Gefühle* (*The Power of Emotions*, 1983) showed that Potter included her film in a politicised avant-garde community still thriving, and producing feature-length films, in Eastern Europe. Two films that stand on the boundary between experimental and arthouse cinema, and whose production crossed national and political boundaries, also featured. *Le Procès* (*The Trial*, 1962) and *Der Stand der Dinge* (*The State of Things*, 1982), like *Saragossa Manuscript*, have spiralling structures that explore, respectively, the byzantine folds of state power and of filmmaking (something that *The Tango Lesson* will echo).

Maya Deren's dance film *Study in Choreography for the Camera* (1945) and Yvonne Rainer's film about dancers *Lives of Performers* (1972) acted as a bridge between the avant-garde works and Potter's selections from the broad church of musicals. Classical Hollywood was represented by *The Gold Diggers of 1933* (1933), *Dance, Girl, Dance* (1940), *Hellzapoppin'* (1941) (screened as a double bill with the Deren film) and *Singin' in the Rain* (1952). By 1983, the musical was no longer a functional genre or production mode in American cinema, although *The Gold Diggers* is far from nostalgic for the days of big-budget production line musicals. *Kuhle Wampe* (1932), a musical after a scenario by Bertolt Brecht, positioned *The Gold Diggers* in a narrow lineage of avant-garde and politically-inflected musicals, while *The Red Shoes* (1948) showed that it was possible to fuse ballet with the form of the musical.

As in the backstage musical, *The Gold Diggers* features several characters who are conscious of themselves as performers and through them it questions gendered cinematic conventions. Patricia Mellencamp argues that the film plays off the 'masculine' thriller against the 'feminine' musical to offer Celeste and Ruby a way out of the trap of cinema, by reconnecting silent and modernist film to their forgotten roots in live performances such as vaudeville and music hall (see 1995: 159–69). Whether or not it is a musical on the terms of any of the films Potter selected for her season, *The Gold Diggers* is 'musical'. 'The performance of song and dance ... does not simply disrupt the narrative flow, it represents an eruption of anarchy and disorder that condenses the film's own refusal of convention' (Tincknell & Conrich 2006: 5). Its spiralling, improvisatory structure of parodic reversals upset all kinds of power relations.

It climaxes, like a typical costume drama, with a ball. Except here the tailcoated men dance happily with each other, and the women in ballgowns are sliding down the banisters, whooping with joy. When Celeste and Ruby ride off from the ball together on a white horse, what begins as a parodic reversal goes beyond the laughs to find a tone that is both dreamlike and earthy. Cinema 'give[s] back ... pleasure' to viewers who want romance and joy without stereotypes and what Rich calls mainstream film's 'melodramatic myths' (2007: 23). In place of the final kiss, *The Gold Diggers* sets an interracial lesbian couple riding off into the sunset and skinny-dipping in the moonlight, in a closing scene that could be a dream – as could much of the film. The madcap, in which everything could become something else, is matched by a non-linear narrative structure in which nothing is what is seems.

As in the most recent films of David Lynch, whose structure and symbolism would seem to owe Potter's film a significant debt, there is no 'real' story that can be unravelled from the repetitions, inserts and interruptions. Defiantly non-realist, *The Gold Diggers* is a fantasy film in the truest sense, but also fantastic because it offers an inventive, inquisitive tour of the feminine and feminist cultural imaginary. It builds its world by using, questioning and giving rich new meaning to tropes associated with the feminine: dance, costume, ornamentation, water, gardens, motherhood and dreaming. Following a fantastical *Alice in Wonderland*-like spiral logic, it traces Celeste's and Ruby's journeys on the boundary between interior and exterior. Investigating their places in the capitalist economy, they develop an alternate economy of the imagination in which they are able to repeat their actions again and again until they get the desired result.

The first time that Celeste rescues Ruby, Ruby is not ready to go further than Celeste's flat, where she spends time trying to remember who she is. Celeste is still caught up in her job doing data entry for a bank. Like Ruby, she has to become more than a conduit for other people's ideas. Their investigations drive them into the night-time city, where they are driven by pursuit. In keeping with the *noir* aesthetic, both protagonists are stalked by the group of men who will become Ruby's audience. They are stalking Ruby because she is too valuable to be wandering free and they are stalking Celeste because she has stolen Ruby. A black woman who asks questions and refuses her subservient role, Celeste represents a threat to the dominant order. Going even further than in *Thriller*, Laffont's presence refuses the negative stereotypes for black women in cinema. Neither a downtrodden seamstress nor a sex kitten, Celeste is the romantic lead, the black knight who sweeps in to rescue the white princess. She does not act as Ruby's mammy or magic Negro; her humour and compassion give Ruby the space in which to rescue herself, inspired by her attraction, across lines of race and class, to Celeste.

Celeste's first rescue of Ruby results from her observation of a curious ritual in which Ruby is being carried through the streets on a palanquin in an elaborate, bejewelled dress and headgear. Celeste comes to understand the function of this ritual when she interviews the Expert (David Gale), who ends his paean to money's power to make the world go round by stroking a doll-scale model of Ruby in the palanquin. It allows Celeste to put together the connection between Ruby and gold that will make the next rescue attempt more successful. The viewer, like Celeste, only glimpses Ruby in her palanquin at the start of the film. When the scene repeats later, several shots from different angles show that Ruby is like a Catholic saint's statue being carried in a parade. As Potter points out, 'a religious icon has no financial investment in it but has enormous metaphysical, spiritual and psychological investment in it' (in Cook 1984a: 15). The palanquin represents a possible route to freedom from circulation for Ruby and the female film star, a metaphysical meaning beyond Foucault's 'equivocal glitter' of two-dimensional beauty. Yet it is also a trap: the palanquin looks like a jewelled bird-cage and Ruby is being carried alongside a stretcher piled high with gold bars. Both the star and the gold are going to be deposited in the bank to preserve their value. The bank turns into a ball where Ruby arrives as the star guest and circulates from man to man, devaluing their female partners whom they leave standing to get a chance to dance with the star. This exchange increases her value to others while maintaining the 'values' of patriarchy: beauty, whiteness, thinness. No wonder the men in suits are hunting her down. When the men finally get her back to the ball, Ruby drops her male partners to the ground, literally causing the marriage market to crash.

Ruby is finally ready to take up the challenge Celeste offered her with her daring rescue. In the second ball scene, she completes the process that began when she sat in Celeste's flat and opened herself to fragmentary flashbacks to her childhood. A memory about her mother makes her cry and prompts her to change from her ballgown into a trenchcoat and beret that is equal parts *noir* detective and 1960s Godardian It girl. Fleeing from the stalkers who shadow her, Ruby inadvertently slips into a theatre where she sees a key scene from her childhood played out like a silent film. The performer playing her child self is, in fact, her. Understandably astonished when she realises this, she runs out of the theatre, only to find herself backstage and then thrust onto the stage to take the role of her child-self in the play. When she catches the eyes of audience-Ruby, the cycle starts again. Audience-Ruby runs out of the theatre down the same alleyway as before but does not find herself backstage. Instead, she enters a series of corridors that leads her back to the landscape of memory that the play was staging. This is a ramshackle log cabin set in frozen wastes as seen in the credit sequence. Watching as her younger self plays with the toy horse that was seen buried in snow, Ruby relives her mother's desertion, which was partially remembered in the opening sequence and the play.

Kaja Silverman's reading of the film compares Ruby's search for the mother who abandoned her with feminism's search for a maternal or matriarchal political order and imaginary (see 1988: 178–86). As her book is concerned with the repressive use of the female voice in Hollywood cinema, Silverman locates *The Gold Diggers'*

Frozen in girlhood: there's no place like home for Ruby (Julie Christie)

maternal in its wonderfully experimental and varied use of voice, sound and music. The unanchored song and voice-overs that open the film work like Ruby's repeated movement through impossible spaces to call into question the boundary between the real and the fantastic. Western rationalism insists on maintaining a firm boundary between interior and exterior and genders the binary: in many societies, women are kept inside or in domestic space while men move through the public outside world. In Ancient Greece, philosophers argued that women had to be contained within physical structures like the veil and the house as well as social structures like marriage because their biology made them 'leaky' (see Carson 1995: 126–7). Women's voices were particularly problematic as they drew attention to sexual difference and the 'other' female mouth (1995: 131). Silverman demonstrates that the fear of leakiness still applies in Hollywood cinema: the threat of the female voice has to be contained by 'leaking' in confession.

The Gold Diggers sets up what looks like a classic confession scene that appears to reveal the maternal as women's dark secret. In Celeste's flat Ruby lies on the floor while Celeste sits in a rocking chair, telling her she has to remember. Ruby then sits at the desk and says 'my mother, yes, my mother', her lips trembling and her huge, kohl-rimmed eyes looking at the camera in extreme close-up. It is an uncanny echo of an early scene in *Doctor Zhivago*, in which General Yevgraf (Alec Guinness) questions The Girl (Rita Tushingham) about her parents, showing her the dreamily gorgeous photograph of Lara (Julie Christie), who may be her mother, on the flyleaf of a book in an attempt to awaken her memories. There is a close-up of The Girl, suggesting that the story that is about to unravel will be seen from her point of view, like Ruby's memories. Instead, she is just a silent audience for Yevgraf's tale about his brother, the poet who wrote the book. Lara is the film's muse, rarely its point-of-view character. In *The Gold Diggers*, it is as if Ruby is The Girl reclaiming those memories of her mother. From the extreme close-up, there is a cut to a home movie-like image of the dark-haired woman from the credits, laughing. This repeats twice, and in the next shot, Ruby is lying on the floor as she was at the start of the scene but Celeste is gone. Confession is not enough: Ruby will have to re-enter her past as a spectator and performer in order to find a way to speak her memories and self beyond the 'talking cure' that lays the blame at the mother's door, and identifies all women as potential hysterics.

The scene also suggests that we have to listen to more than the words the characters speak. In an interview with composer Lindsay Cooper, Mandy Merck comments that most of the music is dominated by 'dance forms … tangoes [sic], polkas, taps and waltzes' (1984: 50). Cooper answers that she researched a lot of 1950s big band music so that her 'progress through the film score mirrored the Julie Christie character going back to her past' (in Merck 1984: 50–1). We can hear Ruby's journey back to her mother and her childhood not in her confession, but reinforced by the score's use of a 'small number of musical ideas and themes [with] … endless cross-references' (in Merck 1984: 46). One musical moment stands out from the tightly-woven net of memories that Cooper's score casts over the film and it comes at the moment when Ruby finally understands her place in the economy of desire. Having rescued Ruby a second time, Celeste sings her 'The Empire Song' from the stage of the bar that appeared in her dream.

In realising her dream of performing with an appreciative female audience, Celeste shows how she has changed through her investigation. The global economy no longer passes through her body without comment. Instead of asking men for answers they are unwilling to give, she spits out what she has learned about how money goes round the world, and for whom it makes the world go around, in a subtle reference to *Cabaret* (1972) as a political musical. Intercut with Celeste's performance are shots of the gold miners who included Ruby's father. Hearing the song, Ruby understands how poverty and international commerce forced her father into the gold rush, and how his sudden wealth took her mother away from her. It enables her to put her mother's decision into a bigger picture about colonialism, slavery and environmental destruction, shaped by gold's power. This gives her the opportunity to decide to be different.

Silverman argues that Potter's and Cooper's sound world is a warm, sustaining maternal space, which appears to be realised in the moment of communion as Ruby listens lovingly to Celeste's inquest/protest (see 1988: 181). Yet its importantly political lyrics are barely audible. What is important – and what communicates clearly to the viewer – is Ruby's reaction, the way in which Celeste's performance allows her to refigure her memories. Cooper comments that she made a mistake 'in giving the song an over-dense arrangement and not foregrounding the voice in the mix' (in Merck 1984: 53). Whereas Cooper's instrumental themes speak intelligibly to viewers of a shared national past, 'The Empire Song' is problematic, its lyrics and music illegible, less easy to circulate. In cinematic terms, it is a mistake, a failure to communicate.

At the same time, the innovative use of sound has a spikier side, acting defensively against easy readings of all kinds. It points to the film's resistance to the circulation into which female bodies and gold are forced to enter.

The film found itself in the same position as Ruby, an aesthetic object tied to hegemonic ideas of use-value. It was expected to be a willing performer in a cultur-ally-constructed narrative, like Ruby when she is thrust onstage in a childlike costume and the make-up of exaggerated femininity. The film as artiste is expected to show itself for sale, and *The Gold Diggers*' economic critique, figured in the song's over-dense sound world, was a deliberate refusal to do so. The BFI's investment was paid back by the film's escape from circulation and the representational economy, like Ruby's escape from the men who have valued and invested in her, believing that they can own her. *Thriller* refigures the artisan as both artiste and artist, while *The Gold Diggers* focuses on the artiste in order to remove her from sexualised circulation. In reclaiming the possibilities of the artiste as self-aware performer, Potter liberates the audience from their part in the cinematic circuits of (economic) trade, advocating a different form of exchange.

At a transitional moment, Ruby encounters another female performer who is trying to find a new language. The first time she goes backstage to find herself, she accidentally enters the rehearsal space of a dancer, played by Jacky Lansley who co-founded Limited Dance Company with Potter. The Dancer is rehearsing in front of a large mirror, in which Ruby is reflected as she looks around the door. The Dancer says that she had to move Ruby's 'things' so she could rehearse; cut to a shot of the stage-Ruby's little girl dress hanging on the wall. Dressed casually for contemporary dance, the Dancer separates herself from the infantilised yet sexualised 'things' of the artiste, a costume in which Ruby will be disguised as herself. The Dancer, who asks Ruby whether she is going 'to get changed', needs no such costume or stage in order to engage in her performance. What she stages for Ruby, and symbolises in the film, is the artiste as process, as liveness, as failure. 'Despite years of research', she cannot remember her steps. Like the Icelandic landscape that dominates the film's opening, she 'freezes'. Her choice of words harks back to *Thriller*'s voice-over description of English as 'frozen in arabesque'.

The Dancer reveals that she used to have a partner, and jokes that dancing solo makes 'some of the lifts difficult', although she wittily improvises solo lifts. Forget-ting is not just a matter of abandonment (as Ruby will discover) but also point of view: it occurs when the Dancer faces the audience. To help with this, Ruby actively becomes the Dancer's audience, carrying the bench she had been sitting on over to the mirror where the Dancer begins to rehearse again. This time there is music to signal a 'real' performance. Just as the Dancer brings Ruby on 'stage' (demarcated by a light bar lying on the ground) and into the dance with her, they are interrupted by the stagehand, who has been watching, and who pushes Ruby into the wings, taking the camera's focus with them. When Ruby finds herself thrown onstage, there is no answering reverse shot of the audience, only of the stagehand as a labouring, partici-patory audience who mugs her cues from the wings. Like Lansley's Dancer, Ruby has forgotten her moves – if she ever knew them – and is frozen, staring at the audience.

Her backstage encounter is like *Thriller*, an experimental dance working itself out with a sympathetic audience at the moment of feminist film zeitgeist. Ruby, like *The Gold Diggers*, works to bring this knowledge from the minimalist, non-narrative space of the rehearsal room that resembles Mimi's attic into the bigger-budget world of narrative cinema into which she is thrust by a male functionary to satisfy a male audience.

Potter worked comparably to transfer her 'years of research' from one medium (performance) to another (film) as the Dancer works to move from partner dance, which is like the collaborative work of a performance company, to solo, which is the way the film industry positions the director. The way in which performance 'leaks' from Celeste's dream sequence into her waking experience with Ruby shows Potter working out a unique triangulation of live performance, experimental film and interiority, in which each comes to stand productively for the other. The film releases the artiste by showing her to be at once a figure for creative process and also for a new relationship between artist and audience in which the viewer, like Ruby, is prepared to immerse herself in another's fantasy.

By investigating dominant culture's fantasies about them, the women have found a shared dream. At the end of the film, Celeste and Ruby swim through the moon's reflection, as a woman (Kassandra Colson) welding plates to a ship raises her visor and smiles at them. For Ehrenstein, it is 'in the smile of this welder that the special kick (and for some the special irritation) of *The Gold Diggers* can be perceived. She is a real person in a real job [Colson was also a member of the film's crew]. She does not "belong" in the cinematic world' (1984: 126). Yet through her work, and her realness, she is a figure of beauty and fantasy, an alchemist striking spiritual gold. The film runs in slow motion, announcing this as dream-space, and reminding the viewer that the welding scene appeared in Celeste's earlier dream. In its fluidity, its abstraction of light moving on a dark ground and its use of slow motion, it represents what cinema can do. As the figures of the women in the water become visible, the impossibility of their swim across the moon winks at Georges Méliès' famous *Le voyage dans la lune* (*Trip to the Moon*, 1902) and the strange, impossible journeys on which film can take us, imaginatively and politically. If as consumers and producers of cinema, we can release ourselves from market-values that equate the female icon and her 'melodramatic myths' with financial gain, this is the cinematic experience that could be realised. It is joyous, quietly erotic, aesthetically ravishing and emotionally engaging.

But it requires the audience to be willing to jump into cinema as a space of fantasy that is immersive but active (like swimming), artisanal (like metalworking), elemental (like water) and, most importantly, shared. It is one small swim for Christie and Laffont, but a giant leap for the viewer, as they dare us to skinny-dip with them in cinema's potential. Some viewers were ready – those, it seems, who had themselves been prepared by the heady years of feminism's insistence that they rethink the old ways and be open to the new. Others were not. They missed the point that the film asserts its right to be what the joke script calls 'flim': a deliberate play on the word 'film' that highlights the medium's ephemeral and playful qualities on the border between high and low art. By reconnecting with film's heritage of live performance,

The Gold Diggers questions the gendered and classed ghetto-isation of such genres as musicals, costume dramas with their balls and silent melodrama. It demonstrated that genres which critics label as 'flimsy', 'flim-flam' or 'flotsam' are actually refusing to play the serious game of use-value. Like the grills of the joke script, they bite back.

And they come back, as Rich infers. Potter's inclusion of Dorothy Arzner's *Dance, Girl, Dance* in her film programme for the NFT suggests that her film's fantastical presence might create future audiences who will be ready to receive it. In Ruby's silent laughter, *The Gold Diggers* pays homage to the earlier film's climactic moment (excerpted in *Rage* (1987)), in which Judy (Maureen O'Hara) refuses to leave the stage when the audience laugh at her collapsing dress straps. Instead, she walks to the apron of the stage and faces them silently and levelly until they go quiet, then berates them for their prurient interest. Of course, she follows this moment of feminist victory by cat-fighting with Bubbles (Lucille Ball), but triumphs in the end, getting both a job and a man. Ruby's laugh *frees* her from that 'happy ending'; when she issues it, there is none of the startled but thrilled applause that eventually greets Judy.

Arzner's film was a massive flop on its first release, despite a risqué performance by Lucille Ball as a burlesque star and Maureen O'Hara in a rare screwball role as a ballet dancer stuck working as Ball's straight woman. In more ways than one, *Dance, Girl, Dance* can be seen to prefigure *The Gold Diggers*. Louisa Cole wrote recently that '*Dance, Girl, Dance* works best ... as a girl buddy-movie, a bit of flotsam within a rich heritage of similar works ... It has even been suggested in a recent study that the friendship between the girls suggests "a possible rapprochement between high and low art forms"' (Alison Butler in Cole 2004). The friendships between Celeste and Ruby, and between Ruby and the Dancer, perform this possible rapprochement, which is also that between the artist and the artiste. Through these friendships the women are, as Celeste says in her final line, 'searching for the secret of transformation'. *The Gold Diggers* shows women trying to unfreeze limbs trapped in the conventions of dance (or cinema). Through connection, they reinvent performance, like the Dancer remembering her moves with Ruby as witness, and through performance they reinvent film. Released from convention, film becomes a liquid medium like the water that is the element of the film's final scenes. Flotsam is, after all, what floats: as *The Gold Diggers* resurfaces it shows film going through an elemental transformation by changing what it means to be a dancing girl.

CHAPTER FOUR

Moving

Slowness in any medium is the most difficult thing. In dance, when you move slowly, you have to exert the greatest amount of muscular control. But only people who know how to move very, very slowly can move very, very fast. It's where you discover what technique you have. Great tango dancers will move with the stealth of a panther around the edge, then suddenly: dagger leg movements, all the *ochos*. The great wind instrumentalists all practice long notes for breath control. You have to keep the energy flowing as you sustain and hold this long movement. That's very hard to achieve on film. Thus the seduction of the language of commercials, covering up with fast cuts and lots of rhythms, or even chucking ideas onto a page. Developing one idea slowly, like [writer W. G.] Sebald, is incredibly impressive. It's about saying: there is time, there is space. It takes away that crazy, commercialised, industrialised busyness, which I think is an anxiety about death. You're pushing back that moment with white noise and activity. All the great meditative disciplines or spiritual disciplines are about slowing down the breath, or opening up space through prayer, meditation or contemplation, to the more sustainable long-term, difficult ideas of time, space, eternity, birth and death.

– Sally Potter, interview with author, September 2006

The witty draft for *The Gold Diggers* might call it a 'flim', but Potter's films undo the pun by sparkling seriously with the gold dust of performers. Rather than razzle-dazzle, performance in her films is a meditative discipline that puts its work onscreen and speaks of what the performer has learned by working with her body. Reviewers who notice nothing else about Potter's films pay attention to her ability to cast and work with performers, whether first-timers or Hollywood stars. In an exuberant preview of *Yes* before the Toronto International Film Festival in 2004, Roger Ebert nominated Joan Allen's performance for an Academy Award. 'Joan Allen is amazing in *Yes*', he wrote, 'and director Sally Potter is amazing in the way she makes her amazing. Has ever a film looked more clearly and with more love at an actress?' (2004). Ebert frames his praise for Allen's luminous performance by putting his finger on Potter's ability to depict her performers 'clearly and with … love'. Potter brings what she learnt about being looked at onstage to her work behind the camera, in order to create a space in which her performers can develop their characters.

In particular, she is drawn to working with well-known female performers looking to redefine themselves by using their 'star power' to explore more challenging roles. In *The Man Who Cried*, for example, Cate Blanchett took her celebrated portrait of Elizabeth as a young woman rehearsing to be Queen in Shekhar Kapur's *Elizabeth* (1998) one step further. Ginette Vincendeau notes that Blanchett 'dominates the picture … *The Man Who Cried* confirms what a gifted actress she is' (2001b: 54). She plays Lola, a White Russian émigré who makes her living as a cabaret dancer and dreams alternately of a wealthy husband and of success in Hollywood. Lola is like a younger version of Christie's Ruby, one still caught up in the circuits of beauty and desire in order to survive in a politically precarious world. As Elizabeth, Blanchett rehearsed her royal mien before the mirror; Lola's rehearsals are more subtle and more telling. With her peroxided hair and garish red lips, Lola thinks she is rehearsing to be a film star, practising her pout. But she has confused performance and reality: what she is rehearsing is her own identity as a woman based on the myths of the silver screen. Lola presages Blanchett's role in *I'm Not There* (2007) as Jude, an artist whose stardom has begun to erase his/her identity. Immensely charming and vulnerable, Lola is one of Potter's most moving performer characters because she never gets to stop performing, not even when having sex. At the moment of her death, she is practising her imitation of Esther Williams.

Synchronised swimming on film captivates Lola as the purest form of Hollywood stardom. In the same way, Potter's films make ambivalent use of many forms of live performance as/at the height of cinema. The ambivalence is twofold. First of all, film and performance have a tendentious history. Secondly, as Lola discovers to her cost, being an artiste has traditionally been linked to prostitution for women and its forms are accordingly devalued as sites of self-expression. Attributed to women, travellers and others who do not have access to official recorded culture, performance has been seen as ephemeral, bodily and meaningless. In the twentieth century, anthropology recognised that performance was not only an alternate form of expression and record to written culture but carried the cultural memory of its community. Diana Taylor, a leading performance theorist and political activist/performer, notes that if 'performance did not transmit knowledge, only the literate and powerful could claim social memory and identity' (2005: xvii). Performance studies developed in the 1960s to understand how performance binds together performers and audiences into a social whole.

The insistent focus on the individual film viewer in film theory marks just how separate film has become from its roots in live performance. Films were first shown at carnivals and in music halls, places where workers gathered for entertainment, and were often accompanied by lectures, barkers, narrators and music (see May 1980: xii). The presenter was part of the act. Gradually, music halls were converted to cinemas and nickelodeons were built as film became genteel and separated out from the more raucous, working-class forms of entertainment. The projector moved from in front of the audience to behind them. With the arrival of recorded sound, live music and narration disappeared. At the same time, influential voices began to argue that film had its own language that was separate from the theatre's. Hugo Munsterberg (*Photoplay*, 1916) and Rudolph Arnheim (*Film as Art*, 1932) both used perceptual psychology to prove, scientifically, that film produced a different kind of viewing than theatre. They were arguing against sceptics who saw film as nothing more than recording everyday life on the one hand, or a derivative and unsophisticated form of theatre or literature on the other. They wanted to show that there were certain things that only film could do, and to do so they cut film off from its relationship with theatre and with liveness.

Film historians such as Tom Gunning have recently done much to restore this connection by showing how early film audiences would have received film as part of a culture of spectacle in which mechanical thrills were integral to live shows. Panoramas and theatrical effects were advertised as novelties to draw audiences. When Potter projected film behind dancers in *Daily* and *Combines*, she was building on a long legacy of technological innovation in theatrical productions. Likewise, her use of performance in film is an acknowledgement of the importance of theatre to film pioneers. Potter roots her film work in live performance more than any other contemporary director, with Robert Lepage – who also trained and practised as a live performer – as an outstanding exception. It is a rare gift. Performances are never just there as spectacle, but as a way of thinking about film's relation to its audience. They slow the films down, and meditatively open up the characters, drawing attention to the hard-earned virtuosity of the films' dancing protagonists.

Just as performance points outwards to signal the films' awareness of their audiences, so it also points inwards. Songs and dances of all kinds are like soliloquies: they give us a glimpse of the private self that the character cannot express through dialogue or gesture. When neuroscientist Antonio Damasio introduces his theory of embodied emotions, he draws a parallel between the experience of emotion, and that of performance/spectatorship. He uses the metaphor to argue for his theory, in which the body, mind and brain work in concert to recognise, process and express feeling, generating consciousness:

> I have always been intrigued by the specific moment when, as we sit waiting in the audience, the door to the stage opens and a performer steps into the light; or, to take the other perspective, the moment when a performer who waits in

semidarkness sees the same door open, revealing the lights, the stage, and the audience. I realised some years ago that the moving quality of this moment ... come[s] from its embodiment of an instance of birth ... stepping into the light is also a powerful metaphor for consciousness. (2000: 3)

His suggestion that consciousness – mind – has a bodily basis not only in the brain, but in the sensory body, is controversial. Its theatricality has a 'moving quality' that seems appropriate to Potter's use of performance to engage viewers' intellect through their senses. Moreover, Damasio suggests performance as a metaphor for consciousness, as Potter does when she has Laffont become aware through English's dance. In Potter's films, we do not identify or connect with star performers because of their celebrity, but because of their gift for expressing, through the discipline of performance, their private selves.

In the films, however, this is not a gift that belongs to professionals. It inheres in the attempt at performance itself. A professional performer like Lola may find herself conveying anxiety rather than the confidence she wishes to exude through her Marlene Dietrich imitation, while the passionate amateurs who fill the milongas, church halls and cafés of *The Tango Lesson* enable Sally and Pablo to reconnect with tango's *pasión* after their failed performance. Potter's background in situationist performance art also leaves its trace in the way in which all and any spaces – a house, a park, a hospital – can contain, or rather be opened up by, performances that bring together the outside, professional world and the intimate, private world. Pablo dances in the kitchen with the lettuce in *The Tango Lesson* as a prelude to asking Sally to dance with him in an exhibition tango, a gesture that is a signal of growing intimacy, and a reincorporation of the bar scene in *The Gold Diggers*. Father Christmas (Lol Coxhill) makes an awkward appearance in the hospice in *Yes* as She has stepped away from the bedside of her dying aunt. His presence marks both the artificiality and the necessity of live performance's celebration in the face of death. His performance is not separate from life, but shows that art's immersion in real life is what film makes possible. Within traditional performance spaces such as theatres and milongas, the non-professional performer has an opportunity to do performance differently, talking back to the audience as embodied in Ruby's laugh.

This is a huge reversal not only of film's exclusion of performance, but of performance's immoral and gendered associations. Performers were outcasts, and 'nice' girls were excluded from careers on the stage. This is part of the shock for the male audience in *The Gold Diggers*: Ruby is precious enough to be kept in a gilded cage, yet she demeans herself (and devalues herself, like putting too much gold in circulation) by appearing onstage. Their reaction reflects on what it means for a woman to be a filmmaker. In speaking for herself like Ruby, Potter puts herself onstage and in the public eye, performing the role of director. Yet as Ruby discovers, through her encounter with the Dancer, live performance can undermine the static, iconic self that the commercialisation of art demands. Through repetition and rehearsal, performance creates a productively unstable plurality of selves that are pulled loosely together into a coherent self by performing for an engaged, empathetic audience.

Performance is used to question the deep-seated connection in EuroWestern thought between women and the body, which excludes women from an association with the mind. The parodic use of men in ballet poses in *Thriller* converts the Artists into artistes. Costume, props, vocal style and gesture are used humorously throughout Potter's work to challenge social gender norms that dictate audience response.

In order to question performance and the body's ambivalent relation to film, in *Thriller* and *The Gold Diggers* these performances mainly occur outside the narrative and in ambiguous relation to it. By the time of *Orlando* they are incorporated into the narrative, often with a reflexive or literal wink at the audience to remind us that we are watching a performance. Most notable in that film is the number of male counter-tenors whose high, cultured voices challenge presumptions about gender and about the artiste. Both *The Tango Lesson* and *The Man Who Cried* openly declare their desiring relation to the musical via their performances-within-a-film. In *The Tango Lesson*, the performer's body is also the writer/director's body, turning filmmaking into a performance and vice versa. In *The Man Who Cried*, everyone is spying on everyone else, so everyday actions become careful performances, while stage performances are demanding work. The only release from being watched all the time is in the moments of spontaneous, communal performance that Suzie shares with her Roma friends. *Yes* contains no staged performances whatsoever. The characters share their private selves with each other and with the audience through social dance, swimming, clothes shopping, cooking and air guitar. They also speak in lyric verse, a kind of linguistic performance that is associated with self-expression and is the form of the Shakespearean soliloquy. Even in this film, where the spoken word is so expressive, the protagonists use their performing bodies as articulations, to put the motion in emotion.

In his article 'Moving and Moving' (2000), Noel Carroll considers the relation between the two. He asks why Yvonne Rainer moved from choreographing as part of the New York contemporary dance movement to making experimental short films. Rainer trained with Martha Graham, one of the pioneers of self-expressive dance that drew its postures and movements from powerful emotions such as grief and desire, but she later rejected Graham's hysterical expressions for a language of everyday gestures. Her later choreography deliberately excluded the exploration of emotion *because* of dance's long association with women's emotional expression. Even so, she found that 'dance is ipso facto about *me* ... whereas the area of emotions must necessarily concern both of us' (Rainer in Banes 1987: 226; emphasis in original). Moving her body was not enough to move the audience. Potter had the insight that film's movement could actually act as a filter through which to look at live performance's mobile body and engaged emotions. By embodying the artiste's private self, performance in Potter's films gives the lie to the dualisms of matter and form, female and male, body and mind, performance and film by building each term into the other.

Body: Building

Potter's first film experiments in the late 1960s and early 1970s took place in and against the vibrant world of Expanded Cinema. Cinema was being expanded specifically by live performance: the filmmaker often performed onstage, coming between the projector and the screen in various ways to draw attention to the conventions of cinema. By standing in the projector's light stream, repeating the actions on the screen or sewing through the celluloid, the filmmaker-as-performer slowed down the automatic circuit between film and viewer. 'For this synesthetic, sensuous, experiential, live and time-based art called expanded cinema, the existential [was] a kind of becoming: for the artist through process, and for the audience through reception' (Hatfield 2006: 186). David Curtis's authoritative *A History of Artists' Film and Video in Britain* lists Potter's dual-screen installation *Play* as an Expanded Cinema event but misses *The Building*, which was screened/performed at the National Film Theatre as part of an Expanded Cinema programme (2007: 231). A touring live performance featuring Expanded Cinema filmmaker Mike Dunford and installation artist Leda Papaconstantinou, *The Building* had the performers deconstructing their gendered costumes in front of a dual-screen projection of their preparation for, and cleaning up after, an earlier version of the event. In a programme note for the Electric Cinema in Amsterdam, Potter wrote that *The Building* is 'about the overlapping area between film and theatre, man and woman, then and now, word and action. It is a four-part performance: 1) make-up – static, silent; 2) step about – tentative, limited; 3) breakout – role destruction, clearance; 4) construction – a beginning' (1971).

Bringing these dualities into productive tension and blurring the boundaries between them, *The Building* can be seen as a sketch for Potter's later film work as well as an intriguing example of Expanded Cinema's commitment to breaking down conventions in order to create something new. Its structure is also the basic journey of each of her protagonists: they start out 'static, silent', which causes them to reflect on themselves; their investigation of the self in relation to itself and the world takes the shape of 'tentative, limited' rehearsals of various kinds of performance; exhibiting what they feel they have learned, the characters 'break out' and often break down as their failure creates a kind of 'clearance'. Finally, there is a new 'beginning', which involves the 'construction' not of a self, but a self-other dyad as a space in which the characters can share their gifts. Cycling through the feature films, this narrative remains present, a flexible spine for the longer works' more complex twists and turns. Likewise, Expanded Cinema's conjunction of performance and projection remains part of Potter's working method as her films explore the more complex task of incorporating the dimension of liveness into conventional cinema.

Few studies of Potter's films take account of the filmmaker's background as live performer. Placing Potter's history as a performer, not least as an Expanded Cinema onstage filmmaker, on a continuum with her film work would help make sense of her decision to play Sally in *The Tango Lesson*. The attendant controversy could be read as part of a history of such charges laid against Potter in specific, and performance artists in general, for foregrounding the (female) body. In August 1978, Michael McNay reported that the 'New Figuration Group', an earlier manifestation of the Stuckists, protested that Arts Council grants were being given to performance artists, including Potter and Limited Dance Company, rather than traditional figurative artists. In a backhanded (and somewhat sexist) compliment, Stuart Brixley, the performance artist who chaired the granting committee, claimed 'only partly in jest, that if Sally Potter's performances that spectacularly use her own torso, not to mention her dance training, aren't figurative, what are they?' (in McNay 1978: 8). Potter used the grant to fund *Thriller*, but the taint of performance and the body would continue to haunt debates about her films being vanity projects that 'spectacularly use' bodies – as if that excluded them from making critical use of film form.

Potter's inversion of 'spectacular' recurs in the way in which she works with female performers, particularly perceptively in casting Lily Cole as model Lettuce Leaf in *Rage* (2009). Potter comments that: 'It's hard to believe someone is a model unless they look like they really could be. When I met Lily it became clear that she was perfect; and she understood the film because she's lived it' (interview with author, December 2008). Potter – and Cole – play with the limits of feminist performance art's use of the self by drawing on Cole's insider knowledge of how models are treated, and her physical training in the comportment of a model. While Cole's unusual and commanding beauty acts as a draw for the film, it is the way in which her involvement in the fashion industry layers her consummate performance that compels the viewer's attention. Lettuce, the vulnerable female model whom we are told is both fashion's victim and its exploiter, finds a way out of the economy of the gaze as Ruby does, by drawing on her 'situated knowledge', in which 'the object of the knowledge is pictured as an actor or an agent, not a screen or a ground or a resource' (Haraway 1988: 592). Haraway's use of the word 'actor' in its legal sense (a person responsible for their actions) is telling: this is a meaning lost in the showbiz bandying of the term.

For both Cole and Potter, situated knowledge comes from being an actor in the term's theatrical sense, redefined as a framework of stringent physical and intellectual work (on the self). Brixley's jest rightly sets Potter's rigorous 'dance training' against the jibes of the New Figurationists, who suggested that performance was neither art nor work. Potter's choreographic works are cited as influential in the three main histories of New Dance in Britain: Stephanie Jordan's *Striding Out* (1992), Judith Mackrell's *Out of Line* (1992) and Emilyn Claid's *Yes? No! Maybe...* (2006). Potter's name appears alongside several of the dancer/choreographers who would later collaborate on her films: Jacky Lansley is hailed by all three as a major choreographer (although her film work for Potter passes unmentioned); Maedée Duprès, Siobhan Davies, Dennis Greenwood and Fergus Early all collaborated with Potter both onstage and screen, as well as establishing important careers in British dance. All three books mention Potter and Lansley's radical focus on gender and politics, in contrast to the dominant abstract mode. LDC's emphasis on play and spectacle as ways of undoing gender, their creative misuse of narrative and their 'intellectual muscle presented economically and with humour' (Jordan 1992: 31) differed substantially from the influential high speed, highly physical choreography of Richard Alston, with whom Potter danced and choreographed for Strider.

Thriller brought the same qualities of play with narrative and/about gender, the same witty economies of scale (staging an opera in a squat with four performers) to film. Elena del Rio's re-evaluation of *Thriller* begins from the insight that psychoanalytic feminist film theorists in the early 1980s 'relegate[d] the sensual and bodily aspects of female subjectivity to a practically irrelevant status', which was, as Brixley's comment demonstrates, a timely and important move away from the association of women with pure, mindless bodiliness (2004: 11). *Thriller*'s investigation of the body through performance, being ahead of its time, got somewhat lost. For feminist theory, the female body's ability to act as a figure for anything other than itself was constrained by what Laura Mulvey called the Hollywood star's 'to-be-looked-at-ness' (1975: 11). Compelling all eyes, the female star's beauty overwhelmed the film's narrative, threatening the order that put narrative above the visual image in classical cinema.

Potter's protagonists all start out caught in the glare of the male gaze. Mimi has been literally turned into no more than a body by her death while Ruby, carried in state because of her beauty, is actually trapped by it. Ruby finds herself frozen onstage and cracks her mask of make-up with laughter in order to find herself. The protagonists undertake training and rehearsal as a kind of self-investigation into how to use their graceful, beautiful bodies so that looking engages the senses and the intellect. Performance theorist Elin Diamond argues that when the process of performance is made visible, the viewer can see the 'possibilities emerging of another reality, what is not there, but could be' (1997: 145). She describes this as 'looking-at-being-looked-at-ness', or 'looking-ness' (in Dolan 1988: 114), a reflexive space in which conventions that frame the body can be undone. Potter's background in performance leads her to undo the problematic body through the body itself.

'Bodies always gesture towards other fields of meaning', as Susan Leigh Foster writes when arguing for dance as a way of understanding history (1996: xi). Dancing, as hard work, structured performance and joyous expression all at once, allows the body to do the talking. When Sally and Pablo argue after the exhibition performance that goes wrong, they make their peace not through words in any of the three languages they speak between them, but through the language of tango. Their relationship faltered when their tango was forced into 'to-be-looked-at-ness' on the public stage. Mirroring Jacob and the Angel wrestling in a painting, their pose is like Diamond's 'looking-ness', a self-aware investigation that shows the 'possibilities emerging of another reality'.

Dance can speak new ways of being in the world because 'the crafting of moving bodies into a dance reflects a theoretical stance towards identity in all its registers' (Foster 1996: xiii). Each of Potter's artistes initially takes to the stage to undertake a performance that moves her beyond the static stage of 'make-up'. As each film develops, and as Potter moves further into filmmaking, performance migrates from the stage to the world, becoming integrated into the way the characters engage with each other. The ironised quotations and pointed deconstructions that marked Potter's early work are shed like the 'make-up' of *The Building*'s first phase. By drawing attention to different aspects of the performing body – or rather, different performing aspects of the body – the films find a way to integrate performance's ability to point outwards to politics of gender and class and inwards to the character's emotional state. The body is the building-block of Potter's work, the tool with which the artiste moves herself from Muse to meaning. She does this by trying on and stripping off the make-up, costume and shoes that constrain and shape her, to find her own (bare) feet. Reconnected to the ground, the performer journeys on to find the elusive 'construction – beginning again'. At either end of the journey is the performer's face: it starts out caught in its own mirror image, like Laffont's in *Thriller*, and ends by coming close to another's.

Face: Make-Up

Potter brings her film and performance training together to think about the role of the face as bearer of meaning. Her first publicly-exhibited film outside the dance world, *Jerk*, was a stop-motion film shot one frame at a time, in which three faces (one male, two female) shot in close-up merged into one. The face/body split represents the 'to-be-looked-at-ness' in which the female performer's face freezes the film. In Potter's films, the face is associated with the moment in which the female icon *realises* she's an icon and begins to move out of that role. Her features continue this through their very precise use of close-ups. By drawing attention to the way that the convention of the close-up cuts off the face from the body, Potter uses the shot as a prelude to re-integration. The face performs a wonderfully perverse reversal in Potter's oeuvre: while it initially summons the cinematic history of the close-up, it does so to rejoin the face to the body, and to its ability to express both movement and thought. Orlando's final gaze to camera echoes and undoes Rouben Mamoulian's instructions to Greta Garbo for the final shot, in close-up, of *Queen Christina*, which Potter quoted in her programme note for the film in the NFT season: 'I want your face to be a blank sheet of paper. I want the writing to be done by every member of the audience. I'd like it if you could avoid blinking your eyes, so that you're nothing but a beautiful mask' (in Potter 1984: 7). By removing its make-up, whether the greasepaint of staged performance or the mascara and lipstick of femininity, the muse's beautiful mask is remade into a living, expressive face.

Rather than a simple critique of the 'beauty myth', Potter explores the way in which women collude in their own masking, and the ways in which they make themselves up as a survival strategy. Through the casting of Jude Law as the supermodel Minx in *Rage* (2009), Potter denaturalises the association of women and make-up. She comments that 'it took me a while to figure out that the most exciting thing was for the part of Minx to be played by a man, and to work with male beauty as a reflection of all of the issues surrounding the construction of female beauty. Jude seemed to me an obvious choice, partly because his beauty has been held against him' (interview with author, December 2008). The film leaves ambiguous Minx's understanding of her sex/gender: Law could be playing a transgendered woman, a transvestite who uses femininity as a pose but identifies as male, or a cisgendered woman (referring to a person whose gender identity is in accord with their biologically-assigned sex; from the Latin *cis-*, meaning on the same side). It is the packaging of femininity into a 'beautiful mask' that is revealed as dehumanising, as Minx refers to herself in the third person as 'she'.

What that pronoun stands for, for Minx, is neither the identification of femaleness with biology and the inescapable body, nor the misogynistic pejorative as used in gay male culture. Instead, it refers to gender – both sign and symptom of appearance – as a willed construction. At the same moment that she drops her faux-Russian accent, Minx also names herself as 'I' and reveals her ruthless grasp of the constructed nature of (cinematic) glamour. She tells Michelangelo to observe 'how the light falls on my face [like] a fucking caress', the only kind of touch that she allows. That paradox of brutal tenderness is the keynote of Minx's character, exemplified in the astounding final vision of her after the bloody dénouement of the third and final catwalk show. Seen from above in the film's only extreme high angle, Minx is a brutalised Cecil Beaton photograph, her head bent over the massive skirts of her blood-spattered white wedding dress. She raises her face to the camera, the tilt adding lines to her forehead, revealed by the loss of her wig. The light may not make 'ugly shadows' on her face, but her cheeks are stained with tear-melted mascara, the most visible sign of the mask and its cracking.

Visible make-up acts as a dividing line in Potter's films, with women who are still caught in the myth of femininity on the made-up side and bare-faced women striking out. Suzie and Lola present the starkest contrast. Suzie is the good girl in *The Man Who Cried*, while Lola is the bad girl. It is Lola, however, who obediently follows the script of capitalism patriarchy and Suzie who resists. Both wear similarly exaggerated make-up while performing, but the dramatic wave of blue eyeshadow suits and enhances Blanchett's classical blonde beauty while making Ricci look pasty. Ricci's youthful appearance gives Suzie a schoolgirl charm that is deliberately at odds with her cabaret lifestyle. Lola, on the other hand, wears make-up to go swimming. Lola's determined performance of femininity is part of her identity and is key to her survival as an immigrant. Rather than naturalise her as a *femme fatale*, the film shows how she composes herself for the role. In one striking sequence, we see Lola practising the gazes and gestures of the female icon, getting ready for a close-up that never quite arrives. The camera never settles for long enough to satisfy our expecta-tion. Lola's repetitions and the camera's glide unsettle the equation of the close-up with iconic perfection. *Yes* continues to undermine the expectations built into the use of the close-up when She is at the bedside of her dying aunt (Sheila Hancock). She is without make-up, sobbing, and snot is falling visibly from her nose. In asking her performers to reach beyond the close-up's association with female perfection to find emotional expression, Potter's close-ups rely on her actors' virtuosity and a high level of trust between performer and director. There is a tension, seen in the anxiety in Lola's eyes as she practises her silent pout, between the skill of the performance and the chaotic emotions that it contains and expresses.

Potter's live work was often based on improvisation and celebrated chaos in an attempt to subvert the perfection of the female Muse. 'Letting go required a rejec-tion of the *desire* to be the beautiful image and all the paraphernalia that comes with external praise', as Claid argues about feminist New Dance (2006: 81; emphasis in original). For Allen to cry in such a whole-hearted way is exactly a letting go, one that is earned through attempts and failures, and finally leads to a remaking. Her path from wifely performance to emotional expression is charted by moments in which She nego-tiates the meaning of the female face through the mirror as she regards her reflection at boundary moments. Early on, She is caught in multiple reflections in an L-shaped wall of mirrors in a hotel's public washroom. She repeats He's flirtatious words in an internal monologue: encountering her alone in the hotel's function room, he told her that he 'wouldn't / Let such a beauty / Out of [his] sight'. In the throes of her affair with He, She looks admiringly at her body in a swimming pool changing room. She is there with her adolescent goddaughter Grace (Stephanie Leonidas), who is envious of her godmother's slender body. Grace's anxiety about her own body and her admiration of her godmother's slim but natural form lay bare the cultural pressures that could cause a gorgeous young woman to consider herself fat. Grace's praise and She's pleasure in her body offer a delightful reversal of the expectation that age will envy youth. Suggestions that Allen seems old for a romantic lead by Hollywood terms are ridiculed by the subsequent appearance of Sheila Hancock, playing her aunt. Hancock's serene, intelligent face is made the more beautiful by the balance of her gracefully stern bone structure and the soft geometry of her wrinkles. Her beauty promises that her niece will only become more beautiful as she grows older – but only if she lives, laughs and loves as fiercely as her aunt. Emotional expression, which cracks the mask of make-up, is the beauty secret that the Aunt shares with us in her voice-over monologue.

There is a connection, in the female face's movement from Muse to agent, between emotional vulnerability and beauty. She tells Grace, 'there is so much more to you / than your reflection'. The next time She looks in the mirror, after her aunt's death, it is this 'much more' that she is seeking. She and He have separated after a bitter argument, shortly after She rowed with her husband. She has gone to Cuba to fulfil her Marxist aunt's dying wish and she is staying in a small family hotel. Unmade up, sweating from the heat, She glows in her new freedom. Having glimpsed her new self in the mirror, she pulls out her digital camera. We see her framed in its small screen, flat and bright, like a new kind of mirror that allows for the creation of a different relation with the face and its beauty. Thinking through recent events, she records a confession to the camera as if it (and the audience beyond the frame) were God. The gaze that would objectify her beauty becomes a metaphysical regard.

Literary theorists Elaine Scarry (2006) and Wendy Steiner (2001) have both suggested that through our ability to appreciate visual beauty we could reconnect to a metaphysical apprehension of the world. Scarry is the author of the groundbreaking *The Body in Pain* (1988), a brilliant study of what happens when the body is subjected to power's desire to destroy it, so her turn to beauty is both astonishing and profound. A truly ethical apprehension of beauty, she suggests, would be the antidote to the objectifying mentality that makes torture possible. Wendy Steiner argues, as Potter did in *The Gold Diggers*, that we also need to dissociate our notions of beauty from economic value. Through works of art that enable this, 'the female subject of art (and ultimately the male subject, too) will be available once again to symbolise a beauty that moves us to pleasure. And that pleasure will be seen as life-enhancing rather than exclusive or oppressive' (2001: xxv). The Red Model in *Rage* (1996) is first seen fleeing from, and then felled by, a sniper. Having represented the death of the woman as Muse and object, her red dress becomes the sign of vengeance as she turns on her pursuer with a gun.

Costume: Step About

Both *Rage* (1996) and *Rage* (2009) take issue – via plots concerned with murdered models – with the fashion industry's manipulation of aesthetic as economic value, showing that turning beauty into money is a deadly serious business. Yet Potter's characters are always beautifully dressed. In her history of New Dance, Mackrell notes that 'to challenge stereotyped attitudes towards women [LDC would] wear extremely glamorous costumes in the context of strange and disturbing situations' (1992: 22). In particular, she refers to *Lochgilphead*, an improvised performance that took place on the west coast of Scotland as part of Edinburgh Arts 1974. So glamorous were the black evening dresses in which Potter and Lansley emerged from the sea, complete with flippers, that the performance featured, accompanied by several photographs, in an article on 'happenings' in *Vogue* (see Howell 1975: 18–19).

Costume's glamour can attract attention that turns the performer into it into an object, like the elaborate dress that mimics Ruby's cage. In the same way that Orlando's to-camera gaze shows that s/he is aware of the convention of the close-up, the glamorous evening dresses in Potter's films always advertise their status as costumes. The red, blue and yellow dresses of the models in *Rage* (1996) are the most obvious, but their slightly fantastical shapes, sheeny fabrics and blocks of single colour are echoed across the films. English refuses the tutu that goes with her arabesque. Ruby discards her flouncy ballgown – but not before she has used her beauty and class to discard all the men at the ball. Orlando struggles to negotiate the enormous eighteenth-century dress that is her duty and burden as an aristocratic woman. Her long,

Throwaway glamour: Ruby (Julie Christie) changes the rules of the dance

slow procession through a hall of furniture that is covered with dustsheets shows the hard work of learning to be female, and how that work incapacitates her for anything else. The dress is effectively a dustsheet, packing away her body until she can use it again when she is naked under the bedsheets with Shelmerdine.

The dress is inherently a demanding performance. After Sally dances in the exhibition with Pablo, we see her reflection in the mirror for the first time in the film. She is wearing a closely-beaded black dress that sparkles in the high-contrast lighting and contrasts with the exhaustion and disappointment in her face. Through her tango training with Pablo, she had been becoming increasingly feminine, wearing dresses and earrings to go out dancing. As she fell in love with Pablo and with herself as a *tanguero*, these accoutrements stopped being dress-up and became everyday wear. Before the mirror, Sally sees that she is wearing a costume, and thereafter she wears jeans and boots during the day. She and Pablo even do a spontaneous tango in jeans, T-shirts and walking boots, de-linking the pleasure of dance from the constraints of high fashion.

High fashion, however, continues to play a role in the films' visual palette even as Potter continues to uncover how its aesthetics control femininity and its economics disenfranchise workers, culminating in *Rage* (2009). As with the problematic female performer, fashion's self-evident 'to-be-looked-at-ness' creates the potential for 'looking-ness'. Jill Dolan, the premier feminist performance theorist, writes that she is 'not ready to give up the intense pleasure [she] find[s] in a powerful female performer' because of her 'power to know, intellectually and psychophysically … how to control the seductions inherent in the frame, and how to speak the language so that authority, seduction and language mean something different about the status of women in culture' (1993: 1). Costume's sparkle and flounce is one of the pleasures that the performer can use, knowingly, to 'control the seductions inherent in the frame'. Recognising costume *as* costume gives the female performer this opportunity. She can try dresses on like identities, glancing at us – as Orlando does – to show that she knows the difference between the costume of gender and the androgynous reality of hir mind-body.

Like dance, costume thinks through identity. 'The physical presence of the dancer – the aliveness of her body – radically challenges the implicit power dynamic of any gaze, for there is always the very real possibility that she will look back!' (Albright 1997: 15). This is what Ruby recognises onstage, laughing both in and at her 'little girl on the prairie' dress. The performer's dress can also be her power. *London Story* (1986), Potter's intermediate short between *The Gold Diggers* and *Orlando*, ends with a dance on the South Bank of the Thames, starring the protagonist Jack (Jacky Lansley) in a brilliant red evening dress. It takes place outside the complex of arts centres, including the National Film Theatre, on the South Bank that, by 1986, had become institutional arbiters of national taste and cultural policy. The film's goofy plot concerns Jack's attempt to change the government's cultural policy by switching a minister's speech. Having identified the minister and found a way to access him through the Door (George Yiasoumi), a parliamentary doorkeeper, she takes him to the ballet where he promptly falls asleep. Levering his speech from his briefcase, she takes it down to the Door, who gives her in return one that her other ally, Mr Popper (Lol Coxhill) has procured. A television report the following day implies that the minister has delivered the replacement speech without a qualm, mandating an arts policy that embraces the UK's Europeanness. To celebrate the success of this deeply wishful plot (1986 was the height of Euroscepticism), the plotters gather by the bench where the Door gave the signal to Mr Popper, and dance.

It is not a social dance like a tango but a formal, frontal performance in which the river is the backdrop and the Royal Festival Hall is the audience. Jack's spiralling solo is offset by the sweetly lumbering dance moves of the two men, who partner each other at times in a reference back to Potter's duet for two male dancers, *Leave* (1973). Jack's dress is similar to the dress that she wore to accompany the snoozing minister to the Royal Opera House, which makes her dance suggestively a substitution for the ballet that remained offscreen. This implies that the substituted speech also advocated a change from institutional conservatism to audacious experiment. The dance is most experimental in its mixture of contemporary dance with steps from musical chorus lines, folk dance and ballet. Just as Jack's dazzling dress reincorporates and alters the meaning of her high fashion disguise, so her dance incorporates the arabesque that is the hallmark, in *Thriller*, of women's subjection to patriarchy. Claid, co-founder of X6 Dance Space alongside Lansley, writes that for the New Dancers, 'the art form of ballet, however, was never the object to be parodied; it was the lifelong performative practices of the images of beauty that had distorted our bodies. We used exaggerated ballet stereotypes to climb out of that history' (2006: 63). Jack climbs out of Conservative Britain by reclaiming the pleasures of ballet.

Lansley's dancing is as brilliant and compelling as her dress. Her virtuosity as a dancer is of a piece with her espionage skills: the artiste's achievement is part of her politics. This is a far cry from the rejection of virtuosity by choreographers such as Rainer as being élitist and objectifying, comparable and connected to feminist theory's neglect of the body as an instrument of sexism. In Potter's films, skill acquired through rehearsal is what allows the artiste to see her body as more than the object of the gaze, as an instrument of her self-expression. The artiste's body is consciously political through its expertise, the opposite of the clumsy Expert in *The Gold Diggers* who attempts to perform his knowledge and ends up sinking the toy ship that represents his investments. Virtuosity is not gendered, however: Pablo's gravity-defying leaps across genres amply proves that. Jack's dance of revolution is preceded by a skating whiz dressed in a bohemian philosopher's black turtleneck, played by dancer Dennis Greenwood, who is responsible for writing the speech. Raskolnikov on Ice cuts a dash both physical and intellectual as he skates rings around the elderly Mr Popper.

Fancy footwork *is* marked by gender difference, though. While the Skater, however faintly ridiculous, has no problem being taken seriously as a fleetfooted mastermind, it is harder for women performers to have the work that they put into performance regarded as intellectual and bodily labour. This is most true of the performance of femininity, which is all about working hard to make the hard work invisible. The star's beauty is supposed to be as seamless as classical cinema. Potter's performers recognise their evening dress as a costume, but it is their shoes that cue the viewer to the precariousness of their performance of femininity. When Grace models high heels for her godmother, her coltish ankles turn slightly as she wobbles through the store in her too grown-up clothes. The inward curve is reminiscent of a shot of Sally's feet, as she bends to and fro on her new tango shoes at the top of Pablo's stairs. In *Rage* (1996), one sign of the models' subjection to dominant discourses of female beauty is their precarious stiletto heels.

It is only when women kick off their shoes that they can really express themselves. The Cleaner lies prone on the floor at the end of *Yes*, her bare feet raised in the air, their movements addressing the camera much as she does. She is not the only bare-foot philosopher in Potter's films: Ruby, beginning to explore her identity through her memories of her mother, props her bare feet on Celeste's desk. Ruby is a reverse Cinderella whose glass slippers lay discarded foreground centre in Celeste's room in the previous shot, spotlit like the slippers in *The Wizard of Oz* (1939). Ruby's slippers suggest they will carry her magically home; instead, they are abandoned as a false trap like the ballgown. Her journey begins not with shoes, but bare feet. Ruby, the prize of the ballroom, is an angel with dirty soles.

Feet: Break Out

Bare feet are one escape from the trap of virtuosity. Boots made for walking are another. Rather than take Rainer's approach of basing her dance on everyday gestures like walking, Potter's 1974 dance piece *Parry Riposte* contrasted a number of types of virtuosity to gently ridiculous effect. Jacky Lansley and Terry Berman performed a duet with movements drawn from fencing. Lansley gave instructions angrily while Berman broke away from time to time to catch a half-dressed Japanese man in mid-leap. Behind them an alternative *corps de ballet* advanced down the stage to the sound of a Zulu stomp dance. The women wore knickers made of black bin liners over the outside of their leotards; according to Potter, dancers used to wear a layer of black plastic under their leotards in class, to make them sweat more and therefore lose more weight (interview with author, September 2006).

Each aspect of the performance broke one of dance's gender rules, from Lansley being in command to the male-male lift to the visibility of the pressures on female dancers to be thin. Perhaps the most dramatic contravention was the juxtaposition of the *corps*, whose name (body) belies the convention by which they are soundless and effectively weightless, with the rhythmic and bodily music. Stomp dancing began as a form of unspoken protest among black mine workers in South Africa against their white overseers, and in *Parry Riposte* it works as a multiple protest: against apartheid, which is practised in a subtler way by the high arts in Britain, where there has never been a black female dancer with the Royal Ballet (see Somaiya 2008), and against the erasure of women's material bodies.

When Potter's protagonists reach the final stage of their journeys and are ready to break out of staged performance, they reach for their walking boots. Sally stomps away from her argument with Pablo and roams Paris by night. She returns to wearing the hiking boots that are identified with her job as a filmmaker, going on location recces. Orlando ends the film in biking boots. Her motorbike and sidecar are a souped-up version of Suzie's pedal-pushing as she rides her bicycle through Paris to find Cesar (and herself). At the end of *Yes*, She pounds the Havana sidewalk in her sneakers, picking up on the hidden stomped rhythms that run through the film. 'Foot rhythm is the basis of music and music rhythm is the basis of speech rhythm, and poetry' (Potter in Mayer 2005: 76). Freedom is movement for female characters released from the constraints of their ballgowns and high heels.

Women on the move are associated with sexual availability and deviance, and so are performers. This negative association led to legislation to keep women confined to the home, which informs Orlando's pleasure in giving up her property and She's delight in leaving husband and home behind. The 'static, silent' associations of home underline why Potter's characters delight in moving, even when movement brings risk and loss. Movement also creates an international community that complicates any easy attraction to the politics of homelands. In 1938 Virginia Woolf famously said: 'as a woman, I have no country' (1977: 146), laying claim to the wandering status accorded to her by dominant society, celebrating her exclusion from the masculine nation. 'Wealthy European men of estate – heterosexual, Christian and adult – have long marked one characteristic in their Other: the poor, the non-European races, women, homosexuals, Gypsies, Jews, hunter-gatherers, the supposed insane and children. Along the strata of power … there is a common factor: a hatred of *nomadism*' (Griffiths 2007: 253; emphasis in original). Jay Griffiths goes on to include 'another class of nomads … the wandering players' (2007: 294), suggesting a further aspect of settled society's scorn for the performer.

Discussing Paul Robeson's career as a transatlantic anti-racist activist, Sukhdev Sandhu argues 'that actors, in comparison with merchants, mariners or sportsmen, are inadequately theorised vectors of new social and cultural possibility … mov[ing] across, within and beyond national boundaries. Their goal, their very essence, is to enact a series of creative negotiations between their core selves and their professional commitment to mutability and shape-shifting' (2007: 12). Potter's dancing men suggest a larger category of movement, that of the nomad. Gilles Deleuze and Félix Guattari famously referred to nomadicism as the condition of postmodernity, in which the very idea of 'home' is undermined by the movement of global capital. Nomadicism is related to deterritorialisation, a concept derived from the increasing loss of (home)land faced by marginal and poor peoples in the twentieth century. Nomad citizenship can be a utopian conception, associated with heterogeneous groups and alliances that go beyond the borders of nation-states (for example, the feminist movement, or the transnational anti-globalisation movement). In *Alienhood*, Katarzyna Marciniak writes critically that '"salutary models of exile" to use Ali Behdad's words … frequently tend to obliterate the discrepancy between *theoretical*, liberatory renditions of mobility; border crossings; ensuing hybridisation and experiences of conflictual emotionality; and the torn sense of belonging, pain and oppressive liminality that forms the experiential reality of many migrants' (2006: 22; emphasis in original).

Pablo and He both experience and express the negative aspects of nomadicism. He speaks eloquently about the political necessity of his flight from Beirut and about the racism with which he has been confronted in the UK. When he returns to Lebanon for a christening, He dances with his friends – but soon retires from the dance floor. Pablo, 'swiftly speaking with his feet' (as Sally sings to him at the end of *The Tango Lesson*), uses tango to obscure his myth of origin and create a space for connection with his partner. He demonstrates his affection for She, and solicits her adoring gaze, by performing a barefoot dance atop a coffee table in his apartment. The scene cuts between – and often superimposes – her gaze and his flashing feet: eyes may be mirrors to the soul, but so are his soles. The dance that He's feet perform is, like tango, a signifier of exile and of hybrid identities. Potter's protagonist-performers begin as exiles, estranged from themselves and their place in the world, with an idea of home as destination. Through performance, they find that destination is not a place but a self/other relationship that creates continual movement.

Face to Face: Beginning Again

The real journeys undertaken by Potter's characters are interwoven with the metaphorical journeys they take. Deleuze and Guattari coined the phrase 'line of flight' to describe how 'connections among bodies … release new powers in the capacities of those bodies to act and respond' (Tamsin Lorraine in Parr 2005: 145). Mimi, Musetta, Celeste, Ruby, Orlando, Pablo, Sally, Lola, Suzie, Dante, Cesar, She, He, Michelangelo and Lettuce are doubly engaged as actors by their lines of flight: on the one hand, they have to perform selves in the strange places that they come to, gradually adapting as Orlando does in Khiva by removing his wig and ostentatious, over-warm English clothes; on the other, their performances keep them on the move *and* in connection.

Rage (2009) ends with its protagonist running away: Michelangelo's film, a succession of different faces, has incited its online viewers to join a protest against the fashion house for which the interviewees work. Amidst heightened paranoia caused by murders at two previous attempts to stage a catwalk show, the protestors break in only to find themselves caught in chaotic carnage, as an attempt on another model's life sparks return fire. Homer (David Oyelowo), the detective investigating the murders – and possibly complicit in shooting a protestor – advises Michelangelo to start running, because he has 'blood on his hands'. Michelangelo begins his flight by examining a hand in extreme close-up, the light coming redly through the skin revealing the blood beneath it. What appears to be the first part of Michelangelo that we have seen is another mask: the hand belongs to Lettuce and is obscuring the camera's access to her face.

The cheeky, self-assured young filmmaker refuses to show us *his* face, too: on the surface to protect himself from the police, but at a deeper level to resist the singular emphasis he had placed on the face, alone, onscreen. Michael Taussig summarises Emmanuel Levinas's notion of the face as 'the evidence that makes evidence possible' (1999: 224). Michelangelo's documentary of faces had become a case file, evidence in a murder investigation. Rather than a brand or a mugshot, Michelangelo's face – in its absence – returns the face to the unknowability of Orlando's final to-camera gaze, informed by the self-knowledge that Ruby discovers in her confrontation with her own gaze. This escape from a fixed identity occurs through his conjunction with the film's other young runaway. Afraid for her life after two models have been murdered in front of her on the catwalk, Lettuce ceases to place her faith in being 'face of the year'. Looking vulnerable and unglamorous in her sweatshirt, she asks Michelangelo in a whisper whether she can hide out at his house. Her face is the last that we see in the film, as she asks Michelangelo to give her his camera. When she turns it on him, what she witnesses and celebrates is a danced quality to his movement, the bodily discipline that she – as a trained performer – can share with the boy whom Homer suggests is a little overweight from sitting in front of his computer. Having learned to 'walk', Lettuce can teach Michelangelo to run.

Looking at nomadism as performance, and performance as nomadism, Potter's films take seriously the painful condition of exile, but also use the history of performance to look critically at the cultural construction of settlement/home as positive and normal, and nomadism/movement as negative/abnormal. Death is related to being trapped, unable to move like Mimi, too poor to leave her attic, or fallen like the Red Model, unable to run in her high heels. Dancing feet celebrate mobility, but they also step out against histories of repression, alienation and loss. Movement is where the potential for connection and transformation occurs. 'We are fully dependent on each other for the possibility of being understood and without this understanding, we are not intelligible, we do not make sense, we are not solid, visible, integrated; we are lacking. So travelling to each others "worlds" would enable us to *be* through *loving* each other' (Lugones 1987: 8; emphasis in original).

Philosopher Naomi Scheman suggests that Jewishness offers, and models, a way of moving across borders. She claims that her secular Jewish upbringing gave her a 'passionately *internationalist*, socialist sense of justice' (1997: 135; emphasis added). Perhaps this is part of what Sally means when she tells Pablo: 'I *feel* I'm a Jew.' She mirrors Pablo's uncertainty about the meaning of his Jewish identity, shifting it from a fixed cultural and geographical marker into a way of being aslant to the mainstream. It is a partiality that is embodied in wrestling with, and travelling through, questions, in the same way that an actor works to constitute and develop characters. Scheman connects her idea to María Lugones' concept of 'world'-travelling, which is travel not around the world as a tourist, but into others' worlds through performance (see 1997: 145). She comments that this kind of travel is a necessity for the marginalised in order to survive, but 'can be embarked on "playfully" by those among the privileged who have the courage and loving commitment to learn how they are seen by those in whose eyes their privilege marks them as other' (1997: 151).

Sally and Pablo 'world'-travel in each others' worlds: Sally entering the world of tango and of Argentina not as a tourist, but a playful participant advertising her lack of virtuosity in Pablo's world. In Buenos Aires, Pablo submits his masculinity and his skill as a performer to Sally's watchful, cinematic eye, learning to follow. This play, Scheman emphasises, is not frivolous but a political commitment to discarding the 'solid ground [of] identity [in favour of] loyalty and solidarity' (1997: 153). Play-acting, 'world'-travel: Potter's nomadic performers express their interiority not as isolated individuals, but through their relationship to one another forged in performance. By connecting with each other, they release new powers of virtuosity that enable them to connect with the viewer. Even Orlando, whose fate is entangled with his Great House, will only be able to express herself once she is free from property's equation of aesthetic and economic value, and of woman and home. Hung with a singing Angel, the oak tree from which she has travelled away and back is no longer England, but nomadic, in flight. It is a magical moment whose wonder is expressed by Tilda Swinton's unblinking gaze to camera, her face no longer the carefully-composed portrait we saw at the start of the film – nor Mamoulian's blank canvas – but the openness of a new 'construction – beginning again'.

CHAPTER FIVE

Orlando

SASHA: Do you know of our poets? Have you heard of our books? Do you know of our mountains? Do you know of our music? Do you know of our suffering?

— Sally Potter, *Orlando* draft screenplay (1990b: 25)

In Potter's *Orlando* archive is a napkin with the words 'the end is the beginning' written on it in her distinctive handwriting. There is no date but it seems like a very first note towards an adaptation that would take forty drafts over four years. The finished film does indeed end where Potter began: by ending with a return to the setting and framing of its opening scene. Virginia Woolf's novel, on which the film is based, also turns in a circle. Orlando starts the novel dreaming of faraway places 'in Africa or France' but, being too young to ride there, he travels in his imagination while romping around the rooms and grounds of his father's Great House (Woolf 2000: 11). At the end of the book, Orlando is a grown woman with a son, having lived through four centuries and at least one change of sex. By having a son she has secured the Great House that Queen Elizabeth gave to her when she was a young man. Returning home from an expedition to London to buy sheets, she walks through the rooms and grounds with a minutely observant eye. At midnight she meets her husband Shelmerdine, a sea captain who has returned from his adventures. A bird springs up over his head and Orlando cries, in her final line, "'The wild goose...!'" (2000: 228). Shelmerdine is the wild goose, the one who flies away and returns in his aeroplane, while Orlando stays at home.

While the book, like the film, ends where it begins, the film ends up in a completely different place from the book: a different era (London in The [postmodern] Present), different events (Orlando has given up her house and has a daughter) and a different tone. How did the adaptation end up so different? Woolf's *Orlando* is subtitled *A Biography* and was called 'the longest and most charming love letter in history' by Nigel Nicolson, the son of the novel's dedicatee Vita Sackville-West (in Bruzzi 1997: 196). It inscribes its love by relating Vita's family history through the figure of Orlando. The original edition was illustrated with paintings and photographs of Vita and her ancestors, representing Orlando throughout the ages. *Orlando* is hardly a conventional biographical depiction but within the romantic fantasy are historical facts about Vita and her family home, Knole. Sackville-West lost Knole because of her gender; the novel restores it to her.

The Great House is the novel's beginning and ending, its gift, which locates Orlando in, and identifies her with, the English landscape. Orlando's magnum opus, which she works on through the centuries and sexes, is a poem called 'The Oak Tree'. This epic tale, of which the reader catches only glimpses, uses the ages and seasons of the great oak tree at Knole as a representation of England and its literature, which Orlando loves. Even when she is farthest from it, travelling through the mountains of Anatolia disguised as a gypsy, Orlando sees a vision of 'oak trees dotted here and there ... and the gentle sighs and shivers of a summer's day in England' that cause her to burst 'into a passion of tears' and demand to go home (2000: 106). Woolf used the name Orlando for its resonance with Shakespeare's Orlando, the nobleman perse-cuted by his older brother in *As You Like It*. Orlando retreats to the Forest of Arden, and there falls in love with Rosalind, who is cross-dressing as Ganymede. At the end of the play, Rosalind reveals herself, marries Orlando, whose domineering brother Oliver has been chastened, and they all return happily to court. Orlando gets the girl (who was also a boy) and returns to home and family, leaving behind the world of naïve shepherds and religious hermits found in the forest, just as Woolf's Orlando does when she leaves the freedom of the Anatolian mountains for England.

Home is Orlando's great 'passion' but the novel contains the hint of another passionate possibility. In the manuscript version of the novel, there is one more line written directly beneath the 'wild goose', "'The secret of life is...'" (2000: 264, n. 39). Could Woolf have been imagining that the secret of life was the goose's flight, not tied to one place, but cyclical? It is this secret that the film takes up. Rather than focusing on Orlando's internal monologue, the film shows us a person changing through 'world'-travel and connection with other bodies on a line of flight. Biography, an objective story focused on a single individual, is as constrictive as a house. Orlando may be the 'same person, no difference at all' after her change from male to female, but she is transformed from a wealthy aristocrat surrounded by servants into a single mother and writer who is becoming part of a community. Change occurs through movement.

Potter's Orlando struggles against the constraints binding women's movement. Corsets, dresses and propriety keep Orlando to, or close to, her house in the eighteenth and nineteenth centuries. She refuses an invitation to sail to America with freedom fighter Shelmerdine, but through their love, they set each other in motion. He sets off with the changing wind, as in Woolf's novel, but it does not bring him back at the end, and they do not marry. Instead, we see Orlando, heavily pregnant, running through the interminable and indeterminate trenches of the twentieth century's wars. Stripped of class, property and even nation, she is a refugee. She survives the war and turns a manuscript over to her publisher, then rides off on a motorbike with her daughter in the sidecar. Between these two scenes of dramatic movement, Orlando sits upright and still on her publisher's sofa as a train is visible through the window behind her head. It is reminiscent of the steam train that Shelmerdine heralded as 'The future!' If the future is movement, then this cinematic Orlando has not written a poem about an oak tree, a fixed point that celebrates a national history, but a travelogue. The film brings out the moving 'secret' inside the novel's housebound biography.

As Jan Morris notes, 'few writers have ever been more powerfully inspired by the sense of place', yet Woolf's only journey outside Europe was 'a fleeting visit to Asiatic Turkey in 1910' (1993: 3–4), exactly the landscape where Orlando is visited by homesickness. Part of the novel's biographical veracity, as Verina Glaessner points out, is that Woolf used the widely-travelled Vita's accounts of 'carriages crossing the frozen river as if it were a road' in Moscow and 'her visit with Harold [her husband] to Constantinople' (2001: 55). Glaessner cites these accounts to contextualise her set visit to St. Petersburg, where Potter and her crew (including ex-Red Army soldiers who styled the snow) shot the scenes of the frozen Thames. The entire film would have been shot in Moscow, after multiple location recces over two years, had the 1991 *putsch* against Boris Yeltsin not caused a scramble to privatise Mosfilm's resources and chaos among the studio's management. Even in these conditions, producer Christopher Sheppard put together the first fully-fledged Russian-British co-production and secured the use of Lenfilm in St. Petersburg, where the management was more or less intact, for the 1610 section (see Glaessner 2001: 54). Ironies abound in the English team's commitment to shooting, in Russia, a series of scenes about a Russian trade visit to England, just at the moment when post-Soviet Russia was opening up to trade with the West. *Orlando* picks up Woolf's transformative meteorological history of the British Isles and people, interlocking the changing weather more firmly with the weather of history: the Russians arrive in London, bringing not only trade (and their own imperial ambitions) but Russian weather. Later, Khiva is too hot for the English ambassador, both meteorologically and politically.

Those ironies are part of the film's internationalism, which itself derives from the love of Soviet cinema and political writing that brought Potter to visit the Soviet Union in the first place. There she met *Orlando*'s (and *Yes*'s) cinematographer Alexei Rodionov, who had shot the '*glasnost* classic' *Idi I smotri* (*Come and See*, 1985) at Mosfilm (Glaessner 2001: 53). The film also gathered together Dutch production designers, performers from France (Charlotte Valandrey/Sasha), Québec (Lothaire

Bluteau/the Khan) and the US (Billy Zane/Shelmerdine) at a moment at which it seemed that the hegemonic nation-state politics of the Cold War were shifting. Potter said of the experience that 'everybody was kind of astonished by the internationalism of cinema ... People from Russia who you'd never met and had never been to the West, you had the same points of reference, you loved the same films' (in Zeig 1993: 25). Orlando is also no longer an English nationalist of the most poetic kind, but an internationalist who is altered by her encounters with faraway places and people who have travelled from them. Potter would later write a tour diary for *Projections*, charting her travels with the film (1994b). Travel also altered the film's relation to the novel. In an interview, B. Ruby Rich puts it to Potter that when Orlando travels to 'central Asia, where he flirts with the Khan [you] ... really began to tinker with the story in earnest' (1993). Potter gives her reason as the novel's 'arbitrary' sex change, which takes place in Constantinople. She 'made it more motivated' by having Orlando choose not to kill in a battle: 'that's the end of the line for masculinity' (in Rich 1993). Only by leaving England can Orlando see reflected back to him the nation-state's expectations of masculinity and find a way to change.

Exchanging Constantinople for Khiva was anything but arbitrary. Rather than shooting Khiva-for-Constantinople, as she had shot St. Petersburg-for-London, Potter relocates the narrative to a khanate, or city-state, that had a very specific place in British imperial foreign policy. A key town on the Silk Road of trade between Asia and Europe, Khiva was known as an intellectual centre from the ninth century onwards. In the early eighteenth century, reports of gold in the area provoked the competing interests of the Persian king Nadir Shah and Peter the Great, emperor of Russia. Nadir invaded shortly after the first Russian attempt in 1717, and laid the city waste (see Wilson 2003: 159–60). The enemy at the gate in *Orlando*, between 1700 and 1750, could be either the Russians or the Persians. The Russians only conquered the city in 1873, before which it played a key role in the Great Game, the complex and ever-shifting network of alliances that the British empire developed as they struggled with Russia for supremacy in Central Asia. In 1839 both Britain and Russia attempted to free Russian slaves held in the city. Russia intended to use the slaves as an excuse to attack and annex Khiva; when they failed, the British, who were caught up in the first Anglo-Afghan war, sent an envoy to the Khan, the hereditary ruler, in order to remove Russia's pretext for an invasion. As King William 'turn[s his] attention to the East', Orlando becomes a precursor of the resonantly-named Lieutenant Richmond Shakespear, the successful second envoy. In moving Orlando's embassy from Constantinople, which was the capital of a massive empire with whom the British had trade relations, to relatively undiscovered (and conquerable) Khiva, Potter looks back over the long history of Anglo-Russian relations to the beginning of the Great Game and, indeed, of the current situation in Afghanistan.

Potter sends up British colonial ambitions – which were never realised in Central Asia – when William gives Orlando a tulip from the palace gardens to take as a gift to the Khan. Orlando arrives in Khiva still ostentatiously carrying the wilted flower. As Anna Pavord points out in her history of the flower, Uzbekistan is, in fact, famous for its valleys of wild tulips. The bulbs were brought to Europe from its native

Turkey, smuggled in the bags of a Belgian diplomat in the sixteenth century. Pavord writes that tulips 'proved a map of the movements of the many people persecuted for their religious belief ... Protestant Huguenots most probably brought the tulip into England from Flanders long before the Dutch cornered the market' (2000: 14). So the Dutch William's gesture is doubly ironic, giving Orlando a Central Asian flower identified with the Dutch, but actually a representation of the nomad.

As Jeanette Winterson wittily demonstrates in her novel *The PowerBook*, the tulip, often punned on as emblem for women's 'two-lips', is also a symbol for gender confusion and profusion. Her unnamed narrator retells Pavord's story of the smuggled tulips, but this time the smuggler is a Turkish girl who brings the tulip to the Netherlands, strapped under her pants. The tulip's 'well-formed fat stem supporting a good-sized red head with rounded tips' disguises her as a cabin boy and – when she is held captive – allows her to pleasure an Italian princess (2000: 12). At the end of the book, the narrator tells a story where the protagonist wanders through the forest like Rosalind/Ganymede, calling out '"Orlando! Orlando!"' to her lost lover (2000: 237). Like Winterson, Potter uses the tulip to queer the history of international (and gender) relations. Even before Orlando is transformed into a woman, he favours a version of the Khan's traditional Central Asian dress, including a turban; the word tulip may result from a mishearing of a Turkish description of the flower's shape: *tulband*, meaning turban (see Pavord 2004: 54).

The idea that East-West relations are necessarily predicated on the 'clash of civilisations' hawked by neo-cons, rather than mutual trade and pleasure, is refuted by another reversal attendant on Orlando's name. Behind Shakespeare's Orlando (and *Orlando*'s trace of Shakespear) stands another poetic lover and warrior, Ariosto's *Orlando Furioso*, the hero of an epic poem that spins romantic stories around the famous eighth-century knight of Charlemagne, Roland, who died in the battle of Roncesvalles. Roland was the great hero of medieval Christian Spain, hymned in the anonymous poem *Song of Roland* for his fight against the Muslim rulers. Interfaith historian Chris Lowney argues that the original French poem presented Roland in a heavily propagandised and 'starkly spotlit confrontation between Christian Good and Muslim Evil' (2005: 120). As Lowney points out, the attack on Roland's forces in Roncesvalles by Basque guerrillas was wrongly attributed to Islamic forces, creating a myth that came to dominate the European imagination as it geared up for the Crusades. Woolf's glancing reference to Orlando's ancestors on the novel's first page, one of whom brought back the dried Moor's head with which the young boy does mock battle, implies that they were Crusaders – and moreover, that Crusading lies at the root of England's development as a nation. When Orlando refuses to fight in Khiva, he also refuses the cultural baggage of the Crusades, in the same way that her later release from the Great House reverses the return home of Orlando in *As You Like It*.

Orlando's failure to join battle in arms with the Khan may precipitate the city's fall, but it also prevents its addition to the nascent British Empire. The Khan comments that he has heard 'the English make a habit of collecting ... countries' but in this case, the collectors go home without their specimen. The failure is of a piece with Orlando's character: he had asked the King for a diplomatic mission because of his failure as a poet and a lover. His choice of poetry as a career was prompted by Sasha's desertion, and resulted only in a squib that is mocked by the experienced writer Nick Greene. His failures in love and poetry are intertwined: in a draft of the screenplay, Sasha suggests that they result from Orlando's lack of 'world'-travelling. He knows nothing of the poets, books, mountains, music or suffering of her Russian homeland. Travelling to Khiva he may fail as a diplomat and a Crusader, but he succeeds on Sasha's terms, hearing traditional *shash maqam* sung in the desert and listening to the Khan recite from the Qu'ran.

Potter may not have become involved in an armed struggle as the Soviet Union broke up, but her time in Khiva did leave a trace in the film: the '*Orlando* in Uzbekistan' documentary on Artificial Eye's two-disc release of the DVD shows Potter and her crew signing the shooting contract over copious shots of vodka at a party in the desert, as Orlando will celebrate the Khivan-English bond with the Khan. Not all of Potter's experiences of travel are so explicitly visible in the film, but *Orlando*'s picaresque journeys undoubtedly reflect the horizon-broadening of a dozen trips to Russia between the end of *The Gold Diggers* and the making of *Orlando* that transformed Potter and her filmmaking. Potter first travelled to the Soviet Union in 1984, after the scandalous reception of *The Gold Diggers*, which itself took form from a trip with the Feminist Improvising Group to Iceland, where the unearthly landscapes inspired the film's eventual look. Perhaps the country's long traditions of democracy and equal rights also helped shape the film's imagination of another possible world.

Potter returned to the Soviet Union in 1985 on a British Council filmmakers' tour led by Ian Christie, where 'as the only gay male and only female directors in the group [Derek Jarman and Potter] became natural allies – laughing together as we spoke for our respective causes and against our oppression' (Potter 1994a: 63). It was Renny Bartlett and Sian Thomas, tour leaders of the 1984 tour, who would first bring together Russia and filmmaking for Potter, securing a commission for a documentary on women in Russian cinema for Channel Four's *Women Call the Shots* series. The documentary's title, *I am an Ox, I am a Horse, I am a Man, I am a Woman* is suggestive of Orlando's multiple identity, and the interviewees talk about being female in terms that go far beyond 1980s Anglo-American feminism, influencing Potter's developing stance on gender. In screenwriter Natalia Ryazantseva's onscreen claim that 'women are better equipped to make … detailed observations' of 'the depths of the human soul' is an echo of Potter's statement to David Ehrenstein, quoted in the introduction, that *Orlando* is not about the sex wars, but the immortal soul.

The interviews also build a comprehensively different picture of the relationship between art and life in a society based on socialist theory and practice. Director Kira Muratova argues that 'filmmaking is not an island. It's part of the historical mainland of human activity.' This striking reappraisal of artmaking as honest labour rather than a dilettantish distraction will also shape Orlando's discovery of her talents. Art's relationship to travelling through the mainland of human activity is captured in an affecting and funny moment when film historian Maria Turovskaya forgets an English word and uses the Russian term instead. From behind the camera, Potter proffers the translation: the word is 'directions'. Turovskaya is talking about historical trends in Soviet cinema, but the English word intertwines historical patterns, individual movement and the craft of filmmaking. Through the documentary, Potter hones her craft as a director to embrace all three meanings, framed by Georgian director Lana Gogoberidze's assertion that she wants her films to be 'individual … and … self-expressive – and I want to express myself as a woman'. With *Orlando*, Potter proclaimed herself an artist by *I am an Ox*'s definition: individual, self-expressive, observing the human soul in work that is part of the historical mainland of human activity.

Shown in 1990, as the search for *Orlando* funding began in earnest, *I Am an Ox* was the crest of a thaw in post-*Gold Diggers* icy relations between Potter and arts bodies in the UK. Its screening on 9 April presaged sparks of press attention as Potter and Sheppard pitched *Orlando* at the Cannes film festival in early May. Trade magazines *Screen International*, *Variety* and *Moving Pictures International* all picked up on the same story: Daniel Day-Lewis had joined Potter, Sheppard and Swinton on the trail at Cannes, and was going to play Shelmerdine. The *Mail on Sunday* and the *Sunday Telegraph Magazine* (see Davis 1990: 40–1; Ferguson 1990: 8) included *Orlando* in their Cannes round-ups while British gossip columnists at the *Daily Mail* and the *Times* picked up on the same story under predictably similar 'Woolf pack' headlines (see Bamigboye 1990: 7; Anon. 1990: 10). The *Times*' Diary has the best line: 'Strange that it should take *glasnost* to bring Virginia Woolf to the screen for the first time' (Anon. 1990: 10). It could equally have been said: strange that it should take *glasnost* to bring Sally Potter back to the cinema screen.

Orlando, though, is a film about long absences and thaws that could be seen as a record of Potter's career. Orlando's dazzling surprise success with Queen Elizabeth, and the double-edged gift of immortality, could be seen as reflecting Potter's experience with *Thriller*, while the 1610 sequence, LOVE, shares a black/white palette and its ice-bound setting with *The Gold Diggers*. Orlando fails to find love when he uses his wealth and sex to lord it over Sasha, a telling parallel with the stark reasoning and didactic aims of *The Gold Diggers*. *Orlando* celebrates the earlier film's visual panache and its reworking of the mythic romance, but also liberates itself from black/white thinking as the ice breaks up. Orlando's first long sleep, after Sasha's desertion, leads him to POETRY. He researches in his library and works at writing in isolation, as Potter did, which leads him to POLITICS in Khiva, a reflection of Potter's many journeys to the USSR, which involved negotiations with byzantine bureaucracies.

Transformed into a woman, Orlando finds herself forced into SOCIETY, whose barbs and constraints could be read as a wry take on the social economics of film festivals and the funding rejections that the film underwent. Orlando rejects the Archduke Harry's proposal that Orlando should marry him because he is England (a rebuff to British national funding?), setting herself free by fleeing the Great House for the wild moors. The SEX that follows could be seen as an analogy for the experience of filmmaking, after the struggles of pre-production: swift, delirious and resulting (after the painful war of editing) in THE PRESENT of the film itself. Shel and Orlando have found a freedom in relation to one another that is like the film's relationship with Woolf's novel, in which the texts come together desiringly, but move on to their own destinies, and to fully-realised selves.

While travel to Khiva begins Orlando's transformation into a woman, and Potter's restatement of herself as a filmmaker, the effects of Orlando's first long sleep are more elliptical. Falling asleep at the end of King James I's reign, Orlando awakens in 1650. He is in the Interregnum that followed the English Civil War, when his prior attachment to Elizabeth I and James I as a courtier would have inclined him to support the Royalists, the losing side. His magnificently flouncy costume alludes to the Cavaliers' sartorial excesses, which were frowned upon by the Puritan Parliamentarians. Orlando could only safely have dressed like that in the confines of his house, under house arrest imposed by the new government or self-imposed out of fear. Under the guise of romantic tragedy, he voices his internal exile by reciting Shakespeare's Sonnet 29:

> When in disgrace with Fortune and men's eyes
> I all alone beweep my outcast state
> And trouble deaf heaven with my bootless cries
> And look upon myself, and curse my fate.

On the surface, the speaker has been dumped, like Orlando. Shakespeare's lover may also have been his patron, so he was 'in disgrace with Fortune' financially and politically, as well. Moreover, the Sonnets were written while a bout of the plague closed the theatres, so he was doubly 'outcast' from his public role. Shakespeare's plays went unperformed through the Interregnum as Cromwell closed the theatres, while the sonnets were unread because they had influenced the politically unfashionable Cavalier poets. The film uses a familiar quotation to say many different things – not least in that it could speak for and from Potter's experience between *The Gold Diggers* and *Orlando*. Orlando's choice of seat, a wooden stepladder, and the black-and-white tile of the library floor are strongly reminiscent of the scene in the Expert's office in *The Gold Diggers*, where the Expert's assistant (Thom Osborn) climbs a ladder to retrieve some information for Celeste, but drops the filebox so she never receives it. The scene in Orlando's library is visually linked back to Celeste's search for an explanation about the politics of economics, making the argument that a poem that appears to speak about intimate concerns of love and grief could also speak to larger political issues.

In particular, the poem asks: if art is part of the historical mainland of human activity rather than a private practice, does that demand that the artist who wants a private life forego her public voice? Reading the poem, Orlando is balanced between publicly visible and privately ensconced. Unlike his earlier quotation from Edmund Spenser at the banquet for Queen Elizabeth, his reading here speaks for and from his private self. He is, in fact, away from the public eye for the first time since the start of the film. As then, he turns to poetry. The library is the only room in the house where we have ever seen Orlando alone; the butler, footmen, doctors and singers are able to enter Orlando's bedchamber while he sleeps. By defining reading and writing as private activities, the gentleman's library or study raised them to professions and conserved them for men (see Wigley 1992). The camera's intrusion underlines this sense of privilege and privacy, pushing in from long shot to close-up. Orlando's gaze to camera, as it often does in the film, italicises a moment in which the artist struggles to give public voice to private experience.

The self-penned poem that he subsequently shows to poet and critic Nick Greene (Heathcote Williams), 'Death of a Lover', while heartfelt and influenced by Shakespeare's song of lost love, lacks style, wit and originality – and earns a savage verse of criticism from Greene (written by Potter, like Orlando's poem). The rest of the poetry in the film comes from others: the Qu'ran-quoting Khan; Alexander Pope's seemingly spontaneous *bon mots* at the Countess's salon; and finally Shelmerdine's quotations from Shelley. Orlando completes the first, chiming with his words, and gently notes the second (as discussed in the introduction) as inappropriate because the poem speaks of night and it is day. The first quotation comes from 'The Revolt of Islam', Shelley's longest poem, which tells the story of two lovers 'who inspire and lead a bloodless revolution against the sultan of Turkey – an idealised portrait of the French Revolution' (Reiman & Powers in Shelley 1977: 96, n.1). Potter's use of the quotation recalls Orlando's role in Woolf's novel, fighting janissaries rebelling in Constantinople. The internecine rebellion of the novel is refigured in the poem as a class revolution. Shelmerdine is intending to sail to America where he will fight for a classless future – but his quotation from a political poem is a prelude to love. When he and Orlando wake together and he realises he has to leave, he quotes from 'The Indian Girl's Love Song', in the voice of a female character who faints, overwhelmed by love, as Orlando had said she would in the previous scene. The Eastern and female poetic speakers with whom Shelmerdine aligns himself echo his claim that 'if [he] was a woman … [he] might not choose to sacrifice [his] life caring … But instead, say, to go abroad…'.

In answer to Sasha's challenge, Orlando has listened and learned from poets of both European and Islamic cultures. In earlier drafts of the screenplay, Orlando kept appearing as an artiste *performing* writing as she performs reading, particularly in a scene that carried her from marriage with Shelmerdine in the Victorian era to the early twentieth century. The direction states that 'ORLANDO still sits writing at the desk but is now in a dress of the early 1900s. Her other self sits watching, still dressed in a crinoline, then rises from the chair, crosses the room and merges back with herself at the desk' (Potter 1988: 147). Although the scene was discarded, and offers too literal a performance of authorship, it emphasises the film's use of movement to arrange the transitions from period to period, most dramatically the sequence that follows Orlando's flight through the maze from Archduke Harry's proposal in the eighteenth century to arrive, in a different dress, on the misty moors of the nineteenth.

In the finished film, movement of diverse and inventive kinds is key to showing Orlando's development as a writer and a human being. *Orlando* may be the only British costume drama in which no one rides in a carriage. In DEATH, all his encounters with the Queen, including her funeral cortège, take place on foot. LOVE sees him on skates and riding a sled drawn over the ice. When he comes to meet Sasha so they can elope, he is leading a white horse – but without his connection to her, he is footbound once more throughout POETRY; Greene would undoubtedly write a couplet about just how leaden Orlando's solitary, home-bound feet are. In Khiva, he travels through the streets in a palanquin and, as a woman, rides back through

Just keep it moving: Orlando (Tilda Swinton) travels through time

the desert on a camel. Once Orlando is trapped in giant dresses, no further dynamic movement is shown until Shelmerdine is thrown from his horse to land next to her. He becomes her passenger on his own horse because of a twisted ankle. Together, they see the train that sets Orlando's future as a writer in motion, paralleling writing with futurity and innovation rather than tradition.

When Potter's Orlando delivers her manuscript, she turns over a marked history to begin again with a blank page. In the film's opening sequence, Orlando begins to write on a blank sheet of vellum, but falls asleep. This is, in fact, the only time we see him engage in literary activity. The next time she picks up a pen is to sign away her house, which is entailed on heirs male of her body. It is the last time a scroll is waved at Orlando on Her Majesty's authority, but not the first: Queen Elizabeth tucked the vellum conveying the Lord Orlando's right to his house into a garter around his shapely calf in 1600; in 1750, two smirking officials stalk Orlando through her gardens to tell her that being legally dead as well as female – 'which amounts to much the same thing' – she cannot hold property. The first document signals the Queen's ownership of Orlando, which is played as both erotic and economic; the second prompts the Archduke Harry (John Wood) to propose, an offer that foregrounds the economics of romantic love. These documents move Orlando *away* from her work as an artist by placing her identity in another's control, and reminding us that as private citizens we are all members of a public constituted by the legal documents that name us.

Poetry takes its place among other documents that shape Orlando's identity, but with a difference. In handing her manuscript to the publisher Orlando fashions herself by giving away rather than claiming ownership. The film takes up the book's added twist, which is that the publisher so keen to take on Orlando's work is Nick Greene, the poet who dismissed Orlando's earlier (admittedly terrible) poetry with a scurrilous verse. Greene bites the hand that has offered to feed him after his magnificently ridiculous soliloquy asking Orlando for patronage. In a further twist, Greene is played by poet and provocateur Heathcote Williams, who is a model of anti-establishmentism and anti-commercialism. Like Potter, he has enjoyed several careers across live performance, writing and film, and is mainly known for his environmental poems (including *Autogeddon*, an assault on the car) and levitating his daughter onstage. He played the magician Prospero in Derek Jarman's *The Tempest* (1979), turning the character into Heathcote Williams, a notorious writer who had retreated to avoid fame. His Nick Greene is exactly the opposite, still caught up in the black cheque rather than the blank page.

Sheets and pages circulate through the film as images of Orlando's coming to self. The blank page is invoked by the brilliant white sheets that appear at various moments, which in turn suggest the white screen on which the film is projected. This is not a structuralist device to draw attention to the film as film, but rather a chain that effectively connects Orlando's writing to Potter's filmmaking without making one an obvious metaphor for the other. The blank page is where the writer starts, as Sally does at the beginning of *The Tango Lesson*, to imagine a new kind of cinema. Perhaps Orlando's manuscript is not a travelogue but a screenplay, a document that charts *cinematic* movement. Unlike the travelogue and biography, a screenplay points not to what has already been accomplished but, like the blank page, to the thrill of what remains to be done.

Orlando's visit to her publisher takes the place of her trip, in the novel, to buy new sheets to replace those that have been marked by the bodies of kings and queens. The clean sheets that Orlando buys in the novel appear in the film as a movement towards freedom. They turn domestic objects and spaces into striking abstract art as dustsheets over furniture in the eighteenth century and also when Orlando returns to the Great House in the present to find the garden's comical topiary draped as if by Christo. These blank sheets, unlike those bought in the novel, foreshadow Orlando's gradual giving-up of her property. As bedsheets, they are tangled up with the line between public and private in Orlando's identity as a woman and as an artist. In Woolf's previous novel *Mrs Dalloway* (1925), the main character Clarissa Dalloway sees her sheets on her single bed 'clean, tight stretched in a broad white band from side to side' (1992: 40). She has the vaunted room of her own, away from her husband, and the sheets become a surface for a projection of a particular memory, of kissing her friend Sally the night before she accepted her husband's marriage proposal. Clarissa does not go on to become a writer, but Woolf suggests that this kind of cinematic remembering of a moment of freedom is a precursor to expressing oneself as an artist. Orlando's transformations likewise take place in bed among white sheets.

The association of blank pages and new sheets as screens for self-projection has a third term in Woolf's novel: ice in thaw. In Marshall & Snelgrove's department store, Orlando thinks that she encounters Sasha, or a woman very like her. This prompts a vision in which ice begins to break up beneath Orlando's feet (see Woolf 2000: 207–10). In the film, the white sheets of ice over the Thames act like a cinema screen, allowing King James I to look down through a 'pane' in the ice at a drowned woman frozen in a lifelike gesture. The ice is also the stage for a tableau and courtly dance performed for the King and court, and for a late-night performance of Shakespeare's *Othello*. As in Woolf's novel, the ice breaks up at the stroke of midnight when Sasha does not arrive to meet Orlando. The film cuts from shots of people stranded on ice floes floating down the Thames to Orlando asleep amidst his white bedlinen. Frozen panes of ice provide static spectatorship based on class, gender and race hierarchies. *Othello* is not just there for the similarity between its protagonist's jealousy and Orlando's, but because the lead actor in blackface makes entertainment out of power asymmetries, like the King's courtiers showing him a poor woman frozen to death.

Thaw, as the 'secret of transformation' for which Ruby and Celeste are searching, is suggested by *The Gold Diggers'* movement from frozen whitescapes to the dark, moonlit sea. In *Orlando*, there is a more subtle shift from the snowy, icy seventeenth century to the damp, foggy Victorian era in which Orlando bathes Shelmerdine's ankle in hot water. The change hinges on Khiva, where Orlando discovers the pleasures of steam in the *hamman*. Wrapped in a white towel that threatens to slip and reveal his (that is, Swinton's) 'real' gender, Orlando basks. Frontally-framed, the shot is reminiscent of Persian miniatures. Orlando is still, unmoving, a passive receptor of new culture posed as an Orientalist fantasy. It will require the movement of the sex change scene to begin the transformation of the blank sheet. The change begins amidst white bedsheets and mosquito nets. Orlando sits up and discards his wig, revealing its pale inside structure, and his red hair flames out, the only colour in the frame. He moves offscreen as he throws off his white nightshirt. Dipping his hands into a bowl of water, the line of her body hovers on the edge of the frame. There's a glimpse of a breast, but the camera glides upwards to rest on Orlando's face.

The white sheets have been discarded for the moment, and in their place is a mirror. Like the 'pane' of ice, it is a screen, but one that neither freezes the action nor creates an asymmetrical looking relation. Slightly rippled and with its ornate frame reminiscent of Arabic arches and fretwork, the mirror means mobility and transformation. Caught between rippled water and clear glass, Orlando seems to have stepped out of Derek Jarman's meditation on translucence in *Chroma*, which he began writing in June 1993, shortly after *Orlando*'s release. Jarman's friendship with Potter extended to a gracious exchange of gifts in October 1989, when she interviewed him for a National Film Theatre 'Face to Face'. At the end of the interview, still onstage and on tape, Jarman gave Potter a first edition of *Orlando* in recognition of the project she had embarked on.

There is a rippled reflection of Orlando in his reference in *Chroma* to 'Della's ladies', the gender-blending subjects of photographs by genderqueer photographer Della Grace (now Del La Grace Volcano). Jarman pairs Grace's endlessly self-transforming 'ladies' with the translucence of mirrors. Through photography, they are also travellers, like Orlando, in time.

> One of Della's ladies
> Crossing gender in time
> With a beard of spun glass
> She slips between my fingers
> Rippling with laughter. (Jarman 1995: 150)

Orlando's transformation is full of ripples: the rippled patterns of nightdress and wig cast on the bed; rippling water in the ewer forming rivulets on Swinton's skin; ripples or dapples of light and shadow formed as the sunlight passes through fine curtains. Orlando's self is similarly set rippling, and the freedom of a self constantly in motion ripples outward to the viewers.

The rippling mirror evokes Jean Cocteau's *Orphée* (1950), in which Death comes through the poet's bedroom mirror as a beautiful woman. The Orlando on this side of the glass could still be male as we do not see Orlando's full-frontal female body directly, only its reflection. Rather than going through the looking glass like Alice, Orlando 'world'-travels into his female self, as his female self travels back through his world of wealth and privilege to discover that, despite being the same person, gender does make a difference, socially and economically. 'World'-travelling in femininity enables Orlando to turn away from her male self's privilege. Looking at the portrait of herself as a young man in the final sequence, she realises that privilege made him a Muse rather than an artist, an object rather than a subject. In its place the film sets a new portrait made by Orlando's daughter (Jessica Swinton) with a video camera. The ostentatious camera movement and crisp brown-gold tonality of the video recall the swaying camera and dry grass of the film's opening, suggesting that the daughter has been, all along, the author of a film portrait of her mother. It is this daughter whom Orlando has been addressing when she speaks to camera, so she is also the audience born within and into the film, and given the tools to leave the cinema and reinvent art. The Angel who sings above their heads is a splash of vivid colour, dressed in gold lamé rather than white robes. The ice has broken and the world itself has become a blank canvas for Orlando's imaginings.

CHAPTER SIX

Colouring

It took me a long time to figure out why I always found colour on film flat, boring and neutral. It has a lot to do with releasing the imagination. I think that the degree of abstraction when you look at black-and-white, the reinterpretation of the world in terms of light and darkness, reflection and absorption, means that there's a kind of psychic translation at work. The mind knows it's not looking at so-called reality, is excited by this, and works on it. A heightened sense of composition and draftsmanship makes shape more visible, so it excites the graphic sensibility. On every film I've worked with a negative palette: it's not so much what's there as what you take out, so what's there becomes very significant. I was always into quite monochromatic palettes, but first became aware of really controlling colour in *Orlando*, as a way of coding the different historical periods. I discovered how radically you could control a palette and still everything would look 'real'. It gave each period an identity, a strength and a clarity, to give a feeling of the big brushstrokes of history. It simplifies, so that you're not dealing the visual clutter that the full range of colour brings. You're dealing with form, but it's still recognisable form. You've gone into a symbolic language, which makes it more contemplative.

– Sally Potter, interview with author, January 2007

Orlando may be about the blank page, but it is a riot of colour. It was shot entirely on colour 35mm, but it contains a wintry monochromatic sequence reminiscent of *The Gold Diggers*. Attentive and attention-grabbing, colour is never just a noun or adjective in Sally Potter's films, it is a verb: an active, conscious choice colouring the screen. Her use of colour could be said to be on the model of black-and-white film: limiting her palette in particular scenes or sequences delimits the information in the frame in the same way that monochrome can. Potter's description of her colour thought process echoes the dialogue between photographer Mark (Jeffrey Kime) and experienced cameraman Joe (Sam Fuller) that echoes the title of *The State of Things*, the Wim Wenders film that Potter included in her NFT season. Mark says, 'You know, I take pictures, photographs, but I never really thought in black-and-white before I saw our rushes. Do you know what I mean? You can see the shape of things.' Joe replies, 'Life is in colour, but black-and-white is more realistic.'

The Tango Lesson, while ostensibly black-and-white, contains several scenes in vivid Technicolor. *The Man Who Cried* and *Yes* both include sequences in black-and-white that mark the presence of other cameras and lines of sight: a cinema screen and later a cine-camera in *The Man Who Cried*, and CCTV footage and a digital camera in *Yes*, echoing the video sequence of the Angel at the end of *Orlando*. The use of different film stocks, and film, video or digital appearing within the frame add to the optical sensations. In *Rage* (2009), the backgrounds of single colours were sampled from the characters' clothes and lipstick – or even irises – and digitally 'poured' over the greenscreen. Costumes, facial features and hairstyles offer graphic shapes and a multitude of textures that add tactility and dimension to the flat blocks of sheer, depthless colour behind them. Such stylised use of colour draws attention to Potter's refusal of what *Orlando*'s cinematographer Alexei Rodionov called 'crawling realism' (in Donohue 1993: 10). Contrasting colour palettes or film grains alert the viewer to pay attention by altering their perception.

As Laura U. Marks notes in her book on film and touch, such 'visual variations are not formal matters alone but have implications for how the viewer relates bodily to the image' (2002: 8). Both colour and black-and-white have a sensory and sensual richness because they are so carefully and deftly lit, designed and shot. Potter comments that Carlos Conti, production designer on *The Tango Lesson*, *The Man Who Cried* and *Yes* is 'really brilliant at [set dressing through] small changes, subtle changes. Rather than putting things in, he declutters, taking colours out, and taking out unnecessary information' (interview with author, July 2005). There are few patterns or ornaments in Potter's *mises-en-scène*, allowing colours, forms and allusions to become clear. Even when working on location, Potter's use of colour and shape draws its richness not only from the surroundings, but from their framing through a wealth of references to the history of cinema and visual arts. The viewer may not travel with the same extensive library of art books that Potter and her production designers took to Russia to communicate with the Russian art director but *Orlando*'s stylised palette, in which each era has its own colour combination for costumes and sets, is still not only visible but meaningful (see Glaessner 2001: 54). Colour has deep and diverse cultural associations, a 'symbolic language [that is] more contemplative'. By stimulating these associations,

Potter's precise use of colour draws attention to specific moments in the films. Colour thickens them to give the viewer a sense of the way that the scene connects to cultural – which is always also social – history.

For Potter, colour choices are an influential element in the film's effect on the viewer. Yet colour has almost as tendentious a place in film history as performance, and for similar reasons. Brian Price, editor of the *Film* reader on colour, relates 'the neglect of colour in film studies' to film's anxieties about medium-specificity with regards to painting (2006a: 2). Yet, as David Batchelor charts in his brilliant study 'Chromophobia' (2006), the history of art has been little kinder to colour, associating it with the usual negatives: feminine, exotic, Oriental, sensual, queer, fantastical. Colour is disturbing because it does not have a fixed meaning, it 'thrives on difference – perceptually, culturally, and as art' (Price 2006a: 8). Film studies inherits this suspicious mindset along with a more pragmatic problematic: as Victoria Finlay charts in her history *Colour: Travels through the Paintbox* (2002), artists have gone to extraordinary lengths, even risking death from poison, to obtain brilliant, stable colours. Colour is a technical and economic problem for film as well as a philosophical one. The first colour processes were so complicated that the developers had to charge a high price for them. Technicolor even insisted that its own colour consultant, Natalie Kalmus, be present on set to design colour and lighting palettes. She sought to allay moral anxieties about colour's cultural instability by drawing up strict schema in which certain colours were always used to signify certain narrative tropes. Technically, she worked to ensure that no incorrectly-lit film had to be developed and that each film operated as a proper showcase for Technicolor, creating lucrative demand. Many filmmakers and cinephiles felt that these specialised systems stunted the development of film as an artform through the creative use of light and shadow in black-and-white. Colour was confined in its early years to populist films like musicals that would make a return large enough to justify its expense, and was seen as an attraction in itself, sending film back to its days as a mechanical wonder.

While contemporary viewers are accustomed to thinking of colour as being realist and representative, viewers and critics in the early colour era saw it as gaudy ornament, not least because of the way that it was trumpeted as a scientific invention and an attraction in itself. Many critics championed black-and-white as more realist. Writing in the groundbreaking film journal *Close Up* in 1930, C. J. Pennethorne Hughes defends 'the dull subfusc tinting generally adopted for films' because it 'gives uniformity' (1998: 260). Moreover, film 'is the dream of the postwar world [and] … it is extremely rare that colours appear in dreams' (ibid.). This unsubstantiated assertion now seems poignant, and suggests that the viewer's subconscious might be shaped by art rather than the other way round. Pennethorne Hughes' references to 'polychromatic spectacles' as 'monstrosities … vulgarities' highlight the moral anxiety caused by colour's bright attraction as it cheapened film's claim to being an artform (1998: 261).

Subsequent technological developments have met with doubt and disapproval because of similar concatenations of economic, moral and aesthetic concerns. Digital video and post-production have renewed and repeated discussions about film's relation to the world and its dreams. Whereas celluloid is covered with an emulsion that reacts to the way light hits the objects that the camera is looking at, digital cameras turn light into a series of zeroes and ones, so there is no direct, physical (what is called 'indexical') connection between the object and the image. Yet, as Price points out, all use of 'saturated [colour] should cue the perceptive viewer to questions about indexicality' because it points to specialist chemical processing of the film (Price 2006a: 2). Through colour, Potter's films challenge the viewer to read what they are seeing as a representation.

Both black-and-white and colour gesture in her work to the history of cinema, reminding viewers that they are watching a film. Black-and-white is now equally associated with classical Hollywood cinema and with old newsreels, and so in Potter's films can represent either flights of cinematic fancy or documentary reality. In *The Tango Lesson* the black-and-white frame narrative starts out as a kind of documentary about a filmmaker whose imagined film is seen in Technicolor inserts. By the end of the film, black-and-white signals that the film we are watching is the one the filmmaker was making all along, so it cues us to suspend our disbelief in the same way that the stylised colour did earlier. In a similar reversal, colour technologies excite Potter not because their innovation promises financial gain but because they are artisanal. Discussing digital colour grading, she comments that 'in a funny way it's [made the process] more craft-based because you start painting. It's just that you don't have a paintbrush in your hand, you have a knob on the colourising palette' (interview with author, September 2006). Colour is a metaphorical, rather than indexical, trace of the filmmaker's labour and care.

It is a signature like the idiosyncratic shapes of an artist's brushstrokes or like Sally's individual and identifiable handwriting in *The Tango Lesson*. So the stylised use of colour marks the films in two ways: it draws attention to particular moments that are layered with art- and film-historical intertexts, and it signs the film as the work of an artist. Both can be described as *italic*, a convention used to stress particular words, effective because its imitation of handwriting contrasts with upright type. Created by Aldus Manutius in 1501, italic was based on a calligrapher's handwriting, itself based on blackletter, which Manutius incorrectly believed to be the calligraphic style of ancient Rome. As well as drawing attention to the words it highlights, italic also draws attention to itself as a form from a specific place (Italy), historical culture (the Renaissance, and behind that, the Romans) and a body, that of humanist writer and calligrapher, Poggio Bracciolini. Potter's use of colour also refers back to the filmmaker's body behind it through the cultural, aesthetic and historical associations it conjures. It italicises moments and, in doing so, causes us to feel them more deeply even if the references are not familiar.

Technicolor's set representative Kalmus claimed that colour would 'augment the mechanical processes with the inspirational work of the artist. It is not enough that we put a perfect record on the screen. That record must be moulded according to the basic principles of art' (2006: 24). She argued that delicate artistry must be used because of 'the appeal of colour to the emotions' (2006: 25). On the other side of the aesthetic and political divide, Soviet filmmaker Sergei Eisenstein 'felt it important to establish *the place of colour on an equal footing with the other elements of montage* within film-making. We have identified it as the necessary and uniquely all-embracing precondition for achieving *total and genuine synchronicity between the sonic and the visual image, between sound and depiction as separate functions'* (2006: 112; emphasis in original). Colour completes the synchronicity that will actualise film's political affect on the viewer. Both Kalmus and Eisenstein see the strategic use of colour as the 'precondition' for film's ability to reach out beyond the screen and affect the audience.

As a representational, rather than indexical, quality, colour in Potter's films reaches out to the emotions, and also to our political sensibilities. Skin colour and the construction of race have been present in Potter's work since *Thriller*, where she lights Laffont's skin in high contrast to comment implicitly on the normative assumptions that shaped the chemical composition of colour film (which continues to dictate settings on digital camera), designed specifically to accommodate lighting white actors amidst saturated colours. As *Rage* (2009) makes manifest, colour on film and in fashion is not just about 'this season', but about power: the models and financiers are white, the seamstress and bodyguard are not.

Rather than presenting a black-and-white division or a Benetton rainbow, *Rage* (2009) – a film of the Obama moment – recognises ethnicity as diverse not only in skin tone but in characters' experience of their identities, shaped but not defined by race and racism. As much as monologues referring to inequity, the film's variegated range of saturated colours, each chosen to complement the individual actor's skin and sampled from an aspect of their costume, problematises the notion of a person's 'colour' meaning their skin. It is at once a witty, provocative essay on the meaning of colour that echoes and salutes Andy Warhol's screen-prints as an essay on celebrity and visibility, and an invocation of the earlier New York School abstract expressionism, which pushed at representation as *Rage* (2009) pushes against narrative.

Brian Price writes that the 'slipperiness of colour ... encouraged a search for order, for a system that might contain, or at least marginalise, its ambiguity' (2006a: 5). At exactly the time that colour film processes were developing, modernist artists, uniquely in the history of art, were exercised by colour's affect. Wassily Kandinsky (*Concerning the Spiritual in Art*, 1911) and later Kasimir Malevich (in *The Non-Objective World*, 1927) produced exhaustive accounts of the way that particular colours resonate with particular sounds, letters and feelings. In her diary, Frida Kahlo meditated on the relation between colour's cultural associations and the emotions that they caused in her (see 1995: 210–11). All of them wondered whether, for example, red and anger had an intrinsic, biological connection. Their feeling for colour has been extended by two remarkable meditations by postwar British artists, both friends and confidants of Potter's: *Chroma* (1995) by Derek Jarman and *I Send You This Cadmium Red* (2000), a compendium of letters between John Berger and the artist John Christie.

To call Potter an artist as a filmmaker, then, is not to invoke notions of Romantic genius or to corral film among the high arts, or Potter's films into the specialised category of art film. Nor is it to assert that her films are only visually thrilling. Rather, it is to say that she is at once an artisanal designer or draughtsman who takes delight in the material processes of making, and a mystic meditating on reverberations between sight and feeling. Both aspects of the artist are expressed through colour, and through both of them her work tends towards political change. In his renowned textbook, *What Is A Designer?*, Potter's father Norman reflected on the question of whether the designer – who, like the film director, does not have his hands on every part of the process – is an artist. He quotes a Toltec poem translated by American poet Denise Levertov:

The true artist: draws out all from his heart,
works with delight, makes things with calm, with sagacity,
works like a true Toltec, composes his objects, works dextrously, arranges materials, adorns them, makes them adjust, invents. (in N. Potter 2002: 65)

Levertov's translation repeats 'works' at the beginning of the middle lines. The artist's recognition of herself as an artisan is linked to a heartfelt expression and delight in making.

The Toltec vision is in strict contrast with ideas about the role of the artist in the postmodern era. Yet Potter has been celebrated for aspects of her work defined as postmodern, notably parody and intertextuality. When Linda Hutcheon invokes *Thriller* as postmodern, she argues, through a quotation from dance historian Sally Banes, that Potter's work:

widen[s] the scope of the term postmodernism in film studies in order to include, for instance, the sort of things which (under the influence, perhaps, of perform-ance art) are considered postmodern in dance: 'irony, playfulness, historical refer-ence, the use of vernacular materials, the continuity of cultures, an interest in process over product, breakdown of boundaries between art forms and between art and life, and new relationships between artist and audience.' (2002: 9)

Colour could be seen as a continuation of the influence of performance art in Potter's films, not only because it notes film's relation to other media and has a bodily affect, but because it is postmodern in ways similar to Banes' description. Rather than winking knowingly at the audience as it italicises an intertext, it extends the possibility that we could look differently, reaching out and inviting us to experience, even touch, the cascading histories, places, texts and emotions that the colour palettes summon.

Brigitte Peucker, investigating 'the problematic space that film occupies between the established arts of painting and literature' argues that they erupt onscreen through their 'conjunction [which] is articulated most persistently through the figure of the human body' (1995: 3). Orlando's Botticelli-like pose before the mirror is such a conjunction, also reminding the viewer that the sex change scene disappears in a hail of euphemisms in Woolf's novel. Whereas Venus is fair, Swinton's Orlando is a redhead. Rage/love, life/death, imperialism/communism: looking at red, the mind is working with contrast. Contradiction heightens engagement, makes us think, makes things present and therefore brings the full body of the viewer into the film, in the same way that colour italicises the presence of the filmmaker's artisanal and performing bodies within the visual artist.

Red: Death/Love

RED CARDINALS BETRAY…
We came to alter the world, not join it,
Curse all assimilationists,
Burn the blue out of Britain,
…
Set the red devils free in the palace
…
Drive the banks into the red.
Proclaim hell on Earth!
Throw red bricks through grey windows. (Jarman 1995: 41)

Red has more contradictory meanings invested in it than any other colour. In film, it is the colour of visibility as affect, most explicitly (over)used in Steven Spielberg's *Schindler's List* (1992), in which the little girl's red coat stands out unsubtly against the grey of the ghetto as both promise of life and foreboding of violent death. Red is, in a sense, most easily read and so jumps off the screen: the colour of volcanic explosions, of blood on skin. It is often the mark of something emerging that should be kept hidden. 'Could it be that red is the one colour continually asking for a body?' asks John Berger (in Berger & Christie 2000: letter dated 1 March 1997). Jarman arrives at the conclusion that red is the blood of the body politic, come 'to alter the world'. In the same way that Woolf's *Orlando* contains the dream of travel within its hymn to the Great House, the film version of *The Wizard of Oz* contains, within its seeming narrative trajectory of 'no place like home', the red shoes that represent 'the joys of going away, of leaving the greyness and entering the colour … a great paean to the Uprooted Self' (Rushdie 1992: 16). Red, like the artiste, is nomadic and voracious, moving across maps like the various Red Armies, from British imperialism to communist China. Its bright shock makes it politically expedient, and vice versa. Red is devil as well as cardinal because of its value and its difficulty to produce. It is the stamp of deviant exclusion for red-headed witches, reds under the beds, and the Red Power movement, indigenous peoples of the Americas who turned on the European colonisers – who colonised the Americas partially for cochineal to make their brilliant reds (see Greenfield 2006: 66–116).

Red is the first colour to appear in Sally Potter's feature films, and it appears as a word. The song 'Seeing Red' is sung over a snowscape, inviting the viewer to read red, as in the old joke, into what seems black-and-white all over. Red is in our imagination, as feminists were frequently told about the kind of rage at oppression that the song expresses. 'Seeing red' means seeing what is and is not there, like looking at colour on film and seeing it as both indexical and symbolic. Filmmaker and anti-racist activist Trinh T. Minh-Ha writes that: 'To say red, to show red, is already to open up vistas of disagreement … since no history can exhaust the meaning of red … The symbol of red lies not simply in the image, but in the radical plurality of meanings … Seeing red is a matter of reading. And reading is properly symbolic' (1991: 82–3). Seeing red is productive: the imagination fosters difference by reading against black-and-white thinking.

Red is *Orlando*'s difference. Regardless of the question of Orlando's gender in the opening scene, his red hair announces that he is different, not least through its colour match with the ginger wig worn by Quentin Crisp as Queen Elizabeth I. Released, in a later scene, from beneath his blonde courtier's wig, Orlando's long red hair is the first signal of her sexual difference. Orlando may not strictly be a witch, but her hair possesses an occult power in its 'radical plurality of meanings': his gift from the Queen, his magically long life, her sex change, her passionate love and the erotic frisson of her gaze to camera. Orlando blends in with the red/brown colour palette Potter uses for the era of his birth, his hair offset by a red-brown doublet and his skin tone warmed by the red-golds of torch light and rich draperies. Out on the icy river of Jacobean London, Orlando's red hair is a slash, a rare hint of heat, and his skin seems deathly-pale offset by black and silver. It is not until Orlando reaches the present that she blends in again: her brown biking leathers contrast with the postmodern silver and glass city, but look right at home next to the oak tree.

Among the contradictory meanings of red in the film's opening sequence is power. Red is the Queen's colour, and the colour of the British empire as it spread symbolically across the map. Even in this, red retains its multiplicity of meaning. As Anne Ciecko (1998) argues, *Orlando* is a film about Englishness that opens the term to a most unEnglish plurality of meanings. Michael Powell and Emeric Pressburger, cited by Potter as major influences, use red to explore a similar internationalist Englishness that they locate in high artistry in *The Red Shoes* (1948). Andrew Moor argues that their films demonstrate that '"England" can be a wide and pluralistic idea, celebrated for its "incomingness", allowing claims to tolerance, generosity and diversity, admitting its post-imperial circumstances, its multi-ethnic communities and its broadening integration within Europe' (2005: 22). In Khiva, Orlando's red hair is the symbol of his refusal to be a good imperial citizen. He first removes his wig when lying by the campfire. Reflecting the firelight in its shade and warmth, his hair signals his emotional response to the Khivan singer, his love of art that will become a refusal of war. There's a similar transnational history of the relationships between violence and desire, imperialism and freedom fighting, art and trade, national identity and international nomadicism in *The Tango Lesson*'s use of red. The first Model wears a red dress, and her rageful rise from the dead to pursue her attacker is the final colour insert from *Rage* (1996). Red's rage and lust for life, rather than its association with death, are shown just at the moment of and as a prompt for Sally's investment of her energy in the project that becomes *The Tango Lesson*.

Through its descent from Spanish flamenco, red is the colour of tango, a connection Potter made in her modernising production of *Carmen* (ENO 2007). Red first appeared onstage on a calendar showing the cheesy image of a flamenco dancer often associated with Carmen. Carmen (Alice Coote) did wear a succession of red dresses that retained their association with the power of desire and with her occult abilities, but they were traps, increasingly sexual and constrictive. In traditional productions,

Carmen dances a flamenco, the Seguidilla, to seduce José into helping her smuggler friends cross the border. Potter replaced the dance with an erotic tussle interrupted by José's cellphone playing the famous snaky refrain that Bizet borrowed from traditional flamenco and made ubiquitous as a symbol of Spanishness. In the bar scene before the Seguidilla, flamenco was danced parodically but elegantly by two drag queens (Saulo Garrido and Amir Giles) in traditional red dresses, made tall by elaborate mantillas and high heels. Red has history in Potter's work: it colours complex gendered negotiations of national and political identity and it infuses politics with feeling. Through its association with passion and with dance, it is also the primary colour of the artist and her struggle to work outside the market economy. Orlando emerges from 'seeing red' in the bomb-fires of war to present her finished manuscript to a publisher sitting pretty in the grey glass palace of blue Thatcherite Britain, paid for with post-Falklands gold.

Gold: Poetry/Politics

> Gold … is never regular: it's varied. As you say it stores and reflects light, but it receives and gives off waves which are not constant – as though its surface was liquid rather than solid … this irregularity reminds us of living skin, of a body. This could be what makes it a sexy colour … Its symbolism of eternal life, which is not only Egyptian but also Islamic and Byzantine, depends upon it combining the corporeal and … the unchanging. A reassurance about the *beyond* and an affirmation, a very calm affirmation of the *now*. Why does everyone want to *touch* gold? I'll let you know what the exchange is tomorrow. (Berger, in Berger & Christie 2000: letter dated 23 November 1998; emphasis in original)

Like red, gold's sheen of politics unites England and the *Internationale*. At the end of the letter, Berger alludes to 'the exchange'. It could mean the Stock Exchange investigated by Celeste or the exchange of letters and gifts between Berger and Christie, who sent him a gold bar. In either case, gold's value – as Lewis Hyde says of the gift – is in movement. Yet the financial Exchange makes its money by stockpiling gold rather than exchanging it. *The Gold Diggers'* investigation of circulation can be applied to the work of the film industry, passing figures with many zeroes through (national and individual iconic) bodies as information with no tangible end product – except Celeste's transformation. Potter, Jarman and Peter Greenaway explored gold's alchemy in their early 1980s films as a reaction to Thatcherism. Alchemy is part of a specifically British inheritance of mysticism via Dr John Dee, one which serves to represent an anarchic, alternative history in which gold is not capital but spiritual wealth, a token of the value of the immaterial symbolic.

Berger qualifies gold's value by calling attention to its plain speaking: 'It's as if all the colours (and particularly the pure ones) are waiting to undress or be undressed. Maybe the colour *gold* is special (associated with magic and the sacred) because it's the exception. What is on the other side of gold is the same as what is on this side.

Gold is naked from the start, the only one' (in Berger & Christie 2000: letter dated 28 December 1997; emphasis in original). Red is polyvalent, but gold's value depends on its stability of meaning: whether it stands for the body (beautiful), for material wealth or for spiritual purity, all references are to the gold standard. It is the colour worn by financier Tiny in *Rage* (2009), flaunting his wealth in suits made of rich fabrics in shades of gold and copper, their cuts referring to the flamboyant male clothing of the European courts epitomised in *Orlando* by William of Orange. Yet material wealth like Tiny's can be seen as spiritual impurity, while spiritual purity may exempt the body altogether, indicating the complexity with which EuroWestern culture regards the value of value. Art and aesthetics are where the complexity is played, if not worked, out. Used in religious art, gold indicates a patron's wealth – and, through his generosity, his spirituality.

Gilding angel's wings, gold's preciousness signifies divinity because of its purity. Yet seductive, shining, rippling gold is the zenith of colour's feminine frivolous decorativeness, quite literally in the form of jewellery or gold leaf. Due to this association with the corporeal and ornamentation, gold can also symbolise cheapness, devaluation or camp parody, like the gold lamé worn by the Angel at the end of *Orlando*. Catherine Clément comments that a musicologist who hates opera refers to it as the Golden Calf, which 'stands for the unclean, for debauchery. Golden Calf, money, wealth, the bank; Golden Calf, capitalism, bags bloated with dollars, prostitution. And for a musician ... opera is truly the Golden Calf; it is facility, scenery, the image made history' (1989: 14). Opera is seen as an *impure* form, commercialised by its spectacular, verbal and narrative trappings. In a scene backstage in *The Man Who Cried*, a French chorus girl reveals both opera's and gold's 'impure' connotations when she asks cattily: 'Who do you think is controlling the money here? Right here in the theatre? I don't think Monsieur Perlman is a Catholic.' Like red, gold has a racist dimension, associated with anti-semitic stereotypes of Jewish avarice.

The film instead slyly decentres the heroic tenor whose voice is the opera's gold, showing that his sense of self is based on his earning capacity. Dante's childhood poverty has instilled in him the sense that money is pure and clean while poverty is morally dirty. He expresses this most fully after Cesar's horse shits onstage after one of Dante's particularly vainglorious performances. The horse's pointed comment on Dante as opera's Golden Calf gives him the opening to associate Cesar, who is Roma, with moral filth, along the lines of Nazi propaganda. Dante's moral order is upside down: he sings cravenly for the Nazi top brass while Suzie and Cesar must stoop to pick coins out of the dirt in order to survive.

The Man Who Cried continues to drive the wedge between economic capital and metaphysical freedom as two modes of valuing the self. Gold symbolises the movement between the two in its appearance as a gold coin, one of the many glistening objects in the visual lushness of *The Man Who Cried*. On its first appearance, it is a rare light in the washed-out sparseness of the shtetl. Its glint presages the fires of the pogroms burning outside as Fegele's grandmother urgently scrabbles it from the sugar jar and sews it into her granddaughter's coat hem. It is supposed to buy Fegele passage to America, its buying power turning it into something akin to a charm to

Guardian 'angle': the Angel (Jimmy Somerville) casts a glittering spell over Orlando

keep the child safe. It is one of the few things that Suzie retains of the child named Fegele that she was. Her English foster parents take it away, but return it to her when she leaves for Paris. In soft Parisian light, Suzie hides the coin in a sugar jar. As a token of memory, it is carried alongside the sepia photogravure of her father. It has been removed from the cash economy to become a gift that gives Suzie back her child self, and with it the freedom and determination to move on and to survive. Before she leaves Paris, she slips the coin into Cesar's pocket as he sleeps after they have spent their last night together.

The gift of the coin is both monetary and memorial, as it was when her grandmother sewed it into her hem. It could mean survival as a bribe in the wartime economy, but it also has a magical power, reminding Cesar of Suzie and of their transformational effect on one another. It suggests their joint cultural history in the lost East European past. Alluding to the fortune teller's request ('Cross my palm with silver'), it intimates a future. In doing so, it recasts the crane shot that first looked down over the head of Dante and the false angel of Justice or Liberty exactly between the chorus girl's comment about Monsieur Perlman and Cesar's horse's comment about Dante. The shot appears overhead like Big Brother several more times, monitoring a series of tense conversations. Finally it frames Suzie as she packs her bags for America just before Cesar arrives. The glint of gold and the high angle are evocative of Orlando's coming to self beneath the oak tree and an angel dressed in gold. Jacqueline Haigh jokes that, seen in a rare crane shot, the Angel is in fact Orlando's 'guardian angle' (2008). The gold coin that Fegele's grandmother hoped would watch over Suzie turns the shot retrospectively from creeping surveillance to guardian 'angle'.

Irregular yet unchanging, the angel falls into the corpo-real of history in *The Man Who Cried* through touch. Batchelor notes that in *A Matter of Life and Death* (1946) and *Der Himmel über Berlin* (*Wings of Desire*, 1987), two films in which angels fall to earth from a heaven filmed in black-and-white, colour is 'a fall from the disembodied all-observing spirit world into the world of the particular and the contingent, a world of sensuous existence ... most of all it is a fall into a world of desire ... a world of consciousness and self ... made with the explicit purpose of losing the self in desire' (2006: 71). Colour causes us to fall because it takes the gold standard and unsettles it, turning it into other colours and meanings. The Ancient Greek word for dye or paint is *pharmakon*, the root of pharmacy. Like the word drug, it can mean both a poison or a cure. Colour's effect on our bodies is overwhelming. Like a drug, it mingles pleasure and danger. Roland Barthes writes of colour as 'a kind of bliss ... like a closing eyelid, a tiny fainting spell' (in Batchelor 2006: 69). The bliss of desire and the body is ambiguous in a materialist world. Dante and Lola are one side of the coin: he wants to buy her like a beautiful object, she pretends to desire him because she wants the security of money. Cesar and Suzie are the other, finding a place through mutual desire that is outside the Parisian wartime world's corrupt exchange of money, touch and glances.

Jarman plangently imagines such a place in *Chroma*, written in his last months as he was dying of AIDS-related illnesses. He paraphrases the funeral song in Shakespeare's play *Cymbeline*: 'Gold discs for golden lads and lasses, who unlike the incorruptible metal must come to dust' (1995: 143). In Jarman's *Caravaggio* (1986), streetwalkers-turned-muses Ranuccio (Sean Bean) and Lena (Tilda Swinton) kiss lazily in a hammock as they pass a gold coin between them, payment from the artist for modelling as angels. Bliss is short-lived. The artist's money comes between them and they violently 'come to dust'. When money enters the world of pastoral bliss it turns desire into murderous passion. But it is also the promise of passion's ability to create another world in which gold is the symbol of constant, blissful exchange and transformation.

Purple: Society/Sex

> Purple is passionate, maybe violet becomes a little bolder and FUCKS pink into purple. Sweet lavender blushes and watches. (Jarman 1995: 127)

In 'Alchemical Colour', Jarman notes that purple was the final stage in the alchemical process: 'Iosis, the colour of kingship' brought the adept to the philosopher's stone – the Ruby – and thus to gold (1995: 76). The Ancient Greek word for red, *croceus*, could mean any shade from golden yellow through pinky reds to deep purple, the colours of the crocus, whose stamens made the expensive red/purple dye, saffron, which was the gold of the ancient world. Associated with value because of the rarity of saffron and the rare Murex dye used to produce Tyrian purple worn by royalty in the ancient Mediterranean, purple's desirability made it the colour of passion and sexuality. 'Purple prose', used to describe ornate writing, derives from a Horace poem, where it implicitly compares the use of ostentatious and gaudy language in another poet's work to Roman social climbers wearing imperial purple. In modern criticism, it is most often used to suggest that women's erotic writing is both too overt and too coy: throbbing and blushing at the same time. Like red, purple offers a glimpse of that which should be hidden, an inside brought outwards, an intensity exhibited, and so it becomes symbolic of the work of the artist. Jarman has fun with the decadent associations that accrued to purple when it was taken up by the Victorians. Despite Horace's disapproval or rather because of it, purple in its decadence, passion and corporeality was used by the symbolists as the flag of art for art's sake (see Jarman 1995: 130).

Potter's films are rarely given to purple passages that aestheticise sexual passion. Even *Orlando*'s steamy romance with Shelley-spouting Shelmerdine is tempered by witty asides. Their bliss is almost without colour, sprawled on white sheets. When Potter next imagines two blissful lovers in bed for the first time, in *Yes*, the framing is strongly reminiscent of the overhead shot of Orlando and Shelmerdine in bed, which was widely reproduced on DVD and book jackets. The 'allusion is a shortcut to giving memories a new life, relying on remnants of common sensations' (Biro 1982: 14). In *Yes*, the overhead shots of He and She curled up post-coitally are on a more intimate scale, and their difference is marked by colour: not only the rich polychromatic scarf with its intricate Arab geometries that He has pinned to the wall in place of a headboard, but the iridescent purple of the cover beneath which they curl. Red and silver pillows nestle their heads. This profusion of colour contrasts with She's house, rendered frigid in minimalist white, and with her skin's whiteness.

In contrast to both Hollywood standard euphemistic framing and lighting and the defiantly anerotic new European arthouse hardcore, Potter offers sensual allusions to sexual touch. The scene summons sensations in the viewer's body through its attention to textures and small movements. 'The oscillation between [haptic and optical] creates an erotic relationship, a shifting between distance and closeness. But haptic images have a particular erotic quality, one involving giving up visual control' (Marks 2002: 13). Through multiple slow superimpositions the viewer gives up control of the image. The shots touch one another and create a haptic experience through the blurring of body into body and moment into moment. The framing draws on a common memory of *Orlando* while the gestures and superimposition draw on 'remnants of common sensations' of sharing intimate space. We feel with, and as, He and She as we see them arranged variously against and around each other, slowly opening and closing their eyes.

The sequence is meltingly erotic because rather than rehearsing a performance of sexual touch, the film conjures it through colour, music, light, framing and *mise-en-scène*. In her feminist phenomenology of film, Vivian Sobchack speaks 'quite literally of our capacity to feel the world we see and hear onscreen and of cinema's capacity to "touch" and "move" us offscreen. As philosopher Elizabeth Grosz puts it: "Things solicit the flesh just as the flesh beckons to and as an object for things. Perception is the flesh's reversibility, the flesh touching, seeing, perceiving itself"' (2004: 66). The play of light over the purple silk in *Yes*, the play of limbs indenting it here and there, and the play of glances as eyes and bodies caress each other, create a texture that solicits a viewing touch. Texture speaks of bodies and love's delightful confusion of physical and emotional interiority.

The startling colour difference from the famous *Orlando* shot draws the viewer's haptic gaze, while the characters' repeated opening and closing of their eyes affects us kinaesthetically. That is, it causes you to mimic their gestures (as when someone near you yawns). Close your eyes, look again: the light has changed but the purple is still there, even more itself, ever more bodily, ever more beautiful. Purple is beautiful perhaps because it is so passionate. The wordless, repeated-with-variation shots in this sequence invite the gaze by taking the time to take note of what is beautiful. There is nothing flashy or awe-inspiring here. Slowness links beauty to awareness and engagement, rather than casting beauty as decadent, élitist, commercial or unattainable. Colour italicises beauty, making it open and available to the viewer. Its sensuousness delinks beauty from the female body's associations with economic value and the oppression of the male gaze. Delight in beauty is uncoupled from the fantasy of unattainability and connected to the more complex fantasy of intimacy, of having and touching in the moment. This is Wendy Steiner's hope when she argues that the 'experience of beauty involves a challenge to achieve the value or beauty of the Other. This elevation requires effort – interpretation, openness – but once achieved, however fleetingly or vicariously, the result is a pleasure different in kind from normal experience' (2001: xxiii–iv).

Part of that pleasure is in sharing and comparing subjective experiences. Colour is experienced subjectively, influenced by culture, biology and individual experience, and purple, through its associations with desire and aesthetics, is the colour of subjectivity. Brian Price argues that 'the subjective expansion of colour abstraction counters the increasingly conventionalised narrative form of global cinema', which challenges viewers to produce their own subjective readings rather than mandating that they 'submit such works to transcendent critical procedures' (2006b: 86). Individual and intimate readings of purple have to find a shared language, so 'the subjective optics of colour make perceptual multitude not only possible, but inescapable', motivated by eros 'as an animating impulse' (ibid.). Jarman put it more celebratorily and succinctly: 'Colour seems to have a Queer bent!' (1995: 58). No colour more than purple, perhaps because it mixes 'feminine' red and 'masculine' blue. Purple's beauty is in its defiant evocation of a lost value of the ancient world. Purple was, as Price suggests of colour abstraction, once a form of international trade, deeply associated with the 'wine-dark sea' from which the Murex whelk came, and across which Phoenician boats carried the bolts of dyed fabric. In *Yes*, it stands exactly for a language of intercultural exchange between an Irish-American woman and a man from Lebanon, once Phoenicia. Like Suzie's gold coin, purple's travels bring awareness and offer safe purple passage, welcoming the viewer's senses aboard.

Blue-Green: [Becoming]

> It is not enough for a blue or a green to bolster the film's expression; they bring with them new ideas, their presence at a specific moment evokes an emotion *sui generis*. (Rohmer 2006: 123)

It is difficult to read blue onscreen without reference to Jarman's majestic *Blue* (1993), which fulfils Eric Rohmer's dictum beyond all expectation. For 75 minutes, a pure blue screen undulates with 'emotion *sui generis*', resonating with passages from *Chroma* spoken in voice-over. Like purple, the film is full of that which dominant society considers unspeakable, and would like to remain unspoken. Blue, like purple, speaks out(ness). For Jarman, informed by a profound knowledge of Catholicism and its aesthetic heritage, blue is a queer version of the ideal Marian Christ: 'the universal love in which man bathes – it is the terrestrial paradise' (1995: 108). Connected to sky-heaven and the sparkling sea, blue 'transcends the solemn geography of human limits' (1995: 109). Commenting on the prevalence of blue in *Yes*, Potter muses: 'Blue, blue sky, blue the sea, blue of her eyes, blue the horizon, the blue room where we ended up [for the Havana sequence]. Joan [Allen] looked good in blue. And blue is considered to be the colour of eternity – what's above and what's beyond' (2005b: 88). Cinema, in Jarman's film, is saturated with this blue that is his voice.

Blue, in its openness and saturation, has something queer about it. Referring to the sea and sky, it suggests an expansive becoming that is also an elsewhere, an alternate world. One of the most startling visual images in *Rage* (2009) is italicised by its reference to Leigh Bowery's most iconic look, combining blue body paint with cheap Indian jewellery from Brick Lane and gay club leathers. The performance artist and queer provocateur dubbed this style 'Pakis from Outer Space'. Outer Space is at once 'out' queer subculture and the 'over-there' of the former British Empire, spaces provoking fear and loathing as they intruded insistently on 1980s Britain.

Bowery's look has been appropriated by Merlin, who asks Michelangelo, in their first interview, 'You like blue?' in reference to the screen behind him. 'Very sophisticated', he responds to the unheard answer, suggesting blue as the colour of aesthetic discernment. Then he turns sharp, asking, 'What background will you give me, then? Desert with camels? Or Swiss mountains?' He laughs hoarsely, almost hysterically, at this joke about his (indeterminate) ethnicity and its stereotyping. Yet Merlin, as he shows in using Bowery's look, is not above manipulating such stereotypes, nor above commodifying the postmodern protest of an outsider artist, in order to sell clothes. Painted onto Vijay's body, Bowery's look confronts us with multiple layers of Orientalism.

Vijay is the first character we see in one of Merlin's designs. Wearing an open leather jacket and a pair of blue Y-fronts, he is covered in cerulean body paint and heavy metal jewellery. The intense blue both obscures his skin colour and – in its evocation of Krishna – redoubles it. He looks ill-at-ease, not just because he is almost naked (and the only character to appear so exposed in the film), nor because he is a pizza deliveryman pulled into modelling, but because his bike ride on the catwalk is implicated in model Dorothy's murder. The blue of eternity and the godhead is turned – by its commodification – to the cyanotic blue of shock and death. Yet in the echo of both Krishna and of Bowery, there is a resurgent sense of blue's queer protest, its insistent liveliness.

Taking over the screen – or emerging, revealing the blue-screen behind so much of the contemporary cinematic image – 'Blue [is] an open door to soul / An infinite possibility / Becoming tangible' (Jarman 1995: 112). When blue is foregrounded onscreen as a single block of colour, it appears to stand for cinema itself. The rectangle of the swimming pool, which appears in *The Man Who Cried* and *Yes*, suggests the purest function of the cinema screen: a surface for the play of light. It infuses this function with a watery, luminescent blueness, a turquoise or blue-green that recurs in Potter's films from *Orlando* onwards in a very specific manner. Ranging from light blue to a dark, mossy blue-green, it is the colour of the world in which her protagonists find themselves. Elemental self-fashioning makes an ironic reference to the essentialist identification of women and the natural world that Orlando parodies in her Brontë-esque cry to the moors: 'Nature, Nature, I am your bride.' Yet her green bridal gown, with its pagan associations, remains resonant.

Blue-green is the colour in which Potter's pale-skinned women dress, and therefore make, themselves up: Orlando, venturing out for the first time as a woman, wears a pale green crinoline that is transformed into a blue-green wool plaid as she flees through the maze of gender constraints from an awkward proposal in the eighteenth century to love at first sight in the nineteenth. Suzie, playing the wallflower at a glittering boat party, looks over the Seine in a dark green evening dress, wondering if the gypsy figure she sees on the bridge is Cesar. In *Yes*, She switches from the grey sweatpants she wears in her first onscreen appearance to a shimmering deep blue evening gown similar in cut, colour and fabric to Suzie's. The dress is both armour and seduction: she is attending a function with her husband shortly after discovering his infidelities. She confronts him unsuccessfully, but later catches the eye of He. If purple is the colour of desire, then blue-green is an aquatic shock of love, of immersion in the Other.

Blue-green is therefore the colour with which the films' female protagonists think about the relationship between self and world. 'A blue dress ceases to be purely blue when it follows the form of a live body' (Berger, in Berger & Christie 2000: letter dated 13 April 1997). There is a tension in Potter's films between the character's embodied sense of self and the history of the dress. 'In building [Joan Allen's] character, one searches for her range of colours: what goes with the way she looks, the colour of her eyes, a certain coolness, a certain Nordic look that she has. You think about Hitchcock's heroines and what they were like and what they wore. There are some clues for her in that lineage' (Potter, interview with author, January 2007). She's blue dress connects her to a 'lineage' of female cinematic heroines known for their icy intellectual cool and horrible fates. Yet the dress's obvious status as costume suggests that She is aware of, and manipulating, this performance.

In *The Gold Diggers*, the viewer can imagine the changing weather of Julie Christie's famously intelligent blue eyes as ballgowned Ruby cries, laughs and smiles at her escape from a Hitchcockian fate. The blue dress refers to the woman as muse and object of circulation and display, but its witty deployment argues for the woman as artist, fashioning herself as cool (rather than red-hot and emotionally labile) to meet the world's gaze. The blue-green dress is associated with the natural world's blue sky and green trees, yet it is also defiantly crafted, aesthetic because of its shape and shine.

As a solid block of repeating colour, it operates chromatically, foregrounding the female protagonist as cinema: a blue screen onto which she is projecting herself.

Black-and-White: The Present

> Iceland in winter is a monochrome world. When you're in the snow, you're in a black-and-white universe. So it is a magnificent place if you're in love with black-and-white film, and you're in love with light and shade, with reflected light. When you've got snow on the ground, you've got light ground/dark sky, relatively. Consequently you've got all kinds of reversals. (Potter, interview with author, September 2006)

Iceland's monochromatic landscape is the location for Ruby's memories of childhood in *The Gold Diggers*, memories that she is able to re-enter as an adult woman through the fraught experience of performing in a stage version of a black-and-white silent film based on her life. Initially, these monochromatic memories appear to associate black-and-white with the past, and with a kind of home-movie documentary authenticity. The radical simplicity of the Icelandic landscape swept by magnificent pans is reminiscent of *McCabe and Mrs Miller* (1971), invoking Christie as a figure of and for cinematic history. But the film does not switch to colour when, after the opening song, it enters the narrative of the present. The snowfields are exchanged for the shadowy urban spaces of *film noir*, another kind of black-and-white cinematic past. Ruby's memories emerge into the present, and in doing so set her free by undoing the vengeful spiral of *noir* in which the present is punished by the past.

Celeste's appearance, with a dramatic, distorted shadow of her face thrown over a blank white wall in an alley is reminiscent of *Thriller*, and Laffont's role therein. It offers a hard look at the absence of black characters in *noir* and undoes the nostalgia of silent film for whitewashed pre-industrial America. The reversal of the convention of dark ground and light sky sets in motion many others that upend the moral associations of dark and light. Both Celeste and Ruby escape from propriety to become 'shady ladies' as they pursue their investigations. Each time they run through the alley, their shadows are so elongated and intense as to become doubles, emphasising the female performer's absent presence. The lady vanishes when the light is not on her. Like memory, the female icon is substantial enough to cast a shadow – and yet she has no more substance than the shadow she casts. As in *Thriller*, however, these shadows point the characters' way to becoming.

Black-and-white points to what is missing, what needs to be investigated and found. The missing/unmade film-within-a-film in *The Tango Lesson* is brightly coloured, and the main body of the film, which is the film Sally eventually finds, is black-and-white. Black-and-white groups that film with *Thriller* and *The Gold Diggers* as the spiralling tale of a woman searching through/for her own identity in urban settings. It shares a palette (and Paris) with the *Nouvelle Vague* films that were themselves inspired by *noir*. As in those films, black-and-white is a hallmark of 'cool', an auteurial style that signals a love of cinema as artform. In *The Tango Lesson* black-

and-white evokes the urban – Paris style, Buenos Aires tango films – but goes deeper, thinking about what might be missing from this black-and-white world. At first, Sally brings the brilliant primary colours of *Rage* (1996) through the interstices, but tango draws her deeper into the shadows until the final scene risks almost complete blackout. Its monochrome has a different quality, rarely invoking the harsh shadows of *noir*. Velvety depths and shimmering shades of silver-grey echo an ethical world view that has become more complex since the black-and-white gender politics of Potter's first two features.

Set in 1940, *The Man Who Cried* shows a world in which film was on the edge between colour and black-and-white. The film's lush, saturated look was created by digital grading so that the Paris scenes achieved the look of 'some of the photographic techniques of the 1930s and 1940s' (Loshitsky 2003: 66). Black-and-white offers a fantastic escape from this intensely-coloured reality. Lola watches, enraptured, as an Esther Williams film plays at the cinema in Paris, immersing herself in the scene of bathing beauties to such an extent that the black-and-white clip fills the screen, intercut with her vision of herself in a brilliant white bathing suit. This flash of black-and-white hints at the visual sources that inspired cinematographer Sacha Vierny's development of the film's look: Henri Cartier-Bresson's 1930s Paris documentary photography, and Josef Koudelka's portraits of Eastern European Romanies (see Loshitsky 2003: 65). Loshitsky quotes production designer Carlos Conti's comment that the sets were designed to evoke 'a lost world, perhaps, or the intense quality that memory brings to places' (in ibid.). Suzie's memories of her shtetl childhood are desaturated to a palette of greys and greens that is somewhere between the stark colours of Paris and Lola's cinematic black-and-white. Suzie will rediscover her past in America, as she moves towards a white-green hospital ward from the Technicolor world of the Hollywood studio, which appears to represent film's future.

Hollywood is not the scene of a screen debut, however. Lola achieves her desire of being a celluloid star in Paris, when she waves flirtatiously at a camera whose presence is marked by the film's transition to sepia, and the absence of any sound but a camera whirring and clacking its reels. A reverse-shot reveals that the camera is wielded by a young German soldier, engaged at once in the tourist's recreational capture of the sights, the filmmaker's response to beauty, and the police state's circuits of surveillance. The reverse-shot condenses these multiple operations and uses of film, unnerving the viewer. Fascism is paired with the camera at the exact moment that the film makes the apparatus-within-the-apparatus visible.

It is particularly – and pointedly – jarring with the knowledge that Vierny is behind both cameras. The sight of German soldiers with cine-cameras harks back to Alain Resnais' chilling documentary, *Nuit et brouillard* (*Night and Fog*, 1955), which moves between colour footage shot by Vierny in the remains of Auschwitz in 1954, and black-and-white footage shot in Paris and elsewhere by the Nazis in the 1940s. Writing on the use of similar archival footage in Harun Farocki's film *Bilder der Welt und Inschrift des Krieges* (*Images of the World and the Inscription of War*, 1989), Kaja Silverman describes the reframing of a photograph, taken by an unknown photographer, of a Jewish woman arriving at Auschwitz. Silverman argues that the woman offers the camera a 'resistant look', making herself visible to the historical viewer. Her look italicises what the camera cannot see or show, and indeed hides: the absent photographer and his destructive politics (1996: 153–4). Black-and-white operates in Potter's films as a similar 'resistant look', resistant both to conventions of filmmaking, and the conventional invisibility of the filmmaker.

Its appearance is designedly unsettling, bringing us into presence and the present. Unsettling surveillance appears in black-and-white in *Yes*. A CCTV camera positioned above the grand stairway of the hotel where He works and She is attending an official dinner catches, in time lapse, the moment at which She begins her affair with He, handing him her phone number. The footage was shot in colour and desaturated almost to black-and-white, with traces of colour like the washes used on some early film. Rather than being shot in black-and-white with colour, *Yes* comes close to being shot in black, white and colour. *Yes* makes striking use of white through the whiteness of She's house, crisp white shirts, white sheets and, finally, dazzling white sand. In contrast to scenes of luminous whiteness, which are associated with She, there are three scenes of night darkness, associated with He, whom we first see dressed in the black bow-tie and tails of a head waiter. After he connects with She, He is shown in chef's whites and in a white shirt.

When He is later fired from his job after a racist altercation, he wanders the city in the dark coat of the *noir* loner, beginning in the alley behind the restaurant, which is stacked high with black garbage bags. He's journey is cross-cut with She passing through the fluorescent whiteness of her empty laboratory, and then fighting with her husband in the refrigerated, museum-like whiteness of their house. He descends into the darkness of the London Underground like a mythological hero, and emerges at the intersection of Shoreditch High Street and Hackney Road, with a black-fronted lapdancing club in the background and St. Leonard's church before him. Ascending a short flight of steps, he walks towards a lit-up nativity scene. Intercut with close-ups of He in tears are wavering close-ups of the plaster and paint figures who watch him with compassion. The final close-up focuses on the plaster figure of a Wise Man, Melchior, who has the dark skin of Saharan Africa. His dark skin connects him to two other figures in the sequence: for He, the figure might recall Virgil (Wil Johnson), the Anglo-Caribbean kitchen worker, who hangs his head in sympathy when He is fired. The viewer is also reminded of the black cleaning woman at She's laboratory. In the scene between He's firing and his encounter with the Wise Man, the cleaner 'interrupts' She's phone call to He by overhearing it. The cleaner fills the foreground in the final shot of the laboratory sequence, black skin against institutional white. She is the only one of the choral cleaners whose appearance punctuates the film who does not look at the camera, despite being in the far foreground. She is also the only cleaner of colour: her skin tone highlights the tension between physical visibility and cultural invisibility.

He's association with night and with dark-skin invisibility continues when He argues with She in a car park whose murky darkness is cut by only neon exit lights. The film finally undoes the lineage of black's negative associations of race, night-time, depression, garbage, hell and invisibility in one last night sequence. Having left London to visit a friend in Beirut, He is shown walking through a series of leafy streets at dusk, greeting people, playing football with two children. In the next shot, the camera is positioned and angled as it was for He's descent into the Underground, at the bottom of a flight of steps looking up. Instead of walking down into the depths as he did then, He runs up the steps and out of shot into the Lebanese night. The film cuts to a shot of She – perhaps imagining this entire sequence – and then back to He, walking through an alley to find not garbage, but the friends he has come to visit. Welcoming him inside, they close the circle that began with his exile from the restaurant kitchen.

The Tango Lesson closes with a similarly celebratory night-time sequence, in which the inky dark of Buenos Aires' sky dominates the frame. The film begins, like *Yes*, with a predominantly white screen. In conventional iconography, the white screen or page indicates blankness requiring completion, matter without form, a *tabula rasa* associated with femininity. *The Tango Lesson* makes a joke of this, beginning literally with a white table being cleaned. Isaac Newton demonstrated that white in fact indicates the presence of all colour. So the '"white out" of the image does not introduce an abstract field beyond representation. On the contrary, it usually invades the whole image and eradicates all lines and contours' (Lundemo 2006: 97). *The Tango Lesson* begins with white sheets of paper on a white table, a signal that the full colour palette is present, if latent. It is waiting to be filtered by the filmmaker-artist in collaboration with the viewer. Both are summoned to alertness, their eyes opened – rather than blinded – by white light.

CHAPTER SEVEN

The Tango Lesson

The soul is not really united unless all the bodily energies, all the limbs of the
   body are united.
Rabbi Zusya said, a short while before his death: 'In the world to come, I shall
   not be asked, "Why were you not Moses?" I shall be asked, "Why were
   you not Zusya?"'

— Martin Buber, in Potter 1995: 1

Just as white light contains all colours, the blank pages on Sally's table at the start
of *The Tango Lesson* contain a multitude of stories. It is a film about writer's block,
or rather about how writing can *become* a block. Sally is a filmmaker and her new
screenplay proceeds in tune with her interest in learning tango. As she becomes more
fleet of foot, her pencil starts to feel increasingly leaden, burdened with the expectations of Hollywood executives and those of her dance partner Pablo, to whom she has
promised a role in the film. Eventually she sets aside the page and finds her film in
the world, and specifically in the world of tango. The final act of the film takes place
in Buenos Aires, in spaces not usually seen by tourists, rising to the performance of a
four-person 'Libertango' in an empty warehouse. The tangos that structure the film

into its twelve 'lessons' are more than incidental music: they are the film's 'bodily energies', bringing Sally and Pablo into communion with each other and with the world. Tangos by Astor Piazzolla, Carlos Gardel and Osvaldo Pugliese are the texts behind the blank page.

In Robbie Müller's (credited as Robbie Muller) astute, dramatic and inviting cinematography of Buenos Aires, too, there is an implicit homage to Gardel's tango films. Potter may have seen them at the 14th Internationales forum des jungen films in Berlin in 1984, where *The Gold Diggers* screened as part of the Forum. In her copy of the programme Potter has circled a programme that included several Gardel films as context for Humberto Ríos' *El tango es una historia* (*Tango is a History*, 1983). Ríos' documentary intercuts historical footage showing the changing political climate of Argentina with interviews with three tango musicians, including Pugliese and Piazzolla (composer of the 'Libertango'), pairing the documentary footage to the dates at which their music was written. The idea that tango can subtly shape and document a historical moment in a turbulent country is woven through *The Tango Lesson*. Yet the film has none of the didacticism of *The Gold Diggers* or *Thriller*. When she abandons *Rage* (1996) to make a new, more engaged film, Sally does not read from the 1969 manifesto 'Towards a Third Cinema' by Argentinians Fernando Solanas and Octavio Getino. The Forum programme included Solanas's film *Tangos: l'exil de Gardel* (1983), in which some Argentinians exiled in Paris stage a tango-ballet in honour of Gardel.

Unlike *Orlando*, *The Tango Lesson* is not an adaptation of a pre-existing text, nor does it contain poetic quotations and literary references. Two books appear onscreen: Marlon Brando's autobiography *Songs My Mother Taught Me*, which Pablo reads in the bath in a sly wink at the most famous film to associate tango and Paris, and Martin Buber's *I and Thou*. The film cuts between Pablo reading the former and Sally reading the latter. In an interview with film theorist and feminist theologian Ulrike Vollmer, Potter described how the book came to be part of the film:

> It was my favourite book when I was about 16, and I read it a lot of times. Then I put it away and didn't come back to it again until I took up the tango [after *Orlando*]. So it was a long time afterwards. Something in me was drawn to it, as a way of trying to find words that would express the experience I was having ... I think I probably had a very personal relationship with *I and Thou* when I first read it. I remember looking at the cover many times, studying Buber's face, wondering about him as a person, and feeling that his words and his work were speaking directly to me. (In Vollmer 2007: 230–1)

It may seem unlikely that someone would reach for Buber's densely poetic meditation on the human relationship to the divine in order to think about the tango. Erin Manning, as both a dancer and a thinker, suggests that tango stands as an alternate conception of human spirituality, undoing Christianity's association of touch with sin to re-imagine a 'politics of touch' in which closeness and exchange mediate individual and national encounters (see 2007: 49–52). Tango is directly associated with a constellation of the intimate, cross-cultural and spiritual when Sally and Pablo strike the pose of Jacob and the Angel beneath Eugène Delacroix's famous painting. Shot in black-and-white, Delacroix's painting is literally a fulcrum in Potter's oeuvre, as she moves from black and white dualities of gender and class towards more complex depictions of the range of human feeling. Male and female, secular and sacred, Global North and Global South, movement and stillness are present, but the film is an attempt to find a balance in which they can reflect each other, rather than Orlando's joyous blurring of all categories. Jacob's tango with the Angel – and its situation in Saint Sulpice – is Potter's model.

Delacroix was commissioned to paint two murals in Saint Sulpice in Paris in the 1850s, after it had been declared a secular and political space, a post-Revolutionary Temple of Victory. *Jacob Wrestling the Angel* is in the first chapel on the right of the main entrance, the Chapel of the Angels. On the chapel's opposite wall is another Delacroix mural showing the Syrian envoy Heliodorus being thrown out of the temple in Jerusalem by an angel; and there is an older painting of St. George slaying the dragon on the ceiling rotonda. There are several contradictory, angelic messages in this small space, about failing and carrying on, struggling and giving in, rejection and acceptance. The chapel is also the seventh Station of the Cross on the route that proceeds clockwise from the altar. It is called 'Jesus Epuise Retombe', the point at which Jesus, exhausted, falls again. As the seventh station, it is the midpoint of the pilgrim's route, a transitional or balancing moment. Jacob and the Angel are shown in a similar balance, and the church itself is divided down the centre by a gnomon, a metallic strip used like a sundial to determine the solstices. It is a pagan trace, like a tango pose, in a Christian space, one of the many contradictions that the pose beneath the painting embodies.

In the transept window is another duality: the letters P and S. Dan Brown drew flocks of visitors to the church by claiming, in *The Da Vinci Code* (2003), that the letters stand for 'Priory of Sion', the secretive organisation that runs the world. The church insists that they stand for Peter and Sulpicius, the two saints honoured therein. Pablo and Sally suggestively take on the roles not only of the Biblical characters in the painting, but also the two saints whose initials 'embrace' in the window. Read the other way, the initials stand for 'Sally Potter', implying that the film is Potter's attempt to make both parts of herself fully embodied as separate beings, rather than repeating the twinned and doubled dark lovers (Sasha, the Khan, Shelmerdine) who are almost interchangeable in *Orlando*. For Sally to be Sally, Pablo has to be, fully, Pablo. Tango's lesson, it turns out, is that when 'all the limbs of the body are united' in the dance, Rabbi Zusya can become Rabbi Zusya not by wanting to be Moses, but by dancing with – and so listening – to him. Tango 'can also be the deeply satisfying acknowledge-ment by an other that I have been heard, if only for a moment' (Manning 2007: 17). It is only in the *I-Thou* encounter that the self can come together. 'As I become *I*, I say *Thou*' (Buber 1958: 11). Rather than being autobiographical, *The Tango Lesson*, like *Orlando*, is about the journey to find the self and the voice in which to speak of it. Beyond that, in the attempt to say *I-Thou* the internal search for self is balanced and pivoted by opening up to the Other who listens *and* speaks for himself.

At the start of the film, it appears that the two protagonists have found their voices. Sally is a successful filmmaker with Hollywood executives on the line, caught up in imagining her new film. When she first encounters Pablo, he is tearing up the stage and thrilling a Parisian audience in a tango show with his partner (Carolina Iotti). Sally and Pablo are both consummate artists and they have what they need: respectively, a project and a partner. By the middle of the film, Pablo's partner has left him and Sally's film is disintegrating. They come to realise that they were both saying *I-It* in their creative process, treating project and partner like objects they could bend to their will. Through tango's improvisatory spirit, they can approach art and each other attentively by saying *I-Thou*. As Sally learns to follow in the tango and Pablo learns what it takes to collaborate on a film, they discover that saying *I-Thou* alters their sense of self as well as their relationship to the other.

Pablo, the breathtaking soloist, has imagined that being a film star will confirm him as the centre of the attention he craves to assuage his sense of not belonging, while Sally's sense of accomplishment in mastering tango initially gives her the confidence to fight for her film in LA. Yet tango has also undermined her sense of herself as a director, as she becomes a performer rather than a filmmaker, and a follower rather than a leader. Pablo, meanwhile, discovers that film acting is hard work because it is collaborative and means following direction. Not only that, but Sally's attention discomfits rather than comforts him. He is uneasy being the subject of a gaze that asks him to be open to it and so brings his vulnerability to the surface. Following and leading have gendered dimensions. For both Sally and Pablo, following initially entails giving up power and therefore the right to name themselves artists. The auteur is a particularly masculine figure of power, so Sally's internal battle is the more obvious and political, reflecting women's struggles for all kinds of equal access. By mirroring Sally's struggle with Pablo's, Potter looks at the damage that patriarchy does to masculinity in demanding that it conform to an ideal of force, *machismo*, that cannot admit vulnerability.

In the mirroring a possible way out appears: not to abandon the languages of tango and cinema, but to rethink them so that 'following' is accorded as much respect as 'leading', whether on the dancefloor or in politics. In the notes to the film's published screenplay, Potter cites the quip that 'Ginger Rogers did everything Fred Astaire did, only backwards and in high heels' (1997b: 84). Celebrating the skill of following, Potter draws attention to the need to be 'completely centred and balanced, yet able to move at a moment's notice ... completely in control of your body, yet [able to] surrender control of where you are going ... completely mentally alert, yet your mind must be empty' (1997b: 85). It is a state of paradox, of finding the powerful balance between two forces, like tango itself. As a woman, Sally has a cultural experience of following that first makes her resistant, and then permits her to understand where its strength lies and to share this strength with Pablo, who has given her the opportunity to rediscover her body through tango.

Looking at Pablo with her filmmaker's eyes, Sally creates a space in which he can see his whole self. Potter describes this as a 'look of respect and openness, a kind of unconditional awareness and appreciation' (in Vollmer 2007: 222). Its unconditionality allows Pablo to accept, explore and voice his vulnerabilities. His final lines in the film are a moving admission that: 'J'ai peur … d'être quelqu'un sans racines … J'ai peur de disparaître sans laisser aucune trace.' He is 'afraid … of being someone without roots … afraid [he] will disappear without leaving a trace' (in Potter 1997b: 78; Potter's translation). *Disparaître* calls to mind the Spanish word *desaparecidos*, bringing a trace of the men and women 'disappeared' by the *junta* subtly into the film. Pablo's fear of disappearance is a part of his Argentinian identity, even as it is part of his sense of exile. By speaking his fear, he makes both kinds of disappearance audible, giving them presence. Following Pablo's lead rather than her own artistic will, Sally answers his fear by making him visible on film. Pablo's rootlessness is part of his vulnerability but also his strength, as symbolised by his many lightfooted leaps into the ether. Unlike that of Orlando's angel, his flight has not been a hymn to the coherent, multiple self because it is part of his narcissistic, anxious soloism.

Sally angrily rebukes Pablo that 'tout ce que t'interesse c'est qu'on te regarde', that he is 'only interested in being looked *at*' (1997b: 53; Potter's translation). Pablo experiences a hard fall to earth as the eyes that watched him adoringly are withdrawn. Sally is in a shadowy phone box on a deserted Parisian street, and Pablo is on his cellphone at a bar. Everything around him glitters – light striking mirrors, bottles, glasses. It is supposed to be his moment of triumph, but its glitter is false. Rather than finding a balance while dancing with Sally, he was like St. George slaying the dragon. The scene ends with Sally defeated, withdrawing from language and language's possibilities altogether in a bitterly ironic refusal of her own voice: 'There's only one thing left to say. Goodbye.' Language, her power as a writer, has failed, following on from the failure of the tango exhibition that has caused the argument. So she turns back to her power as a visual artist, going into Saint Sulpice to look at Jacob and the Angel. The painting stretches up to the church's vaulted ceiling, too large to be captured fully in a shot scaled to the human figure. In this moment, Sally realises that it is not enough to think of film as a visual medium, imbued – as she imbues Pablo – with 'to-be-looked-at-ness'. To reconcile with Pablo, she has to share the painting's figurative and narrative aspects through language. She tells him a story that draws on the church sermon and the oral roots of the Old Testament.

Jacob's all-night wrestling match is a story deeply concerned with language. At its heart is a moment of naming in which a single, hard-won word, Israel, gives an identity not only to Jacob but to the Jewish nation he will found. In the Biblical version of the story, when the Angel realised he could not defeat Jacob, he signalled his resignation by touching Jacob's thigh. Jacob then asked for a blessing in reward, and in recognition of the young man's strength, the Angel named him Israel. In Delacroix's painting the Angel is gripping Jacob's thigh: it shows the Angel's moment of resignation. Potter's use of the painting is implicitly informed by the political use made of Jacob's naming, which is interpreted militantly and nationalistically by Zionists and millenarian Christians with an investment in the State of Israel. Israel's meaning, however, 'one who has struggled with God', points not to certain victory, but to the importance of engaging in struggle. Potter draws attention to the important place of 'doubt in Judaism. It's okay to be Jewish and doubt that God exists, or to argue with God. It allows for the role of reason. It doesn't demand a blind leap of faith or expect a sort of complicit passivity' (in Vollmer 2007: 214). Her retelling of the story in the film emphasises Jacob's doubt and humility, grounding Pablo's 'blind leap[s] of faith' in himself – and her own over-confident leap into tango and her new film.

As Sally looks at the painting, her voice is heard in voice-over asking in doubt: 'Pablo, are you there?' There is no response, leading the viewer to think that this may be an internal monologue. Voice-over/off often has an unstable attribution in Potter's films, being less concerned with establishing the identity of the speaker than creating a space of listening, a shared identity in the story. The spectator 'recognises the voice [off] as consciousness, as both "I" and "other", and thus sustains the paradox of difference in a positive sense' (Sjogren 2006: 15). Sally responds to the silence: 'Perhaps not', noting Pablo's absent presence, which could be compared to that of the film's viewer. 'I want to tell you a story', she continues, as the film cuts to show Pablo listening to the answerphone in his apartment. Sally's story is a prayer to an absent God, or a modern confession to a priest hidden behind a screen.

Yet the film moves to and focuses on the recipient, altering visibility's balance of power away from the speaker to foreground the act of listening. The camera stays on Pablo, caught in profile, as Sally tells her version of Jacob's story, in which 'as dawn broke Jacob realised he could never defeat the stranger'. This inversion of the Biblical story sounds out Sally-as-Jacob's humility, creating a space in which Pablo-as-the Angel's blessing of seeing/naming her would come from generosity rather than defeat. The film cuts to Sally, again with the sound bridge of her voice, to reinforce the suggestion of simultaneity. Standing in another phone box, she is not abandoned in the dark this time but gently lit by the Paris dawn as a flock of small girls in Confirmation dresses pass between the phone box and the fountain next to it. The Christian ceremony passes alongside Sally's telling of what she calls 'a Jewish story' through the secular prayer of the answerphone. The juxtaposition is an echo of the painting's location of the birth of Israel in a church that is itself a tourist attraction. Rather than a dualism of Jew and Christian, the film points to a shared narrative heritage that goes beyond faith into the secular world through its influence on the visual arts, and in its location in lived, urban space.

The answerphone becomes a secular angel, messenger of God's word. Sally's voice acts as a sound bridge to suggest that Pablo is listening 'live' – that is, not to a recording of Sally's voice, but listening as she speaks and is taped by the machine. It suggests that he is choosing to 'perhaps not' be there, to register as an absence, but also as an audience. In not answering the phone, he makes a space for Sally to tell her story, and then treats it with respect by listening intently. Sally's story blurs the roles of leader and follower, but also the nature of the fight, questioning whether 'the stranger was an angel. Or God. Or perhaps all along, Jacob had simply been wrestling with himself.' Angel and human, leader and follower, are one and the same. Listening takes them beyond perceived dualities and received narratives. In adopting the Angel's pose, Pablo recognises that he mirrors something in Sally as he has demanded that she reflect him as his tango partner.

When Sally finishes her startling interpretation of the story, she turns its end into a beginning. She tells Pablo: 'It's dawn now, and I want stop fighting … [and] begin again' by meeting at Saint Sulpice. As in Jacob's story, dawn, as night's end, is the pivot on which Sally's and Pablo's relationship turns to reconciliation. Night is the time of tango, of excitement, elegance and romance in the film's first act, while day is the time of hard work, either in lessons, location recces or on the resistant screenplay. Sally returns to her hotel from a wild night of dancing to be met by the receptionist's raised eyebrow and a pile of faxes that mar the beautiful dawn light. The bright sunshine of LA confirms the dichotomy: night is aliveness, day is deadening. As tango becomes Sally's day job, however, night begins to lose its charms. Pablo stands her up on New Year's Eve and then the evening of the tango exhibition is a disaster. The high-contrast lighting of the exhibition sequence, with its harsh stage lights flattening dead the black of Pablo's tails and Sally's dress, makes it the blackest of nights. In the first act, Sally and Pablo literally danced through the Paris night, waltzing on the bank of the Seine, but at the end of the second the darkness is compounded by her lonely walk to Saint Sulpice.

The woman walking alone through the night is usually punished for being sexually available, as the 1970s 'Reclaim the Night' protests stated and worked to change (see Solnit 2002: 232–46). Potter has been concerned, since *Thriller*, to Reclaim the Night cinematically by refiguring *film noir*, not only formally through the use of shadowy urban spaces shot in black-and-white, but also setting her female characters on a journey through the genre's associative complex of metaphysical ambiguity, eroticism and self-investigation. Like a classic 'fallen woman' (danced in brothels, tango was associated with prostitution), Sally has walked, confessed and sought a complicated forgiveness. She will, however, continue to dance and to love Pablo, unpunished. Sally makes it to dawn. She is a Queen of the Night, to borrow a term from cultural theorist Elisabeth Bronfen, whose book-in-process on Queen Elizabeth I as the first diva must surely draw some of its inspiration from Quentin Crisp's Queen in *Orlando*. In a profound reading of the Queen of the Night in Mozart's opera *The Magic Flute*, Bronfen queries the cultural opprobrium heaped on the solitary powerful woman like the diva or the Queen. She looks at a number of more contemporary texts that rewrite the powerful woman's journey through what the German philosopher G. W. F. Hegel called the 'night of the self', an experience that he associated with the void of the maternal womb, and contrasted with dawn as Enlightenment and rationality (see Bronfen 2004: 306). Dawn offers Sally an opportunity to 'start again', but does not require her to become a rationalist. She retains her pleasure in night, tango and femininity *and* reawakens her passion for her 'day job' as a filmmaker by bringing together her intellect and her embodied senses.

For Bronfen, this reconciliation is the magic wielded by a contemporary Queen of the Night like Frannie (Meg Ryan) in Jane Campion's *In the Cut* (2003), for whom 'waking up and walking into the dawn of morning might just as well mean preserving the dialectic between night/day rather than insisting on a violent repression of the nocturnal side of the psyche. It might well mean focusing on the partial darkness [that] inevitably accompan[ies] all hopes and anticipations connected to love, on the partial light illuminating all sense of vulnerability and anxiety' (2004: 313). Night's vulnerability comes partially from its association with the body and its relations:

Gracías: Sally (Sally Potter) and Pablo (Pablo Veron) begin again

tango, touch, exchange and love. It is in exchange that Sally and Pablo will find their film.

Outside the church, Sally and Pablo 'baptise' each other with water from the fountain in the partial light of a grey Paris dawn, incorporating the ritual of confirmation as a rededication of their relationship to each other rather than God. Sally then lowers her face into the water of the fountain. Glowing blue fills the screen. The use of colour is a sign that we are in Sally's internal point of view, as in the colour scenes from her discarded film *Rage* (1996). A tail-coated Pablo swims towards the camera and upwards towards a red light spreading on the surface. Pablo shapes Sally's cinematic attention, not because of his angelic elevation but because of his human willingness to wrestle, to exchange and to follow. Pablo's placement onscreen and breast stroke are visually similar to the shape of the Angel/Jacob pair in the painting. Sally's imagination has been informed and infused by her contemplation of the painting, and *The Tango Lesson* takes shape in relation to Delacroix's source, its story, and Sally's experience of it, rather than the artificially-composed, highly allegorical events imagined for *Rage* (1996). It is the first moment in which Sally's imagination stops leading and begins to follow the world.

'Above all', Potter writes of the art of following, 'you must be completely in the present. Without the sheer now-ness you cannot follow at the speed and with the precision that is required' (1997b: 85). Her vision of Pablo in the fountain shows that she has begun truly looking 'in the present'. What she has learned from Pablo is an awareness that gives her the ability to respond to what is around her. While learning tango in Paris, she had also been location scouting. Cuts to colour film showed her peopling the Parc de St. Cloud with imagined models and assassins. The *Rage* (1996) sequences are spectacularly, classically beautiful. Their stylised Technicolor, dramatic framings and urbane locations have the feeling of a studio musical. What they lack is a score of their own. Distinctive music, similar to the breathy score of *Orlando*, begins to play over Sally's attempts at writing in the black-and-white world of *The Tango Lesson* and carries over into *Rage* (1996), marking the scenes as reveries or projections. When Pablo appears in the fountain, a heartbeat pulsing on the score, like the one that beats through *Thriller*, suggests that we are not only in Sally's point of view but in her body. 'This scene was based on what some psychologists have said a baby might "see" in the womb: light shows (red) through the stomach wall' (Potter, notes to author, April 2008). Sally's film is literally reconceived and – as Pablo swims towards the surface – reborn. In 1993, Potter mentioned to B. Ruby Rich that her plans for future projects included '*In the Beginning*, a musical about "an epidemic of immaculate conceptions"' (1993: n. p.). That is not the film that takes *Rage*'s (1996) place, but the birth-like vision generously includes another abandoned project as part of the journey to *The Tango Lesson*.

In a tactical document prepared for potential funders, Potter stated that there would be colour sequences (of an unspecified purpose) running through *The Tango Lesson* as 'a dreamy thread [that] will counterpoint the body of the film like a vivid inner eye' (Potter 1995: 17). That early treatment gave the film a classic three-act structure that ended with Sally and Pablo mounting a triumphant tango performance in Buenos Aires after Sally throws her film to one side for good. It had not yet brought together all the limbs necessary for Sally, Pablo or Potter to say 'I' fully. Using the colour sequences to show Sally's visions of *Rage* (1996) points to her self-identification as a *visual* artist, acting as a counterpoint to the tangoing physical 'body of the film'. They become a reminder that filmmaking is part of that body. The fountain sequence marks the point where film transforms from Sally's 'vivid inner eye' to unite with her bodily eyes – that is, the eyes she has learned to use by rediscovering her body through tango. What she sees is a way towards reconciling the dualities that the painting implies: heaven and earth, human and divine, sacred and secular, light and dark. The sequence is utterly unlike anything else in the film, and yet the red/blue contrast is reminiscent of the primary colours of *Rage* (1996).

Red is the trace of *Rage* (1996) but also the suggestion that it contained the seed of *The Tango Lesson*, as the model's red dress bears a resemblance to the flamenco dress that migrates into tango. Tango's association with red lies in the film's conception of tango as a marriage of passionate emotions and magnificent artistry. This reverses the narrative that *Thriller* investigated, where being an artist and loving with one's eyes is incompatible with loving with one's heart. The tactical document reveals that red is also the trace of this story as it is told in Powell and Pressburger's *The Red Shoes*, a key film for Potter, and one she cites in the document as a conscious intertext for *The Tango Lesson*. One of the first films to integrate dance numbers into a psychologically complex narrative, *The Red Shoes* is based on Hans Christian Andersen's fairy tale about a girl who falls under the spell of a pair of red shoes. The spell is so powerful that she wears them to her Confirmation and thinks of them when she receives the Host. Cursed by an angel barring the way, the demonic shoes literally dance her to death as she cannot remove them. Having travelled around the world, she returns to the church to see her funeral mass being celebrated. She cannot enter, but the town executioner cuts off her feet, which dance away. Having asked God for forgiveness, she dies (see Andersen 2008: 251–62).

The film takes Andersen's morbid tale about worldly desires causing spiritual damage and updates it to the 1920s. They transpose the girl's longing for the shoes into a longing for fame – a longing, as Sally accuses Pablo, to be looked at. The girl becomes a talented dancer called Victoria Page (Moira Shearer, then the Royal Ballet's prima ballerina), for whom the red shoes are the shoes of the prima ballerina, and the vengeful God is replaced by composer Julian Craster (Marius Goring), the jealous husband who resents her success. She is torn between her love for Julian (and a certain amount of propriety that dictates she stay at home as a wife) and desire to dance the role of the Girl in a ballet created for her by charismatic impresario Boris Lermontov (Anton Walbrook). Victoria's dilemma is realised in a cinematically innovative sequence in which the performance of a ballet of *The Red Shoes* takes flight from the stage into a surreal world that conveys her internal experience of dancing the role. Julian appears to walk from the conductor's stand onto the stage, bringing together the fantastic spaces of the ballet's world and her internal imaginings. She initially chooses Julian over dance, but is drawn back to the stage to perform the ballet that made her name. After a confrontation between Boris and Julian before the curtain rises, Vicky dances to her death in order to escape her dilemma.

Sally survives Victoria's fate in the same way that she survives the fate of the woman alone in the urban night: through her regard for Pablo that enables her to give him direction and learn from him at the same time. While the tactical document sets Act III's 'let's put on a show' happy ending in Buenos Aires, the finished film avoids *The Red Shoes'* climactic confrontation and performance, making something more complex and resonant from Sally's trip to Buenos Aires with Pablo. They tango spontaneously in the rain as well as at milongas where Pablo is welcomed as a prodigal son, the local boy made good as a *tanguero* in Europe. The film suggests lightly, but not superficially, the post-colonial tension towards Europe specific to Argentina. Unlike many Latin American countries, Argentina continues to pride itself on having been a European colony. Despite being the nation where Third Cinema originated, with the aim of bringing about change through solidarity with the indigenous peasants, Argentina never experienced a socialist revolution, despite widespread Marxist organising (see Solanas & Getino 1983). Its political élite are of European descent and its connections to Spain remain strong.

Like Orlando in Khiva, Sally is not there to colonise. She is not undertaking the tactical document's plan that she bring tango back to Buenos Aires. On her previous trips to Buenos Aires, Sally was a student learning from two of Pablo's acquaintances, Gustavo (Gustavo Naveira) and Fabian (Fabian Salas). With them, she observes and participates in the tango culture, 'world'-travelling in a spirit of openness. When she first arrives, she goes to a café where her limited Spanish fails her. She asks for a croissant in English, with a hand gesture curving upwards. The waiter gives her the word: 'una mezzaluna', a half-moon (as *croissant* means crescent). It reawakens the meaning of the French word we use in English, giving the pastry back its poetic association. Tango playing in the café evokes love songs in which the crescent moon hangs in the night sky as lovers dance beneath. The translation also makes audible the various stories behind the croissant: its crescent shape marks an association with the Levant, where many delicacies are rolled into crescents. The crescent is the symbol of Islam, and the pastry's shape is said to commemorate either the defeat of Islamic forces at the Battle of Tours, or of the Ottoman armies who besieged Vienna. The stories are unsubstantiated, but the pastry's shape and name reveal both imperial histories and cultural exchanges, rather than a unidirectional imposition of the coloniser's culture.

Tango's invention is equally rich and vexed. It is Carlos Gardel's love song to his home city, 'Mi Buenos Aires Querido', that plays over the café scene. Calling Buenos Aires tango's 'home' destabilises the word, however, as tango was forged by people without homes, immigrants landing on Buenos Aires' teeming docks. In her notes to the film's soundtrack, Potter writes that:

> Controversy surrounds the origins of the tango. However, most researchers agree that the earliest tangos were danced in the streets, bars and brothels of Buenos Aires around the 1800s. The vocabulary of the dance and rhythms of the music that accompanied it echoes the ethnic origins of its proponents … African slaves from Argentina had brought with them the rhythmic patterns of the *candombé* and later black Cubans brought the *habanera* … together with the polka and the mazurka [they merged into a new dance] known at the time as *milonga*. (1997e: 2–3)

Tango not only sounds out the colonial origins of Buenos Aires, but the legacy of slavery. It remained associated, like jazz in the US, with brothels and bars until it returned to Argentina in the mid-nineteenth century as a 'new' European sensation popular in Paris, which made it fashionable with the middle classes.

'Tango always symbolises a certain exoticisation of an other, brought to bear through external imperial interventions' (Manning 2007: 26). *The Tango Lesson* recognises and foregrounds the imperial legacy that always dances in the tango in order to dramatise Manning's assertion that 'tango as an *improvised* encounter challenges this model of colonisation/imperialism' (ibid.; emphasis in original). Marta Savigliano is more cautious: 'Tango started as a dance, a tense dance in which a male/female embrace tried to heal the racial and class displacement provoked by urbanisation and war. But the seductive, sensual healing was never to be complete and the tensions resurfaced and reproduced' (1996: 202). Carine Perelli writes that in Argentina during the post-*junta* show trials of the late 1980s, 'there was not much space left for dialogue, negotiation or reconciliation among the actors involved' (1994: 60). Tango is allusively a 'space left for dialogue, negotiation and reconciliation' in Potter's delicate allegory for a 'politics of touch' that might meet the need for reconnection and communication in Argentina. Tango can, potentially, bring down hierarchies and open up listening because its lesson is collaborative improvisation, constant awareness and constant movement.

Through improvising with each other, Sally and Pablo find they can improvise their selves, keeping in motion their multiple roles and identities by recognising tango's hybrid origin. The tango embrace is a potential space in which the 'seductive, sensual healing' can occur. Pablo's eventual tango with the camera is therefore very different from his tangos with the mirror that punctuate the early part of the film. In the bathroom, in the dressing room, in the living room, in the rehearsal room, Pablo is constantly checking himself out in the mirror. Like the Dancer in *The Gold Diggers*, he is a solo performer engaged in perfecting his steps. He uses the mirror as an audience and a teacher. In his vanity and virtuosity, Pablo appears constantly vulnerable to the fear that he is performing at less than his best. Sally, on the other hand, is extremely timid about looking into the mirror. When she buys tango shoes, we see her feet reflected in a low mirror. Before her New Year's Eve date with Pablo, we see her face and torso briefly, and on a diagonal, as she leans in towards the mirror to put on earrings. Her body is fragmented despite her engagement in dancing and dressing-up, because she is not seeing it with her filmmaker's eye. It is only after the 'Libertango', which magically turns a location hunt in Buenos Aires into the fully-fledged film that Sally wants to make, that she can regard herself face-on, candidly and compassionately, in the mirror.

She is invited there by Pablo's movement from self-regard to watching her pay attention to something other than him. He observes, on the edge of jealousy and interest, as she turns her filmmaker's eye on Gustavo and Fabian as they dance for her. When she senses Pablo's attention to her reflection, she turns to watch him as he watches her watching his friends, then she crosses to stand behind him. She repeats his level gaze into the mirror, reflecting it back to him. Looking into the mirror face-on, Pablo addresses her reflection with a defensive Travis Bickle impression: 'Are you looking at me?' Unlike Bickle, Pablo is not talking paranoiacally to himself. Sally replies 'Yes', but Pablo feels alone because Sally is seeing him as if 'onscreen' as she looks at his reflection framed in the mirror. 'Then you are not here with me,' he replies. His narcissism is finally revealed as an anxiety about being alone.

When he complains that Sally has abandoned him for 'Work! Only work!' the camera pans to move behind Sally as she turns to face him. Face to face, their position is reminiscent of their stance beside the fountain where they baptised each other. The framing is tighter on their faces here, excluding the mirror. Even the tango music cuts out. Sally asks him what else he wants, and he responds: 'I want to know why we met.' It is a newly-reflective Pablo who asks the question. Having looked into each other's reflection, they have seen that each is a reflection of the other. So they are able to look at their own reflections and become them, looking out from the mirror to the world.

Feminist philosopher Marilyn Frye writes that the way to the self is through such a mutual regard. 'The loving eye is a contrary to the arrogant eye ... [it is] the eye of someone who knows that to know the seen, one must consult something other than one's own will and interests and fears and imagination' (1983: 75). Sally's 'will and interests and fears and imagination', which are the subject of *Rage* (1996), are transmuted by the 'loving eye' into *The Tango Lesson*. Sally 'know[s] the seen' through following in the tango, while Pablo knows it through being the camera's subject.

They travel towards each other through the looking-glass – but not into a fantasy realm. In his late lecture, 'Of Other Spaces', Michel Foucault describes this magical mirror-travel as a *pas de deux* of the self: 'Starting from this gaze that is, as it were, directed toward me, from the ground of this virtual space that is on the other side of the glass, I come back toward myself; I begin again to direct my eyes toward myself and to reconstitute myself there where I am' (1986: 24). Sally and Pablo 'come back toward' each other through the mirror, not quite reconciled but, through their level gazes, finding another moment to begin again.

The mirror could be described as a heterotopia, Foucault's concept of a space that is other or more than the place that it physically occupies. Tango, always referring to elsewhere even in Buenos Aires, is a kind of heterotopic gesture. The closing scene's tango, whose music carries over the credits, ends the film with a beginning. It takes place not in the magical space of the mirror, but, in another Brando reference, on the waterfront where the historical tango began amidst the poverty, pain and opportunity of immigration. In the only extreme long, high-angled shot in the film, Sally and Pablo walk through Buenos Aires' docklands. The romance of Seine-side Paris where Sally and Pablo had danced earlier is here transmuted to a deeper *noir*. Among the cranes and ships, Pablo speaks of feeling lost and vulnerable, echoing the prior shot that had made the human figures tiny. In answer, Sally joins him in a tango, which she also sings. Unlike the swiftly-edited, feet-focused sequence of the tango exhibition, the cinematography now focuses on faces and torsos in two-shot.

Sally echoes the Angel's song to Orlando with her song's first line: 'You are me / I am you.' Orlando's bi-gendered self is split, in *The Tango Lesson*, into two fully-realised individuals united in an act of supreme musical fantasy that shifts the film from being a quasi-documentary about a filmmaker making *Rage* (1996). It goes beyond the Borgesian conundrum in which 'Libertango' showed the film-in-process-of-becoming. 'Libertango' is framed by Sally explicitly asking Pablo to set up a rhythm with Gustavo and Fabian and, while exuberant in its energy and dazzling in its use of a single long take, it is possible and probable within the world of the film. When Pablo and Sally tango on the docks as Sally sings, our belief is suspended like the extreme long, high-angled shot. This would be how angels see life: as cinema. The improbabilities in which cinema delights have moved outwards from Sally's vivid inner eye to become integrated into the film itself through a combination of Sally's prowess and Pablo's. Her words to the song, his dance for it.

Before they dance through the docks, they visit a synagogue, alluding to the church that the Girl cannot enter at the end of *The Red Shoes*. There is a cut from Pablo's desire to investigate 'why we met' to a shot of the synagogue, as if it might contain the answer to his question, and the questions of destiny, identity, heritage and location within it. The camera is behind Sally and Pablo as they hesitate on the threshold, as if their commitment to dance might prevent them from entering. But Andersen's punitive God is absent: they walk through the front doors, holding hands. A similar shot framed and followed them as they entered the stage for the exhibition, but here the camera pulls back as the doors close. Pablo is wearing a *yarmulke* in the first expression of his Jewish background since he told Sally that he was a Jew in Paris.

His confession was prompted by Sally's discussion of free will, which she ends by saying she is an atheist, but qualifies that she 'feel[s she's] a Jew'.

Jewishness is connected to profound emotion, intertwined with a stance of radical doubt. In the synagogue, as in the café, Sally and Pablo look at each other with tears in their eyes, which seem to express a historical grief. When Ulrike Vollmer asks what it means to feel that one is a Jew, Potter says that she 'grew up, as anybody did who was born in the second half of the last century, under the shadow of the Holocaust, and therefore tried to make sense of it ... I think we are all haunted by the deaths of the Jews' (in Vollmer 2007: 214). To be haunted by the deaths of the Jews can be to feel, in solidarity, like a Jew. Potter suggests that this fellow-feeling could be an activist strategy: 'the attempted extermination of the Jews could never have happened if everybody said "I'm a Jew"' (in Vollmer 2007: 213).

Visiting the synagogue is not an attempt to unify or sanctify Pablo's individual identity but, as through Sally and Pablo's shared tango, to constitute a new kind of political identity that Manning suggests could be called a politics of friendship. Friendship is a way of saying *I-Thou*, a thirdspace between *eros* and *agape* where love (or spectatorship) is transformed into mutuality rather than dominance and possession. In friendship, Sally can be Sally and Pablo can be Pablo because they have travelled imaginatively and actively through each other's reflections and listened to each other's words, and to the vulnerability behind each other's words. In listening to each other they take on and model the role of the active audience. Listening silently to Sally's story, Pablo suggests that the viewer is like God: 'perhaps not' there, but the film addresses them anyway, inviting them to meet down on earth. Saint Sulpice might be where Pablo descends as the Angel, but his and Sally's mutual baptism takes place in secular water. The synagogue is also earthly rather than heavenly, placing Sally and Pablo in the histories of violence, oppression and exclusion that group together Judaism and tango. Judeo-Christianity's God is absent. In His place, the film speaks *I-Thou* to the audience.

CHAPTER EIGHT

Listening

I want to try and create openness that might then have a small part in the transformation of the individual life of the viewer. You work for so long alone on a film, imagining the audience. When they're finally there, it's incredible. You're confronted with their real responses and there's so much to learn and to absorb from them. That's fantastic: I'm not afraid of people's feelings. What I've come to understand is if people are coming up to me full of love, it's not really me. It's the need for a focus for their feelings, and I'm wearing the robe at that moment. But I go home and I take off the robe, and I'm just me at home in my dressing gown. But at that moment, I've got the robe on and I will fulfil the role, because I see how powerful it is for people. It's like a ritual: I'm like a channel or a vessel at that moment, or both receptor and giver. I don't take it personally and start thinking I am a priest. I'm just a person that made a film that had this effect. People are watching the distillation of hundreds of hours' work. When I get up at the end to do a Q&A, I carry those years of complete dedication to the project. I think that's what people are linking into. It's like you're a messenger. It's not something that people talk about in connection with film at all, because you're hidden away as the director, you're not the one in view – that's why *The Tango Lesson* was different.

– Sally Potter, interview with author, September 2006

Although Sally is a filmmaker, the director is 'perhaps not' there – or, at least, not visible – in *The Tango Lesson*. The film explicitly raises the question of what constitutes filmmaking. When Sally and Pablo argue in *The Tango Lesson*, he stings her by saying he has not seen her direct in all the time they have spent together. Sally retorts that he is too busy looking at himself to observe what anyone else does. When he observes her in the mirror in the barbershop, as she watches his friends dance, it is not only a significant change in Pablo's self-involvement, but it draws the viewer's attention to the kind of direction that the film puts on show. There is no iconic image of the director behind a movie camera or yelling through a megaphone. When Sally is looking for locations in Buenos Aires, she no longer even has the compact camera with which she took photographs in Paris.

Her one attempt to give Pablo direction, suggesting that he might cry in a scene, leads to an argument that ends with Sally storming off, shouting at Pablo: 'Because of course, I haven't been doing anything this last year, have I? I haven't been watching you, preparing you, creating a role in my head.' As she walks away, there is a cut to a shot of her hand moving over paper, and then a cut out to show her in a hotel room rather than her study. It is the last of several hotel rooms in which we have seen Sally working. On every previous occasion, the camera was by the door, looking sideways on at the bed. In this moment of transformation, it is in the 'guardian angle' position, looking down from the ceiling, slightly canted like the repeated shot that showed Sally at work on *Rage* (1996) in her study in London. Indeed, here in Buenos Aires she is surrounded by a similar mass of paper: writing and images are strewn over the bed. She is not writing, however, but sobbing, hard and messily.

Shrill phone rings cut into the sound of her sobs. Phones have been instruments of miscommunication throughout the film, even as they held out the promise of connection. Sally answers, in a medium close-up that suggests a movement from the God's-eye-view idea of the director to a perspective that reflects engagement and exchange. Through the conversation with an American movie executive who thinks the new film 'sounds kind of intriguing' and wants bankable stars, Sally moves from a quietly contemplative tone to a firm, clear one in which she delivers the kiss-off: 'I thought after the last film you might trust my decisions.' Dropping the receiver, she leans back and watches the play of light on the ceiling. Sally finds her voice by asking another to trust in it. By refusing the misdirections of the executive she reconnects with the source of cinema, the play of light over surfaces. There will be no more location photographs, no more note-writing, no more shutting herself away in her room and no more creating roles in her head. Like Orlando, she finds her voice by looking at the world and letting the world take the lead.

Filmmaking is distilled to a remarkable essence: following. Directors are usually seen as leaders, decision-makers. This is especially true of directors who, like Potter, are referred to as auteurs. The phrase *politique des auteurs* was coined by François Truffaut in 1954 when he was a young critic writing for *Cahiers du cinéma*, and wondering how directors such as Howard Hawks and John Ford produced consistently excellent and idiosyncratic movies across a number of genres despite working on the studio system's production line. Before Truffaut mooted that the internal consistency of a group of divergent films might point to their director as being their author, responsible for their meaning, commercial directors were seen as players in a system. Truffaut and several other *Cahiers du cinéma* associates – including Alain Resnais, Eric Rohmer and Jean-Luc Godard – went on to make films that were infused with the sharp visual style and verbal panache of their American heroes. They combined an avant-garde hands-on approach to filmmaking with feature production, often writing their own films. They became the first generation of directors-as-stars, as *Cahiers du cinéma* continued its auteurist tradition by seeking out interviews with directors in order to create a two-way conversation between audience and author. Godard went on to participate in group-authored film projects around 1968, deflecting auteurist attention as part of his larger Marxist desire to undermine hierarchies, at around the same time as French literary studies was declaring that the author was dead.

Auteurism began as an important way of understanding and valuing the work of directors dismissed as cogs in a machine. In doing so, it argued for the director as an artist comparable to a painter or literary author, someone whose mark was on every aspect of their work. It inspired filmmakers around the world to strike out independently of national or commercial film finance and to take control of the filmmaking process. Yet filmmaking is not unidirectional: while there may be only one director on set, ideas flow in multiple directions. Collaboration is the practical expression of *I-Thou* auteurism during the production process, and it leaves its narrative trace in Potter's films. Each of the films leads its protagonist from inventing a language for solo lifts to mirroring others in a Libertango. When asked whether she considers herself an auteur given her emphasis on collaboration, Potter replies that 'everybody that we think of traditionally as an auteur also collaborated, perhaps even more than I do. So, I don't see them as contradictory ideas' (in Widdicombe 2003). Kristy Widdicombe asks why this is not more generally acknowledged, and Potter goes on to say that 'maybe female directors are more willing to give credit to the people that they work with because women know that there is an enormous amount of invisible labour involved in cinema, and women historically have usually done the invisible work in the home and the workplace' (in ibid.).

The feminism of naming collaboration prompts Corinn Columpar to name Potter an 'auteure' to mark the difference of her approach (2001: 108). Columpar relates this to Potter's use of the dancing body in *The Tango Lesson*, arguing that her 'attention to corporeality [acts] as a horizon of possibility for the articulation of a female subjectivity grounded in [the] embodiment' that Sally learns from Pablo (2001: 113). The body as symbol for the 'invisible labour' behind the camera defines Potter as an artisan; attention to labour redefines the artiste as a serious collaborator; and performance's ability to reshape the gaze changes the definition of filmmaker as artist. It allows the auteure to express herself not only through her own body, but through its engagement with others. Collaboration is signalled to the viewer through different kinds of touch, whether it is a tango or the simple gesture of Sally and Pablo holding hands as they walk into the synagogue. Formally, this is visible through a repeated movement from shot/reverse-shot editing, as in the arguments between Sally and Pablo, to shots in which both characters are equally in the frame. With cinematographer Alexei Rodionov on

Orlando and *Yes*, Potter experimented with various swaying figure-of-eight-like shots that circle between two characters, creating loops of linked close-ups and two-shots that allow for a focus on each character, and yet unite them at the same time.

This spirit of collaboration is given voice in the songs that close *Orlando*, *The Tango Lesson* and *The Man Who Cried*. Not only do the lyrics bring together I and You, but the songs in *Orlando* and *The Tango Lesson* create a listening space shared by the characters and the viewer due to their ambiguous relationship to the narrative world: is there really an angel at the end of *Orlando*, or are we in Orlando's imagination? Does Sally really sing to Pablo, or is this a magical scene from her imagined film? The ambiguity, not the answer, is what is significant. It subtly advertises the ways in which only film can create this specific kind of shared space through its combination of word, sound and image projected through time to an imagined viewer. Blurring the character's interior and exterior worlds, it also blurs the line between film and viewer, pulling us in even at the moment – just before the credits roll – that it is supposed to be pushing us out. Playing on our ability to listen, it asks of us an openness like the film's and the filmmaker's.

The conceit of *Rage* (2009) is that we are watching a film as an unseen filmmaker called Michelangelo shoots it on his cameraphone. We are in Michelangelo's point of view but we know nothing about him. He is not a grandstanding documentary-maker who signs his films by appearing in the frame. Even his lines are inaudible because they come from behind the phone, whose small lens and microphone are pointed at the people he has come to interview. It is rare that his questions need to be audible, however: his interviewees, even those initially reluctant to talk, tell him that they come to talk to him because of his ability to listen. Many of them underestimate him because he is a child and brown-skinned. They see him as passive because he listens rather than intervening.

The course of the film reveals that listening is an act of non-violent resistance: Michelangelo's presumed passivity induces frank confessions about oppression and abuses in the fashion business from his interviewees, which he posts online. The web's democratisation of journalism, which is happening at the same time as conventional journalistic outlets are increasingly muzzled by big business, has created an avid audience listening out for exposés like Michelangelo's. People log on to hear the fashion industry confess its sins, and they act by arriving to protest outside the company where Michelangelo has been making his film. Like Potter's, his auteurial presence is that of the listening ear. At the same time as it redefines the auteur as someone who listens rather than whose word is God, it draws attention to the root meaning of audience: those who listen.

Towards the end of *Yes*, She literally calls the cinematic audience God when she turns on her digital video camera, places it in the foreground so that its screen fills the frame and she appears as an image within the image. 'God, if you exist', she says, 'I need to confess.' Having established this connection between God and the audience who watch her pixellated form on the camera's screen, she stops speaking out loud. The rest of her monologue is delivered as a voice-over rather than to camera and so shares the same blurred status as the songs 'Coming Through' and 'I am You'. The scene draws on, and draws together, the cinematic convention of the internal voice-over, which has been used throughout the film and particularly for the Aunt's dying monologue, and traditions of speaking inside one's head to a divinity. She's thoughts are tied up in the contradictions that bind together cinema's absent presence (the performers and audience never coincide in time so each has to imagine the other) as she meditates on her lack of faith in the God she is addressing. Yet she begins her internal monologue with another kind of spiritual language, a request that could be seen as the artist's plea to an imagined audience and, at the same time, the essence of prayer: 'Please speak to me, just once.' The desire to be heard and the desire to be answered are interconnected, as they are when Pablo asks, 'Are you looking at me?'

She ends with a paradoxical request, out loud once more, that God forgive her 'for not believing in you'. Addressing God as 'you' creates an intimacy by refusing the shock and awe implied in using the capitalised, gendered and singular He. In the film, He is the name given to her lover, who arrives immediately and surprisingly as she asks her final question. Is He the sign from God that she has been forgiven, or at least heard? Perhaps He has overheard She's final question, and by announcing his arrival marks his forgiveness for her initial inability to see and believe in him as more than a figure of Orientalist fantasy. If He has been listening offscreen, then he is sugges-tively aligned with that other divine He. God and the power of forgiveness are made human and loving, in the same way as Pablo brings the angel and its blessing down to earth. This is the power of listening. The audiences who gather around Potter after screenings may not realise it, but as they are looking to her as a conduit of emotion and affect, she is looking to them as the same. The viewer is the only one who can speak back to the film, who can listen, understand and bless it with her presence. For Potter as an *I-Thou* auteure, each film is a small prayer risking the absent audience not listening.

Quejas de Bandoneón: Struggling

Potter's films, from *Thriller* onwards, have intertwined protest and prayer in a kind of liberation theology, in which the struggle against oppression can become collabo-rative and recuperative action by being voiced and shared. 'Quejas de Bandoneón', composed by Juan de Díos Filiberto, is the tango that draws Sally in to witness Pablo's performance at the start of *The Tango Leson. Quejas* means complaints, an allusion to the tone of the bandoneón, 'a larger, more expressive version of the accordion, prob-ably brought to Argentina by the earliest immigrants from Germany, [which is] the key instrument and identifiable sound of the tango' (Potter 1997e: 3). Right from the start, Sally is compelled by tango's plaintive expression of the pain of lovers and slaves. Tango's ability to move its listeners' bodies and hearts is rooted in its ability to voice pain. As Sally will discover, the bandoneón also complains because it is the voice of the lover who has been unheard or misunderstood. Sally and Pablo enjoy many ecstatic dances, but age, gender, class and national identity create tensions that lead to tears in rehearsal when Pablo pushes Sally too hard, and jealousy in the milongas when Sally dances with other men. Tango tells of imperfect communication and the dance itself does not always say what it means or mean what it says. A protest against slavery and poverty that was received as colonialist spectacle in Europe, an equality between leaders and followers that has been portrayed as – and used to portray – violent gender inequity, tango brings this conflicted history into each dance. As it resonates with the private selves of the dancers, it can set up further miscommunication.

Tango might well model a 'politics of friendship', as Erin Manning suggests, because that politic 'is about disagreement, about misunderstanding, about the necessity to listen in order to be heard in order to listen again' (2007: 46). Manning's politics could describe the arc of Potter's films. Listening in order to be heard acts as a hinge moment in each narrative, an auteurial trace of Potter's collaborative practice. At the heart of *Yes* is the scene on which the whole film hinges, the argument between She and He in a car park, in which he rejects her as a 'bitch' and she calls him a 'terrorist' and 'bigot'. She lets go of her rage at He's sexual insults when he speaks of his loss of 'pride and honour in this game / Where even to pronounce my name / Is an impossibility.' Rather than projecting his loss by rejecting her, he names his vulnerability as racism and Islamophobia (and her part in them through her white-skin privilege). She responds: 'I hear you. Tell me more.' A face-to-face circuit of communication has been created with great difficulty, after an argument predicated on deep fears that set man against woman, poor against rich and East against West. When He compares She's hurt pride to his daily experience of racism, they can find a common ground in realising the similarity of their fears. As tears gather in his red-rimmed eyes, he describes, haltingly, how he 'fight[s] / For every little thing', only to be interrupted by her cellphone. She answers to receive the news that her aunt is on the verge of death in a hospice in Belfast, and upbraids herself 'I didn't call. / Oh why didn't I call?' There is more listening to be done.

One urgent circuit of communication has been interrupted by another that reminds She of her failure to communicate. Like the telephones in *The Tango Lesson* and *Yes*, language is fraught with risks of miscommunication. It is a vessel, like a telephone or the filmmaker, through which communication occurs. Language requires the same virtuosity and mutual understanding as *ochos*, dagger-like tango steps that could injure the performers or make them look astonishing. Risky and glorious, spoken and written language stand in Potter's films for the difficulty of communication: that is, the difficulty of filmmaking. Comparing film to literature, Potter asks: 'What about the editor of the novel? What about the publishers of the book? What about the teachers of the writer who wrote the book?' (in Widdicombe 2003). Even writing, the most auteurial of activities, is manifestly a collaborative exercise in listening. Writing is crucial to Potter's auteurial identity. It is the moment when the filmmaker has the most control over the direction of the film. As *The Tango Lesson* shows, writing and rewriting makes up the bulk of the writer-director's working life and so stands in for the whole process of filmmaking.

Writing is like a solo lift: inventive and innovative, a generative area for the filmmaker to play with ideas. Like a solo lift, however, it is very different from the collaborative process of filmmaking and can often obscure or vitiate it. When Pablo refuses Sally's direction, she realises that by creating Pablo's character in her head she has been as narcissistically self-determined as Pablo and his constant rehearsals with the mirror. Like the mirror, the script and the writing identity have to be discarded for the film to come into being. As Potter explains:

> I realised that filmmaking was always going to be an expensive, slow, arduous, uphill bloody battle. The only part of my craft that I could keep practising everyday was writing. So it actually *is* what I do – that's the loneliness of the long-distance filmmaker. *Orlando* took seven years of writing, ten weeks of shooting, three months of editing. So *Orlando* consists of the consequences of work done in writing: that's where you organise and refine visual, conceptual and aural information. It manifests on paper as an instruction, but it's really a means of thinking. To paraphrase Gertrude Stein: 'The thought occurs at the moment the pencil hits the page.' That's the moment of 'is-ness'. But it is absolutely true that at the moment of the beginning of the shoot, all that writing is but a snakeskin to be shed in order for the other thing to emerge through the multiple decisions that a director makes. The director's work is, I totally agree with auteur theorists, another form of writing, and editing is another. You reorganise and reshape and therefore rewrite what you wrote in the first place. It's not finished when the film is over. You start writing director's statements and giving interviews in which you try and rewrite what you were doing. So that rewriting goes on and on. (Interview with author, September 2006).

Writing is a rehearsal, and like dance rehearsal, it can be painful. As the bandoneón's moan is essential to tango, writing's pain is part of its importance in the crafting and narratives of Potter's films. Writing is a way of listening in order to be heard, listening for the 'thought [that] occurs the moment the pencil hits the page'. That listening could teach the writer to listen to others – collaborators, critics and viewers – as they contribute to the process of rewriting.

Zum: Critiquing

'Zum' soundtracks the Fourth Lesson, in which Sally and Pablo dance together for the first time in a 'politics of friendship' rather than as teacher and pupil. Both the spiralling piano solo and its dance accompaniment exemplify the circuit of constructive criticism and/as collaboration. This piece, like 'Libertango', was composed by Astor Piazzolla, celebrated (and fiercely criticised) as the inventor of modern tango as a compositional and experimental form, and it is played here by Osvaldo Pugliese, considered to be Piazzolla's greatest interpreter; the two men recorded a legendary 1994 concert called 'Finally Together' (see Beach 2001). Shaped by Pugliese's more traditional playing style, Piazzolla's inventions were able to enter tango's mainstream, modelling the writer-performer relationship as a collaborative dialogue, one in which critique occurs through conversation. Such dialogue is always present for Potter's onscreen writers, who model their vocation not as auteurial control, but as a performance in which – like Sally in Hollywood – they speak truth to power.

The speechwriting Skater (Dennis Greenwood) in *London Story* and a journalist (George Yiasoumi) in *The Man Who Cried* draw attention to writing's public and political function as critique. Devastatingly honest fashion critic Mona Carvell (Judi Dench) in *Rage* (2009) brings together the artistic and journalistic aspects of writing. She talks specifically about fashion as a language that, because it is metaphorical, communicates and miscommunicates its designer's auteurial vision. As an 'internal' critic, Mona begins as a caricature whose name – moaner cavil – is an unsubtle dig at the unsubtler critics who have attacked Potter over the years. Mona, with the full force of Dench's waspish and regal intelligence, spits provocation and cynicism presented as the honest truth. Intent on effect, she delights in taking oppositional positions for their own sake. Condemning the emptiness of Merlin's grand designs, she is like the child in Hans Christian Andersen's 'The Emperor's New Clothes' who takes delight in pointing out the emperor's nudity (see Andersen 2008: 3–16). Mona draws attention to Michelangelo's similar role as he points the camera at the fashion industry and lets it reveal its naked ambition – and beneath that, its naked vulnerability. As Hollis Robbins argues in her fascinating reading, 'The Emperor's New Critique', the child's desire to 'speak truth to power' could also be read as the conservative response to experimental artists who are like 'Emperors, cloistered in [their] closets … sifting through and trying on new ideas' (2004: 662).

Together, Mona and Michelangelo investigate the nature and effect of criticism, moving away from the value of voicing a single truth. Mona is talking to Michelangelo when the final attack, on the third catwalk show, occurs. Her customary moue of disdain shocked from her face by the offscreen sounds of shots and screams, Mona offers her final verdict on Merlin's work: 'His clothes are shrouds.' She salutes Merlin's ability to speak of and for the 'age of AIDS and the century of terror', but beyond that she accords his clothes a ritual significance, an ability to contain the naked fact of death that has haunted her monologues about ageing and decay. Mona's commentary stands as the most thorough account of Merlin's unseen collection, a little like the critical accounts that stand in for *The Gold Diggers*. Mona's fierce commitment to her own voice makes her sympathetic when she finds herself cast as oppositional by Tiny, who decides to buy the magazine for which she writes, and to offer editorial 'advice' on her column. She positions herself as a particularly active, expert viewer, one who participates in making the meaning of Merlin's work; because of the film's form, her act of collaboration takes place on the same plane as Merlin's, that of verbal description. This is the substance of the labour done by the weavers in 'The Emperor's New Clothes', who spin in the contemporary political, as opposed to traditional material, sense. Every character in *Rage* (2009) weaves their work in words. Even shy seamstress Anita de los Angeles (Adriana Barraza) describes – rather than doing – her invisible hems for the camera. *Rage* (2009) is a text/ile, a film (in the sense of a translucent fabric, as well as a work of cinema) of words, in which each speaker's contribution is an equal thread.

This lively cluster of competing and complementary voices, among which the viewer finds her own truth(s), was described by Mikhail Bakhtin, with reference to the novel, as 'dialogism'. Bakhtin, writing in a totalitarian state, was fiercely resistant to the coercive monologic truth of the kind shouted by the child. In *Subversive Pleasures*, Robert Stam undertakes a pioneering look at cinema as a dialogic form. In a counter-argument to the general suspicion of language, and film theory's in particular, he revives Bakhtin's thought that 'we do not "fall" into language/the symbolic, but are enriched and fulfilled by it' (1989: 5). His argument resonates with Potter's love of enriching her films with verbal language, and with her films' demonstration that, through dialogic exchange, we 'mutually "author" one another ... by revealing oneself to another, through another, with another's help' (1989: 6). Bakhtin's phrase 'the mirror of others' words' seems particularly poignant in *Rage* (2009), where the characters never interact onscreen, but only in our imagined collation of their words (in Stam 1989: 5).

Stam points out that the 'Bakhtinian predilection for aural and musical metaphors – voices, intonation, accent, polyphony – argues an overall shift in priority from the visually predominant logical space of modernity ... as a way of restoring voice to the silenced ... Voice suggests a metaphor of seepage across boundaries' (1989: 19). In *Rage* (2009), in particular, the polyphony of voices – which Bakhtin, for their different accents and class registers, would call heteroglossic – stands as an alternative to the visual register, a 'metaphor of seepage' in contrast with the fixed iconicity of the image. Potter's films use writing (and its relations, language and music) as a way of rethinking film's fixity from within film itself. Screening the act of writing subtly presents Potter's theorisation of herself as a filmmaker always on the move across boundaries. When Sally leans over her handwritten pages to write and rewrite, we are seeing Potter thinking through and talking about the act of filmmaking as change.

With *The Tango Lesson*, Sally is not writing an autobiographical film, but rather a meditation on what it means to make a film about filmmaking as a female, collaborative filmmaker. Potter is struggling with the conundrum that she describes to Widdicombe: 'auteur is much more readily used as a term for male directors than female directors because people don't concern themselves with the profound collaborations that men have. But as soon as a woman has a collaborator it's thought of as "Oh, it's not really hers then"' (2003). Orlando learns to listen and collaborate through becoming female; that is what makes her a writer, in Potter's version. *The Tango Lesson* expresses a similar arc through the revaluation of following – and of filmmaking. Putting writing so visibly onscreen as an activity that precedes and prefigures filmmaking, Potter connects it to labour, performance and the artist's identity. Writing is like the 'invisible labour' done by women, in the world and behind the camera.

Making visible the behind-the-scenes labour of writing draws attention to other forms of invisible labour. Writing is aligned, from the start of *The Tango Lesson*, with cleaning as well as with tango. This is what the Hollywood producers fail to understand. Their focus on Sally as auteur is gratifying, but revealed to be disrespect for the source of her voice in labour and in community. When Sally puts the phone down on the producer, she moves from auteur to *auteure*, taking off the glamorous robe of the Director in which she has become entangled. That means rethinking conventional cinema's hierarchy of listening and speaking, seeing and being seen. Tango gives Sally a poetics that is also what contemporary poet Joan Retallack calls a *poethics*, in which 'the pursuit of the good and the ethical are inextricably tied up with ... avant-garde poetic practice' (1994: 371). A poethics 'locates the making of meaning in a collaborative engagement with interdynamically developing forms' because it prizes the work of listening and investigation (1994: 355). Poethics moves writing from an auteurial, performative command to the creation of a space for collaboration.

El Flete: Moving

When it is collaborative and deeply heard, language – as a form of 'world'-travel through dialogue and translation – offers an ethical solution to the pain of solitary labour. Pascual Contursi's lyrics for Vincente Greco's 'El Flete' suggest that is what tango can offer in the song's recommendation that when you are done being lied to and beaten by the bosses, you should take a transport (*flete*) 'pa' la otra poblacion', to another town. Tango's contained movement is an analogy for such a healing escape. Sally dances to 'El Flete' when she visits a milonga in Buenos Aires. It is the sound of opening up to strangers rather than her chosen teachers, of 'surrender[ing] to the subtle signals in the private world of the dance' (Potter 1997e: 12). These wordless surrenders find their parallel in Sally's final tango with Pablo, where she sings to him. Language in Potter's films is at its most responsive, and therefore healing, when it is sung or recited. Song condenses and crystallises language, and demands a clarity of expression that is allied to its association with self-expression. In song, language collaborates with music to move.

Potter has said frequently that all of her films aspire to be musicals, where song brings together moving (physical) and moving (emotional). Potter's voice-overs and monologues have a musical quality, in that they act like 'numbers' punctuating and narrating the film, and in their deft, compelling attention to language's sensual as well as intellectual qualities. A process of integration and communication develops from *Thriller*, where all gestures are stagey performances, towards full integration of music, movement and poetic speech in *Yes* and a striking combination of documentary tropes and theatricality in *Rage* (2009). In *Thriller*, Mimi's voice-over stands literally outside the film and *The Gold Diggers*' confrontational 'Empire Song' uses the language of jazz improvisation to stimulate the audience to political thought by presenting information with a difference. The interiority it expresses is not one of emotional subjectivity, but of critical thought. Its distinct rejection of the prettiness of melody charms Ruby as she struggles to escape from the association of prettiness with vacuity.

In *Orlando*, singing is the work of professionals, allowing Orlando to develop his skill as an audience from sleeping through the Herald's song to opening up and allowing the Khivan singer's performance to alter him. John Durham Peters describes this kind of audience as 'in contrast to the distraction theorists, who see in popular entertainment exile from authenticity' (1999: 34). Orlando becomes like Peter's nomadic 'campers ... [who] see neither loss nor lamentation, but lightness' (ibid.) in allowing themselves to be absorbed in the moment through a performance. With the dance in *The Tango Lesson*, it is clear that Potter has moved from *The Gold Diggers*'

Brechtian use of song to using 'lightness' to engage the viewer. Tango's pleasures bring together the 'lightness' of dazzling dance with the music's 'loss and lamentation'.

The Man Who Cried employs Roma music as part of a cinematic language in which sensory pleasure and serious political storytelling are combined. Singing is naturalised in the film in two ways: as professional performance at the opera, and as an intimate communication. There is a sharp contrast between the costumes, sets and stage necessary to arrange listening in the opera house and the spontaneous culture of song and audience in the shtetl where Suzie grows up and the Roma encampment where she sings with Cesar's friends. Her father sings her a lullaby, while the Roma later sing a lament as they march in a funeral procession. These are perhaps the most embodied and expressive of Western musical forms, and they are dismissed because of their attribution to women and non-white others. Suzie is a singer, and sings more than she speaks. Her two key songs, 'Dido's Lament' and 'Gloomy Sunday', carry loss and lamentation in their titles, moods and musical modes. Potter takes the negative cultural associations and makes them positive, contrasting the emotional connection and healing that comes through lamentation's integration into lived experience with the opera company's false equation of art and money.

Suzie's songs are explicitly affective, performed to constitute a community of feeling. David Abram, working to recover the place of the sensorium in Western culture and discourse, writes that the phenomenologist Edmund Husserl 'discerned that there was an inescapable affinity, or affiliation, between … other bodies and one's own. The gestures and expressions of these other bodies, viewed from without, echo and resonate one's own bodily movements and gestures, experienced from within. By an associative "empathy", the embodied subject comes to recognise these other bodies as other centres of experience, other subjects' (1997: 37). As an auteure, Potter works to find a form of self-expression that is centred through gesture and sound in affect's associative empathy. Orlando's openness occurs outside the conventional high art song of his culture, at a moment when the linguistic content of the song is incomprehensible to him, and to most viewers. Yet the emotional content and the performer's incredible vocal skill are both in abundant evidence, and his willingness to understand the song on its own terms, rather than translating it into his, is what allows him to be moved.

Listening gives song its ability to heal because it recognises it as a gift, uniting the word's senses of *present* and *talent*. To listen is to keep the gift in circulation. Suzie's voice is her passport through Europe, not because of its authenticity of self-expression, but because of its ability to respect and reflect the identities of her audiences. Her gift as a performer is to be able to make a gift of her beautiful voice. She acts as a channel for the Welsh music teacher who heals his own hurt at being forced to speak English by teaching Suzie English songs so she can express herself. Singing with Taraf de Haïdouks, she accepts the invitation to be part of the community when she contributes her voice to the song. Their performance is also a contest in which the prize is the respect of the listeners, yet bravura performance is a form of self-expression that is not unproblematic. Dante, who is in some sense Suzie's reflection, believes that his voice is a gift from God, and this makes him an authoritarian bully because it stops him listening. Rather than keep to the pure, European vocal line she had been taught, Suzie imitates – or rediscovers – an Eastern vocal break that draws on her talent without showcasing it. By not holding back, and by listening, Suzie finds her voice.

Pensálo Bien: Translating

Rage (2009) is entirely built from a series of soliloquies that showcase Potter's ear for writing in multiple registers of language, on the edge between representation and parody. These numbers are bravura performances by writer and actor. We hear languid model-speak, peppered with 'like, you know', pretentious designer gibberish and the ridiculous banalities of marketing. There are also surprising, poetic uses of language to reveal hidden depths to the characters, as when seamstress Anita weaves metaphors in her broken English of the immigrant's visibility and invisibility by describing her work. Detective Homer is known as the Bard for his frequent quotations from Shakespeare. Literary quotation makes him stand out from the repeated platitudes of PR man Otto (Jakob Cedergren), which he thinks are sparklingly original but are evacuated of meaning. Shakespeare sounds only one register of Homer's authentic voice; he can also speak street, appealing to Michelangelo 'brutha [chest thump] to brutha' to hand over his video footage in brown-skin solidarity, an invitation that Michelangelo refuses.

Homer, like Michelangelo, is an outsider in the fashion world, a world that he views with some disdain. He also doubles Michelangelo as an investigator; however, he is searching for a single truth not defined by his own desire to become, but by the state for which he works. In a revealing monologue, he sets out the choice he made as an adolescent, that he would 'rather be the chaser than the chased'. In order to survive with 'the cuffs in [his] hands and not on [his] wrists', Homer has accepted dominant culture's binary, expressed pithily by George W. Bush as 'you're either with us, or against us'. Dressing increasingly in conscious imitation of Shaft in order to shore up his identity as a lawman, Homer appears unsettled by Michelangelo's observant neutrality, his gradual attempt to find a third space between criminal and cop, visible and invisible, power and powerless. Oyelowo plays one of the film's most layered roles with verve, inhabiting the black cop with an almost Brechtian awareness of the blaxploitation cliché, suggesting the way in which his character, despite his self-assurance on the side of the Law, is wearing a mask and acting a part. It is his delivery of the smartly-written dialogue, accenting the quotations with Ebonics to suggest and renew the energy with which Shakespeare forged his language, that makes him so compelling and his character so fascinatingly fluid. His articulacy draws, as hip-hop does, on the reincorporation and mash-up of the dozens, while his fluency as a translator stems from his situated knowledge of both sides of the class and ethnicity divides.

Yes showed likewise that authentic dialogue does not have to mean inarticulate realism. He's co-workers Virgil, Whizzer and Billy all speak in the same iambic pentameter as the lovers, with their own intonations and registers. Virgil (Wil Johnson) has the rhythms of a gospel preacher while Whizzer (Raymond Waring) sounds more like a grime MC, using swearing as punctuation. A Glaswegian lost soul, Billy (Gary Lewis) is like a Ken Loach character with stories to match, poetically sung in a colloquial lilt. The men tell stories about their fears and disappointments through descriptions of their relationships to women. The way in which Potter threads hints of vulnerability through what seems like macho posturing and sexist banter shows that both her relationship to identity politics and her ear have developed a depth and sensitivity. Perhaps her ability to listen to men – especially working-class men – began in listening to tangos that combine a lightness of footwork with a record of 'los pesaos, patoteros y mentaos', the burdens, bullies and liars that make the struggling immigrant singer of 'El Flete' want to take a transport to the next town.

Listening to tango is a little like Orlando listening to the Khivan singer. Its mood imparts a general meaning, but the lyrics, especially those of older tangos, are almost untranslatable because they are written in a dense Argentinian Spanish slang that developed of a piece with the musical form. Not understanding is a familiar and educational experience in Potter's films, which include a startling array of languages in contravention of the received wisdom that the English-language film market abhors a subtitle. English and French are the primary languages of Potter's films, but a viewer could also hear Icelandic, Russian, Turkic, Spanish, Italian, Yiddish, Roma and Arabic, as well as a parallel diversity of musical 'languages', modes or tonalities. The interchange and exchange between languages and their speakers in Potter's films is always both freighted and fraught, summed up by a scene in *The Man Who Cried*. Lola teaches Suzie all the French she needs in a single line: 'A very important word that you must know is *amour*.' Love is rooted in communication, which is sited in the proliferation of languages rather than a reductive monolingualism. *Amour* is Lola's way of communicating that she has listened to the men around her and understood. It is her plan for survival.

'Pensálo Bien' soundtracks a scene in *The Tango Lesson* that suggests learning to translate the language of love is exactly a form of survival. At a milonga, Pablo leaves Sally without a word, crossing the floor to dance with his former partner. As Sally watches them with an unreadable expression, an English tango fan offers her a translation of the song's lyrics. '"Think hard before you take this step. / Because once you've taken it, there may be no turning back. / Think hard because I've loved you so much, / And you've thrown it away, / Perhaps for another love."' These are the only tango lyrics that we hear translated into English. They seem to speak Sally's inner thoughts as directed at Pablo. As the singer's voice and the translator's voice are both male, they also suggest Pablo's thoughts, warning Sally to think hard before she confuses, in the title of another tango on the soundtrack (performed, like 'Pensálo Bien', by Juan D'Arienzo), 'Amor y Celos', love and jealousy. It is not the only moment of connection and openness that happens through translation. When the waiter offers Sally her 'mezzaluna', he translates her wordless yet eloquent gesture into Spanish. He is at once listening to her body's communication and suggesting that she has the ability to understand Spanish within her, if she can listen to tango as he listened to her gesture.

Gallo Ciego: Flying

Much later, after her journey through listening with Pablo, immediately after she puts the phone down on the Hollywood executive, Sally takes a taxi through the Buenos Aires night. There are multiple layers of reflection in the rearview mirror and the windows. The patterns and shine repeat the play of light on the hotel ceiling as a visually stunning equivalent for Sally's new-found meditative attitude to her film. But the scene shifts from reflection to engagement when she catches the driver's eye in the rearview mirror. With two Spanish words (and one Italian one), she bridges the divide between the white tourist lost in her thoughts and the Argentinian driver. '"Gallo Ciego." Pugliese.' It is the name of the tango on the radio and its composer, the legendary band leader Osvaldo Pugliese. The driver is so surprised that he stops the car so he can turn around to talk to his passenger, whom he has presumed is just a tourist. In a version of Sasha's lost comment on Orlando's lack of knowledge about Russia, he tells her that one has to have lived and suffered to understand tango. Sally does not retort with an account of her suffering with Pablo and the film, but listens instead to his comment and to the tango.

There are no lyrics, only music, but the title, which means 'Blind Cock', is a richly suggestive comment on masculinity. It is a party game, the Spanish equivalent of Blind Man's Bluff, whose name derives from a situation in cock-fighting, which was popular in Buenos Aires into the twentieth century, in the same working-class milieu as tango. Cocks that got blinded and continued to fight were described as 'pelear de oído', fighting by ear. So the tango's name is a mixture of bravado ('gallo' was often used to mean tough guy in folk songs) and vulnerable dependence on listening (see Gesualdi 2004). The tango gives Sally a space to forgive Pablo and herself and to become ready to hear his vulnerability before the mirror. Through her interactions with the tango and the taxi driver, she is able to see beyond Pablo's 'gallo' stance. He becomes the first fully-fledged male-bodied character in Potter's work because he is situated, via tango, in a community of working men.

Working class Buenos Aires, where tango originated, was a hotbed of extensive strike actions in the early twentieth-century among the strongly-unionised European immigrant proletariat. Between 1901 and 1907, mass strikes occurred regularly, with a total of 170,000 workers involved in 231 disputes in 1907 alone (see Mason 2007: 128–9), many on the docks where Sally and Pablo dance. Sally encounters their actual and metaphorical grandsons: the waiter, a shoe salesman, the cleaner at the hotel, the taxi driver, her tango teachers, the dancers in the milongas. Pugliese's name suggests that he was a descendant of the many working-class Italians who sailed for Buenos Aires. He was as well-known for his politics as his music, having been blacklisted for his membership of the Communist Party and occasionally jailed for such socialist gestures as paying his accompanists the same wage as himself. Pugliese gives his flightless, grounded rooster, the worker blinded by capitalism's burden, a sprightly, seductive tune, one of the most instantly recognisable of all tangos.

It is one of many paradoxical associations between birds, flight and song, on one hand, and masculinity, struggle and speechlessness on the other, that run through

Potter's oeuvre starting from her performance work. In *Auk* (1973), a collaborative performance piece devised with the John Bull Puncture Repair Kit Company, a man carrying suitcases tenderly encouraged a suspended chicken to fly and talked to it about his mother, a seagull. The angel in *Auk*'s companion piece, *Fallen Angels* (1973) wore a 'White Bathing Cap – which hides all his hair. He wears a pair of Flying Goggles, White Underpants and is otherwise naked. He has a pair of White Angels [sic] Wings strapped to his back. His body is patterned with "FRAGILE" sticky backed labels' (Potter, Lansley and Diana Davies in Jordan 1992: 31). These winged but wounded beings represent the male principle in Potter's films, their vulnerable grace in contrast to conventions of gender.

Both *Orlando* and *The Tango Lesson* use male performers to give body to the angel, reconnecting the abstract ethereal being to a fleshly, vulnerable world. The Angel in *Orlando* is preceded by the distinctive song of peacocks, which is first heard when Orlando is first weighed down under her immense crinoline. Peacocks, the male of the species, are flightless because of their massive ornamental tails which, along with their fluting call, form their mating display. Orlando is likewise disabled by the dress that is both a sexual and an economic mating display. Famous for ostentatious show being the male's role, the peacock in *Orlando* audibly marks the historical moment just before male clothing in the West shifted from ornamentation to drab conformity. The twentieth century Angel, by contrast, wears a fabulous costume that evokes Barbarella's futuristic sexuality and gay clubwear (London's best-known gay club, frequented by Jarman, is called Heaven) as much as it does medieval paintings. Embracing ornamentation's femininity has allowed him to fly, just as embracing androgynous fashion has given Orlando mobility. Pablo is a more multilayered angel: his leaps are graceful, ostentatious and seductive, like a flighted peacock. When he embodies Delacroix's Angel, he does so by recognising the Angel's humanity in struggling with Jacob. Through the rest of the film, he works to bring together his masculinity and his angelic side, not as a show of force but of struggle and reciprocity. He is a blinded (pea)cock who reveals narcissism as the protection of a 'body patterned with "FRAGILE"' because of its race and class history.

Angels in Potter's films are neither the (female) wishy-washy wish-granters of new age popular culture, nor the (male) militaristic muscle visible in graphic novels and films such as *Constantine* (2005). They are not Wim Wenders' distant observers or a heavenly choir. Instead, they are reconnected by their androgyny to their Biblical role as messengers. David E. S. Stein, the editor of *The Contemporary Torah: A Gender-Sensitive Adaptation*, makes two important notes about angels in the Old Testament. Its Greek translation reflects the Hebrew by using 'the same term (angelos) either for a human or a divine messenger ... one term that the Bible often uses for messenger is "ish" ... [which] would have reliably evoked in the audience's minds the sense of "ish as representative functionary"' (2006: 406–7). Both men and women could send representatives in the ancient Near East, men sending men and women women. 'To the extent that the Torah presented its God as *beyond* gender ... God [was portrayed] either as an equal-opportunities employer of messengers or as dispatching non-gendered divine agents' (2006: 407; emphasis in original). Pablo comes to hover, like Orlando's Angel, between masculine and feminine as he reveals his vulnerability. Rather than feminising vulnerability, Potter transforms it. Having experienced the feminised position of following, Sally is able to hear Pablo's 'fighting by ear' and recast it as part of his febrile brilliance.

Milonga de Mis Amores: Collaborating

By ending with a tango, Potter advertises the film's co-authorship: while Sally sings Potter's words, she is dancing on Pablo's territory, moving in his idiom. Pablo and Sally become the collaborative auteur of *The Tango Lesson* when Pablo reveals his "FRAGILE" label in the final scene. Their final conversation is in French as a declaration of a shared space. French has been a *lingua franca* in Potter's work, not only between Pablo and Sally, but between Orlando and Sasha over the heads of the boorish English court. It is a mark of Orlando's sophistication and openness that he speaks another language. As he tells Sasha, 'la plupart des Anglais ne peut pas, ne veut pas, parler d'autres langues' ('Most English people can't – don't want to – speak another language'). Ginette Vincendeau notes critically that *The Man Who Cried* is 'a film set in Paris and made with some French money and behind-the-scenes French personnel,

Milonga de Mi Amor: Tango offers Sally and Pablo a 'politics of friendship'

but no French is heard save a couple of arias' (2001b: 54). French, however, is exactly the language that cannot be used in the tense atmosphere of *The Man Who Cried*, where being overheard and understood is a threat, not a route to communication. It is the only film in Potter's oeuvre where 'collaboration' has a negative meaning, given that Dante's collaboration with the Nazi invaders threatens Suzie's life. There can be no *lingua franca* – freely-shared tongue – in such a poisoned atmosphere.

Cesar speaks to Suzie in Roma, a language that neither she nor the audience can understand and that is not subtitled. The film guards its meaning closely despite the number of languages heard and written in it. Yet it has a similar arc to *The Tango Lesson* in many ways and, as an expression of Potter's auteure-ism, is the closest her films have come to a big-budget Hollywood musical, complete with showgirls in sequins and fan tails, however ironised. It brings the subtle depths of *The Tango Lesson*'s historical soundings into the foreground to make a clear statement about how the fear of the Other comes from not listening. Informed by her collaborative 'world'-travel with Veron, in *The Man Who Cried*, Potter creates an ensemble of historical characters who are outside her experience, with no source text but history books. Whereas Orlando arrived in the present, and Ruby, Celeste and Mimi were of both the present and the past, Suzie, Lola, Dante and Cesar stay inside their historical moment. Each character has depth and shade, even Lola and Dante who present themselves as all surface.

Their richly-coloured world is a dramatic contrast to the black-and-white, both film stock and racial, of *Thriller* and *The Gold Diggers*. Potter had made an important intervention into race politics through her collaboration with Colette Laffont, but from the Khan in *Orlando* onwards, her films develop a regard for non-white men on a listening curve shaped by global change. *The Man Who Cried* and *Yes* contain nothing as schematic as the mirror moment when Sally and Pablo act as each other's reflections, but are predicated likewise on a white woman and a non-white man journeying towards a liberating collaboration. *Rage* (2009) completely alters the colour balance of *Rage* (1996): rather than the stark, dramatic contrast between brilliantly-coloured dresses and white skin, there is a narrative about racial identities differently inflected by place, gender and class. Bringing together male performers of colour Simon Abkarian, John Leguizamo, David Oyelowo and Riz Ahmed, it makes the vulnerabilities of non-white men in the contemporary West the motor of the drama. It places Michelangelo's brown male hand on the camera.

Through their developing regard, Potter's films become 'accented', in Hamid Naficy's term for cinema from the developing world. They speak with an inflection that is heard in her use of multiple languages, in her attentiveness to the cultural history of the music and colours she uses and in the way in which her male protagonists come to speak for themselves. Their accent marks them out, deliberately, from mainstream cinematic production. André Aciman writes of the immigrant's life that an 'accent is a tell-tale scar left by the unfinished struggle to acquire a new language. But it is much more … An accent marks the lag between two cultures, two languages, the space where you let go of one identity, invent another, and end up being more than one person though never quite two' (in Moor 2005: 205). The accent acts as a reminder that, as Sara Ahmed observes, 'there is more than one *and* more than two in any encounter' (2000: 141; emphasis in original). In *Yes* all the one-to-one conversations refer outwards, and the lovers are catalysed by their effort of listening to the political histories behind each other's accented speech. The rhyme of iambic pentameter sounds out the film's focus on romantic love and the (dis)place(ment) of the accented other.

Ella Shohat observes that in mainstream depictions of relationships 'between Third World men and First World women, national identity (associated with the white female character) is relatively privileged over sexual identity (associated with the dark male character) … Third World men['s] punishment for inter-racial desire is simultaneously accompanied by gratification for a male sexual gaze as ephemerally relayed by a darker man' (1993: 64). From the moment that Orlando refuses to consummate imperialist or sexual desire in Khiva, Potter's films are working their way out of this conundrum. By *Yes*, it becomes the central expression of her auteurial listening. Potter not only inverts the classical Hollywood paradigm as asserted by Shohat, but – through her use of the iambic form – sets her lovers against the persistently tragic model of interracial love and imperial politics given its most influential form in Shakespeare's *Antony and Cleopatra*. In a recent NPR broadcast discussing *The Sheikh* (1921) in the context of contemporary anti-Arab prejudice in the US, presenter Neda Ulaby asked Jack Shaheen for his opinion of the film. Shaheen, a Palestinian-American professor who studies and advises TV shows on representations of Arabs in popular media, commented that 'he hadn't seen a feature film challenging the notions of love and ethnicity put forth in *The Sheik* until three years ago, when *Yes*, with Joan Allen, was released. "I think it's interesting to point out it took nearly a century to see a man from the Middle East honestly loving an American woman"' (Shaheen in Ulaby 2008). To get to *Yes*, Potter's poethics altered from 'how do I make a film about being a female artist?' to 'how do I make a film about the developing regard between a white woman and a non-white man?' Rather than a belief that gender is the only axis along which the world divides, what Potter derived from second-wave feminism was the value of process, of collaboration and of making visible the invisible, even – or rather, especially – when those suppressed in invisibility do not look or sound like her.

Listening for what is comprehensible in the Other is the key to the film's connection to the viewer, its ability to solicit her listening by awakening her memories of misunderstanding and being misunderstood. When Sally and Pablo tango in the rain after their reconnection at Saint Sulpice, their taxi's radio plays José Maria Contursi's 'Milonga de Mis Amores', in which the singer returns to the dancehall in which he danced with his past lovers. At the end of the second verse, he apostrophises the dancehall, which has fallen into disrepair, as 'you': 'sin embargo te olvidaron y en el callejón / tan sólo una guitarra te recuerda, criolla como vos, / y en su gemir tiembla mi ser.' 'Ah', he sings, 'they [his exes] have forgotten you, and in the alley / a lonely guitar remembers you, Creole like yours / and in its moan my being trembles' (author's translation). The guitar remembers by playing a tune that is creolised like tango.

The music stirs the singer's memory and shakes him open even though he wants to forget the memories of connection and community that the milonga symbolises. Music's profound connection to cultural and individual memory links *The Tango Lesson* and *The Man Who Cried*. Their demand that the audience engage in difficult listening, perhaps to languages or music that they do not understand, is part of Potter's radical reconception of auteureship. Erin Manning asks whether we could 'conceive of hearing as that which might lead us (if we listen carefully) to a notion of friendship that would circumvent the concept of hearth, of presence, of resemblance, affinity, analogy' (1997: 42). Potter's films ask if we could conceive of hearing as that which might lead us (if we listen carefully) to a notion of both love and auteur(e)ship that would circumvent the concept of the author/lover as a God who can only make the world in her own image.

Instead, the filmmaker is a human being wrestling with a wounded angel, who is (and is not) what Walter Benjamin, in his 1940 essay 'Theses on the Philosophy of History' called the angel of history, blown into the future by a 'storm … from Paradise' (1992b: 249). Histories blow through Potter's films as a storm of language and music. The auteure is borne aloft not by her power of annunciation, but her willingness to listen.

CHAPTER NINE

The Man Who Cried

SUZIE (voice-over):
And when he spoke it
Spoke my name
I heard my language
Once again
A music in
My inner ear
A voice was singing
Loud and clear.
 – Sally Potter, voice-over draft: Scene 142/143, *The Man Who Cried*, 2000c

The Man Who Cried began with an act of listening. In liner notes to the soundtrack, Potter writes that 'the original impulse came from music' (2000b). She wanted 'to find a way of telling the story where music was carrying emotional and spiritual truth with as much force as the image and characters' (ibid.), an unusual approach in a cinematic culture that values image over sound. Corinn Columpar notes that 'the soundtrack ... comes to assume an unprecedented prominence in this film insofar as it exerts a structuring influence on the narration. Music is woven throughout the entirety of the film, not only occasioning but also driving multiple incidents of cutting between one narrative high point and the next' (2006). Not only are the main characters all involved, in one way or another, in performing music, but their complex identities are represented and their relations negotiated through music that moves between opera and folk music, between the classical repertoire and new compositions, and between diegetic and non-diegetic.

Far from working merely to underscore plot or intensify audience emotion, music is the film's narrative. *The Man Who Cried*, more directly than any of Potter's other films, tells a story. Its temporal signature is not like *Orlando*'s, which spans centuries, nor does it have an intercutting narrative like *The Tango Lesson*'s. Unlike *Thriller* and *The Gold Diggers*, it happens in linear time, and although, like *Yes*, it is a politicised romance, it has a sense of urgency where the characters' arcs are dictated by the anticipated onrush of historical events. Unlike *Yes* and *The Tango Lesson*, *The Man Who Cried* is set in the historical past. Even more than *Orlando*, it is a period piece. It aspires to the emotional sweep and realism of a Hollywood war drama.

Its music is not conventional aural wallpaper, but nor is it melodramatic manipulation: it is a cry, a passionate articulation of the events of World War Two that focus the narrative, and of the emotions that exceed narrative's framework. The cry sounds out what cannot be spoken but demands a hearing. Potter writes that 'a cry is also another word for the voice in song, celebrating and expressing that which cannot be expressed any other way; the longing to be connected, the longing to transcend pain and oppression, the longing for joy and for love' (2000b). This is a film about the cry, which is at once 'a "voice" for those who were (and are) silenced; mourn[ing] for those who were lost; and celebrat[ion of] the survival of those who lived' (ibid.).

Describing the emotional force of music in *The Man Who Cried*, Potter comments that a 'voice in song can express truth and longing more clearly than in everyday language' (2000a: x). The cry's emotional truth and longing can also be a political and historical truth. In the 'Lav Angle' (Introduction) to *The Romano Drom Song Book*, Roma scholar Thomas Acton tells a story that speaks directly *The Man Who Cried*:

> When the [Roma] delegate from Macedonia [to the World Romani Congress],
>   Abdi Falk MP, returned, a young Rom called Oskar Mamut sang of him:
> 'Gelo sar bilbili
> Ano dur drom,
> Gilo te gilavel,
> Pe hike te rovel,
> Lacipe te anel.'
> He went like a nightingale, on the long road, to sing a song, *to cry for you*, to bring good fortune … Oskar Mamut intended this as a picture of all the work done at Congress. (1986: 2; emphasis added).

One of the book's editorial advisers was Donald Kenrick, an ethnolinguist who has focused his career on Romani. He advised Potter on *The Man Who Cried*, and it is possible that, through him, Potter encountered this song fragment. Its image, of an MP moving and moving, walking the long road to cry at a world congress, crystallises the power of song as both emotional expression and political force explored in *The Man Who Cried*. The listeners at the Romani Congress were able to understand Falik's cry, as Mamut's listeners were able to hear in his song the significance of Falik's action, because they were listening as part of a community for whom music and oral storytelling is of central importance. In their eyes, Mamut uses an appropriate form to relate the history of Falik's journey, and Falik used an appropriate form to address the Congress. It is unlikely that such a cry could have been heard and understood at the United Nations, or even – in all its emotional, communal and political dimensions – in mainstream cinema, where both music and tears are associated with the body, femininity, the non-white Other, sentimentality and overpowering states such as grief and madness.

Falik's cry is both tears and music, both the emotion and the artistic form used to express it. In *The Man Who Cried*, the line between a song and a sob is blurred as songs inspire, and often sound like, tears. The film's sound world includes operatic arias that imitate powerful emotions within the conventions of European high art, as well as Yiddish and Roma music that is associated, culturally and because of the terrible events of the Holocaust, with an overwhelming sadness. Music's plangent moan refigures the tears cried by the men in the film as a kind of music. Male vulnerability is heard as artistic self-expression in tears, while Suzie's self-expression develops as she learns the songs that shape her.

Just as tangos shape and describe *The Tango Lesson*'s trajectory, so in *The Man Who Cried* song is associated with journeying on. The 'numbers' do not halt the plot, they move the characters both emotionally and kinetically. Suzie's ability to move her listeners becomes her passport. Music moves us emotionally because it travels, from singer to listener and from country to country. Suzie is a figure for music's survival through collaboration and cultural exchange. As Alex Ross describes in *The Rest is Noise*, many prewar twentieth century classical composers revivified traditional forms with an infusion of folk sounds, a project that was used for propagandist purposes by both fascists and communists and their ideas of the 'volk'. In the face of fascism's insistence on purity, *The Man Who Cried* sounds out miscegenation, subtly tracing the way in which culture is always a product of movement, change and exchange.

Only once does Suzie sing something that the viewer has not seen her learning from another character. In the mid-Atlantic, she sings for her supper with the ocean liner's band. Her choice of song is not designed to cheer the diners, however. 'Gloomy Sunday' has been haunted by morbid rumours since its composer's suicide. Suzie sings Billie Holiday's 1941 version, which used Sam Lewis's translation of Lázló Javór's Hungarian poem, with its invented third verse: 'Dreaming, I was only dreaming / I wake and I find you asleep in the deep of my heart, here / Darling, I hope that my dream never haunted you / My heart is telling you how much I wanted you / Gloomy Sunday.' In place of Javór's fantasy of desertion and suicide is a dream that awakens the singer to a renewed love. Singing 'Gloomy Sunday', Suzie travels away from the last night she spent with her lover Cesar and voices her legitimate fear that he may be deported or killed by the Nazis who have invaded Paris, but also her hope that her dream will never haunt him and that they will meet again. Like Mamut making a song of Falik's cry, Suzie bears witness to the tears Cesar shed as she slept in his arms.

The scene in which Cesar embodies the film's title draws the viewer's attention by being unlike anything else in the film. Its wordless simplicity is in contrast to the operatic emotions of much of what has gone before. Suzie's room is bare apart from the narrow bed and her battered suitcase, cast into deep chiaroscuro by the pre-dawn gloom. Her face is turned to Cesar's chest so that his face and tears, which catch the fragile light, are all we have to look at. The scene uses Depp's beauty to draw and hold the camera in its long push-in, the only push-in used in the film, on the sobs that distort and shadow his face. The scar that slashes diagonally across Cesar's face, repeated by the tracks of his tears, is the flaw that denotes Potter's reflexive awareness of the dangers of taking beauty at face value. At the same time, the scene's silence marks it out as a rare, simple moment of unadorned beauty, in contrast to the sets and costumes of the opera world. Depp's physical beauty infuses Cesar with a humanity in deliberate contrast to Dante's racist association of gypsies with dirt.

Yosefa Loshitsky finds Potter's depiction of the Roma stereotypical, and argues that she displaces their narrative in favour of a Jewish narrative carried by Suzie (see 2003: 66). Cesar's tears counteract Loshitsky's charge, taking place in one of the few scenes that occurs entirely outside Suzie's consciousness. When the film does show action away from Suzie's point of view, it is intercut with Suzie to give the sense that it is filtered through her real or imaginative point of view. When Lola attends the cinema, her stargazing is intercut with Suzie listening to Dante sing. When Dante prays to Mary that the Germans will come, it is intercut with Suzie's awakening to the sound of German boots stamping towards Paris. There is no intercutting when Cesar cries. It is Cesar's moment alone and his cry is a summation of the film.

It anticipates Suzie's father's tears when she sings to him, and recalls the tears of Suzie's classmates and teacher when she sings to them. It also recalls the cries of the Roma orkestar (played by Taraf de Haïdouks) as they walk and sing in a funeral procession for a Roma boy killed by the Nazis when they come to steal the Roma horses. His is the only death directly caused by Nazis, and his is the only ritual of grief. While a single death cannot approximate the horror of the Porrajmos (the Roma word for the Nazis' ethnic cleansing), it is the most explicit representation of Nazi genocide in the film, and it has a significant place in the chain of men who cry. Cesar's tears are those he could not cry in the funeral procession: Suzie's trusting sleep creates a space in which his feelings – and through them, an acknowledgement of the coming Porrajmos – can be voiced. In her celebrated novel *Fugitive Pieces*, Anne Michaels describes a scene in which a Jewish Holocaust survivor and his wife share a bed. She powerfully evokes the stakes held by Cesar as he holds Suzie: 'one stares, one sleeps, both dream. The world goes on because someone is awake somewhere' (1997: 194). Cesar bears the most important role in the film, that of witness. He stays awake to preserve the world, and cries because he knows he cannot. The tears draw lines on his face that parallel and repeat his scar, making visible forms of bodily memory.

Rather than unmanly sentimentality, tears are a form of awareness and a searing, scarring pain, inscribing the night onto Cesar's body. Suzie's performance of 'Gloomy Sunday' suggestively sounds out the trace of his tears, giving voice to the nightmare that they mourn. In an inversion of the scene, through the song she imagines being awake as her lover sleeps, sharing in the work of preserving the world. By singing she remembers Cesar and, moreover, wills his survival by continuing his voice through hers. That Suzie learned 'Gloomy Sunday' from Cesar's cries is suggested, lightly, in Potter's liner notes. She writes that, while drafting the screenplay, she listened repeatedly to 'an instrumental gypsy arrangement of "Gloomy Sunday"' (2000b). Although Iva Bittová does not sing this arrangement on the film's soundtrack, the song's route into the film is marked by its Roma origins. The recording prompted Potter to research Roma music, attending a London concert by gypsy orkestar Taraf de Haïdouks, which they opened with a version of 'Gloomy Sunday', accompanied by the Kronos Quartet and arranged by Argentinian-Jewish composer Osvaldo Golijov.

Taraf, Kronos and Golijov all became involved in the film, with Taraf appearing as the musicians at Cesar's encampment and Golijov composing all the incidental music and arranging. Through Golijov's innovative intercultural arrangements, the Roma heritage of 'Gloomy Sunday' spreads affectively through the rest of the soundtrack. In 2000, the year that the film opened, Golijov premiered his *St. Mark Passion* 'which trumpeted ... the end of European hegemony over modern composition ... with a barrage of Latin-American sounds' whose creole nature is reminiscent of tango' (Ross 2008: 520). At the climax, Golijov placed 'a softly lamenting Kaddish for the man on the cross. Suddenly the language is Aramaic, the cantillation is Jewish' (ibid.). Whatever was sung at the crucifixion, its language probably was Aramaic and its cantillation Jewish. Like Potter, Golijov practises a passionate and precise syncretism that smuggles marginalised modes into the centre of high culture in order to reveal that they were always there, and always emotive.

The man who cried (Johnny Depp) ... and the woman who listened (Christina Ricci)

Music, cultural memory and emotion are intimately involved in *The Man Who Cried*. Golijov discovers and makes audible the traces of Roma and East European music within the two key operatic pieces: Suzie's version of 'Dido's Lament' and 'Je crois entendre encore', the Bizet aria sung by her father and Dante. 'Je crois entendre encore' is first heard in the credit sequence, which is arguably the earliest memory of the young woman who is close to drowning in the film's opening scene. Her father's performance is scored only by gesture and expression. Its silent film-like compression signals the strange, paratactic structure of the film, where narrative links depend on careful listening. The sensation that the story leaps across gaps, leaving viewers to intuit the temporal, and sometimes causal, relation between scenes works effectively to mirror Suzie's own state of being cut adrift, without linkages, but is also the result of Working Title demanding that Potter excise a substantial number of scenes from the shooting schedule, just before she went into production (Potter, interview with author, September 2006). Voice-overs, written and recorded during post-production, would have provided some exposition to help the viewer connect across the more compressed version of the story that resulted from the shoot.

They were discarded, and instead the credit sequence offers viewers a guide as to how the film works through responsive listening. It is music that answers the 'longing to be connected' that Potter describes in her liner notes, not only on a cultural level, but by providing ligatures between scenes (through repetition), between characters and between film and audience. The use of shot/reverse-shot in the credit sequence demonstrates how the film will solicit the viewer's listening ear. The technique, which splits the scene even as it is bridged by the aria, intensifies the longing that leads the small girl watching intensely from the back of the party to cross the line from Fegele the silent audience to Suzie the performer. Shot/reverse-shot shows the gulf traversed by listening to memory: between passive and active, between suicide and survival.

Potter rarely uses shot/reverse-shot for such a sustained and affective sequence, but it appears again in the film's final scene, to underline the responsive, respectful and reciprocal work by which listening allows another to find their voice. Suzie follows a nurse down a hotel corridor, in one of the film's few unscored scenes. The corridor is blue-grey-green, a cool palette that recalls the twilit pine forest in which she had, as a child, played with her father. The tracking camera stops as Suzie reaches the threshold of a hospital room, and there is then a glance-object cut from Suzie's pale, silent face to a hospital bed, its occupant obscured by a busy nurse, who moves away. From this brief glimpse, the viewer recognises Suzie's father (Oleg Yankovskiy), before there is a cut to his point of view as he sees an unknown young woman looking at him gravely as she crosses to the bed. The second time the shot reverses to Suzie's point of view, her father looks up and says her name, 'Fegele'. The shot reverses to show her reply, also in Yiddish: 'Tateh' (father).

The powerful, moving reunion of a daughter and a father who believed that she was dead echoes *King Lear*. In Oleg Yankovskiy's performance, it carries the charge of his two best-known film roles, both for Russian director Andrei Tarkovsky (see Bergan 2009). He played the father in *Zerkalo* (*The Mirror*, 1975) and the exiled poet and musicologist Andrei Gorkachov in *Nostalghia* (*Nostalgia*, 1983): both roles echo and refract, in the filmmaker's typically elliptical and compressed manner, Tarkovsky's memories of his own father, poet Arseny Tarkovsky. Yankovskiy condenses, via his cinematic performance history, an association between fathers, exile, memory and – embedded in Gorkachov's musicological research – the ritual and emotional affect of music and sound.

Had the voice-overs made it into the final cut, Suzie would have exclaimed at this moment that 'when he spoke it / Spoke my name', her father not only named her – and saw her – truly for the first time since the pogrom, but that by listening to his language, she could name him. Yiddish sounds out both her place of origin (Eastern Europe) and her cultural heritage as a Jew. Fegele, in Yiddish, means 'little bird'. Her destiny as a singer is implicit in the name he returns to her. Language is a 'music in [the] inner ear', a private music made audible to the viewer as Suzie, at the sight of her father's tears, swallows her own sobs and sings to him in Yiddish as he sang to her, when she was a child, on the night she heard him planning to leave for America. The song is forgiveness for his desertion and healing for the suffering it caused him: when he imagined Suzie to be dead, he lost his faith in God and stopped singing. She turns his tears, and her own, into a song.

The songs that Suzie learns teach her listening ear that the marginal – emotions, women, non-white people – are always being pushed from the centre, and that they survive in and through music. By enabling her to survive, the songs are her story. When Suzie is returned to being Fegele, she is able to inhabit fully her longing to give voice and body to emotions before a responsive audience. Her previous performances connect the lullaby beyond the survival of father and daughter to the survival of the communities threatened by the Holocaust. Like Sally in *The Tango Lesson*, Suzie is a good performer because she is a good listener. By echoing his, her voice saves her father's life. Singing the lullaby puts together pieces of the puzzle shared by Suzie and the viewer: the lullaby's tune has been heard throughout the film as a delicate recurring piece of atmospheric guitar music by Potter's long-term musical collaborator, Fred Frith, at moments when something awakens Suzie's childhood memories. It is the sound of memory, of reconnection to the self.

The film is a hall of echoes that leads the listener's ear, following Suzie's, deeper into the story. The lullaby's association with Suzie's sustaining memories of her father contrasts with the misleading spiral turned by repetitions of 'Je crois entendre encore'. The father's syncretic version, aligned with the sepia-toned credit sequence of the wedding party, is set against two more traditional performances of the same aria by Dante, whose beautiful voice is at odds with his fascist beliefs and selfish behaviour, and his habit of turning everyone into an audience for his performances. The viewer first encounters Dante, as the other characters do, through her ears. Before his identity has been established, there is a brief shot of him being introduced by the hostess of a grand Parisian party where Suzie and Lola are performing a tableau with fireworks. A cut shows Suzie, Lola and Cesar, on horseback, relaxing as the audience at the party turn their attention away from the performers standing in the cold to the singer warming up inside. Cesar jettisons the torch he has been holding, and it arcs over Lola, who is shaking out her long limbs. The arcing camera then crosses to Suzie, who has turned away to remove her ridiculous headdress, as Dante sings his first notes. Suzie's indrawn breath is audible, cueing a cut to Dante. He is framed against a grand piano and a large gilt mirror that reflects back the party audience but not the camera, creating an illusion of 'pure' performance. Dante sings only a couple of words before there is a cut to a close-up of Suzie turning towards the camera in slow motion, trembling.

A cut back to Dante confirms the connection: he is singing 'Je crois entendre encore' – in French, but still it calls Suzie out, music in her inner ear. Dante's reprise of her father's song floods Suzie, folding her back in her memories. It brings her into contact with Dante, who gets her a job with his opera company. Through that job she gets to know Cesar, who is the opera company's horse wrangler. Their connection is implicit in the moment of the aria, as Cesar places a hand on Suzie's shoulder when he sees her trembling. Despite the linear narrative events set in motion by Dante's echo, the musical spiral is a miscommunication. Dante will only lead Suzie back to her father obliquely, by betraying her. The second time Suzie hears Dante sing in the same apartment, he is accompanied on the piano by one German army officer and is moments away from revealing Suzie's Jewish identity to another.

Dante's involvement with the Nazis opens up the film's themes of recognition and relation, like collaboration, to negative meanings that can be heard in the story of the aria itself. In Georges Bizet's opera *The Pearl Fishers*, Nadir, a pearl fisher, has sworn a solemn bond with his best friend, the chieftain Zurga, never again to see Leila, the beautiful princess that they both loved. Shortly after Nadir and Zurga celebrate their oath in song, Nadir recognises a veiled temple priestess as Leila. He sings: 'Je crois entendre encore / Caché sous les palmiers /Sa voix tendre et sonore / Comme un chant de ramiers' (I think I hear again / Hidden beneath the palm trees / Your tender and resonant voice / Like the song of ring-doves (author's translation)). He recognises the specific 'tender and resonant' timbre of her voice before he sees her face.

Nadir, the gentle lover, is a surprising role for Dante. He seems to favour the bravura tenor roles of artistic bombast such as the pompous artist Cavaradossi in *Tosca* and the titular troubadour Manrico in *Il Trovatore*. Verdi's opera has many tantalising parallels with the film: Manrico, a nobleman, is raised by a gypsy woman and is executed for remaining loyal to her. Rife with betrayal, passion and revelation, the opera has been used several times in cinema, including a chaotic performance in the Marx Brothers' *A Night at the Opera*, one of Potter's favourite films. Lucino Visconti's *Senso* (1954) uses a performance of Act III, Scene ii at La Fenice as its opening scene, presaging the film's story of deception and desire set against the last days of the Austrian occupation of Venice. As both film and opera show, love is a matter of great political significance. In *The Pearl Fishers*, Nadir's determination to reunite with Leila brings down Zurga's rule.

Dante reprises his Nadir onstage for Felix Perlman's opera company, where Suzie and Lola work in the chorus. While Dante sings the aria, we see four different models of audience, in which listening, betrayal and love are differently entwined. There is a stagehand in the wings, who is framed as part of the production by a side-on long shot past Dante. Perlman (Harry Dean Stanton) stands at the rear of the stage with his back to the scenery in front of which Dante performs, not quite part of the scene but responsible for and aware of its construction. His obscured position and worried gaze suggest that he imagines himself as Leila, his Jewishness 'revealed' by Dante. In a front view of the stage from behind the conductor's podium we see the silent Leila, trapped on papier maché rocks as she listens to the man who has found her out. Nadir's insistence on revealing Leila will lead both of them almost to their deaths at Zurga's hands.

After the long shot of Dante singing, there is a cut to Lola in the audience, watching fascinated – but the play of lights over her face reveal that she is not at the opera, but at the cinema. The screen fills with the almost abstract image of synchronised swimmers from a black-and-white film, and then Lola's imagined image of herself swimming alone replaces the Hollywood film. Lola, the fantasist, is incapable of being an audience. Even as adoring looker-on to Dante's fame she is performing to get his attention. Lola is the Musetta to Suzie's Mimi. Like Mimi, Suzie lives in a Parisian garret, but *The Man Who Cried* answers *Thriller*'s question about what might have happened if Mimi and Musetta had become friends, as Lola moves in with Suzie, befriends her and then – to ensure her own security – betrays Suzie's identity as a Jew to Dante. Potter does not cast Lola as a 'bad girl' like Musetta because she is an artiste who uses others through her beauty, but because she is a bad *performer* who performs constantly to be the centre of attention.

In Blanchett's performance, Lola is as mesmerising to men (and viewers) as Marlene Dietrich's Lola-Lola in *Der blaue Engel* (*The Blue Angel*, 1930), an iconic character recalled by Lola's name and bleached-blonde hair. In her desire to seduce all eyes, she literally poses as a listener to Suzie's performance of 'Gloomy Sunday'. The camera lingers on her porcelain skin and ruby lips as she pouts and poses, casting her eyes sideways to observe the impression she has made on fellow passengers. After the show, Lola explains to Suzie that the new man she has captivated will take them both to Hollywood, and then once again abandons Suzie, who stands on deck in the rain while Lola imitates Esther Williams in the ship's art deco swimming pool. Beautiful Lola in her white swimming costume cutting through the gem-like turquoise of the pool contrasts sharply with drab Suzie left in the damp shadows. Lola is in the pool when the ship is struck by a torpedo, which is dramatised by the sudden rushing and bubbling of the water around her. The beautiful pool is as treacherous as the beautiful garments bought for her by Dante, material objects that isolate Lola and prevent her from building on her affinity with Suzie. It is as if she believed in the opera costumes as a true representation of history, and likewise believed Dante to be as heroic as his roles and as beautiful as his voice. Lola is taken in by the world of surfaces, and her fate is never to surface.

As in *The Tango Lesson* and *Orlando*, water has a profound symbolic role in *The Man Who Cried*, which – like *Yes* – looks critically at the association of the marginalised with dirt. The driving rain that soaks Suzie is 'cleaner' than the artifice in which Lola seeks to submerge her sorrows, and to reinvent herself. The camera dwells on Lola's languid turns, which dramatise the way in which she is turning her body and persona into those of a movie star, just as the swimming pool attempts to conceal and is destroyed by the sea of live water beneath it. Water's mythic associations with feminine beauty are troubled because it serves to isolate women. After Lola first leaves Suzie in order to move in with Dante, she languishes in the bath, bored and alone. She had announced her defection as Suzie was washing her face in a basin of water. Suzie barely listened to Lola's apologies, caught up in her memories of her first sexual encounter with Cesar the previous night, by a bonfire. Fire (strongly identified with Cesar and Suzie as outsiders and observers) and water meet in the opening sequence, which is repeated after the swimming pool is torpedoed. Suzie's elemental submersion in the burning ocean recalls the patterning of fire and water in *Orlando* and *The Tango Lesson*, particularly Sally's self-baptism in the fountain outside Saint Sulpice and the red-tinted underwater vision that triggers her new film.

Suzie's survival is another strike against purity: just as music moves most when it is infused by exchange, so the elements are at their most benevolent when they come together. Lola is identified with water alone, while Suzie bridges fire (associated with listening to her father and with Cesar) and water (being alone with herself). Just as Lola drowns when water rushes into water, so fire alone is a symbol of destruction. Fire erases the government archive in Paris, where Suzie watches officials burn boxes of papers just before the Nazis invade. The fire that spreads across the courtyard, watched by a solemn-eyed Suzie as others flee the city, is reminiscent of the lurid fires of the pogrom that chased her from her village as a child. Fire is the harbinger of war as well as passion and memory. Both Holocaust and Porrajmos mean 'burning'. The film asks: after this burning, what can remain?

The answer circles back to the opening of the film in the burning ocean, and to Cesar's tears: what remains is what has been witnessed. Seeing, however, is not enough. It has to connect to listening. The day before Suzie sees the burning government documents, she catches a glimpse of her Jewish landlady being taken away by that same government. What Suzie sees warns her of her own potential fate, but more immediately recalls to her what she will no longer hear: Mme. Goldstein's Yiddish epithets and music. Her last cultural connection has been severed. Alone in her attic room, Suzie speaks out loud to her father's photograph, the only fragment of memory that now remains. '*But the photograph remains mute and impenetrable*', reads the direction (Potter 2000a: 60). Although it preserves her memory, the photograph of her father cannot sound in her 'listening ear'. Mute as they are, the Hebrew characters spelling out her father's name on the back betray her Jewishness to Lola, who betrays it to Dante. Dante appropriates the photograph's meaning, rifling Suzie's intimate memories by examining it when she is not present. When Suzie shows the photograph willingly, she can control its meaning. It defines her as an individual, rather than one of those people who use Hebrew.

It is only when she shows the photograph to someone who can read the words that the final spiral of her journey begins. In New York, she talks to a woman activist at an archive collecting the details of Jewish immigrants from Eastern Europe, who is able to point Suzie in the direction of the garment factory where her father worked. This scene echoes the archival images of garment workers in *Thriller*. *Rage* (2009) blends the two in Edith Roth's (Dianne Wiest) memories of her parents' garment factories on the Lower East Side. Edie's memories pick up on *The Man Who Cried*'s inclusion of a Jewish history that is not often told side-by-side with the Sho'ah, that of the Jewish diaspora beyond Eastern Europe, a product of widespread European anti-semitism predating the Sho'ah. Suzie's journey to New York extends the film's frame historically as well as geographically, putting cultural survival and destruction side-by-side. The archive and the garment factory, like the survival of Yiddish into the twenty-first century, are evidence of a thriving diasporic Jewish community.

Movement and change are, once again, shown to be survival strategies. They are echoed in Suzie's ability to learn from the operas that she hears and avoid their heroine's fates. As she escapes the tragic fate of Leila, who is almost burned at the stake with Nadir for betraying her religious vows, so Suzie also escapes the fate of the character whose famous aria she sings twice in the film. 'Dido's Lament', Suzie's signature song, originates from Henry Purcell's 1689 opera *Dido and Aeneas*, the oldest surviving opera with a libretto in English. The opera adapts an episode from the *Aeneid*, Virgil's epic account of Rome's Trojan founder Aeneas. Dido, Queen of Carthage, offers shelter to Aeneas and his band of Trojan refugees when they are shipwrecked on her shore. Dido and Aeneas fall in love due to divine (or in Purcell's opera, magical) interference in order to humiliate the queen and delay the imperial founder. A divine reminder breaks Aeneas from the spell, but Dido is still bewitched; when he abandons her, she kills herself by turning Carthage into her funeral pyre. Like *La Bohème*, it is an opera concerned with power versus love, female frailty and male stoicism, abandon and propriety.

The opera's theme of exile and empire is echoed in Suzie/Fegele's own journey to the moment where she sings the song. A refugee who dreams of travelling onwards, Suzie is as much Aeneas as she is Dido, the African queen shamed for her choice of lover. Dido's lament is sung in the final act of the opera as she prepares to kill herself in grief over Aeneas's desertion. Despite its anguished narrative, the opera was written for performance by a girl's school, and it is in school that Suzie learns it. It is disquieting to witness the grave-eyed Claudia Lander-Duke, who plays the young Fegele/Suzie, in her drab 1930s pinafore and braids, move from singing the loving Yiddish songs of her childhood, to rebelling against being taught hymns, to singing in unaccented English on the school stage:

When I am laid, am laid in earth
May my wrongs create
No trouble, no trouble in thy breast.
Remember me! Remember me!
But ah! forget my fate.

This song of adult passion and tragic suicide is inappropriate in the mouth of the still, serious child, even as it seems to predict her likely fate as a Jewish woman in Europe in the 1930s: betrayed to death. The lyrics are sadder still because they were written by Nahum Tate, who famously revised *King Lear* to give Cordelia the same happy ending that Suzie and her father will find. The sequence cuts, with the song as sound bridge, from Lander-Duke singing at school, to Ricci singing the final lines of the song in what turns out to be a cabaret audition in the hopes of earning enough money to go to America and track down her father. Although it is not her voice that gets her the job, but her awkwardly-revealed legs, the song thematises Suzie's desire to *move*. The song enables her to move – and so connect with – those with whom she could not communicate, and it voices what she cannot: her longing to find the first man who cried in her presence, her father.

The viewer learns to hear and understand through repetition ('entendre encore') how song can archive traces of individual and cultural memory. Rebecca Schneider notes that in Western thought, performance is linked to disappearance as the archive is linked to preservation, a binary that erases performance-oriented cultures; part of Pablo's fear of disappearance is, perhaps, that dance leaves no official trace. Schneider argues that it is important to subvert this damaging construction by 'articulat[ing] the ways in which performance ... begins again and again, as Gertrude Stein would write, differently, via itself as a repetition ... as an echo in the ears of a confidante, as an audience member, a witness' (2001: 106). Throughout her oeuvre Potter articulates performance's Steinian repetition as a series of echoes carried in bodily gestures and attitudes, nowhere more importantly than in rethinking the depiction of the Holocaust. The musical archives opened by the films are poignant 'host[s] to a collective memory' (2001: 103). Both Yiddish and Roma songs operate as powerful records of prewar cultures erased by the Sho'ah and Porrajmos. Unlike the burned documents in Paris, they are living archives preserved and altered by performance.

The second time Suzie sings 'Dido's Lament' it opens up the bodily archive through repetition with a difference, based on her ability to listen. The Roma musicians she meets at Cesar's encampment are improvising around a communal table by firelight, recalling the party of the credits. There is a dramatic contrast with the look and editing of previous sung scenes in school and at the opera, which depended on shot/reverse-shot between audience and performer. When the Roma sing, a fluid camera movement circles clockwise then anti-clockwise around the table, embracing performer and audience in the same shot. There is no line between performers and audience here, as Suzie discovers when the men who have performed for her as their guest turn and invite her to sing for them. As Suzie begins to sing, in her high, clear voice, the camera frames her in close-up, alone, and there are cuts to reverse shots of her audience. At 'May my wrongs create', the accordionist walks around the table to stand behind her, and the half-circling shots resume. She has been accepted.

Suzie's ability to respond to the situations in which she finds herself is an aspect of her position as an exile. It can be heard in Purcell's music, which employs dissonance and ostinato (one syllable sung over many notes) to suggest Dido's Otherness as an African woman. Susan McClary suggests that in ostinato, which is mainly given to female characters, 'each potential moment of closure is simultaneously the moment that guarantees continuation' (1991: 125). Its otherness is an image of pleasure in a seventeenth-century opera like *Dido*, but in later operas comes to denote 'grief, erotic transport or madness ... always associated with some obsessive condition' (1991: 192, n. 17). When she sings with the Roma musicians, Suzie begins to sound out the root of ostinato's association with the Other, and its negative associations. As it spreads out from the repetition of 'no trouble', it symbolises affect, collaboration and cultural memory, bringing the sobbing sound of Yiddish music into her voice. Performing ostinato with the Roma musicians, Suzie builds an alliance that sees affect as passionate expression rather than an 'obsessive condition'.

In the pleasure of listening arises the possibility of refiguring mourning as loving witness rather than madness. When Suzie reaches 'ah!', she extends it with breaks between the descending notes, a sobbing sound that persists through a newly-plangent, drawn-out and loud 'forget my fate', whose passionate sorrow prefigures the inhuman scale of forgetting that is gathering in the film's historical background. Poet J. H. Prynne argues that 'ah!' is a sound spoken at the edge of impossible expression, a hinge 'between the pathos of individual sensibility and the ethos of concerted human action' (1987: 165). 'Ah!' sounds the interconnection of a feeling too personal to be expressed and the pressing need of its outward expression. It hinges together Suzie's artiste-like performance; her complex intermeshing of the artisanal in crafting the note; and her artistry in finding her own voice. It could be called an auteurial 'ah', a mark of individual style emerging from collaboration.

Importantly, it also hinges 'remember' and 'forget'. Suzie's plangent 'Remember me!' asks for recognition of individual deaths and cultural specificity, while the descending spiral of 'forget my fate' asks, through its incorporation of a Roma musical line, that identity politics be set aside, and that survival as well as erasure be celebrated. When she sings, it is an act of both testimony and alliance-building. Suzie uses the gift of her voice not to draw attention to herself as an individual, but rather to participate in a communal moment of memory, and to respond to her audience's need. The use of echoing musical performances in *The Man Who Cried*, each with an audience that is affected by what they hear, makes the cinematic audience into a confidante rather than a passive viewer of an epic history. Collaboration is reinterpreted as active, empathetic and ethical. When the Nazi invasion of Paris is shown only through the characters' reactions to the sound of tramping boots growing louder, rather than revelling in stupendous Leni Riefenstahl-like depictions of storm and glory, the film models the kind of listening that it demands.

As well as being dramatically (and cost-) effective, the decision to sound out, rather than show, the troops may be the realisation of a long-term thought process about the relationship between film and viewers' emotional reactions. Potter drew a symbol in the margin next to a quotation from Alfred Hitchcock in Peter Gidal's article 'Film as Film'. Gidal, a fellow member of the London Filmmakers' Co-op, condemns 'the condescension of making a product which forces people to react in more or less the same way at the same time ... [as] authoritarian facistic [sic] control' (1972: 13). He then quotes Hitchcock indicting himself as such a fascistic filmmaker: 'instead of Hitlerian troops marching, I want everyone in silent breathless hysteria at the edge of their seats' (in ibid.). Potter kept the issue of *Art and Artists* in which this appears in an archive of magazines that mention LDC and her other performance work, but there is nothing in this issue that refers to her work; her marginal squiggle seems to be why she kept it. Gidal cites the shower sequence in *Psycho* as the '*sine qua non*' of authoritarian filmmaking, which connects to *Thriller*'s rethinking of Hitchcockian 'thrills' (ibid.). The fact that *The Man Who Cried* creates a minimal staging of 'Hitlerian troops' through sound (starting very faint, becoming louder as each character hears and reacts) suggests that the film is reaching for a third way of active, empathetic listening between Gidal's structuralist anti-instructionism (which informed *Thriller*) and Hitchcock's project of manipulation.

For the viewer who observes the film's lessons in listening, from Fegele's attentive gaze in the credit sequence to the exchange of regard between Suzie and her father at the end, music not only moves the narrative, but opens it out as an 'archive of feelings'. Coined by Ann Cvetkovich, the term describes an unconventional form of witnessing that, unlike records of dominant history, is not concerned with objective facts but rather with subjective memories. She connects it particularly to ephemeral forms such as performances, flyers and diaries that show personal emotions suffusing political events and vice versa. They are particularly produced by, and important to, marginal communities whose identities are excluded from the mainstream, partially because of their association with 'feeling'. Suzie's 'ah!' layers her recall of her Jewishness, her association with Cesar and his Roma family, as well as a release of grief for her loss and loneliness, that it is simultaneously an expression of community and solidarity. The viewer prepared to become audience *hears* and is moved to solidarity by the narrative's spirals when her ears are pricked by musical repetitions.

Potter describes such an audience in the short story that was the first version of *The Man Who Cried*. The boat passengers listening to Suzie sing 'Gloomy Sunday' in the mid-Atlantic 'pause for a moment ... to listen to this dark-eyed girl, soothed and fortified by her lovely voice; a voice with a sob in the throat, a voice that somehow transforms the popular songs they thought they knew into something else, something resembling a prayer' (Potter 2000a: viii). Suzie has taken on the communitarian role as cantor that her father, in exile, has cast aside. The 'sob in the throat' that is Suzie's memory of Cesar's tears, and a trace of their Roma-Jewish affinity, restores the sanctity of music without endorsing a particular form of belief. 'Remember me', it asks, 'but forget my fate', for no fate is singular. Through the story of one woman and those affected by her voice, Potter attempts to find a new way to mourn the Holocaust and to celebrate the fragmented survival of the cultures that it came close to eradicating. The listener prepared to open her body to the sounds and textures of almost-forgotten communities may find that the film moves her to tears that, like Suzie's 'ah', are both an emotional and political cry.

CHAPTER TEN

Feeling

If someone attaches electrodes to the right place in the brain, and reads the brainwaves as somebody imagines eating a particular piece of food, the brainwaves will be the same as if they were eating that same piece of food. Remembering a traumatic experience creates the same chemical reaction in the body and the gut as the actual experience. Memory and imagination are on some physiological level as real as the real. You have to create the conditions of emotional and psychic readiness in the viewer so that they are going to be ready to receive the experience. The tenderness with which, as a filmmaker, you communicate with your unknown audience may be what allows someone to be open or to be resistant. That's where you're starting to work on the subtle body.

                                           – Sally Potter, interview with author, January 2007

Potter's films resonate, in novelist Shauna Singh Baldwin's phrase, with 'what the body remembers'. This is often what the conscious mind – personal or socio-cultural – has forgotten, and what resurfaces through sensory triggers of the kind that cinema can evoke: touch, smell, taste. Potter's films reach out through labour/hand-crafting, performance, colour and sound to work on the 'subtle body'; that is, the spirit or psyche. The films' unusual intensities and rhythms, which move the viewer to be open and receptive, make her feel that she can not only see and hear, but *touch* what is onscreen because the careful attention given to framing and pace solicits recollections of similar textures and experiences, which are in turn bound up with emotions. Laura U. Marks suggests that certain films are particularly touch-oriented or *haptic*. She focuses on films that actively seek 'different' audiences, because of their oppositional politics or because they come from the margins. These works, she argues, are committed to evoking touch and scents that stimulate memories of a shared culture, realising a form of spectatorship that is more embodied without being less intellectually precise. Through their formal difference and their invitation to shared memories, these films 'can be tactile, as though one were touching a film with one's eyes' (Marks 2000: xi). As Potter expresses it, 'if you photograph a texture, people will experience the information in their body not vicariously, but actually, by being open to it' (interview with author, January 2007).

Creating the viewer's openness is the developing project of Potter's use of music throughout her oeuvre, from *Thriller*'s intercutting of Puccini and *Psycho* through *Orlando*'s history of the male falsetto and a tangoing history of Argentina. *Oh Moscow*, an avant-jazz song cycle that Potter wrote and performed with Lindsay Cooper in the mid- to late-1980s (including performances in Berlin in 1989, both before and after the Wall came down (Potter, interview with author, September 2006)), meshes a socialist history of Europe in the twentieth century with an improvisational approach to music. Improvisation, the ability to adapt by listening and collaborating, is a knack shared with Potter by Celeste and Suzie, among other characters. It allows music to change, so it is not only receptive and interactive, but actually able to document the differing circumstances of its performance, to stay live and alive. African-American intellectual Cornel West famously defined jazz 'not so much as a term for a musical art form but for a mode of being in the world, an improvisational mode of protean, fluid and flexible disposition towards reality' (1993: 150). Potter's film work makes use of her jazz training as a 'mode of being in the world': because it is based in change and in the moment, it can open up the listener's emotions towards a desire for political change. Like West's 'jazz freedom fighter', Suzie takes up 'Gloomy Sunday' (recorded by African-American artists Paul Robeson and Billie Holiday) to protest against history's violence, and perhaps to change it.

Potter's films could be called 'jazz documentaries' in which the fictional form represents a 'flexible' approach to official, objective definitions of reality. Ann Cvetkovich argues that experimental documentary film and video are an important part of the archive of feelings. By using performers, music and other affective elements, such documentaries question the idea of the 'objective' documentary, and in doing so 'extend the material and conceptual reach of the traditional archive … [by] incorporating a wide range of traditional and unorthodox materials … including clips from popular film' (Cvetkovich 2003: 244). Potter's television documentary series *Tears, Laughter, Fears and Rage* mobilised clips from popular films to make a sophisticated philosophical and political argument about the place of emotion in British public life.

Tears, Laughter, Fears and Rage is an archive of feelings and also, importantly, an archive of cinematic expressions of emotion. The film clips are framed by the documentary to reveal the presence of emotion in public life and to show how that presence has been repressed by official histories. 'Hollywood film fills in for historical gaps, substituting for the losses of cultural dislocation and secrecy' (2003: 261). The film clips offer viewers a way in to the arguments in *Tears, Laughter, Fears and Rage*, jogging memories of their own cinematic experiences of emotion in the private spaces, such as darkened cinemas, where the Western viewer is allowed to feel. The film clips demonstrate that emotions have long been present in cinema and therefore in public life. In doing so, they incorporate the viewers and their emotional reactions into the films, making them part of both cinematic and political history.

Potter's films not only put onscreen scenes of emotion, but are structured – rather than punctured – by them. They do not stall or stand outside the narrative but act as crucial pivots and ligatures. They arise as part of a chain of sounds and images that narrate the way in which emotion is produced by, literally, touching the deep structures of memory. As in the depiction of the lovers amidst the purple sheets in *Yes*, these scenes invite us not only to touch with our eyes open, but to touch and *remember* with our eyes closed, bringing together the two meanings of 'feeling'. When Suzie loses herself in the scent and feel of the pine needles, her fingers possess both touch and emotion. Fred Frith's arrangement of the lullaby 'Close Your Eyes' plays on the soundtrack, its title (a translation of the song's opening lyric) suggests the relation between film and dream, between looking as a viewer and closing one's eyes to allow personal memories to return. There is individual memory at work, but also cultural memory, as the music vibrates with its missing Yiddish lyrics and the trees stand for the country from which both Suzie and Lola have been exiled. The combination of delicate, allusive guitar and the rhythmic movements of Suzie's fingers allows the viewer to share not only Suzie's memories, but the interior space where sensation, emotion and memory spark each other.

From *Thriller*'s laughter, Potter's films have become more openly emotive until *The Man Who Cried*, *Yes* and *Rage* (2009) name, in their titles, the emotional responses that they contain. Like the films that Marks discusses, they solicit their responses by summoning and depicting communities and traditions on the border between remembering and forgetting. As well as inviting the viewer to touch the film with her eyes and ears, haptic expressions of emotion – like tango or Suzie's 'ah!' – summon histories and memories that are at once individual and cultural. In *The Man Who Cried*, the cry stands out as being at once the sound that affects the listener and also the listener's response. Memory and feeling are specifically brought together through sound.

J. Edward Chamberlin looks at what it would mean to take such a claim seriously in Western culture in *If This Is Your Land, Where Are Your Stories?* Chamberlin argues that Western culture suppresses the centrality of performance, oral storytelling and audience reactions to its legal forms such as parliament and trials. If the importance of orality could be re-established, it might provide a place in which legislators could learn to listen to and recognise as valid and important the non-written legal and historical discourse that remains central in many non-Western cultures. He tells the story of a Canadian trial judge who stopped Mary Johnson from telling her *ada'ox* in court. Johnson is an elder of the Gitksan, one of the First Nations of what is now called British Columbia, and the *ada'ox* are song cycles that record, as mythic stories,

'Mach tsu di eigelech': Suzie (Christina Ricci), touched by memory

several thousand years of Gitksan history, particularly their settlement of an area of land that the Canadian government was claiming. The judge said firstly that singing was not legally permissible evidence, and secondly that he would not appreciate it because he had a tin ear. Chamberlin adds that this 'was a stupid thing to say ... but he *did* have a tin ear, and he couldn't have heard the music even if he *were* interested in it' (2003: 21; emphasis in original).

His cultural tin ear would mean that he could not accept Mary Gordon's *ada'ox* as evidence. To him it was nothing more than a beautiful (or ugly) tune or an interesting performance of anthropological, but not legal or historical, value. The Gitksan land claim rested on a form of documentation that they felt was valid – and more than that, sacred – while the Canadian judge dismissed it. To his tin ear, song was associated with subjectivity and emotion, which are separated off from evidence and rationality. His judgement not only effectively gagged the Gitksan, but pointed to the cultural imperialism that denies songs or cries their function as witness. Silence, as Michel Foucault protested, equals death. The refusal to find a common ground, a shared space of listening and responding feelingly, has implications that extend far beyond film, but that affect it too.

Sound has been film's secret. It is what Jacques Derrida calls a *supplément*, something that appears to be outside and additional to an object that boasts of its self-sufficiency; Derrida's example is that, in Western thought, woman is *supplément* to man (see 1976). Infolded within the original, the *supplément* troubles the original term's boast of completeness. To call sound a *supplément* is to say that film is, and has always been, more than a visual medium. Film theory has been wary of sound, seeing it as supplemental in the colloquial sense because of its late development. Like colour, sound was seen as an innovation that hindered the development of the artform and turned it into a commercial and feminised spectacle. Sound troubles film's claim to be indexical, documenting the world: because it is recorded on a separate track, it could be and usually is recorded in post-production. Sound, like saturated colour, should prompt viewers to be aware of the film as a mediated experience that has an ambiguous relationship with the real. What it documents is not actuality but affect. Potter's films use sound's emotive aspects as a way out of the dominance of the visual, to make audible what cannot be seen. They bear witness to that which is invisible, both literally and culturally. The *ada'ox*, like Suzie's use of 'Dido's Lament', is a statement whose emotional affect is at once a record of a community's past and a political manifesto for its future – but it needs an audience open to it.

The Man Who Cried was developed during a period in which international governance seemed increasingly open to listening to such cries. From 1996, the Truth and Reconciliation Commission made public its hearings about apartheid-era violence in South Africa. Rather than trial and punishment, the Commission used storytelling and listening to alter the balance of power, and create a public legislative space for sounding out feelings ranging from rage and guilt to sorrow and forgiveness. In 1999, the International Court of Human Rights tried Slobodan Milošević in his absence for war crimes and found him guilty. Yet the announcement coincided, almost exactly, with the start of the Kosovo war and further 'ethnic cleansing' in the Balkans. *The Man Who Cried*'s critical statement about listening and/as empathy that could circumvent racist politics came at a crucial time, joining the chorus of the TRC and ICHR against ethnic violence. Yet the primacy of written history, and its emphasis on the victors' narrative, continues to make it culturally difficult for that chorus to have any widespread preventative effect.

Through its cinematographer, Sacha Vierny, *The Man Who Cried* is part of a distinguished lineage of films that investigated and preserved the memory of the Holocaust in an attempt to stop the events from occurring again. For Alain Resnais' *Nuit et brouillard*, Vierny shot several days of footage at the abandoned remains of Auschwitz, ending with a sequence of shots of a guard tower. It asks whether, from our vantage point historically and in the cinema, we could use the film's archiving of the events in danger of being forgotten to help us see – and act – if genocide happened again. Potter's films are not documentaries and they use different strategies to inform and mobilise the viewer. Her films do share certain stylistic traits with documentaries, though, that work to connect them to history and the real, including to-camera address and location shooting. In Potter's films the cry is a documentary. Rather than showing us what is in front of our eyes, by documenting what others have felt, her films awaken what we can feel.

Tears

> Tears are precious – they are one of the gifts of the Almighty. The rabbis tell us that all the gates in heaven are closed except the gate of tears.
> – Rabbi Rabinowitz, Chief Rabbi of Britain, in *Tears*

Tears makes a powerful argument for the cry's heartfelt prayer. Quoting tears from across the cinematic canon, it looks particularly at audiences crying in reaction to art. A clip from Yiddish classic *Dybbuk* (1937) anticipates Potter's construction of a similar scene in the opening credits of *The Man Who Cried*. Made in Poland in 1937 (although based on Sholom Ansky's play written 1912–17), the film is a testimony to a community about to disappear. It was aimed at Yiddish-speaking audiences beyond Eastern Europe, particularly in North America. Yiddish connects the film to the 'old country', but also shows feeling's ability to create continuity and community through art. In the clip, the cantor's song meshes the old story of a wedding with the wedding happening around him. His song provokes the bride's mother's tears, which are shed noisily and communally, in strong contrast to those cried in Hollywood melodrama: they are not lonely, melodramatic or passive. Instead, they are communitarian, pleasurable and celebratory, a model for and reflection of the tears that the film's audience might shed for their memories of the old country. Being an audience is associated with emotional openness; this is something that Potter stages in every film, inviting the audience in the cinema to learn from, and share with, the audience onscreen.

Tears picks up on interviewee Michael Powell's comment that 'most people don't have the chance to express their emotions … but they have their emotions in their dreams', by suggesting that cinema functions as an archive of the more emotionally expressive world that people experience in their dreams. Powell's involvement in the documentary is highlighted in *Tears* by clips from his films, made with Emeric Pressburger, *The Life and Death of Colonel Blimp* (1943) and *The Red Shoes*, that contrast men's and women's tears. The clip from *The Red Shoes* follows and bears out an assertion by another interviewee that in Western culture tears have been the only emotion available to women, and therefore used as an expression of impotent rage and fear as well as grief.

A sobbing Victoria Page is the focus of the clip, as she is of the narrative, which is reaching its climax in this penultimate scene. It offers a telling insight into one of the fragmentary ideas Potter describes in notes to her screenplay for *The Tango Lesson*: 'an image of a woman crying. *Really* crying. As if her heart was going to break. River of water cascading from her eyes and nose' (1997d: 95). This fragmentary suggestion, which is echoed in *The Tango Lesson* by two scenes in which Sally cries 'as if her heart was going to break', could be a description of the scene from Powell's film. Vicky is already in make-up to reprise the role of The Girl that she created and that made her a star. Her false eyelashes and the mascara of a silent screen star heighten and make visible her melodramatic sobs, as she raises her face to the high-angled camera. The excerpt in the documentary ends with ballet impresario Boris's command to 'put on the red shoes' against her husband's wishes. They will dance her to her death, a fate that *Tears* ellipses, as does *The Tango Lesson*, which continues in the tradition of Potter's earlier work in claiming the role of artist for women, arguing women can have both love and creativity.

Potter's films ask the question of what it means to cry as a woman and as a man. When Sally cries in imitation of Vicky's tears in *The Tango Lesson*, she is deliberately, dramatically loud, an assertion of women's right to make their strong feelings heard. Women are expected to cry (politely): at sad events, at happy events and at films. Their tears are used to diminish genres with which they are associated, like melodrama. 'This, too, is part of trauma's affective archive: the resistance to vulnerability for which the dismissal of sentimentality and the canon of women's popular culture serves as a touchstone' (Cvetkovich 2003: 25). It makes it hard to show women's tears on film without falling into the trap of making women no more than hysterical bodies. For a woman to cry, like She or Sally, loudly and without vanity, is to demand a hearing, to refuse to remain attractive to the camera with a single, stylised tear falling down her cheek. A scene in an artfully-framed Parisian café in *The Tango Lesson* parodies exactly such a stylised moment from *The Third Man* (1949), which is excerpted in *Tears*. Reflective, transparent, stylised, Sally's tears in the café are a screen onto which emotion is projected. In their silence, they are a reflection of the Hollywood heroine.

Yet they are shared, in an inversion that threatens to destabilise Pablo's masculinity. When He turns to the camera with tears in his eyes in *Yes*, he names himself 'un-manned' by being invisible in white English culture. Yet his tears, far from unmanning him, make him visible, make him tender towards She, and enable him to articulate his feelings. His tears, like Cesar's, are a deliberate act of witness, a kind of unsettling affective evidence. *The Man Who Cried* is particularly eruptive in assigning, from its title onwards, the act of crying to men. Cesar's tears close a circuit of male emotion as record of authenticity, commonality and spontaneity in the film. That his tears are soundless underscores, literally, the Roma struggle to enter their story into official annals, a struggle complicated by orality's primacy in Roma culture. In the short story that accompanies the film's published screenplay, Potter notes that the Roma had been forced by the French to carry identity cards and live in cordoned settlements even before the Nazi invasion, two trappings of the *gadje* obsession with official recording that they hated and resisted (2000a: xxviii). Cesar's tears leave a watermark on the film, a clear but ephemeral space in which the Porrajmos can be witnessed in an appropriately Roma form.

Cesar cries for his own, and his family's, probable death, and for the lack of a trace it will leave. 'Not only does performance act as a repository for ephemeral moments, it can also make an emotion public without narrative or storytelling; the performance might just be a scream, a noise, or a gesture without sound' (Cvetkovich 2003: 286). Archives, like libraries, are expected to be silent out of respect for the weight of history, and yet that silence points to another, the voices they do not contain, silenced by dominant culture. All the elements repressed by the official archives – song, performance, emotion, sexuality, and those people associated with them – erupt in the archive of feelings as symbols of each other. The archive that Cesar's tears form is different from the unreliable official archive. It does not assert a single meaning, but rather points forwards to a number of possible readings, highlighting their absence from dominant narratives. It is exactly a counter-archive of feelings, a documentation that cannot be collected, preserved, filed or read in a conventional sense. Yet Cesar's tears do collect, bear witness to, make accessible and invite us to remember.

Tears and other expressions of emotion function archivally in a metaphorical sense in Potter's films, but they also assert their place in the historical archive that seeks to exclude them. Cesar's tears are more affective and effective than a list of statistics. Appearing on film as part of an actor's performance, they are halfway between the body's repertoire and the recorded archive. Diana Taylor (2005) argues that the performance's 'repertoire' of bodily, oral and ephemeral forms offers resistance to the archive by slipping away, constantly changing meaning. Feminist performance theorist Peggy Phelan made a revolutionary argument in *Unmarked* (1993) that performance's affect consists in its refusal to remain and enter into the dominant archive. Its disappearance makes it vivid and urgent, like life's urgency in the face of death. Rebecca Schneider, like Cvetkovich, worries that this means that cultures in which performance predominates risk erasure. She emphasises that central to performance is its ability to make its audience remember. 'In such practices [as rituals] ... performance *does* remain, does leave residue. Indeed, the place of residue is arguably *flesh* in a network of body-to-body transmission of enactment' (2001: 102; emphasis in original). Rather than moving performance's residue into the fixed archive that props up official narratives, Potter's films work to record and continue 'body-to-body transmission' by locating their affect in onscreen performances of music, story and emotion.

Bodily gestures and emotions in her films can surprise the viewer into thinking about the political reasons for their absence from the archive and/of dominant culture. Women's loud sobs and men's soundless tears are politically disruptive. Tears streak the surface of the films to reveal their depths of historical and political feeling, as tangos break open the archives of the *junta*. Making their presence felt, Cesar's tears point to their absence in official histories of Nazi France and of cinema. Paris's historical narrative and cinematic tradition define it as an archive of love and freedom. Cesar's Paris is absent, however, from the great tradition of French cinema. A Jew and a gypsy hold each other in a garret, as archetypal as Mimi and Rodolfo, except that their story was untold until Potter imagined it. Breaking injunctions against crying in public, Potter's films are an affective archive to which the viewer can add their own protest of weeping.

Laughter

> If you're laughing, you're in control, you're free.
> — Inez McCormack, trade union leader, in *Laughter*

Tears are not the only 'felt thought', or emotion in motion, in Potter's films. Tears are feminised because they are a moment of submission, of lack of control, giving in to the film – particularly to the sight of another crying, and its kinaesthetic effect. Yet tears, as Claudia Gorbman argues in *Unheard Melodies*, are a deliberate product of cinema, and particularly of cinema's use of non-diegetic instrumental music at moments of intensity (1987: 5). Tears type the films that work to produce them as gendered. Similarly, laughter types the film that produces it by class. Comedy, associated with cinema's origins in vaudeville, is viewed as *déclassé*, low brow, of limited intelligence. Since Mikhail Bakhtin's assertion in *Rabelais and His World* that the belly laugh is a protest against power (see 1984: 59–144), discussion has raged about whether comedy is the purest form of entertainment, or political subversion. The pleasures of laughter are at the very least suspiciously bodily and anarchic.

Physical comedy is one of the strongest traces of the place of the body, and of performance heritage, in both classical cinema (Charlie Chaplin being a key figure) and contemporary cinema. The clips in *Laughter* run the gamut of humour from *Carry On* upwards, including the Marx Brothers, inspiration for the name of one of Potter's improvisational performance groups – although she commented that she wished she had named them the Marx Sisters, for the added comedic value of the twist (interview with author, September 2006). Slapstick offers the possibility of social, as well as narrative, anarchy for Potter. Although physical comedy of this kind rarely appears in her films after the Expert scene in *The Gold Diggers*, the spirit of comedic juxtaposition between gesture and *mise-en-scène* is evident on a smaller scale in the Cleaner's gestures in *Yes*.

Physical comedy also draws a line between 'serious' performance arts such as dance (associated with the middle class), and working-class pleasures such as burlesque, vaudeville and gross-out movies. Yet Emilyn Claid believes the 'cathartic pleasure of laughter is an engaging component in performer-spectator relations that is far too often denied by dance makers and performers in Western culture's efforts to establish dance as an art form of the highest order' (2006: 64). She saw – and recorded others seeing – the funny side of Limited Dance Company's anarchic combination of radical Marxist feminist politics, ballet steps and critical theory. By her account, their wacky humour derived, in the tradition of early film comedy, from inventive use of props and costumes, failed performances-within-the-performance, shock tactics, winks to the audience and intertextual juxtapositions. Describing LDC's *Mounting*, Claid writes that 'we laugh – and our laughter is then undercut by the final violent images of blood trickling from mouths and legs accompanied by the music from *Jaws*' (2006: 65). The subversive humour continues in the incorporation of a highly identifiable film score, in a way that prefigures Potter's use of the *Psycho* theme in *Thriller*. In each case, the thrilling strings are removed from the unthinking, manipulative shock value they have in the original films. Through witty juxtaposition, they are used to prompt spectatorial engagement with larger issues.

In 'On Shows', Potter draws a strong connection between successful perform-ance and humour in engaging the audience beyond laughter. 'Many comedians and others working in theatre tread an extraordinary line that engages an audience on many levels at once ... The audience can laugh or cry *and* think. The function of the joke (when its [sic] not at the expense of an oppressed group) can be to open out and stir up those places in people where thinking has stopped' (1980: n. p.; emphasis in original). This intelligent laughter differs from the instinctive reactions courted by the gross-out humour and insulting language that pervade much contemporary comedic cinema. Potter's belief in the political affect of humour is apparent in the judicious arrangement of interviews in *Laughter*, and particularly the presence of Inez McCor-mack. The Northern Irish trade union leader offers a potted history of her work with both labour unions and feminist consciousness-raising groups in the 1970s and 1980s. She argues that laughter brought women together and empowered them in the face of male domination and the Troubles.

Potter's cathartic humour has a similarly political affect. One of the first arti-cles written on her work, Jane Weinstock's 'She Who Laughs First Laughs Last', draws attention to the place of laughter in *Thriller*. Weinstock associates Colette Laffont's laugh with the anti-patriarchal concepts of French feminism. She hears Hélène Cixous' 'laugh of the Medusa', with which Medusa looks at herself in the mirror and does not turn to stone, and an echo of Julia Kristeva's claim that 'oral eroticism, the smile at the mother, and the first vocalisations are contemporaneous' (in Weinstock 1980: 108). She suggests that Laffont's 'smile at the mother' starts to undo Freud's claim that jokes are told for male pleasure at the expense of female unpleasure. Weinstock ends by asking: 'If laughter and humour are not in step, have I chosen the wrong pretext? If so, the joke's on me' (ibid.). In so doing, she inverts the relationship of critic and text, suggesting that maybe Laffont, in laughing at Tel Quel's *Theorie d'Ensemble*, is laughing at the kind of theory Weinstock employs. At the same time, she suggests smartly that Laffont's laughter is about something more than either the pretentions of high theory or its juxtaposition with the physical pantomime of the Artists carrying Rose English from the room.

Perhaps her laugh can be re-read as threatening like *Psycho*'s strings, the 'thrilling' sound of the madwoman in the attic whom we know not to be mad – or to be mad in the sense of full of anger. Ruby's soundless laugh onstage is a parody of her mother laughing in *The Gold Diggers*' opening sequence. It brings up and questions the French feminist associations of laughter with the nurturing maternal. The male audience rightly perceive it as threatening anger, a sign of 'seeing red' at the same old story in which Ruby has been trapped. It also expresses her pleasure at reaching this realisation. McCormack describes similar moments in which women laugh together out of relief as they come to understand that many of the hardships of their lives are not their fault, but the product of systemic oppression and inequity. 'Through laughter, not only can politically subversive statements be made, but also the object of anger can be disrupted and displaced' (Claid 2006: 61). In the middle of the sad, silent play about maternal desertion, Ruby's mad laugh is just such a disruption.

Moments of cathartic onscreen laughter are rare in Potter's oeuvre, compared to instances of tears. Unlike tears they are not kinaesthetic (causing the viewer to mimic them), working instead to highlight laughter's association with anger and its subversive potential. This is reflected in the many moments in her films that – without enforcing humour – solicit laughter, and cause the viewer to think about what her laughter is doing. Orlando's to-camera observations, already a subversion of film form, are often witty comments on social expectations of gendered behaviour. Like Cesar's tears, Orlando's glances stand outside narrative, and thus release the viewer's laughter. Their impact is like a punchline to a long build of humorous dialogue, edits, intertexts, gestures, expressions and *mises-en-scène* within the narrative flow. They create laughter by cutting against expectations, even within the film. When Orlando confides to the camera that her love for Shelmerdine has made her 'so happy [she] think[s she's] going to faint', she ironises a rare moment of gender conformity even as she experiences it. Her conscious apprehension of her emotional state is the exact opposite of the unconsciousness she announces, so her reflexive awareness of the cliché is even more delightful.

Humour in *The Tango Lesson* and (more subtly) in *The Man Who Cried* comes from the films' awareness of clichés about race and gender, and their refusal to fulfil – or even parody – such expectations. *Orlando* parodies both 'Johnny Foreigner' and Brit-twit conventions of British comedy when Vere (Matthew Sim) speaks loud, slow English to Sasha after Orlando explains that to communicate with non-English speakers, the English 'parlent anglais plus fort'. Pablo and Sally communicate with each other across three languages, but humour does not relate to comical misunder-standings of this kind, arising instead because Potter takes herself as 'subject of [her] own work', as Claid argues about 1970s feminist performance (2006: 61). As in *Orlando*, there is humour in *The Tango Lesson*'s casting: not only is Potter knowingly playing a version of herself, but Heathcote Williams appears as a cowboy builder who gets in the way of Sally's writing. It is funny because he is a writer, and played one in *Orlando*, and also because sucking his teeth and talking in a Cockney drawl draws attention to the actor's own rejection of his aristocratic background.

Sally's patient, pained conversations with her cowboy builder, uncomprehending Hollywood executives and Pablo are, like the 'hapless ballet *pas de deux*' that Potter failed to direct very visibly in *Mounting*, failed performances-within-a-performance (ibid.). Embedded in a narrative that moves towards successful communication and joyous performance, they are invitations to see 'laughter, like tears, [as] a healing agent for emotional pain' (ibid.), as they implicitly replay incidents drawn from Potter's own struggles to make *The Tango Lesson*. The film itself is gentle parody rather than autobiography, made funnier because Potter has the courage to make herself the subject if not of the joke, then of the humour.

In a parody of Potter courageously casting herself as Sally, Dante unintentionally makes himself the butt of the joke in the way that he insists everything is about him, when nothing really is – a comment made amply by Cesar's horse. His pomposity is offset by Potter's acknowledgement of the ridiculousness of opera, with Suzie and Lola as singing pike-carriers in stick-on moustaches. Like Laffont's laughter, Dante's buffoonery is not innocent: his self-belief is reflected in his embrace of fascist politics. Michael Powell comments in *Laughter* that 'laughter keeps us sane. Hitler had no sense of humour', a thought borne out by Dante's inability to laugh at himself or anything else, other than out of cruel mockery.

The sanity of that laughter circulates in *Yes*, in two ways: through the onscreen moments of laughter in the film; and through the deadpan to-camera delivery of Shirley Henderson as the Cleaner, a bravura stand-up/lie-down comic performance of witty dialogue and strange, obsessive gestures. The Cleaner's meditations on dirt at first seem ridiculous, but that thought reveals the viewer's shallow assumption that cleaners can only be light relief. She comments, pointedly, that many people think that 'those who clean are small', socially and intellectually. Her metaphysical monologues combine humour and thought in their juxtaposition of macropolitics and microscopic particles. They offer astonishing insights that bring laughter as their beauty and their ethical profundity is couched in Henderson's idiosyncratic whispered delivery. Expatiating on international politics and embryology in the language of Shakespeare and Joyce, *Yes* roots its politics in its emotional affect. This serious exuberance remakes the lineage of the romantic comedy, inverting the trend for flip high school Shakespeare by returning to the mordant political themes of the playwright's comedies.

She and He earn their joyous, erotic laughter of reunion on the beach. Embracing *From Here to Eternity* (1953), *Yes* uncovers the pleasure of love and emotion that is part of melodrama's appeal. The lovers' laughter refers back to an earlier moment of laughter onscreen, one that makes the later moment possible. It is a generous parallel that recognises the danger in the anarchic diversity of laughter's meanings. The earlier laughter is that of a seemingly shared community, the male kitchen workers including He. It is Christmas Eve, and the kitchen and workers are decorated with cheap tinsel, highlighting the fact that they are working while others enjoy themselves as part of the holiday. Virgil is talking about finding Jesus – an appropriate subject for the date – while Whizzer mocks him and religion, comparing the Christian God's mercy to his own job as a dishwasher: 'I'm God, you're dirt, I wash you in the sink / Of holy fucking water.' A series of exchanged glances suggest both that this is a commonly repeated exchange, part of the rhythm of the job, and that He finds it amusing, even when Whizzer turns on him and on Islam.

'Oh, infidel!' He exclaims, twirling his moustache, parodying clichéd representations of Middle Eastern villains. He continues to humour (or taunt) Whizzer until Whizzer associates him with terrorism. Whizzer rants at him, and He comments perceptively that the young kitchen worker 'celebrate[s] his ignorance with joy' when he 'should be studying'. Lack of education has curdled Whizzer's opportunities for pleasure into a bitter racism against those whom he has been told have deprived him. His violent language finally incites He to threaten him back. He is fired, which leads to his confrontation with She, and eventually to their laughing, loving reconciliation on the beach. Violent humour made out of jokes at the expense of other people is where the lovers' trajectory begins, in humour's association not with joy, but with fear.

Fear

> Sally Potter (off-camera): Have you ever set out to create fear?
> Michael Powell: Yes, in *Peeping Tom*.
> Sally Potter: Why?
> Michael Powell: To see if I could do it.
>
> – in *Fear*

Peeping Tom is a film about how classical cinema turned something joyful (love, the appreciation of beauty) into fear. The story of Mark (Carl Boehm), a photographer who murders his models with his tripod so he can take a picture of their agony, was censored for indecency and practically ended Powell's career. Some feminist theorists, however, saw in the film an exact reflection and a sympathetic exploration of the sadism of their experience of cinema: the film represented the horror of the female viewer confronted with her own tortured image on the screen (see Silverman 1988: 32–41). Through Mark, it showed how patriarchy cultivates fear of the female body, of sexuality and emotions and projects its fears through cinema as violent hatred. Whizzer, like Mark, turns his fears into hate and violence.

The hate language that Whizzer plays for cruel humour does a poor job of masking the deep-seated fears played on by right-wing politics. Whizzer's rant alludes to the subtle ways in which contemporary political rhetoric echoes Enoch Powell's 'Rivers of Blood' speech, the nadir of anti-immigrant racism in British politics. Yet the speech was delivered in 1968, the year of student uprisings that began in France as anti-colonialist protests and in the US as anti-Vietnam and civil rights marches. The speech's reactionary fear was emphasised by Enoch Powell himself when he warned that Britain would end up like the US, referring to the incremental successes of desegregation. 'Politics is riddled with the use of fear', comments black British politician Paul Boateng early on in *Fear*, making an implicit reference to Enoch Powell. Fear, suggests Boateng, is manipulative, even as it points to issues that need to be addressed (like Whizzer's lack of opportunity), which he differentiates from real threats that need to be contained (his racist and nihilistic beliefs in the causes of his lack of opportunity).

Fear's manipulation is so powerful because it is not only an emotion, but a physical sensation. Shivers, or 'thrills', are the sensation that locate fear in the body, as tears do for sadness. Fears in Potter's films rarely translate into shivers for the viewer, but they do speak insistently of the characters' bodies: Pablo's fear of crying, Grace's fear of being fat. *Thriller* dispenses with the manipulative physical cues of the thriller, and in doing so allows the viewer to step back and think about the source of filmic fears. This distancing, like *Peeping Tom*'s explicit display of cinema's mechanisms of subjection, allows us to 'focus on emotions as mediated rather than immediate [to] remind us that knowledge cannot be separated from the bodily world of feeling and sensation' (Ahmed 2004: 171).

Not being conscious, not knowing, is a state of fear for Potter's characters, as is the feeling that other characters know more than they do, or more about them than they would wish. This is most pervasive in *The Man Who Cried*, in which Suzie's life is put at risk because of Dante's knowledge that she is a Jew. In the short story, Suzie joins an early French resistance group as a liaison to Cesar and the Roma, who have been intelligence-gathering through their trans-European network (2000a: xxxii–xxxvi). In the film, this is symbolised by Suzie walking with Cesar behind the funeral procession of the boy struck down in a Nazi raid. As they walk, she and Cesar speak of fear, and of actions taken in fear. The film draws a distinction between the cowardly acts of someone like Dante, who collaborates out of fear that he will not be able to show off his singing voice, and Suzie, whose escape to America perhaps saves Cesar from death by association.

Suzie derives knowledge, and indeed courage, from her fear. According to neurologist Antonio Damasio, fear acts as an early warning system, a form of embodied knowledge (see 1999: 61–7). Being able to name one's fear consciously, as Pablo does at the end of *The Tango Lesson*, is a sign of self-knowledge that could save your life. Potter's films argue that fear can direct us outwards, to explore and connect with the world. The thriller genre's structure of investigation motivated by fear is the backbone of the body of her work, but is tempered by melodrama and the musical. These genre hybrids, which mix melodrama's emotions and musical's spectacle into the thriller, suggest that fear works by closing us off, excluding the (feminised) elements that might help us discover a way out.

Ruby is drawn into the dark alleys and stalking footsteps of *noir* as she searches for memories of her mother. Her loss motivates her search although she does not know what she is searching for. Mimi's memory is supplemented by photographs from productions and archives that point to the gaps that they cover over in her account of *La Bohème*. Suzie's photograph of her father serves a similar purpose, having become a simulacrum of a memory that has disappeared. Mary Gordon, an archivist who turned her professional skills to the search for her own father, writes that 'all of us in the archives are acknowledging the insufficiency of memory. The falseness of the myth of continuity. The loss of living speech. Our own inability to live with the blanks. To live in the enveloping whiteness of imagination and of love' (1996: 239). Fear is an expression of discomfort at archival blanks. It points to the incompleteness of memory, and to the way that the body remembers through 'imagination and … love'.

'The loss of living speech', memory and connection is the deepest source of fear in each of Potter's films. Characters die or come near to death, but death does not generate fear because it is grotesque or repulsive. It is death's threat of disappearance, of being forgotten, that is fearful, as in Pablo's confession: 'J'ai peur de disparaître sans laisser aucune trace' (I'm afraid I will disappear without leaving a trace (1997b: 78; Potter's translation)). The Aunt's deathbed interior monologue in *Yes* asks She for a tribute of tears as an acknowledgement of her existence and death. By acting on what she has intuited, She undoes the fear of erasure that death holds. *The Tango Lesson* contains one oblique reference to *Peeping Tom*'s deathly fears. It appears in the film-within-a-film that is not called *Fear*, but *Rage* (1996). Whereas the women who confront Mark are infected with (and die at the hands of) his fear, one of the women gunned down by a photographer in *Rage* (1996) rises up from the dead, like Mimi and Suzie. Rage is a close relation of the inwardness of tears and grief: the Aunt tells She that 'I want to hear you protest / At me leaving … See you kick a chair and punch the wall.' The legion of undead women in Potter's films stand for an angry refusal to die and be forgotten.

Rage

> Knowing you've got emotions is an incredibly important step on the way to thinking and dealing with the situation. Anger can help you work out what needs to be changed.
>
> – Juliet Mitchell in *Rage* (1987)

Rage (1996) itself has risen again from the dead, transformed from Sally's abandoned project to a full-length feature. Among its other innovations, *Rage* (2009) is a thriller whose fearful plot mechanisms are all offscreen. Several deaths and their investigation happen away from Michelangelo's unwavering camera, which is focused on the real, deep source of events in various characters' rage at oppression. *Rage* (2009) changes the form of the thriller because it is a film about how rage can create change.

Despite its genre-coded promise of justice served, *Rage* (2009) ends in tears. The handheld camera (wielded by Potter), swooping into close framing whenever a character expresses a strong emotion, offers a cinematic language for the way in which emotions bring us nearer to each other and the world. It even shakes, a little, at the end when garment worker Anita, the only character who has cried for the deaths of models Dorothy and Bonnie, tells Michelangelo not to cry. The tears are his first expression of affect, his first editorial comment on the material he has been shooting. The circuit of tears, in which we imagine Anita's own tears reflected on Michelangelo's face, is conjured by Ford Madox Ford in his poem 'On Heaven'. He describes the paradigmatic Englishman – symbol of colonialism and patriarchy – spending his life 'in the craze to relinquish / What [he] want[s] most', which is love, symbolised by 'the coming nearer of a tear-wet face' (1997: 101). This expression of mutually-assured humanity, says Ford, is 'what the rest of the world is on fire for' (ibid.). Reflecting on the film's few scenes of overt anger, Potter describes the characters' 'quieter rage underneath, a volcanic heat of rage against an economy that, by its very structure, ruins lives and turns people into things, forgetting what's important about being alive' (interview with author, December 2008). To return us, through rage, to what's important about being alive, *Rage* (2009) draws the distinction between a rage that is 'the craze to relinquish' our vulnerability (whether by acquisition or destruction) and rage defined as what 'the world is on fire for'.

That the film diverts rage *against* into a rage *for* is suggested by the film's very first image: white-on-black letters typing out 'All the Rage'. Cursor flashing and back-tracking, 'All the' is deleted in recognition of the film's inevitable partiality. It is a restoration of vital anger to a phrase used to refer to acquisitiveness; yet at the same time, a comment on the way in which activism, like all counter-cultures, has been branded and trend-tracked by the media. It is hard not to hear, in claims that police are predicting a 'summer of rage' for 2009, rage as this season's hair colour (Brooker 2009). Visible and invisible in its deletion, the phrase also holds up the desiring intimations of 'all the rage' to set against the destructive association of rage and violence, whether anarchic or revolutionary. From her earliest situationist work, Potter has demonstrated a passionate commitment to emotional, rather than physical, acts of provocation as being the root – and route – of change. Cary Nelson, in a study of cultural memory in modern American poetry, notes that 'the protest or picket line, a significant symbol of Depression culture, was a site where women could be found chanting their demands like lines of verse' (1989: 89). Protest as poetry and poetry as protest are intertwined in Potter's filmmaking. Rage is not just an expression, but a form.

Throughout the documentary episode *Rage* (1987), Potter examines the politics of rage, particularly the equation of rage with change through violence. Rage is a signifier of Potter's transformative politics. The most visible and exterior of emotions, its dramatic expressivity makes audible larger political histories that the films hope will connect to the viewer's lived experience. Beneath the rage in *Rage* (2009) is depression. The film explores the word's dual emotional and economic import, revealing the sugar-spun castle of high fashion to be a keystone of the weighty edifice of patriarchal capitalism that bears down on all the characters. While the film remains conscious of the qualitatively and quantitatively different effects that the crisis has on their lives, brown-skinned illegal labourers like Anita and middle-aged white-collar workers like Bradley are united by the consequences of the credit crunch. From that unity emerges the cinematic form of a trade union: by joining Michelangelo's film, the characters implicitly enter into a form of collective bargaining. In the model of the union, Potter locates the conversion of depression into a creative rage as a thread that unites the characters.

Potter's oeuvre dramatises, and proposes, emotions as a connection to others and an opening to the world in two senses: as overwhelming physical experiences, tears, laughter, fear and rage render us vulnerable; and that vulnerability signals our affectivity, that we can be reached by the world outside us, as when She cries so passionately at her Aunt's bedside. Her release of tears does not signal the end of the film, however, nor is it an end in itself, but informs and motivates She's flight to Cuba and reconciliation. Rage is similarly offered in *Rage* (2009) as an epistemology, a philosophy that shapes the characters' actions – but also their thinking. Rage enables Michelangelo to see how fashion connects, both globally and intimately, poverty to the impoverishment of language to issues of ethnicity and identity. Rage's impetus to undo those connections remains, but the film argues that – not least because of the complexity of the interconnections, and the vast number of people that they hold together – such an unseaming has to be a subtle, consensual act of thought and feeling, rather than a vigilante attack on the symbols of capitalism.

Mimi in *Thriller* does not kill the Artists in revenge. She is loving rather than violent, analytical rather than angry. Her rage is expressed by changing the story. The psychic need for a re-visioned history in Potter's work stems from a rage against 'heritage drama' pastness, in which historical subjects are Othered as being distant from us. Potter responds with Orlando's continuous present, and by an investment in the *material* archive that begins with the photographs of garment workers in *Thriller*. Rage against official history is translated into a rage *for* history, for remembering the past correctly, diversely and in detail. Like fear, rage is associated with not forgetting. This can be heard when He tells the story of why He left Beirut: the details convey his rage although his speech is calm. He cooks as he speaks; his chopping knife is associatively the surgeon's scalpel that he was forced to abandon by gunmen, and also the knife with which he will threaten Whizzer for his racist comments.

He's rage at Whizzer spills over into his confrontation with She, who is fuming at a previous argument with her husband. Their anger is spent when each character realises that they are carrying the previous arguments into this one, and She is able to listen when He demands 'respect'. Respect is also the motivation of Suzie's one instance of rage, after Dante had spoken disrespectfully about gypsies. When Suzie speaks angrily on Cesar's behalf, he tells her that he does not need anyone to speak for him – and yet her rage is the beginning of their romance. Sally and Pablo's reconciliation, and Sally's work on *The Tango Lesson*, begins with a blazing row between them, in which Sally refuses to follow. Rage creates the possibility of a relationship by making visible and explicit the inequalities that make communication on an equal footing difficult.

Rage expresses the feeling that someone has done violence to another by taking power; and the way that it is shown through words, music and gestures, rather than violence and explosions, expresses Potter's films' refusal to take power over the viewer. Although they are attentive to histories of political violence, they eschew revolutionary violence. In the refusal to use formal violence such as MTV-style editing, Potter's films underline their refusal of performative violence. Rage is instead expressed through passionate forms such as tango, which translates anti-colonialist rage into a dance of stylised violence and desire. In *Rage* (1987) Inez McCormack observes that 'it was passion that brought [the trade union] movement into being, the passion of fighting against injustice'. Tango brings the two meanings of 'passion' together, reminding us that rage's other face is love. When He describes the anger that drove him from Beirut, he is preparing a Lebanese salad for She. His caring gesture folds love into rage, as Celeste's 'Empire Song' does. Love, as much as fear, is the root of rage. Potter concludes her documentary series with a comment from Boateng that 'love [is] an instrument of change in positive, practical ways. Not as a sloppy sentiment, but as a practical strategy.'

Coda: A Box of Kisses

> It is no longer useful to presume that sexuality, intimacy, affect and other categories of experience typically assigned to the private sphere do not also pervade public life. (Cvetkovich 2003: 32)

Cinema can bring 'sexuality, intimacy [and] affect' into the public sphere, and Potter's films have challenged the cultural politics of love from *Thriller* onwards. When Orlando kisses Sasha on the frozen river it is the first kiss in Potter's oeuvre, and it is brief, plunging Orlando into a melancholy as he struggles with the meaning of his stolen kiss, signifying the desire to *own* Sasha. Orlando and Shelmerdine never once kiss. In Shelmerdine, Orlando meets an equal who, their conversation suggests, may have had a female identity as Orlando had a male – or is at least willing to consider the possibility. In *Orlando*, Potter began to think about whether cinema, with its taint of oppressive heterosexuality, can screen kisses between men and women, a question that is central to *The Tango Lesson*.

The film's published screenplay includes a story called 'The archivist goes to Buenos Aires'. SP, the central character, is struggling with the place of emotion in her film when the Archivist arrives to visit her. She has been developing emotions alongside the film script, and sending them to the Archivist in boxes. The first contains the 'image of a woman crying', the second is a 'box of kisses', and the third holds 'Pablo and SP in the middle of it all, arguing' (Potter 1997d: 94–6). Two of the boxes are opened in *The Tango Lesson*, repeatedly. Sally cries and she and Pablo rage at each other, but they only kiss once. Sally is leaving for LA and Pablo has been dancing through the airport, leaping from luggage trolleys and the travelator to charm Sally equally as lover and filmmaker. The kiss is part of this choreographic sequence and is followed by a comedic moment in which Pablo appears to fall off the travelator. It is part of a performance that refers to the way that Hollywood's Golden Age musicals typically end with a kiss. This embrace is almost at the film's midpoint, the end of the fifth lesson. It comes just before the executives reject Sally's film and she and Pablo become working dance partners, creating a confusion of love and art that is not resolved until the end.

Sally and Pablo's embrace is also a formal investigation of the affect of the musical, because the box of kisses is, in a sense, the essence of cinema, and of cinema's affect. Imaginatively, Potter's films open a treasure trove of other gestures that speak to and of female sexual pleasure. They are rarely 'The End', as either the limit of narrative or form. Mimi's and Musetta's embrace offered one of *Thriller*'s 'thrills' by putting lesbian desire onscreen in the middle of both a canonical opera and a 'theory film'. Their embrace suggests that the box of kisses is the *supplément* within the archives of high art and academic theory, the secret desire that cinema's romantic narratives satisfy. These affective moments are also resolutely public – not in the sense of exploitative exposure, but in their occurrence in cinema's public space. They move outwards, acknowledging their social history and political present in order to build an intimate public sphere. Intimate encounters, 'insofar as they are face to face, are *forms* of (and not supplements to) collective activism … They are never private' (Ahmed 2000: 179; emphasis in original).

It is only in *Yes* that the box of kisses can be opened completely because the film politicises screen romance in two senses: it foregrounds an interracial romance that explicitly invokes, in order to challenge, clichés of Orientalism, and it balances the public archive of historical events with the private repertoire of bodily memory. The partnership of He and She, their path to mutual regard, is marked by stolen kisses: bodily touches that leave their trace in memory. In the most openly, explicitly sexual encounter in Potter's oeuvre, He arouses She to orgasm through a combination of manual and verbal dexterity. 'I am a feeling,' says She, as He's hand moves under her skirt. Her passionate expression of interiority is all the more powerful because of the setting: an upmarket London wine bar with 'yuppie' postmodern décor.

Their erotic encounter is not just public, but marked by references to the public sphere's imposition of economics on desire. Other customers are visible in the far distance behind the couple; a waiter hovers with the bill – which She pays. As She hands over her credit card, She asks He to turn from the lyric, *ghazal*-like language with which he first addressed her to 'names I never would forgive / If spoken to me in the street'. He whispers words that name the abjection she feels, but cannot articulate, for her economic and white-skin privilege. At the same time the words defy the cultural taboos on female pleasure and sexual passion by making the private public. The kiss cannot be contained in the box of domestic space and the fantasy of privacy that remands female sexual desire as shameful.

Her rhapsody, charted by canted-angle handheld shots superimposed over one another, blurs the boundary between the privacy of sexual space (the bedroom) and public space. He is a chef, and the restaurant is a location for work. Female sexual desire is deliberately removed from the private shame of the blank bedroom in the private house – where the sordid evidence of Anthony's affair is revealed at the start of the film – to the complex lived world of work, food and other bodily pleasures.

Bringing She to orgasm, He offers an ecstatic manifesto for what Lauren Berlant calls 'forms of affective, erotic, and personal living that are public in the sense of accessible, available to memory, and sustained through collective activity' (in Cvetkovich 2003: 9). He's words simultaneously make sexual activity and desire public, and render them collaborative in speaking of She as an agent.

> HE: Let the hidden parts be seen.
> SHE: Yes!
> HE: The only
>> Danger is that all the lonely
>> Private places you have been to
>> Might dissolve, and you'll be seen to
>> Blossom. Dancing, singing, humming,
>> Laughing … come here, love, you're coming.

Each of Potter's films could be seen as a dissolution of 'the lonely / Private places' in which her protagonists initially find themselves. In response to He, She lets go of her past self and her resentment of her husband's secret infidelities. Although the language that He and She exchange, and their setting, is marked by gender, race and class asymmetries, in the moment of orgasmic release there is a sloughing of these histories. Potter's cinema, like She, finds a way to open the box of kisses, and 'blossoms' into 'dancing, singing, humming'. The rhyme makes 'coming' a musical performance, a creative celebration of the embodied present. Jacques Derrida defines the gift as 'the "yes" or originary affirmation … the event, invention, the coming or the "come"' (1992: x). Putting female orgasm delicately and lovingly into public space and onscreen is central to the film's 'yes'.

Derrida also notes the double meaning of 'present', suggesting that what the gift – like the orgasm, or the film – gives is an extended now that opposes the archive's insistence on then-ness (see 1992: 9–10). Potter's films exist in the gift of now, in the action of 'coming'. Potter's spirals 'radicalis[e] our relation to the past, which is transformed into that which lives and breathes in the present' (Ahmed 2004: 180). Their interlocking temporal signatures are shaped by love's intensification of the moment, which shares the spiral's association with infinity and with transformation (Weinberger 2007: 126). The body opens feelingly towards a turn in which a past moment that was lost, hidden or secret is opened to the present. Interacting with the archive of feelings through Potter's films, we (like her characters) are reshaped by opening to those feelings and the memories that they evoke and alter. Surfaces and boundaries are breached, infolded by feeling (emotion and touch). The boxes that the Archivist opens are within us.

CHAPTER ELEVEN

Yes

I wear a red yes and how he kissed me under the Moorish wall and I thought
well as well him as another and then I asked him with my eyes to ask again yes
and then he asked me would I yes to say yes my mountain flower and first I
put my arms around him yes and drew him down to me so he could feel my
breasts all perfume yes and his heart was going like mad and yes I said yes I
will Yes.
JOAN: this was the starting point for *Yes* – Sally.

– James Joyce, *Ulysses* (1992: 993), extract on a sheet of quotations from
Irish writers prepared and annotated for Joan Allen by Sally Potter, undated,
Yes archives

The publicity materials for *Yes* were dominated by 'a red yes' in the sans-serif font
designed by Stephen Masters that has appeared in the credits of Sally Potter's films
since *Orlando*. Potter's note to Joan Allen, on a photocopied sheet of cut-and-paste
selections from a dictionary of quotations from Irish literature, pinpoints the starting
point for *Yes* in the most famous 'Yes' in English literature. 'Penelope', the final chapter
of James Joyce's *Ulysses* is an unpunctuated, breathless, bravura monologue by Molly
Bloom, the wife of the book's protagonist (see 1992: 871–993). She is thinking about
her afternoon's infidelity, about her husband and about her adolescent experience of

love in Gibraltar. The onrush of her orgasmic speech ends by turning the repeated word 'yes' into a verb that stands for orgasm as an ecstatic acceptance of memory, the Other and the world. 'I will Yes', she concludes, as if saying 'I will come.' The 'red yes' of *Yes* is likewise affirmation as action: not passive acceptance but a self-determined opening out to the world.

Like Molly, Allen's character She says Yes to and through a romantic and erotic relationship. She falls for He, an Armenian-Lebanese immigrant in London who is reduced to using his surgeon's skills in his work as a sous-chef at an expensive hotel. Their universal names recall *Hiroshima mon amour* (1959) in which Elle (Emmanuelle Riva), a French actress, has a brief affair with Il (Eiji Okada), a Japanese architect whose family died in the atomic bomb blast. Working on a film in Hiroshima in the 1950s, Elle recalls her former relationship with a German soldier during the occupation of her home town of Nevers. Like *Hiroshima mon amour*, *Yes* is a film in which a white woman and a non-white man fall in love by telling each other stories of the past. She tells stories about growing up during the Troubles in Belfast, while He relates why he left Lebanon, a country he loves. Their memories circle through the film, connecting past loves to present, as Molly does in her monologue.

Kaja Silverman offered a fresh reading of *Hiroshima mon amour* in 2005, the year that *Yes* was released. Influenced by current events that seemed to augur the impossibility of dialogue across cultures, Silverman argued for *Hiroshima mon amour*'s pacifist, passionate radical theory of listening, which she calls 'the cure by love' (2005: 41). *Yes* likewise 'asks us to conceptualise love not in the form either of the aggrandisement or rapture of the one who loves, but rather in the form of care for the world. It suggests that creatures and things are in need of this care because without it they cannot help but suffer from the most serious of all maladies: invisibility' (2005: 42). He first notices She when she is standing alone, neglected by her husband, her beauty invisible to him. By listening, She comes to see beyond He's cultural invisibility as a Middle Eastern exile working in a low-status job. Through her relationship with Il, Elle realises that what she has seen in the museums of Hiroshima hides the more significant, intimate and complex invisible consequences of the nuclear attack and its roots in US imperialism and racism.

The historical backdrop of *Yes* is not World War Two, as in *Hiroshima mon amour*, but 9/11. Unlike other 9/11 films such as *World Trade Center* (2007), *Yes* does not visit Ground Zero or its heroes. Kaja Silverman writes that in Renais' film 'the story of Hiroshima and the story of love are linked not through analogy, but rather through *incorporation* ... To incorporate something is to put it in the body of another thing. It is thereby to carry it away from itself – to make it something else' (2005: 36; emphasis in original). *Yes* incorporates the events of 9/11 not only through the lovers' bodies and relationship, but also by incorporating the immediate events within a longer history of relations between Islam and the West. Rather than lecture against racism and Islamophobia, Potter uses references to histories of art, literature and science to show that European culture emerges from an Islamic framework. The intensities of lyric poetry and visual imagery with which we speak of love developed under a Moorish wall.

Molly Bloom recalls her first kiss in a garden on Gibraltar, the first Spanish territory to fall to a Muslim army. Berbers under Arab leadership crossed the straits and defeated the Visigothic King Rodrigo in 711. Gibraltar was the gateway to the Muslim conquest of Spain and the establishment in southern and central Spain of the culture known as al-Andalus (see Fletcher 2001: 1). Based on Qu'ranic precept, al-Andalus' Muslim rulers accorded special status to Jews and Christians as People of the Book. Until Ferdinand and Isabella's final expulsion of the Jews and Muslims in 1492, al-Andalus provided a 'red yes' of *convivencia* (living-togetherness) in which intellectuals, artists, philosophers, poets and scientists of the three faiths shared discoveries. While Andalusian contributions to science are widely recognised, only careful scholarship has traced the roots of the European vernacular lyric back to the songs of al-Andalus. María Rosa Menocal argues that the troubadours were deeply influenced by Arabic poetry. Transmitted 'body-to-body', Andalusian song was itself an expression of *convivencia* because it drew on Arabic and Jewish poetic traditions, and was sung in Arabic and Hebrew, as well as mixed tongues and new vernaculars like Ladino and Spanish. To reconnect to the tradition of oral poetry that came from al-Andalus through the troubadours before poetry became fixed as a written medium in European culture, Potter took her actors to the Def Jam poetry slam in New York (see Potter 2005b: 85).

During the initial development of the screenplay, Potter read *ghazals*, lyric poems that feature Molly's 'mountain flowers' and 'perfumed breasts', both tropes inherited from pre-Islamic Arabic poetry (interview with author, September 2006). *Yes* invokes the *ghazal* form in the dialogue that follows the lovers' first sexual encounter. Their post-coital exchange is a disquisition on numbers that brings together poetry, philosophy, mathematics and love to evoke the riches of al-Andalus' intellectual traditions. The poetic, playful exchange begins in response to She's request to fill a silent vacuum, which recalls the political need to speak in a time of crisis:

SHE: Speak to me.
HE: Of what? What is there to say?
SHE: Too much ... or nothing ... please try, anyway.

He responds that he 'adore[s] ... the number one', and the subsequent playful dialogue tours through her knowledge, as a Western scientist, of mathematics, reproductive science and quantum physics. At the end of the dialogue, which lasts for four minutes – one-fifth of the film to that point – She smiles as He touches her lips with his fingers. Bridged by music, there is a cut from She smiling in He's flat to She smiling while she looks down a microscope in a white-green laboratory. She raises her eyes from the barrel, blinking slowly and luxuriously as she had in the series of embraces preceding the numbers dialogue. She looks down the microscope, followed by a cut to her point of view of cells moving. This sequence of gestures and cuts implies that the previous scene was also 'seen' from She's point of view as a flashback memory as she looked at the cells. It is one of several examples of a lapping, vertical time structure that makes the past fully present by uncoupling it from linear time.

While *Yes* appears to narrate He and She's affair from their first meeting to a final reunion, time does not run straight. The film mingles Resnais' cyclical intercutting between Elle's gaze and her memories with the spiral time signature of Potter's earlier films. While few scenes in *Yes* are shorter than a minute, few are longer than five, and almost none consist of sequences shot in more than one space. They are self-contained, with none of the usual editing ligatures such as match-cuts that structure the seamlessness of classical narrative cinema. Conventional cause-effect structure and linking incidents are submerged as time hovers, moving densely in the scenes between the lovers, and loosely, swiftly otherwise, skipping from rendez-vous to rendez-vous with the rhythm of love. In *I-Thou* time the moment is 'continually present and enduring ... True beings are lived in the present' (Buber 1958: 13). This is the time of love. Love's dreamy present offers an alternative to the narrative pressures of cause and effect that shape tit-for-tat foreign policy as well as Hollywood cinema.

Romance defines form in *Yes*, prescribing not only lyric dialogue, but lyrical camerawork, and a poetically compressed sense of time, place and character. In 1953 Maya Deren set out her definitive theory of poetic film. For Deren, film had two axes: horizontal, which was the axis of realist linear time, and vertical, the axis of the non-linear imagination. A poetic film was vertical, a series of moments concentrated around a feeling or theme, an internal and intuitive movement rather than the requirements of what happens next (see Deren 1971: 174). *Yes* is a poem composed vertically of events experienced with the heightened senses and presentness of love. Bullet-scarred walls in Beirut are shot with the same care and radiance as cherry blossom in London. The pairing acts as homage to the poetic compression and political allegory of Iranian cinema, which Potter deeply admires (see Vollmer 2007: 229). As in the cinema of Abbas Kiarostami, intimate poetic time is not exempt from public history in *Yes*. Instead, it is infolded, uncovering the 'vertical' personal experience of historical events.

The sense of intensified time and presence is created through the use of a form of slow motion, in which film shot at six frames per second was digitally stretched to 24 frames per second. The slower shutter speed saturates the frames with light, intensifying our viewing experience. 'When we care about something, we see it. We allow it to appear ... What appears shines for us; it is radiant. It has the perceptual vividness that we normally encounter only in our dreams' (Silverman 2005: 43). *Yes* brings this perceptual vividness to everything, drawing a parallel between the dismissal of people or cultures as beneath notice and the discounting of what is physically small, like dirt and dust. The film cares for these things, allowing them to appear. The lyrical time signature causes time to slow during the scenes, creating the space for the viewer's attention to light on everything, so the film can make the world visible from the cellular level up.

The cells swarming under She's microscope recall the opening shot of the film, in which the screen was filled with moving, vibrating specks of shadow against a white background. In the following shot they come into focus as dust thrown up by the vacuum cleaner wielded by the Cleaner, who delivers the film's first lines, an opening monologue addressed to camera. She's gaze down the microscope is defini-

'It all depends on your point of view': the Cleaner (Shirley Henderson) gets the viewer's attention

tively connected to the Cleaner's to-camera gaze when the latter's closing monologue includes inserts of cells swarming. They could be read as She's memories of looking down the microscope, or as the Cleaner's access to She's memories. As She's smile down the microscope incorporates the previous scene as a flashback, so the Cleaner's narrative function as a Chorus incorporates She's and He's experiences into her omniscient point of view. Not only can she see microscopic dirt (and, given her to-camera address, the audience), but as Chorus she can see the film's entire narrative. What appears to be an intimate love story is presented as a parable about the physics, politics and metaphysics of visibility and invisibility related directly to the audience by the Cleaner.

The Cleaner works in a continuous, overlapping no-time that offsets and complements the time of love experienced by He and She. She is the first and last character to speak in the film, and she not only takes possession of the screen, but the main space within the film: She's and Anthony's marital home. We only see the couple there together in a single scene, in which Anthony (Sam Neill) arrives late for dinner and then storms out. It is the only sequence in the house in which the Cleaner is not present. Neither She nor Anthony seem at home in their house, in contrast to the Cleaner. She guides us through the spaces of the house in her opening monologue, and appears to inhabit them in her final address. We see her lying (fully clothed) in the bath and on the double bed, a potent figure of belonging in others' intimate spaces. The Cleaner's radical invasion of the middle-class home argues that possession, like love, belongs to she who sees and takes cares. Her minute and unconditional love makes the house into her laboratory, stage or gallery, a site of work, performance and visual pleasure. Like cinema for Potter, the home is the Cleaner's site of investigation and self-expression.

194   THE CINEMA OF SALLY POTTER

For both He and She, home is a problem that closes down their ability to feel. In a series of vertically-related moments, they criss-cross the globe in a vertiginous quest provoked by their own estrangement from any stable sense of home. She was left with her aunt in Belfast as a child, moved to America with her parents as a teenager and now lives in London while working internationally. He left Beirut for political reasons that make it difficult to love the home he yearns for from exile in London. London, where the film begins, is a place where both are strangers. Dislocation makes them strangers everywhere, even at home. In London, He and She carry out their relationship in the temporary places – hotels, gardens, a rented flat, a car park, a restaurant – that Michel Foucault called heterotopias, spaces of otherness. The park, He's brightly-draped bedroom, and the feast He prepares for She are also the traditional sites of Arabic lyric poetry. They weave a sense of place outside time because of their lyric association.

When She reaches four in the numbers game that takes place in He's rented flat, she threatens their temporary seclusion from the real. Four, she says, is 'a house with walls; and with a door / That closes'. He rejects the retreat into home, turning instead to 'the vast and endless state of none'. She replies that '[s]omeone invented the zero', lightly indicating her awareness of Arabic mathematics, but then protests that he 'tricked' her and gave himself 'the source / Of all the numbers'. In response, he returns cyclically, in the language of *ghazals*, to his 'adored' number: 'You are the one. The light of day, / The velvet night, the single rose, the hand / I want to hold, the secret country, land / Of all my longings.' In place of the 'house with walls' is a 'secret country' made of 'longings'. This is the film's true location, in poetic, vertical time and across multiple, magical spaces.

Yes began life as a celebration of a global metropolis like London. It was originally intended for the portmanteau film *Paris, je t'aime* (2006), as one of several shorts about love in and of Paris by well-known arthouse directors, including Gurinder Chadha, whose short *Quais de Seine* focuses on the Muslim community in Paris. Rather than becoming part of a portmanteau that locates love and its politics in a single (European) city, the short version of *Yes* transmuted into a film that discovers love around the globe, in cities that do not as obviously have Paris's cinematic tradition. The short, which was shot in Paris, is tied to the rhythms and urgency of its urban setting, and it turns the romantic conflict into 'real time' reportage shown second-by-second, aiming for resolution. Short, sharp shots follow feet, his and hers, as they pace the metre of the lines through the streets of Paris, past the bases of monuments and famous locations to a deserted, wintry park.

Most of the lines, remarkably close to their version in the finished film, are spoken in voice-over, in separation, as each character walks and rehearses his or her argument. There is no connection between them. The audience are their privileged witnesses, knowing more than either. The city is at first an intrusion and interruption: cobblestones wobble She's (Fiona Shaw) heels and threaten to tumble her; an iced pond comes between He and the meeting place. Their final meeting satisfies both conventions and emotions: the two bodies of knowledge held by the viewer meet and inform a conversation. It is an argument to which we already hold the answers. The public paths and spaces bring together the (unlikely) lovers. Surrounded by bare branches and white sky, they can speak of, and outside, social conditioning. In the silence, She can answer He's rage against invisibility with stillness and listening: 'I hear you,' she says. 'Tell me more.' They embrace and hymn each other in joy.

In the finished film, the same line is delivered after a similar argument, but does not and cannot precipitate the physical and emotional reunion that it does in the short. Nor is the scene shot in a park, but in a car park – a paradoxical place both dystopia and heterotopia, symbolic of movement and stagnation, of crime and protection, of entrapment and freedom. It is a temporary place where no one stays, and yet He and She are caught there on Christmas Eve, stayed by each other's words. There is a sense of expanded time that comes from moving a conversation written to the pace of a journey across a city to a single moment in a single, enclosed space. The short's lyric trappings are slashed, pared back into framing and editing. Faces instead of feet are the focus. It is not the realist setting of the car park that conveys the scene's political intent and historical context, but the hovering, *vérité* camera that stays with the faces that speak passionately.

The film deliberately disrupts conventions of editing and framing to show 'that narrative can be constructed lyrically, that philosophy is contingent, that history can be anachronic, and that the love song and the hermetic poem can be acts of deep political engagement' (Menocal 1993: 141). The formal choices that make narrative lyric and history anachronic (non-linear) are fused with impassioned poetic speech to produce a profound, humane political engagement that goes beyond he said/she said. With its handheld shots, tight framing, medium close-up scale and argumentative dialogue in split verse lines, this scene reasons out the Cleaner's claim for a contingent philosophy: 'It all depends on your point of view.'

Point of view is crucial in the film, moving between extremes of canted, handheld shots that imply subjectivity and rare instances of frontal framing. Classical framing is a trap. The car park argument follows on from another lovers' tiff that self-consciously announced its theatrical conventions through its flawless, symmetrical composition. The theatrical framing suggests that this is a repeat performance. She and Anthony row like a couple in an Ibsen play, over a dining room table that leads from the foreground of the shot to an arch beyond which there is a mirror flanked by vases. Only one instance disrupts the classical frame. When Anthony imagines embracing She, the shot is rotated 180° to show the dinner table behind them. But he lets go or forgets this dreamed insert, and the shot returns to its theatrical framing.

In the car park, by contrast, the camera hovers, unwilling to settle. Even when capturing the performers' stillness it lacks the icy perfection of the white house. There is no arch here, just a number of brutalist concrete pillars. Similarly, there are few level front-on shots, but rather a proliferation of canted angles, overhead shots, eccentric framing and harsh neon light. The setting draws its power from its bare ugliness, its functionality without beauty. There is no city here to be loved. Place has been replaced. 'I was your secret country / Land of all your longings', She protests when He asks for the return of his body from her 'possession'. Her repetition of his earlier line creates a connection between the metaphor of a woman's body as land, and the violent nationalism and imperialism of which each accuses the other.

The word 'land' is used twice more in the scene, both times by He. First, He addresses his sense of being possessed by a wealthy white American woman by comparing it to invasive American military action: 'You want to rule, you want to spoil; / You want our land, you want our oil.' The second time, instead of an attack, He reveals the vulnerability of exile: 'In your land / I am not seen. I am un-manned.' Land has moved from the start, to the middle, to the end of the line (the position it was in when He first named She 'land / Of all my longings'). It is no longer part of a rhyme scheme that foregrounds the macho posturing of nationalism, but its reversal. Land is literally his longing, but also stands in for something larger: to be in one's own land is to be 'seen' for oneself. This is what He demands of She, that she look again, respect him.

They stand facing each other for the first time since the argument began. She's eyes are open, tearily red-rimmed, the still point of a hovering two-shot. It begins at an angle not seen previously in this scene, and circles closer to He, narrowing the gap – garishly lit by a neon emergency light – between them, until their shoulders overlap. The camera's movement appears to alter the characters' physical proximity, and the overlap of bodies suggests the lovers' physical relationship has always been inflected by the politics of boundaries. It is a potent model in a film about land and belonging, because, through a nomadic drift of the camera, it unsettles the notion of the border as a stable zone of separation, or a troubled zone of conflict. Instead there is shifting ground as connection is realised. She's line 'I hear you. Tell me more' inter-locks with the camera movement, bringing the 'you' closer. The you is also the audi-ence, whose various experiences of being unheard, whether in intimate or political situations, rush in.

What She has heard in his plea is that 'to ask for recognition, or to offer it, is precisely not to ask for recognition of what is. It is to solicit a becoming, to instigate a transformation' (Butler 2004: 43). There is a cut from the shot lingering on her listening face to a ten-second silence of regard in which that transformation begins. He looks away from She – and the viewer – initially, and then lifts his eyes. It is the longest take in the scene – thirty seconds – and its stillness and length contrast the searching, doubling reconception of shot/reverse-shot with which Potter frames their argument. It is a pause that invites the viewer (and She) to gather her listening attention. Feminist philosopher Iris Marion Young argues that the kind of listening this scene reaches towards emerges from the realisation that 'if I assume that there are aspects of where the other person is coming from that I do not understand, I will be more likely to be open to listening to the specific expression of their experience, interest, and claims' (1997: 350). Whereas their bodies shared the previous shot in overlap, She is now out of the frame, grouped with the audience as a listener. The camera holds on He alone through his description of loss of identity as an immigrant to the UK.

Even as he speaks of being un-manned by being unseen, he is being seen – not in his macho rage, but in his vulnerability, his ability to be looked at. 'Opening up to the other person is always a *gift*; the trust to communicate cannot await the other person's promise to reciprocate, or the conversation will never begin' (1997: 351;

emphasis in original). This is the playful, passionate work of Potter's films: to turn the gaze, critiqued by feminist film theory, into a gift from character to character, and viewer to film. As in all of Potter's films, the economy of looks is paramount in *Yes*, and is announced early on by the Cleaner's address, refiguring Orlando's, to camera and the audience. The Cleaner speaks from a female body that is invisible, one that is associated with work, poverty, age and dirt. She is one of several cleaners in the film, all female, who turn their silent gaze to the camera as comment. By looking back, as Ruby does from the stage, they refuse to remain invisible, demanding that we rethink the ethics of looking. Their engagement with our gaze renders them visible as individuals, and as a class defined by invisibility.

To be invisible is to be aligned with all things Other: non-white, non-male, non-wealthy. Specifically, there is an association between the unseen Other and dirt that is implied and then upended by the Cleaner. Looking at the racist, sexist and classist fantasies that underpinned nineteenth-century domestic product advertisements, Anne McClintock argues 'dirt was the memory trace of working class and female labour, unseemly evidence that the fundamental production of industrial and imperial wealth lay in the hands and bodies of the working class, women and the colonised' (1995: 154). Dark skin, poverty and sexually-available women are the dirt that needs to be cleaned to render the Empire spotlessly white, but are also necessary – as labouring bodies – to produce that whiteness. Potter's film constellates, considers and disperses these associations. In the car park, He speaks of She as dirty, connecting dirt and female sexuality. To be un-manned is thus to be dirty like a woman, to be the thing that needs to be swept away by the Cleaner. Being 'un-manned' and invisible is also to be without 'land', disgraced because displaced. The dirty, anonymous, transitory setting of the car park reinforces the association. Car parks figure more readily in horror films and thrillers as dangerous sites for women, like the urban night that Sally walks through in *The Tango Lesson*. Yet the car park is *Yes*'s Saint Sulpice, where listening begins.

For both He and She, the car park precipitates a return to somewhere that had been imagined as home. They follow a trajectory from a fixation on home/land to a freedom in heterotopic spaces and movement. This arc can be traced through She's journeys in taxis. Whereas Sally in *The Tango Lesson* is an engaged passenger, conversing with the driver or leaping out to dance in the rain, She highlights the passive role of passenger at first. An official car or limo operates as a trap early in the film when She confronts her husband Anthony about his infidelities. They sit side by side in the rear of a well-upholstered car, speaking without looking at one another, without moving. A few scenes later, She edges towards her own affair with a phone call from the back of a New York cab. Time and space are rearranged by sound: the scene begins with He whistling while he works in a busy restaurant kitchen. His cellphone rings – or so it seems, before a cut to She in the back of the cab, where *her* phone is ringing. The blurring of spaces and characters' experiences is a beautiful analogy for the first use of the six f/s shooting, which turns the grey tunnel outside the cab into light streaks, softening and blurring She's movements. This is the time of love, the sense of connection wittily implied by the illusion that their phones are ringing simultaneously. The sound bridge suggests that this luminous soft vision of She is He's fantasy of her answering his call.

She is in New York to give a presentation on embryology to an American company: she is secure in her identity as a scientist, a globalised citizen who expresses herself in PowerPoint technology as well as lyric poetry. When she next takes a cab, She is caught in the nexus of many identities: as a scientist, as a wife who has fought with her husband, as a lover who has fought with her lover, and a niece worried about her dying aunt. She is also a grown woman returning to the familial city of her childhood: Belfast, itself a city still divided. The cab passes by the 'peace wall' topped with razor wire that still divides Protestant Shankill Road from Catholic Falls Road, despite a dismantlement clause in the 1998 Good Friday accord. The wall is seen from She's point of view in a six f/s shot, over which a shot of her reflection is superimposed. The city is no longer visual wallpaper passing unnoticed while the passenger focuses on herself. She is enmeshed in the city's history, and its story of division is entangled in her thoughts.

The shot suggests that the film's audience could also 'superimpose' themselves on the film in this way, locating themselves in its visual expression of history, feeling themselves as inescapably involved in events and their traces. Whereas She was separate from New York unrolling as landscape behind the cab window, she is inextricably implicated in the walls that mark Belfast, as much monuments of conquest as the Moorish walls that mark Gibraltar. Rather than *convivencia*, with horrible irony the 'peace walls' mark sites of sectarian conflict. They are a visual realisation of the religious walls constructed and dismantled in She's argument with He in the car park.

Potter's choice of Belfast rather than New York for this scene is telling. It bypasses New York's post-9/11 role as shorthand for the dramatic effects of religious intolerance and the need to enforce borders. Radical philosopher Judith Butler returned, in *Precarious Life*, to the headlines of 12 September 2001 that announced 'we are all New Yorkers' to understand how continuing such a political gesture could have radically altered America's subsequent foreign policy. Her central thesis is that 'one insight that injury affords is that there are others out there on whom my life depends, people I do not know and may never know … no violent act of sovereignty will rid the world of this fact … Rather, the dislocation from First World privilege, however temporary, offers a chance to imagine a world in which that violence might be minimised, in which an inevitable interdependency becomes acknowledged as fact' (2004: xii–xiii). American media and politics did not take this path, so New York cannot stand for injury's insight in *Yes*. Belfast is a site from which to begin a conversation between West and East because of its experiences of violence and vulnerability. Like Beirut, Belfast endured decades of reciprocal violence, a history encoded in the walls. When He is shown looking at bullet holes in Beirut, the walls of Belfast are a visual echo.

In Belfast, She begins to acknowledge a personal as well as political 'inevitable interdependency'. She is confronted with her contradictory feelings about her aunt, God and love as she realises that she was absent when her aunt needed her. The superimpositions that charted her journey through Belfast have suggestively opened her to listening. In the hospice she hears – or seems to hear, unconsciously, in her body – her aunt's voice-over. It is very clear, very far forward on the soundtrack. The only previous voice-overs have been She's thoughts, often before she speaks them or a version of them out loud. These locate the viewer in She's consciousness, and suggest that the Aunt's monologue takes place, or at least echoes, there as well. As the voice-over continues after the Aunt dies, it is hard to place it: is it a speech that She is remembering from a previous interaction with her aunt, perhaps an imagined composite of earlier phrases, rebukes and encouragements?

Like She's breathy voice-overs, and the Cleaner's to-camera monologues, this is a moment in which the audience has a privileged entry into the film. The Aunt's monologue is the longest uninterrupted flow of verse in the whole film, ranging through subjects and tones while retaining a clear sense of character and purpose. Its clarity and aliveness restores the dignity of the dying, and offers the comforting thought that a loved one is reproving and loving us as they did in life even when they are beyond speech. It is an extraordinary sequence, marked by careful framing of She's vulnerability as, with snot falling from her nose, she meshes with Potter's image of the woman who cries a 'river of water cascading from eyes and nose, pouring down her cheeks, dripping from her chin' (1997d: 95). Her tears are a response to her aunt's monologue, which demands that she 'cry … tear [her] hair … sobbing, fall upon [her] bed'. Like her Irish sister Molly Bloom's, the Aunt's monologue is 'a red yes', red in passion and Marxist politics. It impels She to answer with her own yes, travelling to Cuba.

In Cuba, She takes her final cab ride in an open-topped 1950s American car. She becomes part of the city that she travels through because there are no windows or roof between her and her surroundings. She is captivated by the city – and captures it, using a handheld digital video camera. As at the end of *Orlando*, the grainy and swooping video 'shot' by a character is spliced into the film. Filmmaking is signalled as a yes, a positive response to lived experience. It represents She's move from still, stilted passenger in the official car taking her to Anthony's function (at which she has no function other than to be beautiful) via corporate citizen immune to New York and local girl reflecting on and reflected by Belfast's scarred walls to a participant-observer, a becoming-artist. She is a film viewer who has become a filmmaker. Completing her filmmaking yes, she turns the digicam on herself in her hotel room to make a video confession. Her poetic self-reflection enters the vertical logic of love's time and He arrives as she turns off the camera.

After reading a 2002 draft of the screenplay, John Berger wrote to Potter that a 'third ending (which is always where the story begins) is possible: They meet in Cuba – after stopping off in Belfast and Beirut – in an *encounter of gratitude*' (2002; emphasis in original). The lovers' return to each other from Belfast and Beirut is a dramatisation of the use of iambic pentameter, in which the couplet is only completed once the speaker reaches the second rhyme word at the end of the couplet. In the hotel room in Havana, He lays his head in her lap in her cool hotel room. The hotel's blue-green then merges into a beach scene, where the lovers enter a suspended time of pleasure: neither holiday nor exile, a dreamy re-placement that repeats the film's lyric emphasis on how love illumines place, how – in the moment of falling in love – everything about the place we are in intensifies, and place itself intensifies desire.

In response to an audience member's question about whether the film was always destined to have a happy ending, Potter replied that she 'wrote a very, very long sequence (which we filmed) where they … decide they've really come together to say goodbye … When I saw it in the cutting room, I said "Out". No explanations are necessary … We don't know what kind of future these two people are heading towards' (2005b: 91). In mainstream cinema, romantic resolution overshadows and simultaneously underscores the restitution of social order at the end of the film. The suspended time of *Yes*'s conclusion offers no such guarantees. Rather than 'happily ever after', the ending offers 'happily for now'. Berger also noted on the 2002 draft that 'in older lovers (after 35) desire offers – from one body to another – a reprieve from the persistent pain of life. And when the offer is accepted or reciprocated, the reprieve and its promise covers two … Desire … is an alternative use of energy – and lucidity – not for the taking of something, but for the bestowing and therefore the sharing (if only for a short moment) of *exemption*' (2002; emphasis in original). By setting its final scene in a place that is neither geographically located nor tied into the film's narrative space, *Yes* makes film itself a space of exemption in which viewers can, briefly, dream.

On the beach where the lovers embrace, the tideline, the liminal zone where sea meets land and infuses it with wetness and light, is inscribed with the word YES, if only for a short moment. Sweetly punning, this literal inscription on the littoral writes an elemental affirmation on the foreshore/foreground. This final Yes answers philosopher Rosi Braidotti's call for 'ways of reworking our relationship to processes of mourning in such a way that they allow compassion and respect for the hurt and wounded … through to an ethics of affirmation' (2006; author's transcription). The glimmer of Yes in the sand is an *I-Thou* moment in which the natural world speaks in a human tongue. With the echo of the Cleaner's 'There is only yes', the spoken and written words rhyme then dissolve. The word, washed by the tide, is temporary, impossible, fantastic, wild time's meeting of moment and eternity. He and She's embrace is the same, an ethics of affirmation saying 'I will Yes' in the vertical time of love suffused in brilliant light.

CHAPTER TWELVE

Loving

What falling in love does is it gives you permission to experience life as it really is, and people as they really are. The veil lifts for that moment, and the glory is suddenly apparent. So it's about putting falling in love on the screen, trying to create the heightened reality that is the awakening. I try and find an essence of place, and then push it further. Removing lots of information from a space means that those elements that remain have been heightened, deepened, saturated. It makes for a non-naturalistic film language even when, as in *Yes*, there's nothing in there that's unreal, there's no special effects. There's some slowing and speeding of film time, but we're not in outer space, people aren't floating above the ground or morphing. They're just ordinary people in ordinary spaces. The house that She lives in is more empty than one would expect of a domestic environment, His is more saturated with colour. Perhaps the blossom is more extreme, but we didn't art direct it, we timed when we shot. I had a spy in the park doing Blossom Report. Nature gave us that, and we stole the moment. It's really just using what's there and pushing it as far as it can go, so you can feel that hallucinatory sense of awakeness.

– Sally Potter, interview with author, September 2006

Talking about the use of verse in *Yes*, Potter told *Cineaste* that 'part of the goal was to evoke a state of mind in which people are thinking and feeling simultaneously, and not just one or the other – reflecting on their emotions as they're having them, a state of loving detachment really' (in Lucia 2005: 29). Verse lines not only reflect love, but contain it in a kind of detachment, in a similar way to Potter's 'charmed spaces' (Peter Cowie in McKim 2006). These are locations and moments picked out through the use of saturated colour, close-ups and focus on light and shape. The charm of space has always been part of Potter's work, from the dance and Expanded Cinema pieces in which she extended the charm of cinema to theatrical spaces, and Limited Dance Company performances that threw the charm of storytelling over non-traditional performance spaces.

The end of *Yes*, like the ends of Potter's other films, is 'charmed': its spaces are constituted as fantastic moments of suspension rather than closure. 'While Powell and Pressburger's films often use real locations, this is never just a matter of naturalistic detail, but is for *effect*, for the cultural, poetic or pictorial connotations of the landscape, for a "spirit of place"' (Moor 2005: 3; emphasis in original). Locations are similar sites of exchange between the viewer's lived world and the film's fantastic world in Potter's work. They are 'cinematic rooms in which to breathe' (McKim 2006). These magical spaces of transformation create a shared or intimate breath, in which the awareness of place springs from, and foregrounds, a loving relationship that is also intellectually engaged. Love, and the lyric as its form, becomes a way of thinking through the world.

As María Rosa Menocal describes in *Shards of Love*, lyric's history is intimately bound up with place, space and movement (see 1994: 121–4). Pre-Islamic Arabic poetry sang of gardens, oases in the desert, for which the lover longed. This longing was sharpened in al-Andalus as the walled garden became an allegory of the Ummayad caliphate in Damascus that had fallen in the mid-eighth century (see Menocal 2002: 61–5). Like Shakespeare's Sonnet 29, as recited by Orlando, lyric comes from an 'outcast state' of longing that interweaves spiritual and erotic love, and personal and political losses. Made piquant by the infusion of Jewish songs about the loss of Jerusalem, the emerging love lyric layered three desires and losses: of the lover, of the beloved place and of God's regard (see Menocal 2002: 161–3; 1994: 65–7, 87–8).

Lover, land and God are conjoined in the lyric forms that resonate throughout Potter's work. Tango is specifically (up)rooted in the exilic music of Spanish Jews and gypsies who emigrated to Argentina, which is blended with the vernacular anonymous songs of the transient working poor, and the reconnection of African rhythms with yearnings that had begun in Andalusia six hundred years before. Its music and lyrics echo the exilic love songs of those Henry Kamen (2007) calls 'the disinherited', the successive waves of Spanish emigrants and exiles, beginning with the Jews and Muslims forced out of Spain in 1492. Tango, like Roma song, is the music of people on the move, encountering new cultures. New languages and old musical forms create a musical version of an imagined home, as Suzie does in *The Man Who Cried*. Suzie's performance with Taraf de Haïdouks, like Potter's use of tangos, is a political transformation on the level of community, through a shared practice of art.

Through these lyric forms, two characters have what Sara Ahmed (2000) calls a 'strange encounter' that revises collective histories, infusing the present with hope. Their transformative potential is made possible by emerging from specific political and historical circumstances, coded by evocative locations. Tango not only sings of the connections between Buenos Aires and Europe in *The Tango Lesson*, it performs them in the locations it unites through longing. The film's locations are divided between specificities of place – the Parc de St. Cloud, where Sally looks for locations for *Rage* (1996), the milongas and streets of Buenos Aires – and the suspended transitional spaces in-between. Hotel rooms, airport travelators, cab rides, telephone conversations: these symptoms of globalisation are suffused with the complexities of movement and connection, as are similar spaces in *Yes*.

Potter's spiritual yet resolutely secular songs specifically do not mourn the loss of an originary home other than the lyric mode itself. Art is the home found and lost, a nomadic home that makes possible affinities with artists and audiences – but it is also a home radically situated in the world. In Potter's films, to make art, or love, is not to be separate from history and politics, but to shape and be shaped by them. Love is made in, and into, a space in which her characters move. Like tango, the transitory spaces of love mark desire as being always in motion, and in relation. These locations are infused with the sensual immediacy that is at the root of lyric poetry, a realisation of the self in the moment of intense feeling.

City: The Romance of Place/The Place of Romance

The spaces of love are presented in a lyric cinematic language that, as Menocal writes of Andalusian lyric poetry, 'glories in the vitalities and the possibilities of its many varieties and of newness itself' (1993: 121). Thinking lyrically about how cinema can transform the world, this language engages the viewer intellectually and sensually. Whether film is extended through verse dialogue, art-historical time travel, tangoed narrative, musical plots or investigative black-and-white, it goes further into intimacy, both between the characters and with each protagonist, through this lyric form, which is deeply rooted in place.

Even as they delight in discovering the wonderful spaces of Buenos Aires, Khiva and Iceland, Potter's films are critical examinations of both the romance of place, and the place of romance in cinema, and particularly in arthouse cinema. Potter addresses the romance of Paris in *The Tango Lesson*, where the city's stringent elegance and history of heterosexual romance is first imagined as an ideal location for *Rage* (1996). As a thriller about the dangers of *haute couture* romance for women, *Rage* (1996) refers back to *Thriller*'s take on the Paris-set *La Bohème*. Paris is literally a stage set for Pablo and Sally's tango romance. Resolution, too, begins in Paris, at Saint Sulpice, but flowers in Buenos Aires, where Sally redefines herself as a filmmaker, and Pablo negotiates his hybrid identity. Tango returns home from the European capitals where it is commodified as an exotic spectacle to the vast, abandoned spaces of Buenos Aires that chart the city's history of immigration, trade and movement: the closed warehouse that Pablo throws open for the Libertango, the almost-empty synagogue and the docks where the immigrants who shaped tango set foot in the city.

Potter's films bring lyric's romance, associated with the pastoral, within city walls, but they also suggest the dystopic urban modernism of Charles Baudelaire and T. S. Eliot. Potter's Mimi fares little better in the squats of 1970s London than she does in Baudelaire's squalid Paris. Yet there is a difference, marked by the archival photographs sourced from collections in London. In the contemporary city that contains, and offers access to, both the Royal Opera House and the National Museum of Labour History, Mimi can begin her self-investigation in the archives. The photographs provide a geographical, historical and social outside to the otherwise claustrophobic tomb of the attic room. At the same time, they are 'inside' Puccini's take on *La Bohème* and suggest the transformation that the film is enacting. The film uses a heartbeat rather than a drumbeat to call for change: an intimate politics based in a belief that political change on the largest scale begins with the human heart.

Final scenes of transformative union do not take place in London and Paris, although they are the two most-used cities in Potter's work. They are emblematic of long cinematic tradition, and are eschewed for spaces that are marginal culturally and geographically: in the water of a feminist utopia in *The Gold Diggers*; by an oak tree that is just a tree, not England, in *Orlando*; on the waterfront in *The Tango Lesson*; on a Caribbean beach in *Yes*; on a wasteground in *Rage* (2009). Even in *London Story*, the glorious final dance takes place by an inglorious bench, not outside the Houses of Parliament but under Waterloo Bridge where the skaters and buskers play. In their search for self, her protagonists encounter romance and the Other in unexpected, neglected urban spaces, such as He and She's sexual play in the restaurant in *Yes* and their car park argument.

This juxtaposition goes back in Potter's work at least to *Wheat* (1974), a serial dance piece that relocated Igor Stravinsky's music for the ballet *The Firebird* to outdoor locations in London's then-derelict Borough Market. Dennis Greenwood, who later appeared as the Skater in *London Story*, danced the Firebird, but the fantastical Garden of the ballet was replaced by urban spectacles such as fire-eating and burning cans of fire, as well as images of the Great Depression (see Jordan 1992: 51). Urban grime and rural poverty were juxtaposed with the ecstatic myth heard in the ballet's music. The ballet's ahistorical romance received a political charge not just from the associations of the Firebird with fires in drought-ridden fields, but through its extraction from the proscenium arch stage into a 'strange encounter' with the city.

When it came to conceiving the setting for her production of *Carmen* in 2007, Potter designed a similar juxtaposition. Gone were verisimilitudinous kitsch stage sets of a Seville-that-never-was. Like Bizet, Potter had Carmen move through a place that gave meaning to the story she wanted to tell. For Bizet, it was the exoticism of Spain, the Southernmost point in Europe with its Moorish heritage. In order to critique the Orientalist fantasies present in the opera's music and narrative, Potter updated the setting to a contemporary city. Act I took place in the zone of construction and gentrification where the fabulously wealthy and the impoverished and dispossessed rub up against each other. 'It's an urban environment, with a high wall with barbed wire on it, a No Man's Land. An urban wasteland that we've created, where those who are outside the law or beyond the law hang out and fight one another' (Potter, interview with author, August 2007). The massive wall that curved across stage left in the first act appeared stage right in Act IV as the wall of the bullring where Carmen has come to watch her new lover, Escamillo. 'It's the Spain we thought we knew from the beginning, but it's outside the arena, the backside, the bit where the hot dogs are, where people throw their rubbish' (ibid.).

Rather than a Seville that contains the 'rubbish' of fantasies about dark-skinned Others, Potter set the opera in a series of dark, abstract spaces that might call up the audience's experience of the contemporary city. She uncovered a narrative about marginal people (gypsies, sex workers, drag artists, mercenaries, smugglers) in marginal spaces and used contemporary urban signs like CCTV and neon light to set up the resonances between Carmen and the migrants and excluded in our cities. Traditional stage productions charm the audience with the romance of place (like *La Bohème*'s fantasy of an artist's well-furnished 'garret'): Potter exploded it. In doing so, she foregrounded the way that the opera draws on the romance of place. Seville, the city of *convivencia*, has fallen (through the fantasies projected onto it) into intolerance and violence. It is a city exiled from itself.

In recognising this exile, a temporary, contingent romance of place becomes possible. Such a place celebrates the present and understands its history, rather than looking nostalgically to the past. This is how Paris is reconceived in *The Man Who Cried*. The most cinematic of cities is only a way station for Suzie, Lola, Dante and Cesar. It arranges the meetings of the four central characters through a series of spectacles: cabaret, fireworks, opera. Cesar first indicates his interest in – and affinity with – Suzie by taking her to a dance *cave*, of the type where the 'ruffian' dance that prefigured tango originated. It is there that we catch the first intimation of a less watchful, shy Suzie, as she dances with a fleet-foot Roma, played by Pablo Veron. As *The Man Who Cried* tips its hat at *The Tango Lesson*, this scene crystallises Potter's vision of Paris as a space of nomads rather than settlers. Dance is the formal expression of Potter's conception of the city as an anarchic meeting-place between people in 'time in its most fleeting, transitory, precarious aspect ... in the mode of the festival', in which all festivals are linked to all other festivals (Foucault 1981: 26). All dances connect to all other dances in ritual time, exactly as Maya Deren described the poetic, vertical time of her films, in which spaces are linked impossibly across the splice by the dancer's step or leap.

'Global cities are linked to each other, sharing more products (including cultural) with each other than they might with the countries in which they happen to be situated' (Taylor 2005: 232). Rather than a stable, corporate location, the city is part of a circuit of wanderers: nomads and exiles, workers and performers. Reconceived as a temporary encampment for nomads, the city is the site of transformation. Potter's Mimi is black, female, an artist, and imagining a relationship with another woman. These possibilities for self-definition note the difference between Puccini's time and Potter's. They also suggest how the city has historically been a space for self-definition and transformation for members of marginal communities, particularly ethnic minorities, queer people and artists. The city is conceived as a site of plurality and redefinition, of permissiveness and inventiveness. For Potter, cities are living, mutable archives that can contain Delacroix's Jacob and the Angel, as well as tango cafés and the games arcade that Pablo visits. In their diversity and layered history, they are spaces of investigation that bring connection. She's cellphone connection to He from a cab in New York makes a virtue of new modes of urban communication that prize the freedoms found in movement over situatedness, networked connection over hierarchical power, affinity over identity. The romantic city is always a token of exile in Potter's films rather than a claim to home.

Hotel: The Self in Exile/Exile in the Self

Hamid Naficy, theorist of 'accented cinema', recalls that 'exile' derives from the Latin root, *salire*, to leap (see 1999: xii). For both Mimi and Sally, there is a danced leap that is also an 'ethical "leap"' in which their self-knowledge is revised (ibid.). In Havana, She leaps into an exile that is also an interior journey. Like Sally, She stays in a hotel, finding not a home away from home, but a room that, in its bright Caribbean colours and simple furniture, is an absolute contrast to her modernist mausoleum in London. Having found a place to sleep and think, She – like Sally – goes out dancing. Potter first made the connection between hotels and dancing/dance partners as transitional, ephemeral spaces in which to rethink the self in her contribution to Richard Alston's site-specific portmanteau work *Interior* (1973), staged at the White Lion Inn, Islington, London (see Kane 1989: 52). Potter's section took place in a bedroom, prefiguring the constellation of the self, dance and the hotel room seen in both *The Tango Lesson* and *Yes*.

The saturated, six f/s scene in which She salsas in a bar, the movement out of step with the pulsing Cuban music, draws attention, in the bright, almost fluorescent pallor of She's clothes, to her whiteness, her status as tourist in a country whose citizens are rarely able to leave except as exiles and refugees. Yet it also draws attention to her tourism as a 'boundary-breaking' act of solidarity: as an American citizen, She not only 'feels a deepening sense of shame' against the actions of the US military-industrial complex, but deliberately breaks the law by leaping into Cuba. That this is a very real offence is demonstrated by the actual shooting location: the Havana scenes had to be shot in the Dominican Republic after the Bush government reinforced the US clampdown on Americans entering Cuba, meaning that Joan Allen could not work on the island without risking prosecution. At the same time, the political situation produced by the invasion of Iraq meant that Potter could not get insurance to shoot in Lebanon, so the Beirut scenes were filmed in Havana (interview with author, July 2005). The substitution suggestively parallels the situation of the Middle East and Central America as targets of US imperialism, as the cities are exiled from themselves by militaristic and economic interventionism. The city is destabilised like its nomadic citizens.

The spaces in which Potter's characters move and connect are rarely those they would call home. Potter's use of location echoes Homi K. Bhabha's famous formulation that in post-colonial fiction, the 'unhomely is the shock of recognition of the world-in-the-home, the home-in-the-world' (1992: 141). Suzie/Fegele is the protagonist who is an exile in the truest historical sense, and she moves through a world of exiles, émigrés and nomads – a category that would, to his disgust, include the international performer Dante as well as the gypsy Cesar. Yet when Suzie heads for 'home', it is in the opposite geographical direction of her childhood dwelling, and the end of the film does not provide the easy satisfaction of finding her snugly housed with her new American family.

While the spaces of home in Potter's films do figure the world, from Queen Elizabeth at the Great House to the Cleaner's political observations in *Yes*, Potter moves narratively outwards from the home, breaking the link between women and domestic space. Her films also argue that home is different for women, as is the world: less accommodating, less reflective. As a woman, Orlando discovers a sense of exile at home, whereas he had come to feel at home in his Khivan exile. When Ruby returns to her family home, she finds a self that is always multiple, and always leaving. In a sequence framed by a static long take, Potter creates a cinematic joke as young Ruby runs clockwise behind the building to come back around as teenage Ruby, who repeats the run, but it is the adult Ruby who rounds the corner. She returns to the city, and to Celeste.

Home is where the heart is, and Potter's heart is in movement. Her films' fluency in many languages and her global use of locations suggests an intellectual restlessness and a refusal of the idea of the national. Englishness is the home that Potter's films resist and disclaim. Despite its critique of nationalism and empire, *Orlando* has subsequently been taken up by national canon-builders as an exemplary 'British' project/ product. Yet Orlando, like Suzie, is a global traveller, one who moves from power and privilege as a male ambassador to disguise as a woman in a war-torn country.

Like her protagonists, Potter takes an ethical leap into an affinity with artists whose work, by necessity, emerges from Naficy's 'interstitial mode of production [of] exilic cinema' (1999: xii). Potter is not, culturally or economically, an exile, although the process of filmmaking, like that of performance, is economically and culturally nomadic. Andrew Moor argues that Michael Powell formed a similar affinity with the Jewish-Hungarian political exile Emeric Pressburger to formulate an exilic cinema within the British nation. Moor writes that, 'following Homi K. Bhabha's recognition of an "anti-nationalist, ambivalent nation-space [which] becomes the crossroads to a new transnational culture", so too can a distinctively national cinema allow for difference, engage with international factors, and be enriched by hybrid and alternative voices' (2005: 9). Orlando expands her national identity through encounters with the 'hybrid and alternative voices' of Sasha, the Khan and Shelmerdine. Sally redefines her filmmaking by travelling from the familiarities of London and Paris to Pablo's world of tango in Buenos Aires. *The Tango Lesson* is conceived and written in hotel rooms in Paris and Buenos Aires.

These hotel rooms, like Mimi's and Suzie's garrets, and Celeste's bare flat, echo Virginia Woolf's call for women artists to have *A Room of One's Own* (1929), but only insofar as they are specifically a room that one does not own, or owns only temporarily through the fruits of one's labour, whether Mimi's flowers or Sally's bouquets of faxes. The room of the self initially stages estrangement, symbolised by Ruby's tears or Mimi's death. Gradually, it becomes a space of reconnection: Suzie relocates sense-memories of her childhood in the Christmas tree that she buys with Lola, then in Mme. Goldstein's kitchen, and finally in the gesture of passing on the gold coin. The apartment that Suzie rents is one of the temporary rooms in Potter's films in which, through the labour of investigation and creative making, the female protagonist owns herself. They suggest that the cinema can be just such a transitional room in which self-fashioning can occur. The sense of self-ownership comes through leaving behind all thoughts of home and its burden of ownership and being owned.

In *Yes*, in the hotel in Havana, She can let go of being a white, wealthy, scientist in control. She enters a time of play and gives up the double meaning of 'proper': the property she owns and maintaining a 'proper' made-up appearance, either physical or psychical. In exile from love, She turns to metaphysics, conversing through her digital camera with the God from whom she has 'strayed far too long'. This exile from the core of her self has been broached through listening to He in the transitional space of the car park, and sitting with her dying aunt in the transitional moment of death. She's voice-over monologue takes up the aural form of the Aunt's, suggesting that the core of the self is not faith in God, but a practice of self-examination. She re-encounters herself in a strange place, and begins the process of change. She gazes directly at the doubled camera and at the audience, working at a return to self through relation with a listening Other. The camera and the mirror that act as She's interlocutors in her internal discussion are reminiscent of the mirror in which Orlando first sees her female body. They are frames or spaces of transition, capturing threshold moments in which a character transforms. When Pablo bursts through the doors of the warehouse in the Libertango, it signals his commitment to Sally's film, and his joy in expressing the world.

Threshold: The Desire of the Frame/The Frame of Desire

Doors are not just entrances to magical spaces, but magical spaces in themselves in Potter's films, playing on the double meaning of *entrance*. Starting with *Thriller*, Potter's characters persistently stand at both literal and metaphorical thresholds as becoming, emergent selves. The threshold is a site of watching and it also offers a position from which to speak of what one sees. Kaja Silverman titles her study of political transformation through the visual field *The Threshold of the Visible World*, taking the lead from Jacques Lacan's remark that 'the mirror-image would seem to be the threshold of the visible world' (in Silverman 1996: 2). Silverman associates the crossing of the threshold with something similar to María Lugones' 'world'-travelling, a willingness to leave behind stable, unitary identity and an ability to enter the Other's space, which Silverman calls the 'active gift of love' (1996: 78). For Silverman, the recognition of this threshold as the space of cinematic spectatorship leads to the formulation of a resistant look distinct 'from the gaze on the basis of the look's emplacement within spectacle, the body, temporality, and desire' (1996: 163). This is precisely the intimate look that occurs on the threshold between the self in exile and the other in the world.

The dual-screen film *Play* was shot with two adjacent cameras from Potter's window. It echoes Deren's description in 1953 of her filmmaking practice as 'standing at a window and looking out onto the street, and there are children playing hopscotch' (1971: 179). It shows three sets of twins playing in the street, using slow motion and looping to express the linked nature of cinema and of children's play. A black woman repeatedly crosses between the two screens as the film loops, politicising the 'threshold of the visible'. In several scenes, the children look directly at the camera; in one, they line up beneath the window as if conversing with the filmmaker. Rather than the frame standing for exclusion in Potter's films, it suggests that a threshold can, by its nature, be crossed. This is the resonance of the door and mirror in *Thriller* as tropes that suggest the protagonists can escape having been 'framed', set up for the crime of being female. In *Framed* (1974), LDC's contribution to the Artists for Democracy festival in support of Chilean resistance, Potter and Lansley examined oppression in patriarchal culture. In a courtyard at the Royal College of Art, the performers, dressed as men, enclosed two female effigies with a white cardboard frame. They also formed a circle of black stockings, finally drawing a red line from a red flashing light beneath the effigies to one in the centre of the black circle. The act of framing points to that which is not allowed to cross the threshold. By pointing out the frame that excluded the audience, LDC hoped to create a threshold moment that would inspire politically committed action.

Just as Potter's protagonists all stand on thresholds, so all the spaces in her films are in some sense liminal. Stylised framing draws attention to the cinema screen as the place in which the spaces all appear, and camera movement and editing set spaces in motion. The screen, and other thresholds, are spaces like the ship as described by Foucault: 'a floating piece of space, a place without a place, that exists by itself, that is closed in on itself and at the same time is given over to the infinity of the sea' (1981: 27). When Suzie arrives in America, the moment is announced by a reflection of New York's skyline cast over her face as she looks out the window of the naval transport ship that rescued her. Watchful Suzie has been no more than a bystander to the narrative of historically loaded events between her entry as a child onto a Russian ship, thinking it would take her to America, and her disembarkation in New York. She is no longer below-decks in a cabin but about to become part of the city. The reflecting window is a threshold from which she steps into the narrative of herself.

Suzie is strongly associated with the threshold: she stands in the curtained doorway of her grandmother's house listening to her father talk about leaving, she hangs on the fence at school to watch the gypsies pass, and again on the fence at the encampment where Cesar lives. Their relationship is framed by conversations at the door of her apartment and of the theatre; she overhears Dante both from her doorway and from the theatre's wings. Her first conversation with Mme. Goldstein (Miriam Karlin) is by the landlady's doorway as Suzie is leaving for the theatre. Suzie's surprise that she can understand Mme. Goldstein's Yiddish is reincorporated in Suzie's recognition of her father from the doorway of a Californian hospital room. All of the doorways and transitional threshold spaces have led to this moment.

Orlando, too, is a film constantly hovering at the threshold, with its repeated frontal establishing shots of the Great House that parody Academician landscape painting. Each time, the symmetrical, frontal, wide-angle perspective of the House is broken – and each time it is a surprise – by a body or bodies emerging from the space off 'behind' the camera, marching into view. When Orlando arrives for the final time, the camera initially offers the frontal, symmetrical framing, but markedly higher and wider, down the gravel path and centred on the doorway. Orlando roars into the frame on her motorbike. There is then a cut to a side-on medium close-up of the bike stopping on the white sheets that cover the lawn and topiary. Orlando throws off her helmet, in a gesture similar to the removal of her wig in the sex-transformation scene. After Orlando lifts her daughter out of the sidecar, there is a return to the frontal wide shot. The camera moves, tracking forward as Orlando and her daughter approach the house, until it finally reaches the usual threshold shot as Orlando's final voice-over narration begins. The voice-over itself is a frame, connecting back to the opening narration that was the threshold of the film, and suggesting that Orlando has been hovering on that threshold of becoming throughout. It marks the cinematic frame as a threshold that Orlando tries to cross with her looks to the camera.

Like Orlando, the Cleaner in *Yes* frequently speaks from the threshold, looking into or out of rooms not her own, in order to form an intimacy with the audience. Strong frames-within-the-frame elsewhere in the film suggest that these other scenes are also seen through the Cleaner's framing consciousness. When He and She first embrace, their arrival onscreen is preceded by a brief shot of a white wall framed by a brown wood upright onscreen right and a shadow screen left. This aperture frames their entrance into a private world of desire. Once She falls silent under He's touch, there is a cut to a shot at a 90° angle that frames the lovers sideways on, looking towards the closed door of He's apartment. We realise that they are standing, kissing, on the threshold (this was used as the poster image for the film in the UK and US). Shimmering music and a series of superimpositions begin to blur the frame, the boundary between self and other.

Doors swing open and closed throughout the film. He gets pushed out of the restaurant door by his manager, played – in a neat twist – by George Yiasoumi, who opens doors in his roles as the Stage Hand in *The Gold Diggers*, the Door in *London Story* and a butler in *Orlando*. When He and She's relationship dissolves, it is also in the threshold space of a car park. It is a dead end in which She stops the car and gets out, forcing them both to take a stand, to get stuck in position. Where the reassuring door of He's apartment stood in the frame, now there is a lurid green emergency exit sign, with arrows pointing away from He and She to the darkness in the background. The car park, with its mesh of verticals, is like a centrifugal version of the frame-within-a-frame in which they first embraced. When they meet again in the hotel and rest in a secular *Pietà* on the bed, the shot is initially framed along its bottom edge by the counter where She rested her digicam, but the camera tracks along the counter and around its far corner. Whereas concrete pillars in the car park acted as barriers between the characters, they are finally framed unmediated. Like Ruby, they have broken out of the cage.

The car park is itself a threshold, a space of suspended motion that takes its place in the chain of car associations through the film, in which the car is a form of cinema. Cinema, too, is a liminal space, a space of immobility like the car park, but one that signals the potential for cathartic movement after witnessing what is played out within the frame. As a space of resolution and transformation, the car park draws out the hidden meaning in its name: not just a space of parked, immobile cars, but a park like the oasis of sensual colour and smell within urban space in which He and She first talked. Its concrete pillars are reminiscent of the maze in *Orlando*, from whose threshold Orlando comically rejects Harry's proposal. It is a space that hovers between car and park, on the threshold of transformation as the gaze of rage is transformed into the active look of love.

Garden: The Transformation of the Senses/The Sense of Transformation

For Michel Foucault, the cinema and the garden are similar 'contradictory sites' that contain the 'totality of the world' within a rectangle. He writes that:

> The cinema is a very odd rectangular room, at the end of which, on a two-dimensional screen, one sees the projection of a three-dimensional space, but perhaps the oldest example of these heterotopias that take the form of contradictory sites is the garden. We must not forget that in the Orient the garden, an astonishing creation that is now a thousand years old, had very deep and seemingly superimposed meanings. The traditional garden of the Persians was a sacred space that was supposed to bring together inside its rectangle four parts representing the four parts of the world, with a space still more sacred than the others that were like an umbilicus, the navel of the world at its centre … The garden is the smallest parcel of the world and then it is the totality of the world. (1986: 25)

At the heart of the Persian garden was a clear fountain, like the fountain outside Saint Sulpice at the centre of *The Tango Lesson*. The garden is a pause, a womb, a space of return, a suspension in which exiles can feel connected to home, as well as a space of change, like the maze for Orlando.

In a programme note for *Park Cafeteria* (1974), Potter describes Englishness as 'a diffuse glow born of mild landscapes and civilisation. Into this two exiles return … searching out the old faces, researching the tea archives, acknowledging the contradictions, lost for words.' Acknowledging the contradiction of the gallery in the garden, of anarchic performance taking place in a Royal Park, LDC worked to erase the contradiction between performer and audience with their continuous musical performance. Its use of space collapsed boundaries between world and performance, self and other. Writing about the changes wrought by performance art, Amelia Jones notes that it showed that the self-other/private-public boundary is 'a fantasy' (1998: 51). Orlando's meeting with Shelmerdine on the heath, or Sally's vision of Pablo in the fountain, both form intimate visions in public spaces. 'Researching the tea

A garden in the house of love: walls come down between He (Simon Abkarian) and She (Joan Allen)

archives', *Park Cafeteria* gestured towards an older, Eastern tradition of the garden as space of meditation in which interior and exterior selves can be fused.

The park through which He and She walk in *Yes* is public, and yet a deeply private connection takes place within it. Their walk is framed *through* the world, with trees and grass rounding and softening the corners of the frame to create the bower at the heart of Arabic poetry. The pink blossom filling the screen in the park scene in *Yes* is thrown into relief when a group of women in black burqas walk beneath it. Troubadours' songs turned the Arabic garden into a *hortus conclusus*, a closed bower in which the woman is trapped, kept away from eager lovers but also from the world. In Potter's films, the garden of love's edgy existence on the boundary between public and private space situates it in historical time. The garden is transformed, as Potter transforms performance and film, from the Enlightenment sublime of to-be-looked-at-ness into a space to be entered actively and interactively.

Asked to write a director's diary about the *Yes* tour for the BBC Film website (2005a), Potter created a mixed-media blog that also featured on the *Yes* website, which was the first film website to feature the director blogging and participating on talkboards. The journal entry is about a visit to Derek Jarman's famous found-object garden at his home, Prospect Cottage, in Dungeness, Kent. A video shot on Potter's cellphone captures the garden's vivid colour and the evocative sounds of the sea. The camera looks repeatedly at the strange miniature menhirs scattered through the garden, and at various flowers, including bright poppies in Jarman's favourite shade of cardinal red. Tracking as far as the cottage window, the camera then falls back, swooping down onto a lavender plant growing amidst the shingle. The short film and the blog that accompanies it suggest that the garden was Jarman's real home and ongoing evidence of his creation, still blooming and changing more than ten years after his death.

Gardens are complex spaces in Potter's films, cast as the natural world framed by human artistry. As Foucault suggests, they are metaphors for cinema itself. Orlando's maze symbolises human achievements in mathematics and design, as well as being a near-universal symbol of spiritual questing. It also signifies mutability, the unchanging fact of change. The topiary that jokily alters to fit the mood of the era in *Orlando* (hedges cut into teacups frame Orlando's invitation to the Countess's literary salon) is a marker of the importance of transformation, and the way that the partiality of the garden and/as cinema can express the totality of a world. Potter's films likewise change with the season, foregrounding their use of photography, video and digital. Digital, like film before it, is transforming sensory apprehension, and posing the same questions about the loss of connection with the sensory world that were raised by the invention of cinema. Potter's cinema redefines as alive a medium often associated with deadening affect and the loss of intimacy. Her hybrid engagement of film, video and digital, as well as her hybrid gifts of direction, music, dialogue and choreography, makes her films gardens, active gifts of love arising as surprises amidst urban *noir*.

Laura U. Marks argues that it is 'most productive to look for objects made for the particular pleasure of making and interacting with them. The artist's love is embodied in the object and translated to the audience or recipient, if not as love then at least as intensity. Love builds, and these works produced out of love do not simply "resist" but actually build new ideas and affects' (2002: xiv). The ecstasy of love amidst the blossom, or next to the fountain of Saint Sulpice, or among Christmas trees that ignite smell-memories symbolises the affect of Potter's films. The Christmas tree memory is reincorporated in the colour scheme of the hospital where Suzie finds her father: through her song she brings the live world into a place associated with death.

The lullaby she sings layers cultural and individual memory, familial and erotic love, the natural world and travel, to suggest a potentially different kind of cinema to the big-budget spectaculars made by Suzie's father as a Hollywood producer. The lullaby, which sings of a father's desire to protect his daughter, ends with the lines: 'Dos land foon khloymess / mooztoo aveklozn / Dein eign zisser haym / vaystoo iz doh.' (The land of dreams / Must let you go / Your own sweet home / Is here, you know.) It is a bittersweet reflection on the heterotopia of cinema as the 'land of dreams'. When Suzie reverses the roles, watching over her father, she suggests that a cinema is possible which, rather than being the land of innocent dreams to which the father's lullaby dispatches the child, can be a provisional 'home ... here', in the very act of attention to place, for these displaced people. This living, integrated cinema is most palpable in the elemental dreamspaces in which Potter's films end with deliberately fantastical celebratory unions, forged from and in spaces that, infused with love, are more than themselves.

CHAPTER THIRTEEN

Rage

Just before I started work on *Rage* I wrote myself a private manifesto. I called it 'Barefoot Filmmaking' and it was a way of reminding myself what I believed in and how to approach work on this new project. It is something I have often done over the years, partly as a way of tracking my own principles and as a way of energising myself when I have felt like an outsider, working against the grain. A manifesto, even when kept private, dignifies an approach which may otherwise remain obscure … I have subsequently revised both how I think about some of these things and what to call this way of thinking. 'Poor Cinema' is my favourite, but in the past, when I started out, I called it 'Kitchen table filmmaking' as that was so often where I ended up working.

                                  – Sally Potter, blog post, 6 February 2009

Sally Potter's manifesto for filmmaking, which she posted online shortly before *Rage* (2009) had its world premiere, infolds and extends her blog post from Jarman's garden at Prospect Cottage (see 2005a). In the centre of that post, in capital letters, she quotes Jarman's adage: 'KEEP MAKING THINGS WITH WHATEVER YOU HAVE.' She writes: 'If it is no budget and a small camera, you make a handheld one-person epic. If you have a patch of shingle and some driftwood, you make a garden' (2005a). When not making films, Potter makes gardens in France and on the balconies of her studio

Barefoot Filmmaking: Sally Potter and Jean-Paul Mugel on set with Lettuce (Lily Cole)

in London (notes to author, April 2008). Potter's films are made like Jarman's garden, with what is to hand: *Rage* (2009) is indeed a 'handheld one-person epic' that sees Potter return to her position as writer/director/camera operator on *Thriller*. She shot *Thriller* on film scrounged from waste bins outside editing studios in Soho and made the *Yes* short for no money with friends and frequent collaborators, shooting on DV over a few days in Paris and editing it digitally (interview with author, September 2006). Technology, like money, does not dominate Potter's concept of filmmaking. Instead, it is raw material, like soil and seeds transformed into a garden.

To the garden, Potter adds two significant spaces of technology and interconnection that ground and make possible the fantastical spaces of her cinema: the internet and the kitchen table. In positing them as filmmaking spaces – as well as cinematic spaces, like the worktable in *The Tango Lesson* – Potter identifies the kitchen table and the internet as possible manifestations of heterotopia, gardens of ideas and exchange. Yet neither of them is a neutral, unproblematic heterotopia of creative energy. When she was shooting *Thriller* on her kitchen table, Potter was both resisting and repeating the kind of poorly-paid homework that Mimi would have done over her kitchen table. Turning a domestic space into a surface for the play of the imagination, Potter underlines the materiality of cinematic labour in parallel with Mimi's work, literally mapping editing onto sewing. It is this physicality that she brings to the internet, which Sadie Plant (1997) links both conceptually, in metaphors of the web and its threads, and in its assembly and operation to female labour in the cloth and garment trade. That labour is disguised by the hailing of the web as a free space of multi-dimensional invention, seemingly the greatest realisation of Foucault's heterotopia.

In the same way that *Thriller* located homeworkers on the Romantic opera stage, disrupting its disconnection from history and lived place, *Rage* (2009) re-places the clothes on our back in the hands of their labourers. It also relocates the internet in the world, not least by suggesting its affinity with the kitchen table as a space for intimate and activist community. In some ways, the film is a hybrid of cinema and internet, intensified by its planned pre-theatrical release, to be streamed online by Babelgum as a seven-episode serial. The release plan (un)cannily mirrors the film's framing device, whereby we are supposedly watching a series of cellphone videos streamed on a blog, filmed by the latest in Potter's series of investigative protagonists, a young man using the name Michelangelo. Potter remarked that she discovered the film's form, after more than a decade reworking the story that appears, fragmentarily, as the film-within-a-film in *The Tango Lesson*, while blogging and interacting with forum posters during the festival tour for *Yes*. A 'profound experience of connectedness with an invisible audience, hidden from view and yet very visible to millions of people, gave me the clue to a credible point of view, a child behind the camera who might be allowed in for a school project about fashion' (interview with author, December 2008).

Michelangelo is 'hidden from view and yet very visible'; although he is neither visible nor audible during the interviews, his responsive framing acts as a constant reminder of his presence, as do the intertitles that mark the start of each day that he documents. Signalled by a cursor flashing white on black, these titles begin with the word 'My' (first day, second day, etc.), positioning the view as subjective, and the viewers as Michelangelo's audience. His rapid typing pauses as each title appears on the screen, and the cursor backtracks to delete a telling word that hints at what is to come. From the first appearance of the cursor, Michelangelo's presence is associated with movement and with knowledge, and with a playful inversion of showing and telling that continues throughout the film.

It is not only the conceptual framework of an internet videostream that provides a unique optic for the film's narrative. Michelangelo's camera remains focused, at all times, on a single character speaking from a set that could be characterised as a digital version of Mimi's attic, a bare studio with a greenscreen backdrop. At first the greenscreen seems like an inversion of the grounded material history of Mimi's space, but even as it turns both set and screen into a literal nowhere, it raises the question of how much 'here' exists not only on a film set (even on location), or on a film or computer screen, or in the diffuse network of the internet itself, but in the visible world that Potter's location shoots so lovingly summon.

As Naomi Klein (2001) and Rebecca Solnit (2002) have both chronicled, public spaces, like the Parisian ones that Sally explores in *The Tango Lesson*, are being eroded. Urban centres are increasingly branded spaces, owned by conglomerates and converted into billboards. In taking the garment industry to task, *Rage* (2009) explores the tectonic shifts that have taken place since civil rights promised to change national and international gender and class relations, by literally changing the landscape. The 1970s eruption of sit-ins, protests and squats, including the former sweatshop where Potter shot *Thriller*, has been erased by globalisation and gentrification as thoroughly as have working-class neighbourhoods. This is the city in which the film takes place: one in which there is, increasingly 'no there there', as Gertrude Stein said of her home town, Oakland. Potter's films, drawing on her situationist performances, have depended on and celebrated the anarchic potential of public space and its long association with nomadic performers. By the time of *Yes*, however, there are few public spaces to be found. Instead, taxis, swanky restaurants, even a car park, become sites of affective resistance as intimate expression remakes the spaces *and* the emotions shared into a common ground.

The last thing that we see in *Rage* (2009) could be the remains of a commons, a piece of abandoned land striped by bright sunlight. Almost post-apocalyptic in its dilapidation, it is both the final erasure of New York and the film's only visible evidence of the city's existence. Tufts of grass are breaking through the asphalt in an urban heterotopia, a space that stands outside the film in some sense: one of only two scenes in which an image is projected over the greenscreen used throughout, displacing it in this instance with a hint of green. For the first time, there is character movement, breaking open the hermetic world of the film trapped backstage. A figure runs towards the vanishing point, and away from the 'action' of a fashion show. We understand the figure to be Michelangelo not because we see his face or hear his voice (as face and voice are the focus of his portraits of all the other characters), but because we see his sneakers. It is a complex recognition that, in the film's final moments, makes profound sense of the film's emplacement in New York and in the fashion industry as a meditation on globalisation's effects, both international and intimate.

Michelangelo is no barefoot filmmaker: for all the activist fervour and aesthetic simplicity of his project, he is inescapably caught in the net of globalisation, posting online films he shot on his cellphone, powered by coltan. This necessary and rare substance is mined in the Democratic Republic of Congo, where global demand has turned it into a conflict mineral. Sneakers, the visible echo of the invisible cellphone, encode this entangled history, and Potter's recognition of *Rage*'s (2009) necessary and impossible complicity in the networks of global finance that the film critiques: they stand as a condensed and complex symbol for what has become the fashion industry as it emerged from what Edith Roth (Dianne Wiest) calls 'the garment trade'. The sneakers' brand is not visible, but in themselves, sneakers have become a brand, a marker of lifestyle and identity. Nike, the most successful brand identified with sneakers, echoes throughout Klein's 2001 study *No Logo*, the definitive account of the shift towards a branded world and of the activism against it. *Rage* (2009) dramatises Klein's thorough documentation of marketing's rise to prominence over production, and in particular the way in which the fashion and sports fashion industries have led the field in selling an all-consuming identity.

In her discussion of Nike's relationship with Michael Jordan, Klein crystallises the way in which the American fashion industry has commodified African-American culture in order to sell it back to young consumers (see 2001: 50–2). Michelangelo's sneakers are thus a double signature of his character as a young male of colour: they are 'street' shoes, but they are an aspect of street culture that signifies his inability to get beyond what Klein calls our 'New Branded World', however far he runs. Even on the wasteground, the sneakers mark him as a 'brutha' (as Detective Homer names him), in that they have been deformed – via the branding of street culture – from athletic enablement to shorthand for violent crime among African-American males (who reportedly killed each other for over-priced sneakers). Sneakers are thus connected to explosive issues of race and violence in both the over-developed (to borrow Stuart Hall's term) and the developing world, where they are made in sweatshop conditions.

Michelangelo's sneakers – the first time we have seen feet striking the ground – are an analogy for the place he moves through: New York, as both the origin point of hip-hop and the location of the first Nike Town. That New York is only visible in the sneakers, while the New York of modernist architecture, high finance and high fashion – Brand New York, as used to market *Sex and the City* – is deliberately withheld. With its reflective surfaces, dazzling at skyline and street-level, that New York *is* visuality, the seen world in all its photographic intensity. Set in New York, and shot in part in photographers' studios in the city, *Rage* (2009) offers what appears to be a perverse take on one of the great cinematic cities. As Potter remarks: 'New York is like the fashion world itself: overseen, oversaturated, over-visible, to the point that it is symbolic beyond itself, linked with the sense – for how long we don't know – that it's a centre of gravity and attraction' (interview with author, December 2008). Eschewing such brilliance and saturation, the film calls it to mind for the audience through glancing references in costumes and dialogue, and in this final flash of light. The sunny ground is an evocation of New York's past (and possible future): as Mannahatta, in Lenni Lenape territory. It resonates with what the Mannahatta Project is uncovering through its mapping of waterways and wildlife: 'A new aspect of New York culture, the environmental foundation of the city' (Wildlife Conservation Survey 2008–09).

Stripped back to the foundations, Mannahatta is radiant. Yet the film does not fall into an ecological nostalgia, offering Michelangelo a barefoot escape into an Edenic past on the 'land'. In his sneakers' flash (which parallels the cursor flash in the film's first frame) the blinding light of the Manhattan Project and the devastating uses of technology are visible. Similarly, the offscreen sounds that convey the chaotic violence that attends the final fashion show resonate with our mental soundtrack for 9/11: sirens, police radio, screams, explosions, helicopter blades. In fact, the offscreen sound world of the final scenes is understandable *because* we have that mental soundtrack (itself shaped by disaster movies). The film is comprehensible because it carefully and cannily sounds out the New York of our image- and sound-banks, drawn from current affairs and culture, from headlines and *haute couture*.

Equally, a new New York becomes comprehensible: a Ground Zero that does not aspire to re-erect the edifices of global financial power, but to speak of its trauma with 'a voice that is paradoxically released *through the wound*' (Caruth 1996: 2; emphasis in original). Cathy Caruth's lucid formulation for individual expressions of trauma seems equally relevant to New York as the unseen protagonist of *Rage* (2009) (doubling Michelangelo), a film deeply concerned with listening as characters speak with a voice released through the wound. The film's paradoxical concept of an invisible New York constructed of signs and whispers is suggestive of Caruth's assertion that in 'trauma, the outside has gone inside without any mediation' (1996: 59). This 'unclaimed experience', as she titles her book, is 9/11; but as in *Yes*, it is 9/11 as the summation and synecdoche for tumultuous experiences of colonialism, oppression, loss and violence. Formally, the film renders an impossibly tight 'inside' of green-screen and close framing in which this experience is at first contained, and can slowly begin to be claimed. It moves from inside to outside through the perfect metaphor of surface, overlaying and deeply imbricated with New York: fashion.

Fashion is what New York speaks, both in the specific sense of clothing and life-style trends and the larger sense of cultural style. In the twentieth century, New York took over from Paris the role of arbiter of fashion. As Alan Howard illuminates in his essay on fashion's place in the new global economy, New York became an 'ideal site for a culture industry with a global focus' because it concentrated not only cultural capital in the form of the art world, but also national media and global finance (1997: 171). Wall Street and the *New York Times*, the United Nations and Greenwich Village: all of these signifiers of New York's centrality haunt *Rage* (2009) and its rage.

Only one character in the film makes a specific locative reference. Tiny's body-guard Jed (John Leguizamo), an ex-cop and coffee addict, claims that he has a mental map of the 256 Starbucks in the city. No other character alludes to the city with Jed's particular combination of addiction and pragmatic awareness. Merlin speaks of it as being 'alive' when his first interview with Michelangelo is interrupted by a wailing police siren, a distinctive sound that conjures television cop shows and the 1970s New York independent cinema that they reference. This aliveness will be reinter-preted as a speaking from the wound as, through increasingly detailed revelations of his childhood memories, Merlin's unnamed home city where death was public and omnipresent is overlaid on New York. Murder and mayhem are recoded: no longer the glamorous, gritty or thrilling stuff of movies set in the city, the murders on which so much American cinema and television is predicated are revealed as no different than deaths elsewhere.

Beneath Merlin's revelations echo two implicit questions: first, why dominant media fetishises violent or unexpected death, when it is both a trauma and a common-place in so many parts of the world (including parts of New York); and second, why there is no equivalence between the unnamed, multiple deaths that take place 'offscreen' from First World consciousness, and the sentimental or gruesome fascina-tion with singular deaths such as Princess Diana's. In order to approach an answer, *Rage* (2009) moves its murders offscreen, like New York. Rather than offering us the forensic detail that we are led to expect by the televisualisation of violent death, *Rage* (2009) returns to the ethics of Greek tragedy, in which deaths happen offstage and are recounted by a messenger: *angelos*, suggestive of Michelangelo's role.

The ethics of bearing witness are argued by Frank (Steve Buscemi), a war(-weary) photojournalist reassigned to fashion because his editors feel he is too old. His cynical yet informed attitude is one of the many threads that ties fashion to the world, removing it from its pedestal and reconnecting it to economic and political events that span the globe. When Dorothy, who is heard but never seen, is shot on the catwalk, Frank rises to the occasion, noting the utility of his camera lens in contrast to the fashion photographers with long lenses, and his willingness – paraphrasing paradigmatic photojournalist Robert Capa – to get close to the action. He chides Michelangelo for his distance from the drama, his lack of usable (sellable) material. Frank is a compelling voice, observing that Dorothy's death is the 'first real thing' most of the fashionistas have seen. Yet his classical photojournalistic ethics, placing the picture above all – and the monetary value of the picture above that – contrast with Michelangelo's metaphorical/metaphysical long lens and thus broader field of vision: his lack of zoom, his focus on individual faces, on what appears to be telling rather than showing.

Certainly, *Rage* (2009) is a 'talkie', fascinated with cinema's ability to show people talking – and particularly, talking about themselves. As well as calling on the anarchic, homemade genre of the video diary, this address to camera is suggestive of Woody Allen's nerdy-wordy New York films, and of the association of New Yorkers with torrents of playful language, an association that has its roots (like Allen's films) in Yiddish culture, but has come to encompass (or perhaps generate) bullish traders and hip-hop flows. Overflowing with language, New York also overflows with languages and accents, a facet of the city that is audible from *Rage*'s (2009) first words, spoken in Indian-accented English by Vijay.

Through Edith Roth, the only character who describes herself as having roots in New York, *Rage* (2009) suggests that the city's continuity lies in its continuously changing communities of immigrants. Wiest's sweet-smart face and soft voice are immediately recognisable, offering the viewer a connection to the world of New York crime via *Law and Order*, where she played D. A. Nora Lewin from 2000–02, and even more resonantly to the world of Allen's semi-autobiographical films *The Purple Rose of Cairo* (1985) and *Radio Days* (1987), fantasias located in the disappearing working-class Jewish community of New York's outer boroughs. Edie's Jewishness is apparent in her surname, shared with one of America's most noted Jewish writers, Philip Roth (who grew up just outside New York in Newark, New Jersey), and her memories of her parents' garment business, which is now the fashion house for which Merlin works.

Edie offers the most nostalgic monologue in the film, recalling a trade in which her parents knew 'every bead and button sewer, every cutter and presser, every janitor in every warehouse, every delivery boy, all by name'. Edie's emphasis on the final clause gestures towards the importance of names and naming in the film, directing the viewer back to mild-mannered Edie's first line, 'My name is Roth', which sounds a lot like rageful 'wrath'. The poetic repetitions lend a romantic authenticity to the Edenic memory of manual labour that both evokes and disguises the darker historical events of Jewish-owned and -staffed sweatshops on the Lower East Side before World War Two. Listing the many specialised employees, Edie illustrates the division of labour that made fashion the model for Fordist production lines. As Andrew Ross writes in the introduction to *No Sweat*, the fashion industries 'have seen some of the worst labour excesses, [and so] they have also been associated with historic victories for labour, and hold a prominent symbolic spot on the landscape of labour iconography' (1997b: 11).

As the inheritor of her parents' business, but also as the first to remark on the presence of the protestors shouting 'Justice for Workers!' outside the venue, Edie stands for a historical lineage that stretches beyond her familial associations with the world of the Triangle Shirtwaist factory where the first union was formed, back towards Karl Marx's concern for the coat-makers who are the first subjects discussed in *Capital* and Friedrich Engels' attention to English cloth manufacturing. Edie offers Michelangelo a multi-faceted take scattered with hints of this history. She speaks thoughtfully of what she has learned from her long association with the business, including – with a gently ironic smile – women's love of adornment for their own pleasure.

She is a model of the feminist whom Angela McRobbie imagines in *No Sweat*, a woman who takes female pleasure and expertise in clothing as motivation to 'bridge the gulf that divides issues of labour from style' (Ross 1997a: 1). Edie is the only character who makes the choice to join the protestors gathered on the final day, their ranks now swelled by the young internet users who have found, and been inspired by, Michelangelo's videostream. Her sense of history is represented, narratively, as a desired connection to offscreen space, which stands as much for her remembered New York of the garment trade as it does for Merlin's more painful childhood memories. Offscreen space assumes dimensions of past time, but – in Edie's reference to her parents' workers – it also encompasses the hidden side of our visible world, both the exploited labourers and the big businesses engaged in exploitation that we push to the corner of our vision.

Through this layering of offscreen space, the viewer is literally dis-Oriented. Rather than offering the comforting fiction of the all-powerful voyeuristic viewer, *Rage* (2009) locates the spectator, by affinity, with those who are powerless. We are at once the working immigrant ghosts of the past summoned by Edie's wistful gaze off, and the vulnerable and terrorised inhabitants of Merlin's childhood home. We are also, in the present, the protestors heard offscreen and the overseas workers on whose behalf they are protesting. We come to realise that as spectators in commercial cinema, our active participation in narrative has been 'outsourced'. Our inability to intervene in the film is layered with all these experiences of being offscreen, and particularly with the most pressing political 'offscreen space' of the developing world.

The film's unthinking of Eurocentrism goes deeper than its references to Chinese labourers through its resignification of offscreen space as, in a sense, cinema's Orient – the direction towards which cinema is oriented, but also the place it denies, suspects and patronises. There are two instances in which the fabrications of Orientalism are made clear in the film, two fashion(ed) objects that make specific references to Merlin's catwalk designs. Their presence underlines the fetishisation stemming from an ingrained association of the imagined East with surface, ornament, fabric and femininity. There is the 'thirty metre long black braid, Chinese reference' that Bonnie is said to be wearing when she is shot on the catwalk. It is woven of multiple strands, not least the persistent Orientalism of the fashion industry. Merlin reverses and makes visible the spectre of the braid – in its punitive weight, associated with gendered social control – when he threatens to redesign his collection as burqas, and then rend them as if in an explosion.

In emphasis – and in the one moment in which we see Merlin at work, designing – he throws his ever-present black sash (usually worn in the style of Byron as Greek freedom fighter) over his head.

In a film predicated on the visibility and legibility of the face, it is a shocking – and thrilling – erasure. On the surface, it is a paradoxical and provocative image of male veiling, in which Merlin apparently signals his origins as (Middle) Eastern. It offers a graphic depiction, in its blurring of the niqab and the hoods worn by the prisoners in Abu Ghraib, of the insistent Western feminisation of Oriental men. Yet it is also an act of resistance and reclamation, instating the veil as a refusal to be the pure surface of visibility with which the Orient is associated. With his gesture, Merlin creates and owns a hidden space, a depth of shadow, in a screen that has been insistently evenly-lit and flatly-coloured. He claims a right to privacy, to be unseen, in the moment that he grieves for his abandoned collection and his lost childhood. What it asserts as a valid human right, in place of celebrity, is the agency of choice. By challenging the validity of visibility, it restores dignity to those who are unseen, whether women in burqas, secret prisoners, labourers in hidden compounds or the audience.

Rage (2009) makes these unseens visible, not through a literal depiction onscreen – where it could only use one face, or one factory, symbolically to tell the story of millions – but through the smallest of changes in the visual field. When Edie compares her childhood memory to a present in which nothing is manufactured in New York, she tells Michelangelo resignedly that everything is made in China. 'Don't believe me?' she asks. 'Look inside your shoe.' The camera dips to imply that Michelangelo is doing just that, a rare and dizzying movement that tilts our vision away from the interview subject, and kinaesthetically moves us to look at our own shoes. It reminds us that Michelangelo's film is a made object in an environment in which very little is made. Klein quotes Nike's president Phil Knight as saying, 'There is no value in making things any more' (2001: 197). *Rage* (2009) is insistently not 'a product without a producer, a discourse without an origin', as Daniel Dayan succinctly describes the 'tutor-code of classical cinema' (2000: 224). Avoiding shot/reverse-shot even more studiously than Potter's previous films, *Rage* (2009) refuses to 'outsource' its source, to disattribute its enunciation and making. *Rage* (2009) has a doubly-visible producer: not only is the filmmaker a named, if never seen, character in the film, but the characters look directly at him when they talk, breaking the cardinal rule of the tutor-code by gazing into offscreen space.

Disconcertingly (un)familiar, this to-camera gaze solicits another associative resonance with Edie's name: Edie Sedgwick, and the Factory milieu of which she has become the decontextualised and much-fetishised symbol. *Rage* (2009) works like an extended narrative version of Andy Warhol's *Screen Tests* (1964–66), mesmerising extensions of Warhol's photo-booth photography, in which Factory visitors – including Sedgwick – were asked to sit, without blinking or moving, before a tripod-mounted movie camera. *Rage* (2009) shares Warhol's interest in duration's effect on the viewer's understanding of the human face, as the representational style associated with still portraits is extended by cinema. Warhol's fascinated fraying at the boundaries between public and private, celebrity and 'nobody', beauty and death – all expressions of the visibility/invisibility dyad that runs through *Rage* (2009) – located itself repeatedly in the form of the portrait, most famously the screen-printed multiples of iconic figures and, later, of car crashes, a progression suggested by the ethical violence of representation and mass visibility.

Supermodel Minx (Jude Law) approvingly quotes 'Mr Andy Warhol's' maxim that we will all be famous for 15 minutes, but later unsettles the value of visibility. Warhol is not the only defining twentieth-century thinker from whom Minx quotes: she also borrows a line from 'Mr Sigmund Freud'. Through their secular priests, she unites the ikon and the confession in her extended meditation on being visible. When Minx confesses that her supermodel career stems from her desire to stop her mother's tears, she is one of several characters – those most powerful and adept at manipulating the audience – who reveals a scene in which he or she was the powerless audience to their parents. Tiny Diamonds, who has recently acquired the fashion house, hints at a tempestuous childhood to explain his desire to purchase beauty and peace. By contrast, in a moment of vulnerability Minx wonders whether the money she earns can buy the tranquil life, and the attentive audience, she was deprived of as a child. In Minx's use of the camera as a reflexive, as well as reflective, mirror, we see her seeing, as if she is on 'our side' looking in. Celebrities, the film suggests, are just a sur/face for our rage against the machine, their massive visibility a distraction from the economic and political power at work behind them.

The film draws on the familiarity of billboard-size celebrity close-ups to draw the viewer into the film, so that at first the strangeness of watching these iconic confessions is disguised by the modes of celebrity and surveillance they critique: the dailiness of vox pops and expert interviews in news broadcasts; the emergence of videocalling; the state's use of biometrics and face recognition CCTV to regulate us by making our faces our identity; and our own willing participation in the relentless faciality of communications media through which everyone's face has become their brand. The stream of faces and voices in *Rage* (2009) at first rewards our Facebook fascination with other people's snapshots and soundbites, with bright colours, snappy dialogue and swift succession keeping our attention.

Rather than taking the characters at face value, Michelangelo's interest shows a persistent, focused, investigative quality that illustrates both the compelling (yet unsat-isfying) nature of confessional reality TV and also the (fatally obscured) difference between documentaries and 'reality-based programming'. What starts out feeling like *Big Brother* shifts, as the characters unravel, to the honest and intensely-felt connec-tion of Michael Apted's *7-Up* documentary series (1964–). Where Apted has worked over 45 years (and counting), Potter allocates herself seven days; the tension provoked by the protestors and the murders becomes the cue for confession. Michel Foucault describes how it appears that 'confession frees, but power reduces one to silence; truth does not belong to the order of power, but shares an original affinity with freedom' (1990: 60); as he continues, however, 'truth is not by its nature free … its production is thoroughly imbued with relations of power' (ibid.). Once Detective Homer arrives to investigate Dorothy's murder, the power apparatus that controls and benefits from the act of confession becomes visible.

In the characters' initial willingness to confess to the camera, something more sinister emerges. In *Giving an Account of Oneself*, Judith Butler argues that 'we become reflective upon ourselves, accordingly, through fear and terror. Indeed, we become morally accountable as a consequence of fear and terror' (2005: 11). This is particularly, and strikingly, true of Merlin's summoning of Michelangelo on the sixth day. His monologue straddles the boundary between a confession that frees and one produced by fear and terror: he wants Michelangelo to record it, he says, in case he is arrested and disappeared as a suspect in the murder of the models. Merlin's fear extends beyond the brown-skin invisibility that He describes in *Yes* into the physical erasure represented by the extra-legal detention used by the US in the 'war on terror'. In his confession, almost a legal deposition, Merlin brings to the fore another disconcertingly familiar form of contemporary confession that is (in)visible beneath the documentary-cum-diary room talking heads. The confession is a pre-emptive version of those extracted by torture. For a moment, the bright box of *Rage's* (2009) static frame, with its sharp, even, high-key lighting, is a torture chamber. In the same moment, it is the desperately necessary record of that which the torturing power does not want to be known.

The moment is both moving and discomfiting. In coming so close to events occurring in the real world, Merlin's words urge us to act – and confront us with the impossibility of doing so on behalf of a fictional character. Bearing witness is a seductively important role for the viewer, but our seduction is undermined by our hunger for the next confession, and indeed for the horrific events at the fashion show on the following day, the projected 'fear and terror' that prompt Merlin's confession. Confession is caught up in, and makes visible, the contradictory realisation that visibility and audibility do not mean power, but subjection to power. The need to be seen is revealed as a cover-up for, and resistance to, all that dominant culture does not want us to see. That such resistance is not successful is manifest in the film's refusal to *show*, as much as in its refusal of conventional narrative outcomes: the murderer is not made visible; neither is Merlin's collection, nor the protest against the company.

Potter makes the film's most moving and emotional scene a rage against visuality that echoes Merlin's donning of the veil and voices the 'fear and terror' implicit in his deposition. Anita de los Angeles, like Merlin, is an immigrant, a person of colour, an accented speaker. Her surname connects her to Michelangelo in his role as messenger and witness. As if to emphasise this, she names him frequently in her dialogue, and is the only character to reach out to him. Her empathy with the boy behind the camera seems like a 'natural' affinity predicated on skin colour, and on her identity as a mother. Yet it is Anita alone who rages against the camera as an intrusion, an interrogation. In their first encounter, Anita shyly tells Michelangelo nothing except the technical details of her work as a seamstress on Merlin's *haute couture* designs. Later, she confronts the camera in a towering fury, *accusing* Michelangelo of making her visible. Her daughter had seen the videostream and said, 'Mom, you're famous.' For Anita, however, visibility means not celebrity but deportation. Like Merlin's on-camera deposition, Anita's interview with Michelangelo is a pre-emptive, and inadvertent, confession, in her case to immigration officers. The screen becomes a cage against which she pushes. Viewers are compelled by the performance but, perhaps, shamed by our complicity in consuming a person against her will. We have to reconfigure our gaze, to unthink the passivity of spectatorship and align ourselves with the characters as subjects of surveillance.

Anita, having altered the audience's perceptions, returns to speak to Michelangelo on future occasions, moving from confession to tearful prayer for the murdered models, and eventually to absolution for Michelangelo when his offscreen tears confess his burden of guilt at the deaths of the young protestors who followed his videostream to the show. Anita's affinity with Michelangelo is that they are among the last people *making* things in Manhattan. It is in our power of making that Potter locates human beings' affinity to the godhead or lifeforce. Potter's is not a transcendent God, a God of invisibility held out of reach by institutional religion to force confession, but an immanent spirit inhabiting bodies at work. This is, finally, why and how *Rage* (2009) is a film about fashion(ing) – one that takes place over seven days, like Biblical Creation. Long before it referred to the marketing of high-end clothing and/as lifestyle, even before it meant a style, *fashion* meant the 'action of process or making', derived from the Latin verb *facere*, to make or do, which exactly translates the Greek *poiein*, the root of the word *poetry*. So *fashion* is equivalent, at root, to *poiesis*, the act of creative making.

What matters to Anita, from the first, is the quality of her work. She speaks in a compressed poetry of doing 'visible and invisible' work, of sewing invisible zips. This worker of the invisible, the least financially-valued of the film's workers, is like Grandmother Spider Woman who weaves the world in Navajo and Hopi creation stories. She performs a new kind of suture that brings Michelangelo – as the viewer's representative in offscreen space – into the film. When the film fades to black on Anita's tearful face, it seems as if she has had the final word: God. As plain as the small gold crucifix she wears around her neck, Anita's statement of faith in what could be seen as the ultimate Offscreen has none of the doubt or investigation of She's to-camera monologue in *Yes*, but it yokes God and the audience in the same way.

Adriana Barraza's extraordinary face, radiant with conviction in a film that works hard to reveal and deconstruct our inevitably knowing pose before the camera, ensures that her words echo as the final scenes play out. A white-into-white fade-through comes up on the palm of a hand placed close to its lens. As the hand moves away, it allows the viewer to take in a scene that has completely changed. The only familiar aspect is Lettuce's (Lily Cole) face, but it is horizontal as she is lying on a flower-patterned rug. The garden has returned, and with it Michelangelo relinquishes the godlike role of filmmaker, the all-seeing, unseen auteur. 'It's, like, my turn,' says Lettuce, reaching towards the camera in a gesture that repeats Anita's.

The image fades out. Then, flashing whitely in sun that striates the wasteground into brilliance and shadow, Michelangelo's sneakers are objects of pure cinema. Rather than making Michelangelo visible to us as a portrait, the sneakers lead him towards the background and out of frame. They draw attention to themselves (and their play with cinema) at the same moment as they almost disappear into the white light of the over-exposed shot. As a 'line of flight', Michelangelo's sneakers are like his cellphone:

a tool for self-expression – and more than that, self-fashioning – however compromised by their source in globalised industry.

Sneakers are thus a signature for the filmmaker and his making, a kinetic metaphor for moving pictures, for the relationship of time to space, and of the body to its image. Michelangelo's sneakers are the key, the final clue given in the final frame: not to the identity of the murderer who stalks through the film unleashing violence on the models, but to the larger mystery – which is not a mystery at all – of power's violence against and exploitation of the powerless, which structures the fashion industry from the production of raw materials through to the modelling and marketing of the end product. The disappearing sneakers, a reference back to Ruby and Celeste riding over the horizon on their white horse at the end of *The Gold Diggers*, note film's implication in those power relations and, at the same time, suggest how we might escape them.

Released from the real time of observation, which turns through the course of the film from feeling like *vérité* documentary to feeling like CCTV at a crime scene, the final shot enters the time of love. It uses the same music (composed by Potter and Fred Frith, and quoted from *Yes*) that has been heard repeatedly, almost subliminally, throughout the film to denote the catwalk show. That music is now fully audible, filling the entire soundspace. Its delirious beats pound in time with the movement of feet in the frame – Michelangelo's feet, we believe – and so are transmitted kinaesthetically to our own bodies. The beat that links heart and feet in Potter's films from *Thriller* onwards provides a jubilant ending to the film, one that tilts the viewer's own body into forward motion, without prescribing a destination. The music turns Michelangelo's 'line of flight' into a catwalk show and vice versa, summoning the sense we might have – when running with headphones on – that we are starring in our own movie, that it's, like, our turn to fill the immense screen space of celebrity and power.

Michelangelo is not running towards celebrity, but away from the camera, away from the fixed location of the fashion show – the scene of his crime – and even away from the fixity of location itself. He is in flight like Pablo and He, leaping into the unknown that is a new kind of cinema *beyond* that rooted in the shorthand of brands and urban cool. To find it, he has turned the camera over to his collaborator, Lettuce, the only character in the film associated by name with the natural world. She is the figure in the cinematic carpet, the flower in the garden, as well as the bad girl, the one who did not die. She is the flame-haired phoenix who rises from her fashionable pose of apathy and passivity, and returns cinema to its affinity with light.

CONCLUSION

Becoming (Part II)

I'm interested in reading Carmen and her sorcery as a key to how to work with theatrical language, which is all smoke and mirrors, like magic. But Carmen's fortune-telling is also related to mythology (and a degree of actuality) about gypsies. It ties into historical themes of women's abilities being punished as witchcraft because people are fearful of them. Through fear, it gets turned into a cliché about women and gypsies and their mysterious powers, but it's really an emblem of female power and knowledge. I think there's a seduction and an attraction in somebody who holds their own ground and refuses to wimpify their own power in that drag act known as femininity. The men want to follow Carmen's wildness and her lack of hypocritical moral constraint. Through her, they want to find that part of themselves that is repressed or calcified. She opens a chink of light, and they go towards that light, that luminosity.

– Sally Potter, interview with author, August 2007

Sally Potter conjures her films, like her 2007 ENO production of *Carmen*, with smoke and mirrors. Her sorcery draws on all the powers of the medium through innovative use of address, performance, colour, sound, rhythm, affect and narrative space. Like Carmen, Potter lays claim to her power as an auteure, refusing to don the drag of either the female artiste (who is only her body) or the genius one-man-band auteur. Her 'mysterious powers' are linked to her 'wildness': her willingness to experiment with film form, narrative and aesthetics, but also her place on the 'wild' margins of globalised commercial cinema. Her films are not National Trust gardens like Orlando's. Instead, like guerrilla gardening, they take neglected or surprising spaces – a squat, a dockside, a family-run hotel – and reveal the wild beauty that is already there. Potter's Carmen did not reveal her fortune-telling powers in Act III's customary grotto in the mountains, but on a walkway over a six-lane motorway, where she watched nervously over the cross-border smuggling operation she had organised. Urban spaces and the natural world are not antithetical in Potter's work, which refuses the strict separation that associates urban space with masculinity and nature with femininity. Her Queens of the Night travel through the city and encounter the wild infolded within it. The fountain at Saint Sulpice creates a 'chink of light' for the viewer through its resonance with what is wild in us.

In a blog for the *Yes* website, Potter describes a visit to a literary festival in Avignon where she discovers a secret place called The Alchemist's Garden. The garden opens with a maze that spells out the word *berechit*, the first word of the Torah, meaning beginning/creation. It proceeds through a catalogue of plants of the world, with a particular focus on the curative and magical herbs of Provence. The journey culminates in an 'alchemical voyage through three inner gardens … The journey through the [third] red garden, governed by the sun, leads you to a state of transformation. You leave it ready to begin your life again' (Potter 2006). Potter's cinema, like the alchemist's garden, offers the viewer a route through a heightened, saturated version of the natural world that 'leads you to a state of transformation'. It is a cinema that asks the viewer to open their senses, as gestures, colour, space and sound solicit the subtle body's response. 'Ecstatic experience is one of total kinaesthesia; everything is alive, quivering, embodied, and it is noteworthy that mystics down through the ages have insisted that the experience is essentially cognitive, a mode of knowing' (Berman 1990: 38). An ecstatic cinema makes the screen into the totality of the world. It is a way of feeling knowing and knowing feeling, through an interrelation of Self and Other. Potter's cinematic gardens transform through the senses, through film's profusion and its growth.

As colour and music draw the viewer's attention to images that are layered with political and aesthetic references, so Potter's specific, idiosyncratic arrangements of narrative time and space centre on images that are rich with intimations of mythology and spirituality. Rather than drawing on a J. G. Frazer-esque universal mythology, Potter is attentive to cultural and historical specifics. Orlando's tree is the English Royal Oak, and it is Woolf's Orlando's poem 'The Oak Tree'. It stands for historical and geographical specificity. Appearing at the beginning and end of the film, it is also the Celtic oak, regarded as a door between worlds. Orlando's sex change reverses that of the oak at Dodona, the oldest oracle in the Greek world (known as early as 2000 BCE), which was originally dedicated to the Mother Goddess, Dione, before it was appropriated by worshippers of her consort Zeus. The oak is transformed from doughty symbol of royal, national, masculine, singular identity back to its wild, plural roots.

Unlike Potter's surface of references to Western high culture, this play of the natural world striates the films and opens them up to viewers across cultures, classes and languages. This is strengthened by a sense of historical ecology from *The Gold Diggers* onwards, which looks clearly at how human cultures negotiate with and are shaped by landscapes. While Potter's films are not explicitly or didactically ecological, they show their respect for and understanding of the physical world by making that world the ground of human relations. Fissile, beautiful, mutable combinations of fire, water, earth and air function to reconnect cinema, as a mechanical process with an industrial product, to lived experience in its physical and metaphysical dimensions.

For Potter the metaphysical is entwined with the physical, arising in bodies and world. In an interview for *Cineaste*, Potter made a compressed comment to Cynthia Lucia that underlines the close connection of 'the visible world' and the transcendent with which her films desire 'to reconnect'.

> In times of political extremity or urgency it is necessary to reconnect with transcendent, metaphysical dimensions – to remember what lies behind or beyond the impermanent, immediate realities ... this is something cinema can do – make links between layers of existence and evoke the invisible world. (In Lucia 2005: 26)

Kristi McKim comments on the interview that 'Potter aspires to nothing less than art that affects the macrocosmic/world by working within the microcosmic/human' (2006). It is an impossibly hubristic claim if understood on politicians' terms. If understood from the perspective of wisdom traditions, however, it is not only humble but intensely humane, and – more than that – a possibility that her films extend to every viewer. By embedding their complex questions of self and world in elemental beauty, Potter's films, and their mutable, engaging protagonists who journey towards openness, hold out the potential for change to each of us. Transformation begins in watching the films and accepting their model of audience.

Each film contains the audiences that it hopes for, from the intensely intimate, affective audiences of *Thriller* and *The Gold Diggers* to the globally, digitally connected audiences of *Yes* and *Rage* (2009). Each of these audiences partakes in Potter's cultivation of an *I-Thou* cinema, one that addresses its viewer as not only an equal, but an equal partner in creation. For Martin Buber, *I-Thou* is not just a word spoken to a human or divine Other, but also to the natural world that is an intrinsic aspect of the divine and the human. Speaking the word *I-Thou*, Potter's films draw on the elemental world to mirror and shape her human protagonists' movement from isolation towards each other.

In their attention to the collaborative, sensual, affective and spiritual, Potter's films align themselves with neglected wisdom traditions. In the West, these have been marginalised and 'feminised' because they imagine the self and world as being united rather than disparate, and shifting rather than static. Esoteric practices have tended to see the male/female principle as a construct rather than a biologically essential dualism, and so have had space for women as spiritual leaders and teachers. Carmen's fortune-telling is a version of such leadership in a post-Enlightenment world that does not recognise it.

Potter has played cannily with the association of woman and sorcery/spirituality since her early work. In the first part of the four-part performance event *Berlin*

Fire and Ice: Sally Potter in *Berlin* (1976)

(1976), the audience arrived at a house where performers Potter and Rose English were squatting. After encountering Potter standing mute, dressed only in a crinoline, in a firelit room, they were led upstairs by English. She stood in front of the bedroom doors, 'below a bulb with the light hitting her forehead; she stood until tears began to roll down her cheeks: the audience was very close, watching, as it were, a cinematic close-up of her crying' (English 1988). *Berlin*'s promenade staging created an emotional meeting between performer and audience mediated by technology's 'smoke and mirrors' summoning of the elemental.

Fire

> Fire is the ur-energy of art ... Fire is a verb, too ... to fire something with love is to intensify it. (Griffiths 2007: 252)

> There, on the threshold, the response, the spirit, is kindled ever new within him; here, in an unholy and needy country, this spark is to be proved. (Buber 1958: 53)

It seems fitting that Potter's interactive digital archive is called SP-ARK (www.sp-ark.org). Fire is at the heart of her work, both visually and metaphysically. Onscreen, it signals the intensity of artistic labour that her films record, metaphorising both the 'spark' of inspiration and the energy of work. Fire's meaning alters to trace the progress of empire in *Orlando*, from the burning torches that herald Elizabeth I to the burning trenches that mark Orlando's passage into the reign of Elizabeth II. Fire burns on ice in the reign of King James, as Orlando falls in love. Fire makes steam in the *hammam* in Khiva. It burns in the hearths of the Great House in contrast to the damp green of the Victorian era as Orlando tends to Shelmerdine's ankle. In early drafts of the screenplay, fire burnt the house to the ground as Orlando's class rage turned her into the first Mrs Rochester. In the finished film, torches burn in the Khan's courtyard just before war breaks out, but fire is never simply associated with danger or madness. It marks moments of transformation.

When fire meets ice, it is an elemental reflection of Orlando's divided self. Flames burn on water at the opening of *The Man Who Cried*. They are like a screen of 'reverie' in which Suzie sees her memories unfolding. Rachel O. Moore compares film to fire in *Savage Theory*, her remarkable account of cinema's ritual significance. Watching film raises the ghosts and dreams of collective activities like sitting round the campfire; watching fire on film even more so. Moore describes the attitude of watching fire as 'reverie', a play of thought, memory, emotion and dream. 'Continually shifting between absorption and attraction, private mental meandering and public ritual, your vision will be yours alone, but the collection of inner speeches will intersect around the ritual's stories, songs and images' (1999: 5).

Fire is the spirit of mutability that runs through Potter's work as a liberatory politics. Moore argues that for revolutionary Soviet filmmaker Sergei Eisenstein, 'fire was an important element … because of its movement, the way the shapes change while we watch it. Like music, its images flow continuously, they are eternally changeable' (1999: 128). Film offers a formal frame for staring into the flames, like the sweat lodge ceremony described by Chicasaw poet Linda Hogan:

> In a sweat lodge ceremony, the entire world is brought inside the enclosure … It is all called in … It is a place of immense community and of humbled solitude; we sit together in our aloneness and speak, one at a time, our deepest language of need, hope, loss, and survival. We remember that all things are connected.
> … The ceremony is a point of return … But it is not a finished thing. The real ceremony begins where the formal one ends, when we take up a new way, our minds and ears filled with the vision of earth that holds us within it, in compassionate relationship to and with our world. (1995: 39–41)

Her description points to the rich traditions of shared experiences of being 'together in our aloneness' in the dark that survive in non-Western cultures, and the possibility of recognising and valuing such a holistic space in our own culture.

Through Potter's work, it is possible to imagine a sweat lodge cinema, in the sense of both medium and building. As in the ceremony Hogan describes, the world is 'called in' through the scenes projected onto the screen, and, if we are lucky, the film speaks with us in 'our deepest language of need, hope, loss, and survival'. It does not, however, provide us with a complete solution or satisfaction, but sends us out fired up to 'take up a new way'. When Pablo swims redly into Sally's vision, it suggests the way in which the vivid images we see in Potter's cinema can carry over into a joyous real.

Water

It's very tempting to work with a figure floating suspended in water. There's one colour across the screen and a human figure in that one moving mass of water. It's very photogenic. And there's so many different resonances in myth, in psychology, in symbology, and in actual places. With Pablo swimming, we've got how life begins in relation to water, and how our bodies are full of water. Water is thought of as the female element, because of the movement of the tides and the pull of the moon, and water coming into dreams. We've also got David Hockney's swimming pools, icons of Western affluence as well as the working-class dream of leisure and the holiday. There's Siegfried and the pool. When you film water, you feel that you're tapping into all kinds of things that people will sense without you spelling them out.

— Sally Potter, interview with author, September 2006

In *Waterlog*, his account of a year-long swim through wild water across England, Roger Deakin writes that 'the beauty of a swimming pool is in its graphic simplicity … What you are seeing is changing so fast your eye can never quite catch up with it. In every way you are dazzled. It is not water you perceive so much as light, and how water can play with it' (2000: 307). Water, like celluloid, is translucent, and its beauty derives from the play of light through and over its surface. At the same time, it is buoyant, literally a medium through which bodies and ships travel. Water bends light, makes ripples. Bodies in water are softened, distorted; sound is reduced to breathing and heartbeat. Potter's films take up the parallel between film as medium for the play of light and water as medium through which bodies pass.

Not only does water ripple across the screen in a movement of constant change similar to fire, but it also offers a metaphor for the experience of spectatorship. Watching a film is like swimming: immersion in an unhomely element rich in associations. Deakin notes that, once in the water, 'free of the tyranny of gravity and the weight of the atmosphere, I found myself in the wide-eyed condition described by the Australian poet Les Murray when he said: "I am only interested in everything"' (2000: 3). He describes lyrically the way in which entering water is always a ritual act, 'a crossing of boundaries: the line of the shore, the bank of the river, the edge of the pool, the surface itself. When you enter the water, something like metamorphosis happens. Leaving behind the land, you go through the looking-glass surface and enter a new world, in which survival, not ambition or desire, is the dominant aim' (ibid.). This immersion is the experience of each of Potter's characters as they 'world'-travel, crossing from being a spectator to a participant.

The difference between fire and water, of course, is immersion. While both are beautiful to watch, fire transmits sensation but is dangerous to touch. Its ritual associations are with sacrifice, and in *Orlando* and *The Man Who Cried* it heralds war. When you enter water 'you are *in* nature, part and parcel of it, in a far more complete and intense way than on dry land, and your sense of the present is overwhelming … Natural water has always held the magical power to cure. Somehow or other, it transmits its own self-regenerating powers to the swimmer' (2000: 4; emphasis in original). Sally's and Pablo's liquid handfuls from the fountain return baptism to its near-universal association with the ritual healing powers of water. Draft screenplays for *Orlando* contain a scene in which Orlando is ritually bathed by women in Turkey. In the finished film, she splashes her face with water at the moment of transformation. Potter's films often invoke ritual bathing, connecting natural water with the water inside the human body, which emerges onscreen as cathartic tears. Weeping in the closing credits of *Yes*, the Cleaner is metaphorically crying the sea water seen a few shots earlier. One way of translating *catharsis* is 'ritual cleansing'.

Symbolising change, water does not infer erasure. If we let the film wash over us and do not swim, we are in danger of forgetting the real. Rather than the threat of Lethe, Potter's films are like the river Mnemosyne, the river of total memory. Mnemosyne, named for the mother of the Muses, is almost forgotten now. Even in ancient times, the river was the secret preserve of Orphic cults, associated with the source of creativity (muses), and specifically lyric poetry and song (Orpheus). Worshipped as the goddess of memory at the shrine of Asklepios, where cult devotees were visited with vivid dreams in sleep cures, 'presumably [Mnemosyne] was expected ... to keep alive the recollection of the dreams in which the god appeared to his devotees' (Zuntz 1971: 379). Mnemosyne's vivid dreams make her, perhaps, the Muse of cinema, and specifically of Potter's lyric cinema, in which seekers pass through a ritual bathing in order to return from the dead. Mnemosyne is the goddess of the experience of ecstatic immersion, and of the moment that we return across the boundary to dry land, transformed.

Earth

> In the punitive austerity of Genesis, the tree represents the 'evil' of sexual knowledge and the woman is sinful. Tree, woman and sex are tied into the damnation of 'the Fall', while here in the [Amazonian] forests the stories tell the exact opposite; the lively flirtatious tree and the laughing sexy woman are the heroes of the story ... in the universal human truth of our long and necessary rapport with trees. (Griffiths 2007: 53)

Potter's films often end where land and water meet, hovering on the boundary. Only *The Gold Diggers* ends in the water. It is a film that works through earth's associations with the female body. The problem is not the parallel between the female icon and the earth or its products, but the way the parallel is used to control, strip-mine and disenfranchise women, as well as the land. Travelling back to see her younger self on the land, Ruby can undo the parallel, making the elements a source of female power. The connection between the body and the earth goes deep in Potter's films, rooted in the scale of her performance work, and its frequent location outside theatrical spaces. The relation of body and landscape is made visible in Potter's films through their resolute refusal of the establishing shot. Apart from the opening of *The Gold Diggers*, in which the camera pans across mountains specifically to intimate their inhospitality, Potter's films open and close on a human scale. 'Bodies are given as having the sense of being earthly bodies, space is given as having the sense of being earth-space' (Edmund Husserl in Berman 1990: 42). The bodily scale is also earthly and earthy, connected to sexual desire.

The park in *Yes* offers a playful scene that resounds with Jay Griffiths' stories of seductive trees. He and She walk, telling stories of their past, and of the other places that they think of as home. The camera hangs back, watching the characters shyly through trees and bushes as they walk a tentative path. When He mentions the 'trees / That blossom in the spring' in Beirut (in contrast to the bomb noise he has just made), and lists the sweet summer fruits that grow on them, the camera slowly moves towards them. It reaches a medium-long shot, directly behind them, as he praises the apricot, telling She that 'you can taste her secret with your tongue'. This association of fruit, trees and sexual pleasure is seemingly too much for the film; a slow super-imposition brings back the shy shot through the branches as She jokingly counters with a hymn to the earthier potato and its political history. The slow superimposition suggests the growing connection between them, even as She's nervous chatter of theology suggests that for her, with her Catholic upbringing, trees retain their association with Eve.

Through the course of the film, She enters further into the garden of her self and her connection with the world, until in the final shots she is laughing and kissing, dusted with sand. The earth, its trees and gardens, are associated with women in their wild states of liberation from culture by desire, or in childhood before culture has constrained them. Orlando is brought back to the tree by her daughter, who runs through the dry, golden grass with a video camera to film her mother sitting beneath the oak. When she points upwards, what her daughter catches on the camera screen is the spirit of air embodied in a singing angel.

Air

> A boy leaping is one of the sublimest images of art, sculpture, poetry, dance. Here is a bomb of male beauty, a perfectly controlled explosion of utmost athleticism and utmost finesse as Icarus leaves the earth and flies to the sun. (Brown 2007: 1)

Potter's female beauties redefine what it means to be metaphorically fertile gardens that are also – like the Alchemist's Garden – journeys of spiritual and intellectual transformation. Her male angels leap but do not repeat the fate of Icarus. Like the films themselves, her male and female characters are suspended between earth and air. At the end of *The Tango Lesson*, Sally asks Pablo in song:

> Where did you come from?
> Where, oh, where?
> From earth, from water,
> From fire, or air?

The rhyme *where/air* suggests Pablo's connection with flight throughout the film. He is often seen leaping – in the airport, onto the mantelpiece, through the warehouse doors. In Saint Sulpice, he takes the pose of the angel. The angel who hangs on the wall in Delacroix's painting, like the Angel who hung in the sky in the closing minutes of *Orlando*, is an artist's fantasy. While *Orlando* uses camp delight to give new, queer meanings to the angels of high art and self-help culture, *The Tango Lesson* re-presents the angel as lover – and love as being hard work, like learning tango. Potter's male, but never macho, dancers reconfigure the myth of Icarus. Eroticism, etheriality and vulnerability mingle and inform each other. The Icarene male body flies down to earth, turned this way and that from the tutu'd Artist in *Thriller* to Cesar riding through the night sky of Paris standing on horseback in *The Man Who Cried*, as well as the angels of *Orlando* and *The Tango Lesson*. In *Orlando*, the buoyancy of song and brilliant colour lifts the Angel's erotic 'coming through' into the ether.

The hard work of transformation is, itself, transformed by angelic grace. The films take delight in transformation, associating it with lightness but not levity. The air around Orlando sparkles with dust at the moment of her transformation, and this sparkling dust is the thread that runs through *Yes*, uniting the Cleaner's monologues about transformation and presence. Dust makes the invisible – air, film – visible, as film makes the invisible – angels, cleaners – visible. This is why Potter's oeuvre features so much doubling and twinning, both within and across films: there is a sense that we are all already doubled when made visible by photography, and before that by the mirror. In *Phantasmagoria*, Marina Warner traces the way in which Western culture has imagined 'soul stuff', from clouds to film. She argues that the coincidence of spirit mediums and the birth of photography lends film its ghostly air, making it the latest in a series of ethereal visions of angels, ghosts and spirits (see 2006: 300–1, 325–7). The sparkling air of Potter's films is where impossible leaps take place. Air is cinema itself in its ability to suspend disbelief in what it makes visible. In this, Potter's films work both to depict and to affect the 'subtle body', the extra-material self or spirit.

'I am born in a beam of light', begins Ruby in *The Gold Diggers*, drawing attention to the way that film is projected through the cinema's air to meet the screen. She is transformed, from the kind of problematic, ethereal screen representation that Lola aspires to become, into a manifestation of the subtle body. Later in the film, she comments in voice-over as she is whirled around the ballroom, 'I project. I am projected.' Ruby's project is to move from 'being projected' through the air on a palanquin to 'project[ing]' her own voice and image. Born in a beam of light, she grows up to become light. *The Gold Diggers* begins with elemental images of dark sky above icy ground: water, earth and air creating a stunning, inhospitable landscape. It ends with an arc of sparks from a welder's gun over dark water. Above all, it draws attention to the cinematic qualities of light, whether through the shadows thrown by bodies against white walls, or the moonlight reflected in water.

In offering this sensual apprehension of film as a medium that moves through air as light, it offers a different visual and sensory pleasure to the hard gold that the miners dig out of the earth and send to the bank. Moving from metal to photons borne aloft in dark water that meets and merges with the sky, Ruby performs a reverse alchemy. On her journey through the backstage labyrinth of her memory, Ruby encounters two younger versions of herself digging in a garden that is housed inside a warehouse.

The startling appearance of the two white-blonde children is Ruby's first physical encounter with her younger selves. In the *Alice in Wonderland* logic of the film, she follows them. Leading her deeper into her memory or dream, they bring her home. Running around the cabin, wind in their hair and boots striking the earth, the three Rubies become, in the Angel's words, 'joined ... one, with a human face'.

Grace

> When [Crop Eared Wolf] rode horses, or watched them running, he felt the spirit alive in him. *Whose* spirit, he couldn't say. But he could say that there was a moment when he felt one with both the earth and the sky.
>
> (Chamberlin 2007: 22; emphasis in original)

Grace in *Yes* and Lettuce in *Rage* (2009), like Ruby, are caught between childhood and adulthood. Both of them seek their identity in being clothes-horses: Lettuce is a model whose identity seems initially to have been shaped entirely by her manager, agent, designer and dressers. Grace worries about her weight and shape, but takes delight in trying on sexualised clothes and high heels on a shopping trip with her godmother, stalking through the changing room like a model to a techno track, 'Fawn', that also denotes the fashion show – and Lettuce's closing film – in *Rage* (2009). Grace is, wittily, shown twice in *changing* rooms, at the pool and the store. In both cases, her adoring gaze suggests she wants to change into her godmother who is on the point of liberating herself through desire. In Potter's films, grace belongs to beings 'fallen' into the sensual, pleasurable and political world. Transformation is the province of those suspended between earth and air, like the three Rubies.

A toy horse is the first human-made, or human-scale, object visible onscreen in *The Gold Diggers*. Half-submerged in snow, it is suggestive of buried memories. Its transmutation into the live horse on which Celeste rides in and rescues Ruby from the ball begins the process of thaw. The horse is the most prevalent non-human Other in Potter's films. In this, it is what Donna Haraway refers to as a 'companion species', particularly for Cesar in *The Man Who Cried*. Whereas Suzie is an expert at listening to human languages, Cesar is an expert listener to horse language. His instinctual relationship with his horse is given its fullest expression in a disquieting scene in which the horse, through its extra-human hearing, perceives approaching German troops and transmits its anxiety to Cesar. Jump-cut canted close-ups between horse and its human partner extend to the viewer an ability to hear what the horse and Cesar hear.

Cesar offers a model of cinematic spectatorship, less verbal and theoretical than Ruby's and Celeste's spiralling riddles, but equally astute. Watching this scene closely, the viewer 'enter[s] the horse's world', which, like cinema, has 'its own grammar and syntax, codes and conventions ... as we learn the new language we find ourselves thinking and feeling differently without even realising it' (Chamberlin 2007: 36). Filmmaker Raúl Ruiz writes that an alchemical cinema would follow Élémire Zolla's conception of alchemy as 'an extension of charity to the animal, vegetable, and mineral reigns. For our purposes, charity will mean simply according attention, or love, to all that is or can be closest to us in the frame. An attention at least equal to that given to the characters in the story we are being told' (1995: 80). In Potter's films, alchemy is charity in its etymological sense of grace: a partnering dance between Self and Other, whether human and human, human and animal, human and cinema, or human and world. The horse/rider relationship speaks, as Potter's films do, in the *I-Thou*. The attention that comes from learning the horse's/cinema's language is expressed in its transformative affect.

Ruby and Celeste, Orlando and Shelmerdine, Suzie and Cesar all meet through a horse's intercession. Despite the romantic cliché of the horse that shapes both the western and costume drama, horses are polyvalent and all their meanings are alive in the films. The films particularly feature white horses, descendants of Arab horses brought to Andalusia and creatures of fairy tale as in Jean Cocteau's *La Belle et la Bête* (*Beauty and the Beast*, 1946). The moving image began with Eadweard Muybridge's studies of horses in motion in 1877, made with the zoopraxiscope he designed to win a bet by securing proof that all four of a horse's hooves are off the ground in a gallop. Mythic horses such as Pegasus can fly, acting as a metaphor for human aspirations. Horses appear in the western because they are symbolic of wildness and of settlement.

Associated with nomadic peoples, horses offer lines of flight. 'John Jennings talks about how the moment of suspension is the moment that matters on horseback, the moment between gathering up and moving out, between the rhythms of the horse's movement and your own, between the earth and the air' (Chamberlin 2007: 38). Riding horses, like swimming in wild water, represents a border-crossing between Self and World. On horseback, Potter's characters are transported, suspended between the two modes that horses represent: the earth of work, and the sky of dance. If the horse is suggestively cinema, then the films offer us a moment of suspension in which we can be transformed. We can hitch a ride into the sunset (without conforming to happily ever after), and find ourselves moved.

When Celeste rescues Ruby for the second time, she rides off with her down a long bower. Unlike the dingy alleyway that the women have haunted and been hunted through, the bower is lit in soft shades of grey. As the horse rides deep into the background, the glimmer of white that is its tail commanding our attention, Celeste speaks in voice-over what she has learned: 'I know that, even as I look, and even as I see, I am changing what is there.' This knowledge is the grace of Sally Potter's films, given both to her characters and her viewers. Even as we look and even as we see, we are changing and changed, a politics of love that locates both personal and political transformation in love's openness to and through fellow-feeling. Judith Butler says of this transformation that being 'undone by another is a primary necessity, an anguish, to be sure, but also a chance – to be addressed, claimed, bound to what is not me, but also to be moved, to be prompted to act, to address myself elsewhere' (2005: 136). Celeste describes how her search for Ruby has wrought changes in her that she in turn will write on the world. Potter's politics of love suffuse the long take with a reverie of slowness, silvery light, whispering trees, gentle humour, a passionate embrace, a musical voice and poetry. The audience is there, moved by the transformations wrought by fire and water, suspended in grace between earth and air.

FILMOGRAPHY/PERFORMOGRAPHY/MUSICOGRAPHY

FILMOGRAPHY

The Building (1968) [Expanded Cinema event]
35mins, b/w
Cast: Mike Dunford; Leda Papaconstantinou.

Daily (1968)
14 mins, colour
Cast: Dancers from Ernest Berk's class

Jerk (1969)
3 mins, b/w
Cast: Mike Dunford; Hilary Dunford; Sally Potter;
    Susan Bocking

Black & White (1970)
10 mins, b/w

Hors D'Oeuvres (1970)
10 mins, colour
Cast: Student dancers from The Place

Play (1970)
10 mins, b/w and colour
Cast: twins living nearby

Combines (1972)
Looped, colour
Cast: Siobhan Davies; Paula Lansley; Ross McKim;
    Stephen Barker; Celeste Dandeker; Anthony
    van Laast; Micha Bergese

Thriller (1979)
34 mins, b/w
Production company: Sally Potter and the Arts
    Council of Great Britain
Producer: Sally Potter
Screenplay: Sally Potter, with the collaboration of
    Colette Laffont, after *La Bohème* by Giacomo
    Puccini
Cinematography: Sally Potter
Editor: Sally Potter
Original music: Lindsay Cooper
Main Cast: Mimi/Musetta (Colette Laffont);
    Mimi/Musetta (Rose English); The Artists
    (Tony Gacon, Vincent Meehan)

The Gold Diggers (1983)

90 mins, b/w

Production company: British Film Institute
    Production Board and Channel Four

Production supervisors: Nita Amy and Donna Grey

Screenplay: Lindsay Cooper, Rose English and Sally
    Potter

Cinematography: Babette Mangolte

Editor: Sally Potter

Original music: Lindsay Cooper

Main Cast: Ruby (Julie Christie); Celeste (Colette
    Laffont); The Expert (David Gale); Expert's
    Assistant (Thom Osborn); Mother (Hilary
    Westlake); Dancer (Jacky Lansley); Stagehand
    (George Yiasoumi)

London Story (1986)

15 mins, colour

Production company: Sally Potter, in association
    with the British Film Institute and Channel
    Four

Producers: Nancy Vandenburgh and Jill Pack

Screenplay: Sally Potter

Cinematography: Belinda Parsons

Editor: Budge Tremlett

Music arranged by: Lindsay Cooper

Main Cast: Jack (Jacky Lansley); Mr. Popper (Lol
    Coxhill); The Door (George Yiasoumi);
    Skater (Dennis Greenwood); Minister (Arthur
    Fincham)

Tears, Laughter, Fear and Rage [four-part television
    documentary] (1987)

4x30 mins, colour

Production company: Working Title, for Channel
    Four

Producer: Sarah Radclyffe

Interviewees: Paul Boateng, Irene Handl, Hanif
    Kureishi, Inez McCormack, Juliet Mitchell,
    Michael Powell, Rabbi Rabinowicz, Barbara
    Windsor

*I Am an Ox, I Am a Horse, I am a Man, I am a
    Woman: Women in Russian Cinema* [television
    documentary] (1990)

60 mins, colour with b/w film excerpts

Production company: Triple Vision

Producer: Penny Dedman

Interviewees: Ina Churikova, Lana Gogoberidze,
    Kira Muratova, Maria Turovskaya

Orlando (1992)

90 mins, colour

Production company: Adventure Pictures,
    co-produced with Lenfilm, Mikado Film, Rio,
    Sigma Filmproductions

Producer: Christopher Sheppard

Screenplay: Sally Potter, adapted from *Orlando, A
    Biography*, by Virginia Woolf

Cinematography: Alexei Rodionov

Editor: Herve Schneid

Original Music: David Motion and Sally Potter,
    with additional material by Fred Frith and
    David Bedford

Main Cast: Orlando (Tilda Swinton); Shelmerdine
    (Billy Zane); Khan of Khiva (Lothaire
    Bluteau); Archduke Harry (John Wood); Sasha
    (Charlotte Valandrey); Nick Green/Publisher
    (Heathcote Williams); Queen Elizabeth I
    (Quentin Crisp)

The Tango Lesson (1996)

97 mins, b/w and colour

Production company: Adventure Pictures, co-produced
    with OKCK Films, PIE, NDF/Imagica, Pandora
    Film and Cinema Project, Sigma Pictures

Producer: Christopher Sheppard

Screenplay: Sally Potter

Cinematography: Robby Müller

Editor: Herve Schneid

Original Music: Sally Potter, with the participation
    of Fred Frith

Main Cast: SP (Sally Potter); Pablo (Pablo Veron);
    Pablo's partner (Carolina Iotti); Builder
    (Heathcote Williams); Gustavo (Gustavo
    Naveira); Fabian (Fabian Salas)

The Man Who Cried (2000)

96 mins, b/w and colour

Production company: Working Title, in association
    with Adventure Pictures

Producer: Christopher Sheppard

Executive producers: Tim Bevan and Eric Fellner

Screenplay: Sally Potter

Cinematography: Sacha Vierney

Editor: Herve Schneid

Original Music: Osvaldo Golijov

Main Cast: Suzie (Claudia Lander Duke and
    Christina Ricci); Father (Oleg Yankovskiy);
    Lola (Cate Blanchett); Mme. Goldstein
    (Miriam Karlin); Cesar (Johnny Depp);
    Felix Perlman (Harry Dean Stanton); Dante
    Dominio (John Turturro); Romany band
    (Taraf de Haïdouks)

Yes (2004)

100 mins, colour

Production company: Adventure Pictures, in association with Studio Fierberg

Producers: Christopher Sheppard and Andrew Fierberg

Executive producers: John Penotti, Paul Trijbits, Fisher Stevens and Cedric Jeanson

Screenplay: Sally Potter

Cinematography: Alexei Rodionov

Editor: Daniel Goddard

Original Music: Sally Potter, with the participation of Fred Frith

Main Cast: She (Joan Allen); He (Simon Abkarian); Anthony (Sam Neill); Cleaner (Shirley Henderson); Aunt (Sheila Hancock); Kate (Samantha Bond); Grace (Stephanie Leonidas); Billy (Gary Lewis); Virgil (Wil Johnson); Whizzer (Raymond Waring)

RAGE (2009)

99 mins, colour

Production company: Adventure Pictures,

Producers: Christopher Sheppard and Andrew Fierberg

Executive producers: Bob Hiestand and Christina Weiss Lurie

Screenplay: Sally Potter

Cinematography: Steven Fierberg

Editor: Daniel Goddard

Original Music: Sally Potter, with the participation of Fred Frith

Main Cast: Merlin (Simon Abkarian); Dwight Angel (Patrick J. Adams); Vijay (Riz Ahmed); Bradley White (Bob Balaban); Anita de los Angeles (Adriana Barraza); Frank (Steve Buscemi); Otto (Jakob Cedergren); Lettuce Leaf (Lily Cole); Mona Carvell (Judi Dench); Tiny Diamonds (Eddie Izzard); Minx (Jude Law); Jed (John Leguizamo); Detective Homer (David Oyelowo); Edith Roth (Dianne Wiest)

PERFORMOGRAPHY

John Bull Puncture Repair Kit (1973) *Auk* and *Fallen Angels*. Perf. Diana Davies, Sally Potter, Dennis Greenwood. Birmingham: Arts Laboratory.

Limited Dance Company (1974a) *Aida*. London: Oval House.

_____ (1974b) *Brief Encounter*. Perf. Caroline Potter. London: Oval House Theatre.

_____ (1974c) *Death and the Maiden*. Netherlands: Rotterdam Festival and De Lantaren.

_____ (1974d) *Lochgilphead*. Lochigilphead, Scotland.

_____ (1974e) *Park Cafeteria*. London: Serpentine Gallery.

_____ (1974f) *Why Film*. Tour of the Netherlands.

Potter, Sally, chor. (1973a) *Interior* [section]. London: White Lion, Islington.

_____, chor. (1973b) *Leave*. London: The Place.

_____, chor. (1973c) *Parry Riposte*. Perf. Jacky Lansley. London: The Place.

_____, chor. (1974) *Wheat*. Perf. Dennis Greenwood. London: ICA and Borough Market.

_____ dir. (2007) *Carmen*. Comp. George Bizet. London: English National Opera.

Potter, Sally and Rose English, perfs. (1976) *Berlin*. London.

Potter, Sally, Jacky Lansley and Rose English, perfs. (1977) *Mounting*. Oxford: Museum of Modern Art.

MUSICOGRAPHY

Aïda (Giuseppe Verdi, 1871)

'Amor y Celos' (Miguel Padula and Alfredo F. Roldán, n.d.)

Carmen (Georges Bizet, 1875)

'Close Your Eyes', *The Man Who Cried* (Osvaldo Golijov and Sally Potter, 2000)

'Coming Through', *Orlando* (Sally Potter and Jimmy Somerville, 1993)

Dido and Aeneas (Henry Purcell, 1689)

'El Flete' (Gerónima Gradito and Vincente Greco, n.d.)

'The Empire Song', *The Gold Diggers* (Lindsay Cooper, 1983)

'Fawn', *Yes* and *Rage* (2009) (Fred Frith and Sally Potter)

'Gallo Ciego' (Agustin Bardi, n.d.)

'Gloomy Sunday' (László Jávor, Desmond Carter and Rezsö Seres, 1935)

'I Am You', *The Tango Lesson* (Sally Potter, 1996)

Il Trovatore (Giuseppe Verdi, 1853)

La Bohème (Giacomo Puccini, 1896)

Les pecheurs des perles (*The Pearl Fishers*) (Georges Bizet, 1863)

'Libertango' (Astor Piazzolla, 1974)

'Mi Buenos Aires Querido' (Carlos Gardel and Alfredo Le Pera, 1934)

'Milonga de mis Amores' (Pedro B. Laurenz and José Maria Contursi, n.d.)

Oh Moscow (Lindsay Cooper, 1991)

'Pensálo Bien' (Juan José Visiglio, Nola López and Julio Alberto, n.d.)

Psycho (Bernard Herrmann, 1960)

'Quejas de Bandoneón' (Juan de Díos Filiberto, n.d.)

St. Mark's Passion (Osvaldo Golijov, 2000)

Tosca (Giacomo Puccini, 1900)

'Zum' (Astor Piazzolla, n.d.)

BIBLIOGRAPHY

All materials marked 'Private archive' are held by Sally Potter. Thanks to Sally and to Adventure Pictures for access to this material.

Abram, David (1997) *The Spell of the Sensuous*. New York: Vintage.

Acton, Thomas (1986) 'Lav Angle', in Denise Stanley, Thomas Acton, Donald Kenrick and Bernard Hurley (eds) *The Romano Drom Song Book*. 2nd edn. London: Romanestan Publications, 2.

Agostinis, Valentina (1981) 'Interview with Sally Potter', *Framework*, 14, 47.

Ahmed, Sara (2000) *Strange Encounters: Embodied Others in Postcoloniality. Transformations: Thinking Through Feminism*. Series editors Maureen McNeil, Lynne Pearce and Beverley Skeggs. London and New York: Routledge.

_____ (2004) *The Cultural Politics of Emotion*. Edinburgh: Edinburgh University Press.

Albright, Ann Cooper (1997) *Choreographing Difference*. Hanover: Wesleyan University Press.

Andersen, Hans Christian (2007) *The Annotated Hans Christian Andersen*. Trans. Maria Tatar and Julie Allen. Ed. and with notes by Maria Tatar. New York and London: W. W. Norton.

Anon. (n.d.) *The Gold Diggers*. Typescript single-page draft with handwritten notes. Private archive.

_____ (1990) 'Woolf pack' [Diary], *Times*, 28 April, 10.

Arnheim, Rudolf (1958) *Film as Art*. London: Faber.

Aston, Elaine and Geraldine Harris (2006) 'Feminist Futures and the Possibility of "We"?', in Elaine Aston and Geraldine Harris (eds) *Feminist Futures? Theatre, Performance, Theory*. London: Palgrave Macmillan, 1–16.

Bakhtin, Mikhail (1984) *Rabelais and His World*. Trans. Hélène Iswolsky. Bloomington: Indiana University Press.

Baldwin, Shauna Singh (1999) *What the Body Remembers*. Toronto: Random House.

Bamigboye, Baz (1990) 'Daniel joins the bizarre Woolf pack', *Daily Mail*, 28 April, 7.

Banes, Sally (1987) *Terpsichore in Sneakers: Post-Modern Dance*. Middletown: Wesleyan University Press.

Batchelor, David (2006 [2000]) 'Chromophobia', in Angela Dalle Vacche and Brian Price (eds) *Color: The Film Reader*. New York and London: Routledge, 63–75.

Baudry, Jean-Louis (1992 [1974–75]) 'Ideological Effects of the Basic Cinematographic Apparatus', trans. Alan Williams, in Gerald Mast, Marshall Cohen and Leo Baudry (eds) *Film Theory and Criticism: Introductory Readings*. New York and Oxford: Oxford University Press, 302–12.

Beach, Clayton (2001) 'Modern Music, Piazzolla, Pugliese and Sexteto Tango'. Listserv message, 3 November. Available online: <http://pythia.uoregon.edu/~llynch/Tango-L/2001/msg00931.html>. Accessed 5 May 2009.

Benjamin, Walter (1992a [1936]) 'The Work of Art in the Age of Mechanical Reproduction', *Illuminations*. Trans. Harry Zohn. London: Fontana, 211–42.

_____ (1992b [1940]) 'Theses on the Philosophy of History', *Illuminations*. Trans. Harry Zohn. London: Fontana, 243–55.

Bergan, Ronald (2009) 'Oleg Yankovsky' [obituary]. *Guardian*, 23 May. Available online: <http://www.guardian.co.uk/film/2009/may/22/obituary-oleg-yankovsky>. Accessed 25 May 2009.

Berger, John (1960) *Permanent Red: Essays in Seeing*. London: Methuen.

_____ (2002) Note on *Yes* screenplay. March. Private archive.

_____ (2005) 'A Letter', in Sally Potter, *Yes*. New York: Newmarket, xi–xiii.

_____ (2007) *Hold Everything Dear*. London: Verso.

Berger, John and John Christie (2000) *I Send You This Cadmium Red: A Correspondence between John Berger and John Christie*. Ed. Eulàlia Bosch. Barcelona and New York: ACTAR.

Berman, Morris (1990) *Coming to Our Senses: Body and Spirit in the Hidden History of the West*. London: Unwin.

Bhabha, Homi K. (1991) 'The World and the Home', *Social Text*, 31/32, 141–53.

Biro, Yvette (1982) *Profane Mythology: The Savage Mind of the Cinema*. Trans. Imre Goldstein. Bloomington and London: Indiana University Press.

Boyarin, Jonathan (1994) 'Space Time and the Politics of Memory', in Jonathan Boyarin (ed.) *Remapping Memory: The Politics of TimeSpace*. Minneapolis and London: University of Minnesota Press, 1–37.

Braidotti, Rosi (2006) 'Transposed Companions', *Ways of Dying*. London, Tate Modern: 14 October. Author's transcription. Audio file available: <http://www.tate.org.uk/modern/eventseducation/symposia/6755.htm>. Accessed 5 May 2009.

Brando, Marlon and Robert Lindsey (1994) *Brando: Songs My Mother Taught Me*. New York: Random House.

Bronfen, Elisabeth (2004) 'Nocturnal Embodiments: Gendering Allegories of the Night', *Edda*, 4, 304–13.

Brooker, Charlie (2009) 'To Politicians, We're Little More than Meaningless Blobs on a Monitor. Bring on the Summer of Rage', *Guardian,* 2 March. Available online: <http://www.guardian.co.uk/commentisfree/2009/mar/02/charlie-brooker-politicians>. Accessed 5 May 2009.

Brown, Dan (2003) *The Da Vinci Code*. New York: Doubleday.

Brown, Ismene (2007) 'Ivan Vasiliev, the Boy Who Can Fly', *Daily Telegraph*, 14 July. Available online: <http://www.telegraph.co.uk/arts/main.jhtml?xml=/arts/2007/07/14/nosplit/btivan114.xml>. Accessed 5 May 2009.

Bruzzi, Stella (1997) *Undressing Cinema: Clothing and Identity in the Movies*. London and New York: Routledge.

Buber, Martin (1958 [1923]) *I and Thou*. Trans. Ronald Gregor Smith. 2nd edn, rev. Edinburgh: T. and T. Clark.

Butler, Judith (2004) *Precarious Life: The Power of Mourning and Violence*. London and New York: Verso.

_____ (2005) *Giving an Account of Oneself*. New York: Fordham University Press.

Carroll, Noel (2000) 'Moving and Moving: From Minimalism to *Lives of Performers*', *Millennium Film Journal*, 35/36. Available online: <http://www.mfj-online.org/journalPages/MFJ35/MovingandMoving.htm>. Accessed 5 May 2009.

Carson, Anne (1995) 'The Gender of Sound', *Glass, Irony and God*. New York: New Directions, 119–42.

Carter, Angela (1979) *The Bloody Chamber*. London: Vintage.

_____ (1996) *Orlando: or, The Enigma of the Sexes. The Curious Room: Collected Dramatic Works*. Ed. Mark Bell. London: Chatto, 155–82.

Caruth, Cathy (1996) *Unclaimed Experience: Trauma, Narrative, and History*. Baltimore and London: Johns Hopkins University Press.

Chamberlin, J. Edward (2003) *If This Is Your Land, Where Are Your Stories?: Finding Common Ground*. Toronto: Knopf.

_____ (2007) *Horse: How the Horse Has Shaped Civilisations*. London: Signal.

Ciecko, Anne (1998) 'Transgender, Transgenre, and the Transnational: Sally Potter's *Orlando*', *Velvet Light Trap*, 11, 19–34.

_____ (2002) 'Sally Potter: The Making of a British Woman Filmmaker', in Yvonne Tasker (ed.) *Fifty Contemporary Filmmakers*. London: Routledge, 272–80.

Claid, Emilyn (2006) *Yes? No! Maybe…: Seductive Ambiguity in Dance*. London and New York: Routledge.

Clément, Catherine (1989) *Opera, or the Undoing of Women*. Trans. Betsy Wing. London: Virago Press.

Cole, Louise (2004) 'Dance, Girl, Dance.' *Senses of Cinema*. Available online: <http://www.sensesofcinema.com/contents/cteq/04/33/dance_girl_dance.html>. Accessed 5 May 2009.

Columpar, Corinn (2003) 'The Dancing Body: Sally Potter as Feminist Auteure', in Jacqueline Levitin, Judith Plessis and Valerie Raoul (eds) *Women Filmmakers: Refocusing*. Vancouver: University of British Columbia Press, 108–16.

_____ (2006) 'The Politics of Beauty in Sally Potter's *The Man Who Cried*'. London: Post-Auteur Auteurs panel, Society for Cinema and Media Studies, March. Unpublished. By permission of the author.

Cook, Pam (1984a) 'British Independents: *The Gold Diggers*' [Interview with Sally Potter]. *Framework*, 24, 12–30.

_____ (1984b) '*The Gold Diggers*' [Review]. *Monthly Film Bulletin*, 51, 604, May, 140–1.

Copjec, Joan (1980) '*Thriller*: An Intrigue of Identification', *Ciné-tracts*, 3, 3, 33–8.

Cuddon, J. A. (1992) *Dictionary of Literary Terms and Literary Theory*. 3rd edn. Harmondsworth: Penguin.

Culler, Jonathan (1981) *The Pursuit of Signs: Semiotics, Literature, Deconstruction*. Ithaca, NY: Cornell University Press.

Curtis, David (2007) *A History of Artists' Film and Video in Britain*. London: British Film Institute.

Cvetkovich, Ann (2003) *An Archive of Feeling: Trauma, Sexuality, and Lesbian Public Culture. Series Q*. Series editors Michèle Aina Barale, Jonathan Goldberg, Michael Moon and Eve Kosofsky Sedgwick. Durham, NC and London: Duke University Press.

Damasio, Antonio (2000) *The Feeling of What Happens: Body, Emotion and the Making of Consciousness*. London: Heinemann.

Davis, Roger (1990) 'In Cannes, you need more than a topless starlet', *Mail on Sunday*, 13 May, 40–1.

Dayan, Daniel (2000 [1974]) 'The Tutor-Code of Classical Cinema', in Joanne Hollows, Peter Hutchings and Mark Jancovich (eds) *The Film Studies Reader*. New York: Oxford University Press, 219–25.

Deakin, Roger (2000) *Waterlog: A Swimmer's Journey Through Britain*. London: Vintage.

Del Rio, Elena (2004) 'Rethinking Feminist Film Theory: Counter-Narcissistic Performance in Sally Potter's *Thriller*', *Quarterly Journal of Film and Video*, 21, 1, 11–24.

Deren, Maya (1971 [1953]) 'Poetry and the Film: A Symposium' [with Maya Deren, Arthur Miller, Dylan Thomas, Parker Tyler. Chairman: Willard Maas. Organised by Amos Vogel], in P. Adams Sitney (ed.) *Film Culture: An Anthology*. London: Secker and Warburg, 171–86.

Derrida, Jacques (1976) *Of Grammatology*. Trans. Gayatri Chakravorty Spivak. Baltimore, MD: Johns Hopkins University Press.

_____ (1992) *Given Time: I. Counterfeit Money*. Trans. Peggy Kamuf. Chicago and London: University of Chicago Press.

Diamond, Elin (1997) *Unmaking Mimesis: Essays on Feminism and Theatre*. New York and London: Routledge.

Dolan, Jill (1988) *The Feminist Spectator as Critic*. Ann Arbor: University of Michigan Press.

_____ (1993) *Presence and Desire: Essays on Gender, Sexuality, Performance. Critical Perspectives on Women and Gender*. Ann Arbor: University of Michigan Press.

Donohue, Walter (1993) 'Immortal Longing' [Interview with Sally Potter], *Sight and Sound*, 3, 3, 10–12.

Dowell, Pat (2002 [1993]) 'Sally Potter: Demystifying Traditional Notions of Gender', in Gary Crowdus and Dan Georgakas (eds) *The Cineaste Interviews 2: On the Art and Politics of the Cinema*. Chicago: Lake View Press, 108–13.

Ebert, Roger (2004) 'Toronto fires starter gun for Oscar race', *Chicago Sun-Times*, 12 September. Available online: <http://rogerebert.suntimes.com/apps/pbcs.dll/article?AID=/20040912/FILMFESTIVALS03/409120303>. Accessed 5 May 2009.

Ehrenstein, David (1984) 'Sally Potter', in *Film: The Front Line/1984*. Denver CO: Arden, 119–27.

_____ (1993) 'Out of the Wilderness: An Interview with Sally Potter', *Film Quarterly*, 47, 1, 2–7.

Eisenstein, Sergei (2006) 'On Colour', trans. Michael Glenny, in Angela Dalle Vacche and Brian Price (eds) *Color: The Film Reader*. New York and London: Routledge, 105–17.

English, Rose (1988) 'Hast Du *Berlin* Gefunden?' [Talk And Interview]. *Archive of the National Review of Live Art*. Transcript of a cassette tape.

Ferguson, Jane (1990) 'Potter and the Woolf', *Sunday Telegraph Magazine*, 13–19 May, 8.

Finlay, Victoria (2002) *Colour: Travels through the Paintbox*. London: Sceptre.

Fletcher, Richard (2001) *Moorish Spain*. London: Phoenix.

Ford, Ford Madox (1997) 'On Heaven', in Max Saunders (ed.) *Selected Poems*. Manchester: Carcanet, 99-110.

Foster, Susan Leigh (1996) 'Introduction', in Susan Leigh Foster (ed.) *Corporealities: Dancing Knowledge, Culture and Power*. London and New York: Routledge, x–xvii.

Foucault, Michel (1986) 'Of Other Spaces'. Trans. Jay Miskowiec, *Diacritics*, 16, 1, 22–8.

_____ (1990) *The History of Sexuality: An Introduction. Vol. 1*. Trans. Robert Hurley. New York: Vintage Books.

Fowler, Catherine (2008) *Sally Potter*. Champaign: University of Illinois Press.

Frye, Marilyn (1983) *The Politics of Reality: Essays in Feminist Theory*. Trumansburg: Crossing Press.

Garrett, Roberta (1995) 'Costume Drama and Counter Memory: Sally Potter's *Orlando*', in Jane Dowson and Steven Earnshaw (eds) *Postmodern Subjects/Postmodern Texts. Postmodern Studies 13*. Series editors Theo D'haen and Hans Bertens. Amsterdam and Atlanta: Rodopi, 89–99.

Gesualdi, Alberto (2004) '[TANGO-L] Gallo Ciego'. Listserv message, 20 August. Available online: <http://pythia.uoregon.edu/~llynch/Tango-L/2004/msg01582.html>. Accessed 5 May 2009.

Gibson, Owen (2008) 'Diversify or die: equality chief's stark message to broadcasting industry', *Guardian*, 17 July. Available online: <http://www.guardian.co.uk/media/2008/jul/17/channel4.television1>. Accessed 5 May 2009.

Gidal, Peter (1972) 'Film as Film', *Art and Artists*. Artists' Films issue, December, 12–14. Marked-up copy. Private archive.

Gilbert, Sandra and Susan Gubar (1979) *The Madwoman in the Attic: The Woman Writer and the Nineteenth-Century Imagination*. New Haven: Yale University Press.

Glaessner, Verina (1972) 'Interviews with Three Women Filmmakers', *Time Out*, 17 March, 46–7.

_____ (1998) 'Sally Potter', in Gwendolyn Audrey Foster, Amy Unterburger and Katrien Jacobs (eds) *Women Filmmakers and Their Films*. London: St James' Press, 340–2.

_____ (2001) 'Fire and Ice', in Ginette Vincendeau (ed.) *Film/Literature/Heritage: A Sight and Sound Reader*. London: British Film Institute, 53–7.

Gorbman, Claudia (1987) *Unheard Melodies: Narrative Film Music*. London: British Film Institute.

Gordon, Mary (1996) *The Shadow Man: A Daughter's Search for Her Father*. New York: Vintage.

Greenfield, Amy Butler (2006) *A Perfect Red: Empire, Espionage and a Quest for the Colour of Desire*. London: Black Swan.

Griffiths, Jay (2007) *Wild: An Elemental Journey*. London: Hamish Hamilton.

Gunning, Tom (1995 [1989]) 'An Aesthetic of Astonishment: Early Film and the [In]Credulous Spectator', in Linda Williams (ed.) *Viewing Positions: Ways of Seeing Film*. New Brunswick: Rutgers University Press, 114–33.

Haffenden, John (1985) *Novelists in Interview*. New York: Methuen.

Haigh, Jacqueline (2008) Essay on *Orlando*. 1 May. Unpublished. By permission of the author.

Hankins, Leslie K. (1995) 'Redirections: Challenging the Class Axe and Lesbian Erasure in Potter's *Orlando*', in Eileen Barrett and Patricia Cramer (eds) *Re: Reading, Re: Writing, Re: Teaching Virginia Woolf*. New York: Pace University Press, 168–84.

Haraway, Donna (1991a) *Simians, Cyborgs and Women: The Reinvention of Nature*. London and New York: Routledge.

_____ (1991b) 'Situated Knowledges: The Science Question in Feminism and the Privilege of Partial Perspective', *Feminist Studies*, 14, 3, 575–99.

_____ (2006) 'Notes of a Sportswriter's Daughter', *Ways of Dying*. London: Tate Modern, 14 October. Author's transcription. Audio file available online: <http://www.tate.org.uk/modern/eventseducation/symposia/6755.htm>. Accessed 5 May 2009.

Hardt, Michael and Antonio Negri (2000) *Empire*. Cambridge, MA: Harvard University Press.

_____ (2004) *Multitude: War and Democracy in the Age of Empire*. New York: Penguin.

Harvey, Sylvia (1996) 'What is Cinema? The Sensuous, the Abstract and the Political', in Christopher Williams (ed.) *Cinema: The Beginnings and the Future*. London: University of Westminster Press, 228–51.

Hatfield, Jackie (2006) 'Imagining Future Gardens of History', *Camera Obscura*, 62, 21, 2, 185–91.

Haynes, Jim (1969) Letter to the Arts Laboratory. 28 October. *The Centre of Attention*. Available online: <http://www.thecentreofattention.org/dgartslab.html>. Accessed 5 May 2009.

Hogan, Linda (1995) *Dwellings: A Spiritual History of the Living World*. New York: Touchstone.

Howard, Alan (1997) 'Labor, History and Sweatshops in the New Global Economy', in Andrew Ross (ed.) *No Sweat: Fashion, Free Trade and the Rights of Garment Workers*. London and New York: Verso, 151–72.

Howell, Anthony (1975) 'Is this a happening?', *Vogue*, 2, 132 (2109), 18–19.

Humm, Maggie (1997) *Feminism and Film*. Edinburgh: Edinburgh University Press.

Hutcheon, Linda (2002) *The Politics of Postmodernism*. 2nd edn. London and New York: Routledge.

_____ (2004) *The Poetics of Postmodernism*. 2nd edn. New York: Routledge.

Hyde, Lewis (1983) *The Gift: Imagination and the Erotic Life of Property*. New York: Vintage.

Internationales forum des jungen films (1984) Programme. February. Berlin.

Jarman, Derek (1995) *Chroma: A Book of Colour – June '93*. London: Vintage.

_____ (1996) *Derek Jarman: A Portrait*. London: Thames and Hudson.

Jarman, Derek and Sally Potter (1989) 'Face to Face', London, National Film Theatre. 27 October. Audio cassette, British Film Institute National Archives. Author's transcription.

Jones, Amelia (1998) *Body Art: Performing the Subject*. Minneapolis: University of Minnesota Press.

Jordan, Stephanie (1992) *Striding Out: Aspects of Contemporary and New Dance in Britain*. London: Dance Books.

Joyce, James (1992) *Ulysses*. Ed. Declan Kiberd. Harmondsworth: Penguin.

Kahlo, Frida (1995) *The Diary of Frida Kahlo: An Intimate Self-Portrait*. Ed. Phyllis Freeman. London: Bloomsbury.

Kalmus, Natalie M. (2006) 'Color Consciousness', in Angela Dalle Vacche and Brian Price (eds) *Color: The Film Reader*. New York and London: Routledge, 24–9.

Kamen, Henry (2007) *The Disinherited: The Exiles Who Created Spanish Culture*. London: Allen Lane.

Kandinsky, Wassily (1914) *Art of Spiritual Harmony*. Trans. M. T. H. Sadler. London: Constable.

Kane, Angela (1989) 'Richard Alston: Twenty-One Years of Choreography', *Dance Research*, 7, 2, 16–54.

Kaplan, E. Ann (1981) 'Night at the Opera: Investigating the Heroine in Sally Potter's *Thriller*', *Millennium Film Journal*, 10/11, 115–22.

Keathley, Christian (2006) *Cinephilia and History, or the Wind in the Trees*. Indianapolis and Bloomington: Indiana University Press.

Klein, Naomi (2001) *No Logo*. London: Flamingo.

Le Guin, Ursula K. (2001) *Always Coming Home*. Berkeley: University of California Press.

Loshitsky, Yosefa (2003) 'Quintessential Strangers: The Representation of Romanies and Jews in Some Holocaust Films', *Framework*, 44, 2, 57–71.

Lowney, Chris (2005) *A Vanished World: Muslims, Christians, and Jews in Medieval Spain*. New York: Oxford University Press.

Lucas, Rose (2005) 'Orlando', in Brian McFarlane (ed.) *The Cinema of Britain and Ireland*. London: Wallflower Press, 217–25.

Lucia, Cynthia (2005) 'Saying "Yes" to Taking Risks: An Interview with Sally Potter', *Cineaste*, 30, 4, 24–31.

Lugones, María (1987) 'Playfulness, "World"-Travelling, and Loving Perception', *Hypatia*, 2, 2, 3–20.

Lundemo, Trond (2006) 'The Colors of Haptic Space: Black, Blue and White in Moving Images', in Angela Dalle Vacche and Brian Price (eds) *Color: The Film Reader*. New York and London: Routledge, 88–101.

MacDonald, Scott (1998 [1995]) 'Sally Potter', in *A Critical Cinema 3: Interviews with Independent Filmmakers*. Berkeley, Los Angeles and London: University of California Press, 397–427.

MacKintosh, Helen and Mandy Merck (1979) 'Rendez-vous d'Edinburgh: A Report of the Festival's Feminism and Cinema Week', *Time Out*, 7–13 September, 22–3.

Mackrell, Judith (1992) *Out of Line: The Story of British New Dance*. London: Dance Books.

Malevich, Kasimir (2003) *The Non-Objective World: The Manifesto of Suprematism*. Trans. P. Theobald. Mineola, NY: Dover.

Manning, Erin (2007) *Politics of Touch: Sense, Movement, Sovereignty*. Minneapolis: University of Minnesota Press.

Marciniak, Katarzyna (2006) *Alienhood: Citizenship, Exile and the Logic of Difference*. Minneapolis: University of Minnesota Press.

Marks, Laura U. (2000) *The Skin of the Film: Intercultural Cinema, Embodiment and the Senses*. Durham, NC and London: Duke University Press.

____ (2002) *Touch: Sensuous Theory and Multisensory Media*. Minneapolis: University of Minnesota Press.

Marx, Karl (2004) *Capital: Critique of Political Economy. Vol. 1*. Trans. Ben Fowkes. Harmondsworth: Penguin.

Mason, Paul (2007) *Live Working or Die Fighting: How the Working Class Went Global*. London: Harvill Secker.

May, Lary (1980) *Screening Out the Past: The Birth of Mass Culture and the Motion Picture Industry*. Oxford and New York: Oxford University Press.

Mayer, Sophie (2005) 'She She She Shine On', *Plan B*, August/September, 76.

____ (2008) 'The Mirror Didn't Crack: Costume Drama and Gothic Horror in Sally Potter's *Orlando*', *Literature/Film Quarterly*, 36, 1, 39–44.

McClary, Susan (1991) *Feminine Endings: Music, Gender and Sexuality*. Minneapolis: University of Minnesota Press.

McClintock, Anne (1995) *Imperial Leather: Race, Gender and Sexuality in the Colonial Context*. New York and London: Routledge.

McKim, Kristi (2006) '"A State of Loving Detachment": Sally Potter's Impassioned and Intellectual Cinema', *Senses of Cinema*. Available online: <http://www.sensesofcinema.com/contents/directors/06/potter.html>. Accessed 5 May 2009.

McNay, Michael (1978) 'Don't shoot the award givers', *Guardian*, 17 August, A8.

McNeill, Isabelle (2008) 'Orlando', in John White and Sarah Barrow (eds) *Fifty Key British Films*. London: Routledge, 195–200.

McRobbie, Angela (1997) 'A new kind of rag trade?', in Andrew Ross (ed.) *No Sweat: Fashion, Free Trade and the Rights of Garment Workers*. London and New York: Verso, 275–89.

Mellencamp, Patricia (1995) *A Fine Romance: Five Ages of Film Feminism*. Philadelphia: Temple University Press.

Menocal, María Rosa (1993) *Shards of Love: Exile and the Origins of the Lyric*. Durham, NC: Duke University Press.

Merck, Mandy (1984) 'Composing for the Films', *Screen*, 25, 3, 40–54.

Michaels, Anne (1997) *Fugitive Pieces*. London: Bloomsbury.

Mishra, Pankaj (2004) *An End to Suffering: The Buddha in the World*. London: Picador.

_____ (2005) 'Introduction', in Sally Potter, *Yes*. New York: Newmarket.

Moor, Andrew (2005) *Powell and Pressburger: A Cinema of Magic Spaces*. Cinema and Society Series. Ed. Jeffrey Richards. London and New York: I. B. Tauris.

Moore, Rachel O. (1999) *Savage Theory: Cinema as Modern Magic*. Durham, NC: Duke University Press.

Morris, Jan (ed.) (1993) *Travels With Virginia Woolf*. London: Hogarth.

Mulvey, Laura (1975) 'Visual Pleasure and Narrative Cinema', *Screen*, 16, 3, 6–18.

Munsterberg, Hugo (1916) *The Photoplay: A Psychological Study*. New York: Appleton.

Murger, Henri (2004) *Bohemians of the Latin Quarter*. Trans. Ellen Marriage and John Selwyn. Philadelphia: University of Pennsylvania Press.

Naficy, Hamid (1999) 'Preface: Arrivals and Departures', in Hamid Naficy (ed.) *Home, Exile, Homeland: Film, Media, and the Politics of Place*. New York and London: Routledge, vii–xii.

Nelson, Cary (1989) *Repression and Recovery: Modern American Poetry and the Politics of Cultural Memory, 1910–1945*. Madison: University of Wisconsin Press.

Noble, Peter (1990) 'In confidence', *Screen International*, 21–27 April, 6.

Ouditt, Sharon (1999) '*Orlando*: Coming Across the Divide', in Deborah Cartmell and Imelda Whelehan (eds) *Adaptations: From Text to Screen, Screen to Text*. London and New York: Routledge, 146–56.

Parr, Adrian (ed.) (2005) *The Deleuze Dictionary*. Edinburgh: Edinburgh University Press.

Pavord, Anna (2000) *The Tulip*. London: Bloomsbury.

Pennethorne Hughes, C. J. (1993 [1930]) 'Dreams and Films', in James Donald, Anna Friedberg and Laura Marcus (eds) *Close Up: A Quarterly Devoted to the Art of Films, 1927–1933*. Princeton: Princeton University Press, 260–2.

Perelli, Carina (1994) '*Memoria de Sangre*: Fear, Hope, and Disenchantment in Argentina', in Jonathan Boyarin (ed.) *Remapping Memory: The Politics of TimeSpace*. Minneapolis and London: University of Minnesota Press, 39–66.

Peters, John Durham (1999) 'Exile, Nomadism, and Diaspora: The Stakes of Mobility in the Western Canon', in Hamid Naficy (ed.) *Home, Exile, Homeland: Film, Media, and the Politics of Place*. New York and London: Routledge, 17–41.

Peucker, Brigitte (1995) *Incorporating Images: Film and the Rival Arts*. Princeton: Princeton University Press.

Phelan, Peggy (1993) *Unmarked: The Politics of Performance*. London and New York: Routledge.

Pidduck, Julianne (1997) 'Travels with Sally Potter's *Orlando*: Gender, Narrative, Movement', *Screen*, 38, 2, 172–89.

_____ (2004) *Contemporary Costume Film: Space, Place and the Past*. London: British Film Institute.

Plant, Sadie (1997) *Zeroes and Ones: Digital Women and the New Technoculture*. New York: Doubleday.

Potter, Norman (2002) *What Is a Designer*. 4th edn. London: Hyphen.

Potter, Sally (1971) Programme note. *The Building. Electric Cinema*. Amsterdam, BBK Aktiecentrum. 3–4 September. Private archive.

_____ (1974) Programme note. *Park Cafeteria. Festival of Performance Art*. London: Serpentine Gallery, 20–26 August. Private archive.

_____ (1980) 'On Shows', in Catherine Elwes, Rose Garrard and Sandy Nairne (eds) *About Time: Video, Performance and Installation by 21 Women Artists*. London: ICA, n. p.

_____ (1981) 'Imaging of Women', *Towards a Living Cinema: Issues in Contemporary Film. No Rose* 3, 26–30.

_____ (1984) 'Gold Diggers and Fellow Travellers', *National Film Theatre Programmes: May*. London: National Film Theatre, 7–8.

_____ (1988) *Orlando*. Unpublished draft. Private archive.

_____ (1990) *Orlando*. Unpublished draft. Script Collection: British Film Institute Library.

_____ (1994a) 'Derek Jarman', *Vertigo*, 3, 63.

____ (1994b) 'On Tour with *Orlando*', in Walter Donohoe (ed.) *Projections 3*. London: Faber & Faber, 197–212.

____ (1994c) *Orlando*. London: Faber & Faber.

____ (1995) 'If Tango is the Answer, Then What is the Question?' Tactical document for funders. Private archive.

____ (1997a) 'Introduction', *The Tango Lesson*. London: Faber & Faber, vii–xii.

____ (1997b) *The Tango Lesson*. London: Faber & Faber.

____ (1997c) 'First Steps', *The Tango Lesson*. London: Faber & Faber, 83–91.

____ (1997d) 'The archivist goes to Buenos Aires', *The Tango Lesson*. London: Faber & Faber, 92–7.

____ (1997e) *The Tango Lesson*. Liner notes. CD. Sony Classical.

____ (2000a) *The Man Who Cried*. London: Faber & Faber.

____ (2000b) *The Man Who Cried*. Liner notes. CD. Sony Classical.

____ (2000c) *The Man Who Cried*. Voiceover draft. Private archive.

____ (2005a) 'Director's Diary 4', *BBC UK Movies*. Available online <http://www.bbc.co.uk/films/ukmovies/filmdiaries/sally_potter_4.shtml>. Accessed 5 May 2009.

____ (2005b) *Yes*. New York: Newmarket.

____ (2006) 'The Alchemist's Garden'. 23 June. Available online: <http://www.yesthemovie.co.uk/ForumDiary/41%7ediary.html>. Accessed 5 May 2009.

____ (2007) '"I have been moved to tears"', *Guardian*. 25 September. Available online: <http://www.guardian.co.uk/music/2007/sep/25/classicalmusicandopera>. Accessed 5 May 2009.

____ (2009a) 'Barefoot Filmmaking'. 6 February. Available online: <http://www.sallypotter.com/barefoot-filmmaking>. Accessed 5 May 2009.

____ (2009b) 'Thank you very much for this'. Response to forum post 'Money, Money, Money'. 16 April. Available online: <http://www.sallypotter.com/node/209#comment-102>. Accessed 5 May 2009.

Price, Brian (2006a) 'General Introduction', in Angela Dalle Vacche and Brian Price (eds) *Color: The Film Reader*. New York and London: Routledge, 1–9.

____ (2006b) 'Color, the Formless, and Cinematic Eros', in Angela Dalle Vacche and Brian Price (eds) *Color: The Film Reader*. New York and London: Routledge, 76–87.

Prynne, J. H. (1998) 'English Poetry and Emphatical Language', *Proceedings of the British Academy*, Vol. LXXIV, 135–69.

Quart, Leonard (2006 [1993]) 'The Religion of the Market: Thatcherite Politics and the British Film of the 1980s', in Lester D. Friedman (ed.) *Fires Were Started: British Cinema and Thatcherism*. 2nd edn, rev. and updated. London: Wallflower Press, 15–44.

Rainer, Yvonne (2006) 'Mulvey's Legacy', *Camera Obscura*, 21, 3, 167–70.

Ramose, Mogobe B. (2003) 'The Philosophy of Ubuntu and Ubuntu as Philosophy', in P. H. Coetzee and A. J. P. Roux (eds) *The African Philosophy Reader*. 2nd ed. London: Routledge, 230–8.

Retallack, Joan (1994) 'RE:THINKING:LITERARY:FEMINISM: (three essays onto shaky grounds)', in Lynn Keller and Cristann Miller (eds) *Feminist Measures: Soundings in Poetry and Theory*. Ann Arbor: University of Michigan Press, 344–77.

Rich, B. Ruby (1983) 'The Very Model of a Modern Minor Industry', *American Film*, 8, 7, 47–54, 64.

____ (1993) 'Sexual Personae', *Mirabella*, May, n. p.

____ (1998) *Chick Flicks: Theories and Memories of the Feminist Film Movement*. Durham, NC: Duke University Press.

____ (2007) 'The Gold Diggers', *Sight and Sound*, 17, 8, 23.

Robbins, Hollis (2004) 'The Emperor's New Critique', *New Literary History*, 34, 659–75.

Rohmer, Eric (2006 [1989]) 'Of Taste and Colors', trans Carol Volk, in Angela Dalle Vacche and Brian Price (eds) *Color: The Film Reader*. New York and London: Routledge, 123–5.

Rosenbaum, Jonathan (1984) '*The Gold Diggers*: A Preview', *Camera Obscura*, 12, 126–9.

____ (2006) 'The Best Film of the Last Two Years', *Chicago Reader*, 6 January. Available online: <http://www.chicagoreader.com/movies/archives/2006/0106/060106_1.html>. Accessed 5 May 2009.

Ross, Alex (2008) *The Rest is Noise: Listening to the Twentieth Century*. London: Fourth Estate.

Ross, Andrew (1997a) 'Preface,' in Andrew Ross (ed.) *No Sweat: Fashion, Free Trade and the Rights of Garment Workers*. London and New York: Verso, 1–2.

_____ (1997b) 'Introduction,' in Andrew Ross (ed.) *No Sweat: Fashion, Free Trade and the Rights of Garment Workers*. London and New York: Verso, 9–37.

Ruiz, Rául (1995) *Poetics of Cinema* Vol. I. Trans Brian Holmes. Paris: Éditions Dis Voir.

Rushdie, Salman (1992) *The Wizard of Oz*. BFI Film Classics. London: British Film Institute.

Sandhu, Sukhdev (2007) '*Borderline* and the Emergence of Black Cinema', booklet accompanying *Borderline* DVD. London: British Film Institute, 9–14.

Savage, Jon (1991) *England's Dreaming: Sex Pistols and Punk Rock*. London: Faber & Faber.

Savigliano, Marta E. (1996) 'Fragments for a story of tango bodies (on Choreocritics and the memory of power)', in Susan Leigh Foster (ed.) *Corporealities: Dancing Knowledge, Culture and Power*. London and New York: Routledge, 199–232.

Scarry, Elaine (1988) *The Body in Pain*. Oxford: Oxford University Press.

_____ (2006) *On Beauty and Being Just*. London: Duckworth.

Scheman, Naomi (1997) 'Queering the Center by Centring the Queer: Reflections on Transsexuals and Secular Jews', in Diana Tietjens Meyers (ed.) *Feminists Rethink the Self*. Boulder: Westview Press, 124–62.

Schneider, Rebecca (2001) 'Archives: Performance Remains', *Performance Research*, 6, 2, 100–8.

Shakespeare, William (1995) *Antony and Cleopatra*. Ed. John Wilders. London: Methuen.

_____ (1996a) *As You Like It*. Ed. Juliet Dusinberre. London: Arden.

_____ (1996b) *Cymbeline*. Ed. J. M. Nosworthy. London: Arden.

_____ (1997a) *King Lear*. Ed. R. A. Foakes. London: Arden.

_____ (1997b) *Othello*. Ed. E. A. J. Honigman. London: Arden.

_____ (1997c) *The Sonnets*. Ed. Katherine Duncan-Jones. London: Arden.

Shelley, Percy Bysshe (1977) *Shelley's Poetry and Prose*. Eds Donald H. Reiman and Sharon B. Powers. New York: Norton.

Shohat, Ella (1993) 'Gender and the Culture of Empire: Towards a Feminist Ethnography of Cinema', in Hamid Naficy and Teshome Gabriel (eds) *Otherness and the Media*. Chur, Switzerland: Harwood Academic, 45–84.

Silverman, Kaja (1988) *The Acoustic Mirror: The Female Voice in Psychoanalysis and Cinema (Theories of Representation and Difference)*. Bloomington: Indiana University Press.

_____ (1996) *The Threshold of the Visible World*. London and New York: Routledge.

_____ (2005) 'The Cure By Love', *Public*, 32, 32–47.

Sjogren, Britta (2006) *Into the Vortex: Female Voice and Paradox in Film*. Champaign: University of Illinois Press.

Skoller, Jeffrey (2005) *Shadows, Specters, Shards: Making History in Avant-Garde Film*. Minneapolis: University of Minnesota Press.

Smith, Caleb and Enrico Minardi (2004) 'The Collaboration and the Multitude: An Interview with Michael Hardt', *Minnesota Review*. Available online <http://www.theminnesotareview.org/journal/ns61/hardt.htm>. Accessed 5 May 2009.

Sobchack, Vivian (1992) *The Address of the Eye: A Phenomenology of Film Experience*. Princeton: Princeton University Press.

_____ (2004) *Carnal Thoughts: Embodiment and Moving Image Culture*. Berkeley, Los Angeles and London: University of California Press.

Solanas, Fernando and Octavio Getino (1983 [1969]) 'Towards a Third Cinema', trans Julianne Burton, in Michael Chanan (ed.) *Twenty Five Years of the New Latin American Cinema*. London: British Film Institute, 17–27.

Solnit, Rebecca (2002) *Wanderlust: A History of Walking*. London: Verso.

_____ (2005) *Hope in the Dark: The Untold History of People Power*. Edinburgh: Canongate.

Somaiya, Ravi (2008) 'Young, gifted – and ignored', *Guardian*, 10 April. Available online: <http://arts.guardian.co.uk/theatre/dance/story/0,,2272145,00.html> Accessed 5 May 2009.

Stam, Robert (1989) *Subversive Pleasures: Bakhtin, Cultural Criticism and Film. Parallax: Re-visions of Culture and Society*. Series editors Stephen G. Nichols, Gerald Prince and Wendy Steiner. Baltimore and London: Johns Hopkins University Press.

Stein, David E. S. (ed.) (2006) *The Contemporary Torah: A Gender-Sensitive Adaptation of the JPS Translation*. Philadelphia: Jewish Publication Society.

Steiner, Wendy (2001) *Venus in Exile: The Rejection of Beauty in Twentieth Century Art*. New York and London: The Free Press.

Swanson, Gillian and Lucy Moy-Thomas (2003) 'Interview with Sally Potter', in Nina Danino and Michael Mazière (eds) *The Undercut Reader: Critical Writings on Artists' Film and Video*. London: Wallflower Press, 194–7.

Taussig, Michael (1999) *Defacement: Public Secrecy and the Labor of the Negative*. Stanford: Stanford University Press.

Taylor, Diana (2005) *The Archive and the Repertoire: Performing Cultural Memory in the Americas*. Durham, NC: Duke University Press.

Tel Quel (1968) *Theorie d'Ensemble*. Paris: Editions Seuil.

Tincknell, Estelle and Ian Conrich (2006) 'Introduction', in Estelle Tincknell and Ian Conrich (eds) *Film's Musical Moments*. Edinburgh: Edinburgh University Press, 1–14.

Trinh T. Minh-Ha (1991) *When the Moon Waxes Red: Representation, Gender and Cultural Politics*. London and New York: Routledge.

Truffaut, François (1954) 'Une certaine tendance du cinéma français', *Cahiers du cinéma*, 54, 2.

Tutu, Desmond (2000) *No Future Without Forgiveness*. London: Rider.

Ulaby, Neda (2008) 'Valentino's Sheikh: An "Other" Made to Swoon Over', *Morning Edition, National Public Radio*. 4 February. Available online: <http://www.npr.org/templates/story/story.php?storyId=18602260&ft=1&f=1008>. Accessed 5 May 2009.

Vincendeau, Ginette (2001a) 'Introduction', in Ginette Vincendeau (ed.) *Film/Literature/Heritage: A Sight and Sound Reader*. London: British Film Institute, xi–xxvi.

____ (2001b) '*The Man Who Cried*', *Sight and Sound*, 11, 1, 54.

Vollmer, Ulrike (2007) *Seeing Film and Reading Feminist Theology*. New York: Macmillan.

Warner, Marina (2006) *Phantasmagoria: Spirit Visions, Metaphor and Media in the Twenty-First Century*. Oxford and New York: Oxford University Press.

Weinberger, Eliot (2007) *An Elemental Thing*. New York: New Directions.

Weinstock, Jane (1980) 'She Who Laughs First Laughs Last (*Thriller* by Sally Potter)', *Camera Obscura*, 5, 100–11.

West, Cornel (1993) *Race Matters*. Boston: Beacon.

Widdicombe, Kristy (2003) 'The Contemporary Auteur: An Interview with Sally Potter'. Available online: <http://www.bfi.org.uk/filmtvinfo/publications/16+/potter.html>. Accessed 5 May 2009.

Wigley, Mark (1992) 'Untitled: The Housing of Gender', in Beatriz Colomina (ed.) *Sexuality and Space*. Princeton: Princeton Architectural Press, 327–89.

Wildlife Conservation Society (2008–09) *The Mannahatta Project*. Available online: <http://www.wcs.org/mannahatta>. Accessed 5 May 2009.

Williams, Heathcote (1991) *Autogeddon*. London: Cape.

Wilson, Paul (2003) *The Silk Roads: A Route and Planning Guide*. Hindhead, Surrey: Trailblazer.

Winterson, Jeanette (2000) *The PowerBook*. London: Cape.

Wollen, Peter (2006 [1993]) 'The Last New Wave: Modernism in British Films of the Thatcher Era', in Lester D. Friedman (ed.) *Fires Were Started: British Cinema and Thatcherism*. 2nd edn, rev. and updated. London: Wallflower Press, 30–44.

Woolf, Virginia (1929) *A Room of One's Own*. London: Hogarth Press.

____ (1977) *Three Guineas*. London: Hogarth Press.

____ (1992) *Mrs Dalloway*. Ed. Claire Tomalin. Oxford: Oxford University Press.

____ (1993) *Orlando, A Biography*. Ed. Brenda Lyons. Intro. and notes Sandra M. Gilbert. London: Penguin.

Young, Iris Marion (1997) 'Asymmetrical Reciprocity: On Moral Respect, Wonder, and Enlarged Thought', *Constellations*, 3, 3, 340–63.

Zeig, Sande (1993) 'Queens of England', *Filmmaker*, 1, 4, 24–6.

Zuntz, Günther (1971) *Persephone: Three Essays on Religion and Thought in Magna Graeca*. Oxford: Clarendon.

INDEX